T4-AKS-132
3 2390 00140 6245

European and American

DOLLS

Written and illustrated by the same author:

Ancient and Modern Dolls
Toys' Adventures at the Zoo
Ladybird, Ladybird
A Book of Toys
Eight Little Frogs
A Book of Dolls
A Book of Pictorial Perspective
A World of Pattern
Dolls of the World

*

FRONTISPIECE (*overleaf*) Bisque Doll, *c.* 1910.
See caption to PLATE 346. *The London Museum.*

European and American
DOLLS
and their marks and patents

Gwen White

New York: G. P. PUTNAM'S SONS

First American Edition 1966

Library of Congress Catalog Card Number: 66-24567

Printed in Great Britain

CONTENTS

ACKNOWLEDGMENTS

The Author would like to thank the Comptroller of H.M. Patent Office for permission to reproduce the Patents and Trademarks and also to thank the many Museums and doll collectors who have allowed her to inspect the marks found on their dolls.

Illustration nos. 162, 240 and 347 are reproduced by gracious permission of H.M. The Queen.

The Author and Publishers would also like to thank the following for permission to reproduce the illustrations appearing in this book:
The Trustees of The National Gallery, London, for nos. 1 and 3.
The Syndics of The Fitzwilliam Museum, Cambridge, for no. 2.
The Director of the City Museum, Leeds, for nos. 4, 40, 62, 100, 235, 236, 238, 338, 339 and 349.
The Director of Brooklyn Children's Museum, for nos. 5, 46, 344 and 345.
The Chief Curator of Landesgewerbeamt Baden-Württemberg, Stuttgart, for nos. 6, 7, 27, 34, 39, 47, 52, 57 and 90.
The Director of Nordiska Museet, Stockholm, for nos. 8, 37, 113, 211–13, 225 and 226.
The Trustees of The London Museum, for nos. 9, 12, 15, 18, 61, 71, 73, 74, 91, 103, 105, 116, 135, 136, 140, 156, 176, 184, 195, 196, 205, 214, 230, 237, 278–80, 287, 307 and 346.
The Borough of Hove, Libraries and Museum Department, for nos. 10, 19 and 169.
The Director of the City Museum, Bristol (Blaise Castle House Folk Museum), for nos. 11 and 337.
Bethnal Green Museum, for nos. 13, 14, 16, 17, 20, 38, 42, 49, 69, 70, 85, 92, 107, 109, 111, 119, 137, 144, 145, 151–3, 155, 163–5, 173–5, 223, 252, 299, 320, 333, 334 and 336.
The Director of the Essex Institute, Salem, for nos. 21, 227, 241 and 350.
Detroit Public Schools, Children's Museum, for nos. 22, 56 and 133.
The Director of the City Museum, St. Albans, for nos. 23, 24, 67, 83, 138 and 139.
The Director of Deutsches Spielzeugmuseum, Sonneberg, for nos. 25, 29, 33, 43, 66, 82, 102, 141, 158, 171, 181, 183, 185, 186 and 281. (Photographs by Claus Hansmann, Munich.)
The Curator of The American National Red Cross Museum, Washington, for nos. 26 and 166.
The Director of the National Museum, Prague, for nos. 28, 31 and 220–2.
The Curator of Saffron Walden Museum, for nos. 30, 32, 44, 45, 108, 110, 148, 149, 239, 301, 302 and 324.
Plymouth Antiquarian Society, Massachusetts, for nos. 35, 41, 104, 106 and 332.
New Milford Historical Society, Connecticut, for no. 36.
The Director of the National Museum of Finland, Helsinki, for nos. 48, 59, 65, 170, 179, 250, 283 and 284.
The Trustees of the Victoria and Albert Museum, London, for nos. 50, 130, 131, 134, 143, 191 and 210.
Kidders Trading Post and Doll Museum, Apache Junction, Arizona, for nos. 51, 172, 177 and 218.
Smithsonian Institution, Washington, for nos. 53, 54, 81, 118, 253, 257, 258, 288, 289, 294 and 295.
Miss Leona Stone Salyer, McCully House, Jacksonville, for nos. 55, 124, 242, 249, 265, 267, 340, 352 and 353.
The Toy Museum, Rottingdean, for no. 58.
Mrs. Graham Greene, for nos. 60, 93, 142, 209, 244, and 248
The Chief Director of Germanisches National-museum, Nuremberg, for no. 63.
Fru Estrid Faurholt, for nos. 64, 68, 77, 79, 80, 96, 97, 146 and 178.
The Curator of the Museum of Childhood, Edinburgh, for nos. 72, 78, 228 and 243.
Mrs. Heather Fox, for nos. 75, 94, 154, 160, 192, 193, 207, 208, 251, 255, 256, 262, 269, 275, 296–8, 300, 312, 341 and 342.
The Curator of Luton Museum and Art Gallery, for nos. 76, 180, 306 and 343.
Miss Ruth Wainwright, for nos. 84 and 86.
Mrs. Lorna Hennessy, for nos. 87–9, 99 and 200–2.
Museum of the City of New York, for nos. 95, 98, 112, 114, 115, 120, 216, 217, 219, 263, 268 and 351.

The Curator of the Red House Museum and Art Gallery, Christchurch, for nos. 101, 132, 150, 168, 277 and 321.
Mrs. Nina S. Davies, for nos. 117, 190 and 194.
The Curator of the Musée des Arts Decoratifs, Paris, for nos. 121–3 and 246.
The Director-General of the Rijksmuseum, Amsterdam, for nos. 125–9.
The Bowes Museum, Barnard Castle, for nos. 147 and 182.
The Curator of the Municipal Museum, TunbridgeWells, for nos. 157, 159, 198, 199, 232, 259, 270, 319 and 348.
The Curator of the Grosvenor Museum, Chester, for nos. 161, 245, 247, 313 and 316.
The Art Director and Curator of the Harris Museum and Art Gallery, Preston, for no. 167.
Mrs. Joan Cope, Flax Home Industry, Grasmere, for nos. 187, 188 and 224.
Honiton and Allhallows Museum, for no. 189.
Miss Muriel Pierotti, for nos. 197, 203, 204 and 206.
The Director of The National Museum of Denmark, Danish Folk Museum, Copenhagen, for no. 215.
Mr. John Noble, for nos. 229, 254 and 323 (on loan to Pollock's Toy Museum).
The Curator of the Colchester and Essex Museum, for nos. 231 and 234.
Mrs. M. E. Dickson, for no. 233.
Miss Irene Blair Hickman, for nos. 260, 261, 271, 274, 276, 291, 292 and 335.
Mrs. Wigmore, for nos. 264 and 266.
Miss Betsy Dean, for nos. 272 and 273.
Miss Faith Eaton, for nos. 282, 285, 286, 304, 305, 314, 315 and 327–30.
The Director of Maryhill Museum of Fine Arts, Maryhill, Washington (The Neva Bunsey Collection of Dolls), for nos. 290, 293, 303, 311, 322, 325, 326 and 331.
Miss Christine Smith, for nos. 308–10.
Miss Alix Boyd, for no. 317.
Miss Moriarty, for no. 318.

From a Silhouette by Edouart

INTRODUCTION

Much time and money was spent on dolls towards the end of the seventeenth century, and Christoph Weigel in 1698 mentioned that 'dolls and playthings were made in part silver, in part of wood by turners, and in part of alabaster by workers in alabaster'. Therefore as dolls are made from many different materials they have been classified as being Wooden if their heads are of wood, Porcelain if their heads are of porcelain, etc., regardless of the substance from which their bodies are made.

The use of the word 'head' often includes the shoulder-piece, which is here referred to as the 'yoke'.

Many elaborate and expensive dolls have survived, and apart from these there are numbers of interesting little dolls which in their day were purchased from pedlars who hawked them from door to door. Unfortunately few early dolls were signed by their makers, and their dates are ascertained by examining their details such as hair, eyes and joints, and of course, their clothes.

The materials from which the doll is made must be inspected, stitches peered at to see if they are hand-sewn or machined, and sometimes even those are difficult to detect. When the history of the doll is known, then dates will be authentic, and some may have the mark of a shop stamped on their bodies.

Dolls were for grown-ups as well as children, and in 1753 Horace Walpole noted that 'confectioners found their trade moulder away, while toymen and china-shops were the only fashionable purveyors of the last stage of polite entertainments—Women of the first quality came home from Chenevix's laden with dolls and babies, not for their children, but for their housekeeper'.

Early in the nineteenth century attention was turned to patenting methods of making dolls, and from this time dating becomes more accurate. The patents collected here continue through to 1910, together with the Marks from four countries, Britain, France, Germany, and the U.S.A., thus covering a period of about 100 years.

A greal deal of the history of dolls may be discovered from the specifications, and in particular the materials from which dolls were made. Metal is mentioned in 1860, silk is sometimes used for covering rubber dolls in 1861, celluloid as early as 1862, whereas leather bodies seem to disappear about 1908.

Patents have been taken out simultaneously in various countries, some having a year or so in between. The drawings accompanying them are often crude, but they are for the purpose of showing that part to be patented, and the dolls themselves when properly made and dressed with care would be beautiful and not like these bare outlines.

The collecting of dolls is different from collecting inanimate objects such as plates or lace, for dolls when looked at can look back, and many hoard dolls simply because they cannot bear the idea of parting from them. They stay as they were made, and do not grow old as we do, and it is a coincidence that one of the finest collections in England is housed at Bethnal Green Museum, which originally was part of a design by Prince Albert as a home for old ladies.

Doll patentees are by no means confined to doll manufacturers, *bimbeloteriers* and such like, for here are the names of engineers, doctors, brush-makers, etc. Emile Jumeau is described as a '*teinturer à Paris*', that is a dyer, and it is interesting to find a William Peck, possibly some relation of Lucy Peck, the wax doll maker of Regent Street, London. Florence Upton, of Dutch doll and Gollywog fame, is also here, together with many ladies who describe themselves as being 'of no occupation'.

The patents for stands for dolls indicate that during the nineteenth century dolls were displayed on stands in order to show their clothes to advantage.

Novelties of this era include swimming dolls, feeding dolls, upside-down-dolls, and a doll whose wardrobe was inside her body, surely the most novel space-saving invention ever devised.

The marks given here also span the same hundred years. In addition those dolls after 1890 will be marked with the country of their origin, for the Tariff Act of that year made this compulsory, and many marks are registered about this time, even though they may have been in use for several years previously.

Mark of C.& H.White

The Tiniest Store in New York, 1889
From *Harpers Magazine for Young People*

I Materials

Wood

Plates 1–32, 231–9

Some of the earliest dolls were made entirely or partly of wood, and those of the sixteenth century differ little from those of the nineteenth dynasty in Egypt. Here were complete wooden dolls with carved head and hands, and with the arms and legs joined to the body with wooden pegs. Other wooden-headed dolls, with stuffed bodies, have been discovered at Akhmin Panapolis dating from about A.D. 600.

Central Europe, a region of forests, produced wooden dolls during the sixteenth century, made by peasants and eventually marketed by agents. From centres such as Berchtesgaden, Oberammergau, Nuremberg, Thuringia, and from the South Tyrol, these playthings were collected and sent abroad. There were 'stump' dolls, 5 or 6 in. high, carved complete with skirt, like ninepins, some being made in Finland and other northern countries—in fact almost anywhere where trees were plentiful.

In England, 'Bartholomew Babies' were carved with bonnet, full skirt, and apron, and these, together with dolls from Holland, crossed the Atlantic during the sixteenth and seventeenth centuries. Early wooden dolls were carved in Pennsylvania from pinewood much in the same manner, with a pleated frilly bonnet also in one with the head. A little paint might suggest the sleeves, but the long dress and apron were similar to those indicated on the Bartholomew Babies. Each doll would vary slightly as they were all hand-carved, the cheaper variety being left uncoloured.

Wooden figures were made for crèches and, although not dolls, they may have been passed on for children to play with, and were often carved with great care.

Contemporary paintings and woodcuts show the larger kind of doll which the richer children possessed—an oil painting by Cranach (1472–1553), in the British National Gallery, is most interesting. These dolls were treasures handed down from generation to generation. In an English will of 1548, a wooden-headed doll with the head slightly carved with a protruding nose and with eyes and mouth indicated, was dressed in a silver and gold gown of the year 1500. This doll was bequeathed to a granddaughter with the request that it be handed on with the estate, and this was done until 1726.

Matthias Schütz, a woodcarver, made and mended toys for the court at Munich in 1670, for these dolls were playthings and even at this early date may have had their limbs replaced and hair renovated.

Turners turned the wooden dolls, which were 'cunningly constructed', some having their

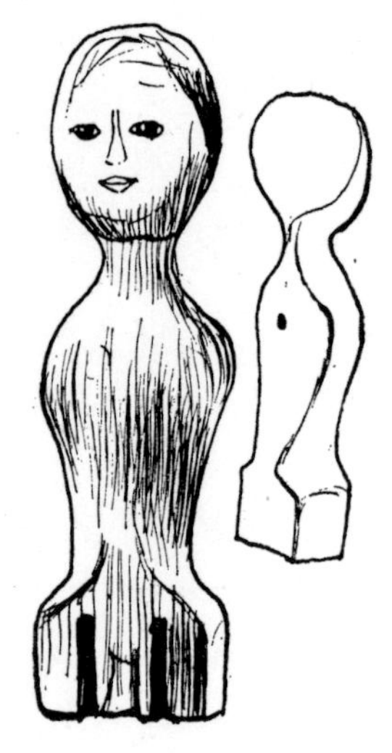

Wooden doll, 1700. Painted gesso, glass eyes

backs flattened slightly with head and body in one piece. Dolls of about 1660 were from 10 to 12 in. high, and had arms and legs attached by strings, or they could move by means of simple joints.

A coating of gesso, that is a mixture of about two-thirds whitening and one-third size, such as was used for mouldings, would be applied to the wooden head and shoulders before painting. Sparse wisps of hair, usually human, poked from under the muslin cap, being either fixed with glue, or nailed to the head with large nails or even hand-made pins.

A twist of padded material formed the upper arms, and a doll of 1688, 21 in. high, had the lower arms carved of wood with spade-like hands and separate thumbs. Later, hands had separate fingers and could be of bone, straw, bamboo, or wood, the latter becoming very big between 1690 and 1700, some being carefully carved with slightly up-turned palms.

In the Fitzwilliam Museum at Cambridge, a beautiful doll is depicted in a picture by Jan de Meyer. Surrounded by four children, she is dressed in an olive-green striped gown with a bodice ending in a V at the waist, the elbow sleeves showing carved arms and hands—in fact she is a typical doll of a wealthy family at the beginning of the eighteenth century.

Beauty patches appeared on the doll faces about 1690, for between the sixteenth and the nineteenth centuries the doll was a well-dressed lady—children were just smaller-sized dolls and those with leading-strings on their grown-up gowns were but three years of age.

About 1710, many dolls had kid arms, and a few had leather bags for bodies. A doll could have knee joints made by a projecting piece of wood with one hole, fitting be-

Wooden doll of about 1800, head painted cream with carmine cheeks, inset eyes of enamel, very white whites, dark iris, black pupils. Kid arms and hands. Wearing a muslin cap with yellow ribbons, a cream cotton dress, printed in a brown repeat pattern. *Haslemere Museum*

tween a piece of wood with a hole on either side of a groove, with a wooden peg pushed through the three holes. The lower leg of a better doll could be covered with silk to resemble a stocking.

Dolls varied between 10 and 24 in. high, and by 1750 there were many with joints also at the elbows. Often mended, often redressed, dating is difficult. Should a wooden hand be lost it might be easier to replace it with one of kid, and should a head be broken off it could be mended with a nail and thus be given a turning head!

Eyebrows were curious, sometimes just a sweeping line of black paint, sometimes with little lines at right angles giving the appearance of blanket-stitch, or even herring-bone, which may have imitated those dolls of stuffed cloth and embroidery which preceded them.

Jointed wooden doll, with inset brown eyes, brown wig and wooden hands. *Haslemere Museum*

Henri d'Allemagne[1] wrote that 'in the eighteenth century the doll-heads were of carved wood, painted with more or less refined art; as for the body it was sometimes formed in the same manner, but, most often, trimmings of material, rolled and held together by a light bond formed the arms, at the end of which were attached wooden hands; with her gown of figured silk or her beautiful French suit, the little personage, thus constructed, was far from being a bad figure. However this type of doll cost a great deal to produce, particularly by reason of the carved parts which had to be done by hand by special craftsmen.'

Large wooden dolls of the eighteenth century had blown glass eyes or eyes of enamel. At first there was no pupil, but by 1790 many eyes coming from Europe had black centres. The diamond-shaped enamel eyes were set into diamond-shaped grooves carved in the wood. They were blue-white in colour or pure white, usually with such a dark brown iris that it is difficult to see if there is a pupil, though on the lighter brown eyes this shows. Blue irises were

[1] *Histoire des Jouets.*

rare at this time. A wooden doll which had glass eyes to open and shut by means of a wire which came out at the base at the back of the body was made in 1826, and patents mention dolls with enamel eyes between 1845 and 1861.

As Queen Anne died in 1714, it would be more accurate to call the 'Queen Anne type' dolls Georgian. They were played with all through the eighteenth century with little change, except for those curious dolls with staring marble-like eyes, and pegged wooden joints, threaded, which appeared during the Georgian period. There are not many of these (the Geffrye Museum has a good specimen), but their clothes with loops, fringes and hand-made lace are very interesting. Their bodies are of jointed wood and are very heavy to hold.

From an engraving of 1821

Apart from the large expensive dolls, there were many small wooden ones from about 8 in. high to as little as ½ in. with jointed arms and legs. These were the 'Dutch' dolls, the Pennywoods and the Pegdolls which were popular on both sides of the Atlantic. Made in quantities in Central Europe and in Holland they were a convenient size for dolls' houses, and varied in price according to how well they were made. Some were crude, others were well finished with glossy painted 'hair', tinted skins and shaped spade-like hands. Some had carved yellow combs on top of their heads and belong to the period between 1812 and 1830. Many had grey curls painted around their faces and all had black shiny 'hair'. The little Princess Victoria dressed dolls of this kind, and the various sizes may be seen in novelties such as 'The Old Woman in a Shoe' where even the tiniest children are jointed.

Charlotte Brontë had about 21 dolls when she was a child, the chief amongst these being a large wooden doll which had been presented to her as a prize for hemming her first handkerchief. Children learnt sewing at an early age, so if she was about five years old at this time, the year would be 1828 and the doll very much like the large wooden 'Dutch' doll of 1830.

In London, in 1851, the principal places for buying wooden dolls were at Alfred Davis's and at Whites, both in Houndsditch, and at Joseph's in Leadenhall Street. The dolls were sold mostly by the people who had assembled them, and could be purchased from barrows, stalls or from baskets carried in the streets. John and L. Poole of Twister's Alley, Bunhill Row, were makers of wooden dolls.

About 1860 some heads were smaller in proportion to the bodies, thus making the dolls appear taller, and many of these were dressed as pedlars. Persons who wished to have more

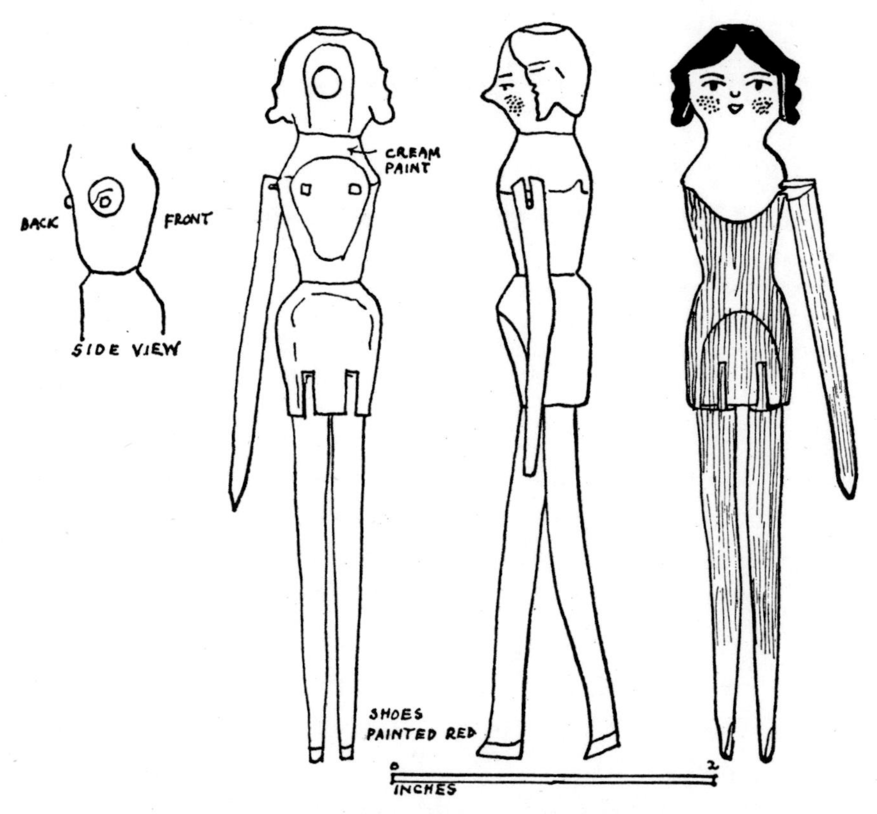

Wooden 'Peg' doll, showing arms pegged through to back. *Haslemere Museum*

pliable dolls would replace the wooden limbs with wire, which they carefully covered with wool or cloth. Gradually papier mâché and wax ousted the larger wooden dolls, though the smaller varieties continued to be made in large numbers by the poorer people.

In Nuremberg, Christian Hacker and Samuel Krautz both registered their marks in 1875, and R. Patzig of Niederneuschönberg, another maker of wooden dolls, registered his mark a little later.

Also in 1875, the Dressel Brothers, Cuno and Otto of Sonneberg, registered their sign incorporating the words '*Holze-Masse*'. *Holz* is German for wood, *Masse* includes materials such as imitation wood or composition. Emil Thurnauer of Nürnberg registered his mark in Britain in 1899 for his wood and papier-mâché toys, and though dolls by then had heads of other material, their bodies and their limbs continued to be made of wood by many doll-makers.

Papier mâché and other compositions *Plates 33–60, 333–4, 348, 350*

'To bring play-dolls within the reach of all purses, attention was given to substituting mechanical procedures for manual work.' This was the invention of moulded cardboard spoken of by Henri d'Allemagne[1] when he was alluding to the passing of the wooden dolls which had been made by hand.

Papier Masse is papier mâché, in other words mashed paper, and as the words 'Fester Masse' mean all other substances or compositions, many recipes come under these headings.

Doll-heads which are cast in moulds are either poured in and made in one piece, in which case the mould opens to reveal the complete head, or they are made in two halves and then joined. This latter method is used for papier mâché and composition.

A model of a doll-head would be made in carved wood or clay, then coated with shellac. This would be completely surrounded by clay which when hard would be cut away in two halves showing the face in one half and the back of the head in the other, the concave 'dishes' looking like the interior of a blancmange mould. Into these would be pressed the composition substance, a method already used in 1698 in Nuremburg for doll-heads and for complete little dolls about 7 in. high.

By using casts and moulds into which the pulped paper was pressed, dolls became a commercial project, and by 1810 papier-mâché dolls were produced in bulk in Sonneberg. These were strong and light to hold and although at first they were crude, better ones gradually became popular. The doll-heads, often complete with yoke, would then be joined to soft bodies of rag or kid, either by stitching or by gumming.

Charlotte M. Yonge, born in 1823, mentions[2] having a 'novelty doll' made of white leather with a papier-mâché face.

From the patent drawings it may be seen that the two halves of the head consisted of the front portion and the back portion, and when the head was sufficiently hard and dry, the halves were joined and later painted.

These composition heads often included the 'hair' which was usually painted black or dark brown, very rarely being fair. The relief 'hair' was moulded in various styles, often incorporating ribbons, combs, and ornaments, and it is from the way in which the hair is dressed that these heads may be dated. Other papier-mâché heads might have wigs added later, and often the edge of the yoke was coloured blue.

Some of these composition heads had inset glass eyes, and in 1840 a doll was made with eyes which could move from side to side, a movement nowadays known as 'flirting eyes'. Soret made his dolls of mashed and pressed paper in 1847 and as these were coloured by hand, small differences occurred making each doll an individual type.

[1] *op. cit.* [2] *Autobiography* (quoted by G. Battiscombe).

Baby dolls of papier mâché were introduced into Germany from England, and later these achieved fame at the 1855 exhibition. The little *Gelenktäufling* were of flesh-coloured papier mâché dipped in wax (*Gelenk* meaning jointed, and *Täufling* a little baptized baby). Some doll makers added a covering such as muslin, linen, or silk which was pasted or cemented to the paper pulp. Greiner did this in 1858, Lake in 1868, and Weigand in 1876.

Many of the recipes show that the doll composition or pulp was put into the moulds in separate layers, each in turn being pressed into the concave or convex contours. This method can be seen clearly in the diagram for Vogel's patent.

Hawkins moulded dolls and doll-heads in 1868, taking out patents in France and the U.S.A. His patents show the hair modelled in one with the head, whereas in that of Reichmann's, the doll is obviously wearing a wig.

The Lake doll-heads were made of buckram, muslin, felted fabric, or other textile and were stiffened with some gluey substance such as starch or size, the fabric being damped and shaped by pressure between heated dies. These heads were formed in two halves as usual and were afterwards joined by heated seaming tools. When William Brock made his hollow doll-heads in 1874 the mould was first lined with tinfoil or leather, so that the stiffening, which was saturated with glue, did not adhere to it.

Many different recipes were tried not only for the doll-heads but also for the limbs,

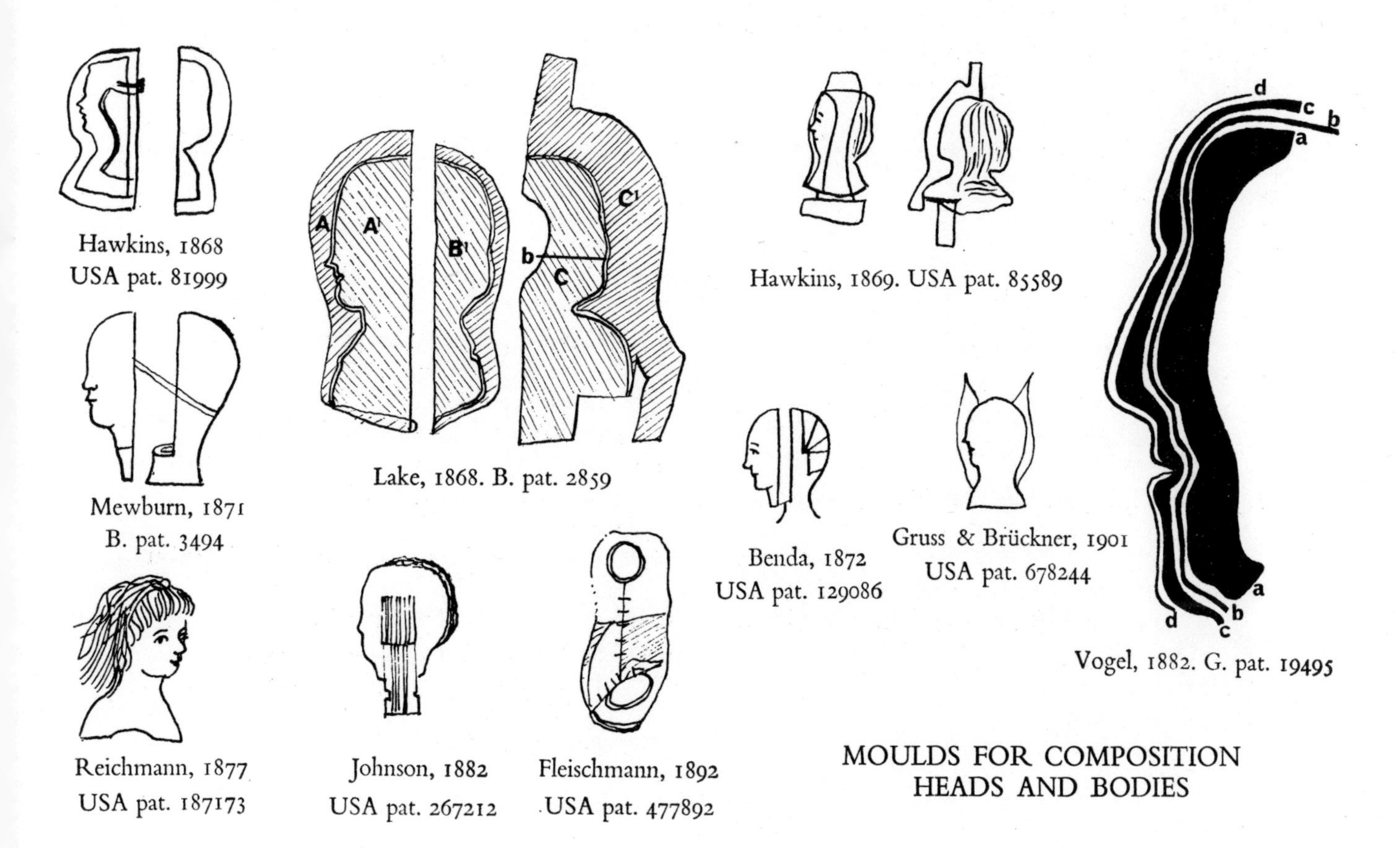

Hawkins, 1868
USA pat. 81999

Lake, 1868. B. pat. 2859

Hawkins, 1869. USA pat. 85589

Vogel, 1882. G. pat. 19495

Mewburn, 1871
B. pat. 3494

Benda, 1872
USA pat. 129086

Gruss & Brückner, 1901
USA pat. 678244

Reichmann, 1877
USA pat. 187173

Johnson, 1882
USA pat. 267212

Fleischmann, 1892
USA pat. 477892

MOULDS FOR COMPOSITION
HEADS AND BODIES

usually the lower arms and lower legs, which would then be joined to stuffed bodies. Reichmann, in 1877, used an inner layer of sawdust, glue, and paste, with an outer layer of beeswax, paraffin, and turpentine. Bartenstein put wax over his composition in 1880, and Johnson covered his wooden heads with what he termed a 'plastic shell' in 1882.

Remignard in 1888, Steiner in 1889, and Fleischmann and Bloedel in 1892, all made a 'pâté incassable' (unbreakable substance) for dolls. This was used for limbs and for bodies which gradually took the place of stuffed bodies, and to which later on bisque heads were added. Fleischmann's patent diagram for 1892 shows the moulded portion of the doll's body with the holes through which the separate limbs would be attached.

In 1892, a recipe was sent from Moscow to the U.S.A. by Samuel Hoffman.[1] This was for 'a method of producing the heads and limbs of dolls which consists of reducing glue, glycerine, zinc oxide, and Japanese wax to a liquid state, and pouring the liquid into moulds. Smoothing the moulded mask, dipping the mask in a bath of glue, glycerine, white zinc oxide, Japanese wax, and colouring matter reduced to a thin liquid, and finally decorating the moulded article, and immersing it in a bath of collodion.'

Gesland, in 1898, the firm of Verdier & Gutmacher, and Gruss & Brückner in 1901, all made unbreakable dolls using stiffened material between glued layers of fabric. Eaton, in 1904, used a mixture 'of paper and glue beaten to a pulp, moulded under pressure, the centre of the cast being filled in with cork. The dolls were moulded in halves and then joined, painted with diluted celluloid and coloured, the final result resembling china.'

However, some compositions were not strong; fingers and toes often broke off revealing a kind of cardboardy substance.

Marian Kaulitz made her heads of papier mâché, adding detail which made each doll into an individual full of character.

Patents

1847 Soret. Papier mâché
1852 Wicks
1853 Richard. Cirico-plastic paste
1854 Guichard. Flocking
1855 Voit. Papier mâché
1856 Brouillet-Cacheleux. Pasteboard
Barth. Moulds
1857 Roy
1858 Greiner. Strengthening doll-heads by pasting or cementing those parts with muslin, linen, or silk, etc.
1862 Souty. Pumice-stone
1865 Clark. Composition
Longbottom. Kampakaon
1866 Darrow
1867 Clarkson. West Indian corkwood
1868 Lake. Stiffened buckram
Champson. Paste
Hawkins. Composition and moulds
1869 Bru
Brock. Stiffened material
1872 Benda
1874 Lacman. Papier mâché, covered with leather
Brock. Moulds
1875 Judge. Moulded paper and paste
1876 Wiegand. Paper and textile in layers
1877 Fischer Naumann. Papier mâché
Reichmann
1878 Jumeau. Papier mâché

[1] See 'Makers', under Hoffman (U.S.A. pat. 480094).

1880 Escher. Composition
Bartenstein. Wax over composition
1881 Bastier. Composition
1882 Johnson. Plastic over wood
Vogel. Compositions in layers
1884 Steiner. Composition
1885 Grumeau. Composition
1887 Thompson. Glazed pasteboard
Schmidt. Composition
1888 Hinde. Pressed pulp
1889 Steiner. Unbreakable heads
1890 Caillard. Composition
Colin. Artificial wood
L'Epine. Composition
Pintel. Composition
1892 Hoffmann. Composition and moulds
1892 Fleischmann & Bloedel. Unbreakable composition
1893 Scott & Seymour. Composition
1895 Doebrich. Composition
Eaton. Dental enamel
1896 Kammer & Reinhardt. Papier mâché
1897 Verdier & Gutmacher. Unbreakable composition
1898 Gesland. Unbreakable composition
1900 Verdier & Gutmacher. Glued fabric layers
1901 Stiefel. Papier mâché
Gruss & Brückner. Textile and paper layers
1904 Eaton. Papier mâché
Wislizenus. Composition
Bernheim & Kahn. Composition
1909 Kaulitz. Papier mâché

Ceramics

Plates 61–123, 240, 244–332, 335–6, 340–7, 352–3

The early Greek terracotta dolls found in the tombs of Athens had been cast in moulds. These jointed dolls all represented females and were called *Neurospasta.* The separate limbs were pierced with holes and connected to the body by strings. Socrates was interested in these playthings, some of which have survived and may be seen in museums to-day and compared with the dolls of our own times.

Clay, porcelain, Parian, and bisque are all materials where moulds are used, and to each of these belong two classes of dolls. There are those completely made in one of these substances, either with or without joints, and there are those with head or head and yoke cast in a mould and which is joined to a stuffed body or one of composition.

To the first class belong numerous little dolls which are mostly found in dolls' houses, including those known in the U.S.A. as Frozen Charlottes, and bisque dolls with limbs joined by wire which were to be found in shops well into the twentieth century.

In the second class are dolls with porcelain, Parian, or bisque heads, with or without yokes, and with bodies of leather, textile, or composition.

Porcelain, commonly called china, is distinguished from pottery by being translucent, some being known as hard-paste and some as soft-paste. Should a doll's head be broken and the chipped edge sparkle like a flint stone and be impervious to staining, then it is made from hard-paste. If the broken part shows a porous surface capable of absorbing colour, then the doll's head or limbs are said to be of soft-paste.

European families of potters worked during the sixteenth, seventeenth, and eighteenth centuries; some made figures, but there is no actual mention of dolls. One such family, the Perottis, worked at Faenza from 1505 onwards, and E. Armand worked at Marseille and Varages in 1698. Potters at Rouen named Armand were mentioned during the middle of the eighteenth century, one being in charge of the enamelling kilns at Sèvres from 1745 to 1788. The Greiner family, with five sons who were painters and potters in Thuringia, were among founders of the great modern porcelain industry from 1764 onwards.

The porcelain and china of Richard Chaffers, sold in Liverpool, was advertised as 'proved with boiling water before it was exposed for sale'; and Mr. Cookworthy of Plymouth patented his hard-paste porcelain in 1768.

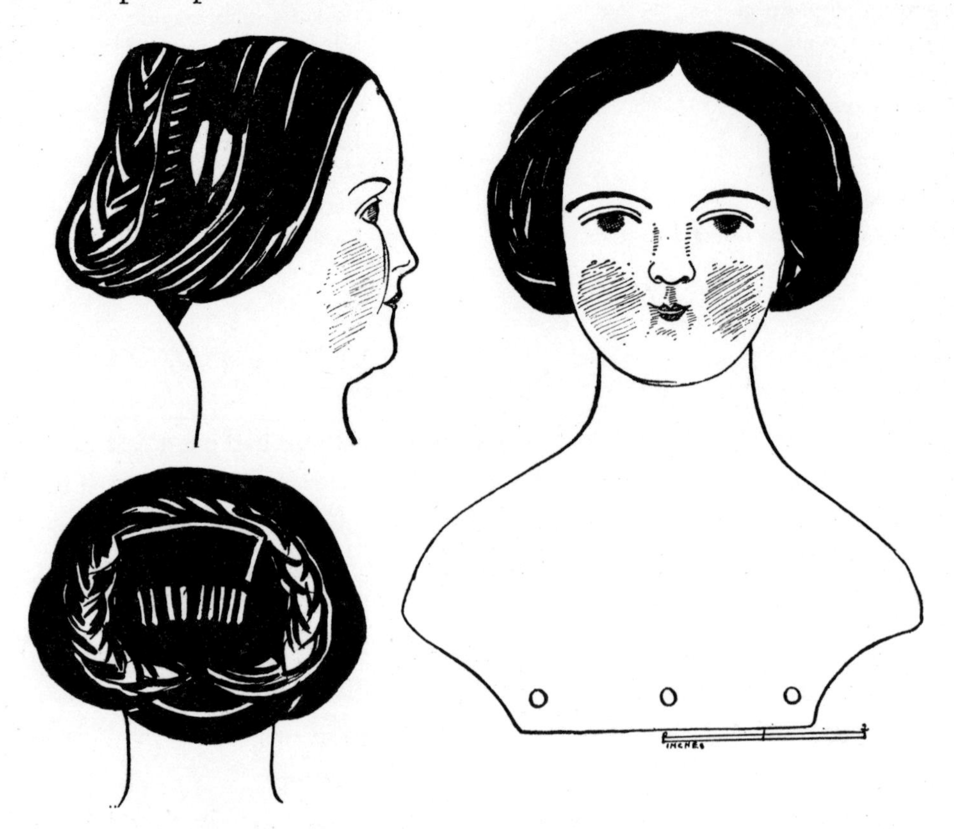

Porcelain head, about 1840. Black hair, black comb, red top lid to blue eyes, pink cheeks.
Belonging to Miss Blair Hickman

Kestner, a German potter, worked at Gardner's factory, Moscow, in 1779, and Francesco Perotti was a potter at Mondovi in 1808. By 1820 there were porcelain doll-heads made in Europe, but unfortunately the makers did not seem to sign their wares.

Jacob Petit made porcelain heads in 1843 and patented improvements in England in 1853, and it is known that he made biscuit figures at first at Belleville and later at Fontainebleau. Other French or Swiss potteries where dolls were made were at Montreux and at St. Maurice. In England, pottery figures were fairly numerous, but although the details of heads, hands, and feet are similar to those of dolls, it is difficult to trace if any were actually made in these places. Ralph Salt and Obadiah Sherratt made figures in Staffordshire in 1840, and between 1845 and 1878 flat-back figures for mantelpieces were made by Sampson Smith of Longton. Other potteries were at Prestonpans and Portobello in Scotland.

The features on the porcelain doll-heads were usually painted, with pale blue eyes with pupils, often a red line defining the upper lid, a sweeping black line for an eyebrow, two red dots for nostrils and a small red mouth painted below. The little mouth was firmly shut and, as far as I know, never had parted lips to show teeth.

One way of dating these heads of porcelain is by the manner in which their hair was moulded and painted black. Some heads were of a pale flesh colour and many had tinted cheeks.

The Limbach factory in Thuringia registered a sign in 1855, and Reidemester and Fischer Naumann made porcelain dolls in Germany in 1860.

Porcelain heads of 1863, with lustre glaze and fair hair, are said to represent the Princess Alexandra at the time of her marriage. They are very beautiful, with coloured glazed ornaments in the hair, and have stuffed bodies with either leather or porcelain arms.

Bisque doll, about 1885. Fair hair wig, dark brown eyes, dimple in chin. Dépose, etc. stamped in light red under wig at back of neck; Jumeau, etc. stamped in blue at base of spine. Wearing a white satin bonnet with pale blue ribbons, a cream corded-silk outfit, trimmed with cream braid. *Bethnal Green Museum*

Doll-heads and dolls of porcelain were made in quantities in Germany about 1873, the later heads being hollowed at the back in order to make them lighter in weight because of custom duties. Unfortunately this tended to make the dolls fall forward and by 1884 to prevent this some porcelain heads were fitted with a piece of lead inside at the back which was covered with a piece of cork.

Late nineteenth-century porcelain heads have an opening at the top to which was fixed a wig of hair or of tow, some having a layer of cork to facilitate fixing. Some have holes in the porcelain, usually one over each ear, one on top of the head, and a fourth at the base of the skull, in order that the wig could be secured.

Entries for trademarks disclose the makers of porcelain dolls, German names being those of Wilhelm Simon of Hildburghausen, Cuno and Otto Dressel of Sonneberg, and Samuel Krautz of Rodach bei Coburg, all of these being for the year 1875. The firm of Schmitt Père et fils advertised their '*Bébés en Porcelaine*' in 1879, and Heubach in 1880.

Bisque doll, 19 in. long. Fair greyish hair wig, painted eyebrows, brown eyes, pale red nostrils and lips. Bru mark on back of neck. 'Serena', *belonging to Miss Faith Eaton*

So far only the porcelain dolls have been mentioned, but alongside these, perhaps at a little later date, are the bisque dolls with fair bisque hair. Some of these are so fine that they have been classed as 'Parians' and, to avoid confusion, all these complete bisque heads have been put in this class. The shiny porcelain dolls had not appealed to everyone, and a few heads were made with glazed hair and unglazed faces, for by now manufacturers were aiming at a flat finish to their doll-heads and limbs.

Parian was a ceramic resembling unglazed porcelain biscuit, and between 1851 and 1866 or thereabouts, doll-heads were made from this fine white clay which was so like marble. Actual Parian ware was dead white and expensive, many ornaments and figurines at the 1851 Exhibition causing quite a stir. It was left unglazed and delicately tinted, and was suitable for very fine modelling, for often a glaze seems to round off the corners.

Ribbons and flowers were modelled into the blonde hair-do's of the dolls and some, in addition, had necklaces and collars. The features were usually painted, though a few had glass eyes and some had swivel necks. Gradually these heads were fitted with hair wigs in the same manner as those of porcelain, and from now on these dolls will be classed as bisques.

Jumeau is accredited with making a 'blonde bisque' in 1856, but it is not until Haag's trademark, registered in 1886, that the work 'biscuit' is mentioned for the first time, and Steiner claimed unbreakable heads both in porcelain and biscuit in 1889.

There were many beautiful bisque dolls during 1870 which may have been made for the International Exhibition held in London in 1872. Very few of these dolls are marked, they have fair hair wigs, inset fixed ultramarine eyes, swivel necks, leather bodies and limbs, many of them have pierced ears and all of them have closed mouths. The faces are of very fine bisque, and most of these dolls are beautifully dressed as fashionable ladies and come from France, often bringing trunkfuls of clothes with them. The kid arms have hands with carefully stitched fingers, the later dolls having arms of bisque and their kid bodies stamped with such names as Jumeau, Simonne, Rohmer, and Cremer.

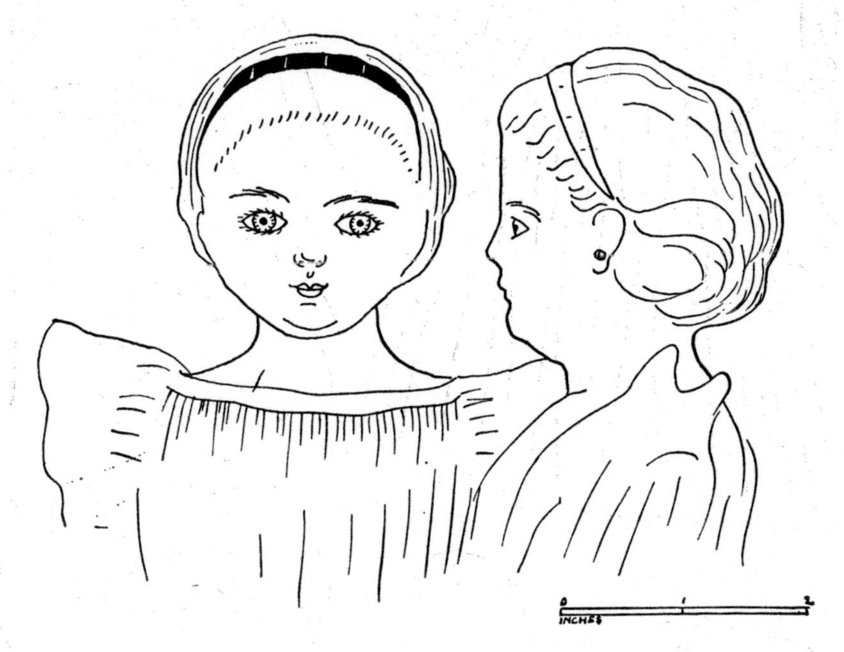

Bisque head and hair, fair ochre, with a black band, cobalt blue eyes, pale pink cheeks. Stuffed body marked on the bust, 1/-. *Haslemere Museum*

It is interesting to note that most of these porcelain, 'Parian', and bisque dolls were dressed as grown-ups, and even those of doll's house size shown in 'the Old Woman in a Shoe' are neither childlike in feature nor in dress. However, later in the nineteenth century heads were made larger, and during the 1880s dolls of these materials were dressed as children.

Since the brown-eyed beauties of Georgian times, blue eyes had predominated, but about 1881 many of the bisque dolls with wigs of fair hair were fitted with brown glass eyes, and by 1891 some brown-haired dolls had dark 'skins' also. Later, many of these were made by Armand Marseille, who gave them pretty eyes of a light brown colour, lighter than their skins.

On the later bisque heads it is fortunate if the maker's complete mark shows, for often it starts right up under the hair wig, which is usually stuck on with such strong gum that the

Bisque doll, $10\frac{1}{2}$ in. long. Hair of animal skin, very soft and fair, brushed forward in the natural way of the fur. Eyes open and shut, painted eyebrows and eyelashes, open mouth showing teeth and tongue, swivel neck. *Belonging to Miss Ruth Wainwright*

mark is difficult to decipher. However, by studying the registered marks, even if only a part of the mark shows, it may give a clue to the identity of the doll.

Dolls had wigs of sheepskin in 1881, and Bru mentioned that his dolls had real eyelashes in 1889. These were on the top lid only and fixed where the painted lid on the sphere ended. The Jumeau dolls had parted lips in 1888, and many dolls had dimples in the chin, but

Jumeau does not seem to mention his well-known dimples until about 1890, by which time he was using jointed bodies of papier mâché.

There is much variety of form and detail in the bisque doll-heads and it may be possible to recognize well-known makes by studying the features. The large liquid eyes of the Jumeau family peer from beribboned bonnets, the Steiner family seem to have inherited rather thick eyebrows, whereas the little Brus appear French and ladylike. The Marseille dolls, although coming from Germany, look particularly English with their fair skins and blonde hair. As all dolls after 1891 are marked with the country of their origin, this makes it easier for identification.

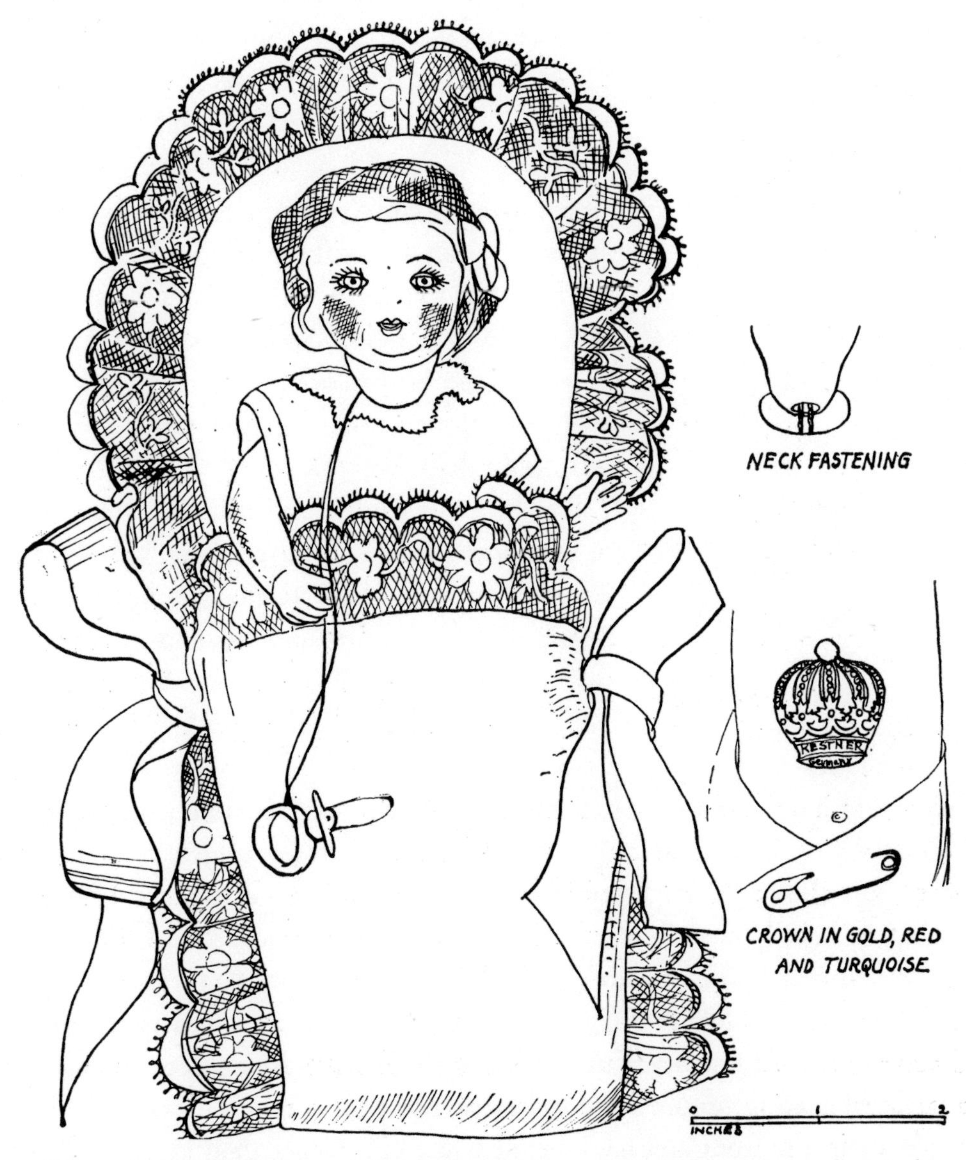

All bisque jointed doll, early twentieth century. 6 in. long, swivel neck, no joints at elbow or knee. Marked in colour with the Kestner sign, which is printed on paper and stuck to the stomach. *Bethnal Green Museum*

Esparza made imitation porcelain in 1888, and both Eaton in 1895 and Zeh in 1898 took out patents dealing with a hard substance for doll making.

At this time, the firm of Verpillier and Graves took out an interesting patent in the U.S.A. This was for a method of colouring doll-heads whereby the porcelain was tinted with water mixed with glue and glycerine, then covered with transparent lac which sunk into this coating. When dry a coating of dull lac made a skin-like effect instead of a glossy.

To all these different kinds of ceramic heads would be joined different kinds of bodies, so it is small wonder that there are so many varieties of dolls.

All bisque, jointed doll with elastic cords.
Belonging to Miss Ruth Wainwright

Throughout Europe and the U.S.A. the separate heads were sold in sizes giving measurements from shoulder to shoulder and from front to back. Those of porcelain or of 'Parian' were cheaper than those of bisque as they had painted hair and eyes.

The bodies could be of kid, muslin, or felt. They varied considerably, as often the soft bodies were sewn at home with beautiful stitches, the later ones being sewn by machine. The earlier models retain their bodies of kid and although Delphieu took out a patent in 1856 in which the leather was replaced by pink textile, kid bodies remained well into the 1890s and were stuffed with bran, hair, or cork.

Ready-made stuffed bodies could be purchased either of fine linen or of calico, which was sometimes glazed. Another material for stuffed bodies was known as Silesia. This was a fine linen or cotton fabric originally manufactured in Schlesien, in east Germany, as early as 1727. It was a kind of thin twilled cotton which was used for linings.

The dolls could have kid arms or hands with or without separate fingers, or the lower arms could be of wood, porcelain, 'Parian' or bisque. Narrow ridges are found just above the elbow, or just above the knee, which enable the limb to be attached to the body, the material being stretched over the porcelain and threads wound around the narrow ridge. Dolls with home-made bodies usually have thick legs and larger feet.

Kintzback took out a patent in 1869 for fastening a leather arm to a porcelain head; that is to head and yoke, for these heads usually included the shoulder piece. Holes in the china, front and back, enabled the entire yoke to be sewn or tied to the body with linen threads or tapes, three holes in the front and back being said to be earlier than those yokes with two. If there were no holes, then strong gum was used, the leather often coming up over the yoke, and finished with either scallops or pinking.

The lower legs are often complete with accessories—in fact they were more often clothed than left bare—and these details were usually coloured. Legs terminated with tiny black boots, quite out of proportion to the doll's head—some with heels, some with brown soles and mostly with white socks which had been made in the mould with the leg. Coloured bows are found tied just below the knee, and these may have lustre added, giving them an elegant finish. Boots may be laced or buttoned—in fact great care was taken in the designing of these details and often they are a help towards dating the rest of the doll.

In the U.S.A. in 1894 the doll bodies were advertised as 'made of white muslin and with arms of white kid'. These had two rows of stitches down the front and across the thighs, and a band with stitches where the knee would be so that it could bend. Bodies such as these were machined right across the shoulders, making an arch-like shape which would fit securely under the bisque yoke.

Other dolls had bodies of coloured felt, complete with bisque head and hands; these were described as 'Knock About Dolls' and could be bought for 45 cents in the U.S.A. about 1895.

At the beginning of the twentieth century many baby dolls had wax faces, but these were gradually replaced by ones with lifelike heads of bisque. At first these babies had stuffed bodies, and were dressed in long-clothes and veils, but at the end of the Edwardian era they had composition bodies and limbs with joints at the shoulders and thighs only. The elbows and bent knees were made in the form of a chubby baby and the curved legs enabled the doll to sit up on its own.

In America china and bisque heads were sold separately and attached to stuffed bodies ready-made or sewn at home.

China heads with painted hair and eyes.
Width across shoulders, 3 in., width from front to back 2 in., price 10 cents.
- Width 3½ in. × 2¼ in., 15 cents
- Width 4 in. × 2½ in., 20 cents.
- Width 4½ in. × 3 in., 25 cents.
- Width 5 in. × 3½ in., 35 cents.

Bisque heads with solid eyes, including wigs of flowing hair.
Width across shoulders 3¾ in. × 2 in., i.e. width from front to back, 60 cents.
- Width 4½ in. × 2½ in., 80 cents.
- Width 5½ in. × 3 in., 1.0 dollar.
- Width 6¼ in. × 3½ in., 1.25 dollars.

Bisque heads with closing eyes, including wigs of flowing hair.
- Width 3¼ in. × 1¾ in., 50 cents.
- Width 4¼ in. × 2¼ in., 65 cents.
- Width 4¾ in. × 2¾ in., 85 cents.
- Width 6 in. × 3 in., 1.10 dollars.

From a Montgomery Ward catalogue of 1894. *U.S.A.*

Kid doll, about 1826. 20 in. long. The leather head seems to be over a wooden base, the leather body stuffed with sawdust and cotton wool. Blown glass eyes with pupils, side combs in hair wig. A boned bonnet is worn over a muslin cap, the long white muslin dress comes to the ground, and is gathered at the waist, neck and sleeves, and all hand sewn. The doll was made for Miss Louisa Parker when she was eight years old, by the ladies of Ashburnham Place, near Battle, from their kid gloves, in recompense for sewing their ball dresses. The doll wears a petticoat, chemise, stays, drawers, and shoes of muslin. *Bethnal Green Museum*

Leather

Plate 230

As dolls are classified by the material from which their heads are made, few dolls come under this heading, though leather was used in many ways other than for heads. Children had played with wooden dolls for years, but even the jointed ones were stiff, and eventually leather bodies replaced the unbendable wood.

Leather dolls, made in Sonneberg in 1820, were very strong and were stuffed almost to bursting point, some having wire inside to make them even stronger.

At first the leather used was coarse sheepskin, the doll body being merely a bag shape. The upper arms were loosely attached to the torso, but the forearms and hands were beautifully

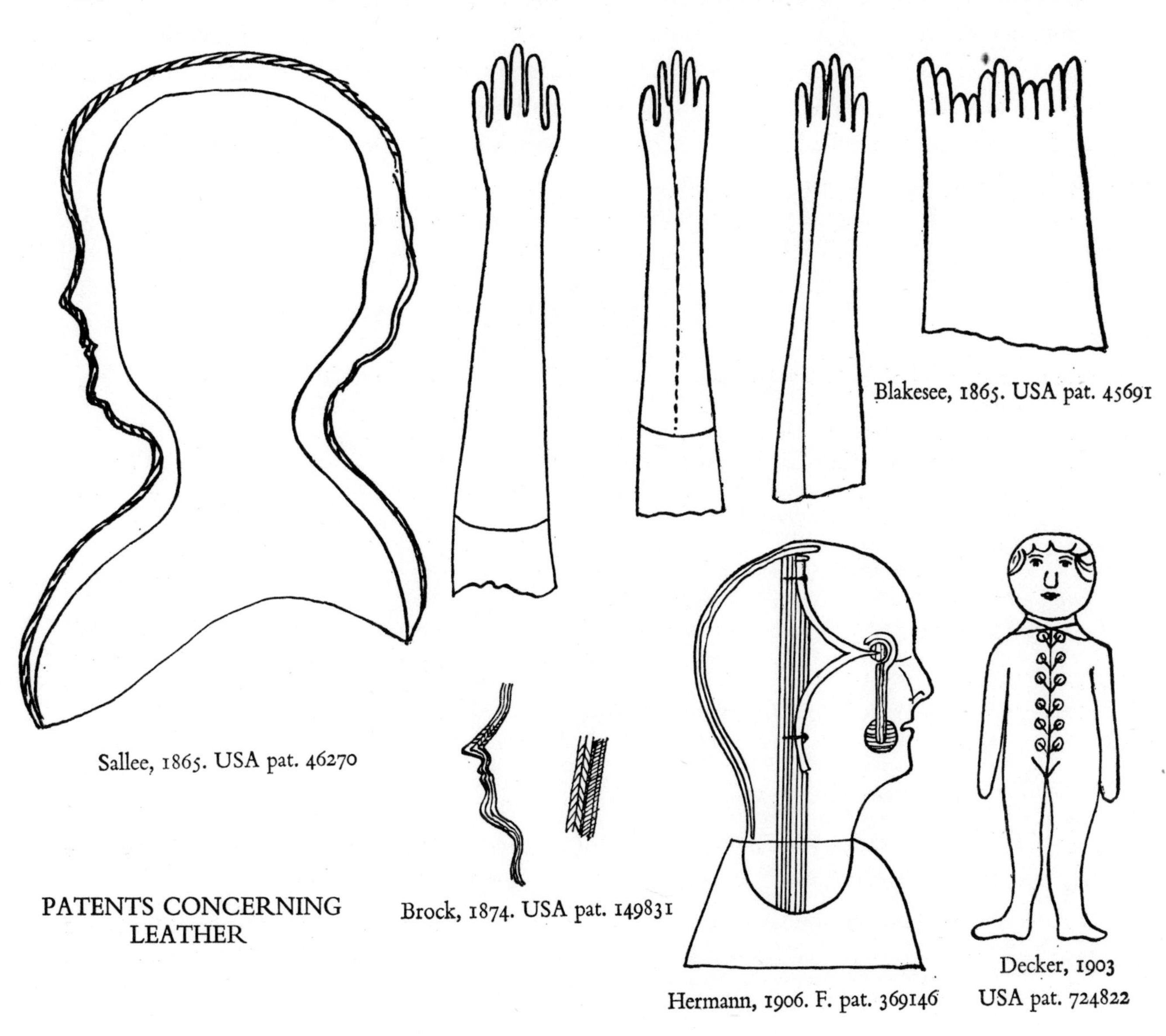

Blakesee, 1865. USA pat. 45691

Sallee, 1865. USA pat. 46270

Brock, 1874. USA pat. 149831

Hermann, 1906. F. pat. 369146

Decker, 1903
USA pat. 724822

PATENTS CONCERNING LEATHER

made. Red, green, blue, black, brown or yellow was used and so the dolls have the appearance of wearing long kid gloves. Early examples have mitten hands, later ones have separate fingers.

Gradually sheepskin gave way to fine kid, some white, some pink; it is interesting that Emile Jumeau described himself as a dyer in one of his entries.

Louis Bauersach, an importer of dolls in the U.S.A., had kid and jointed dolls for sale in the 1850s, but most of these dolls were unmarked and it is only by comparing their seams with those of patent drawings that their identity may be established. Rohmer patented leather arms for dolls in 1857, and between *c.* 1861 and *c.* 1875 Chauvière made jointed kid dolls which were stuffed. In Blakesee's patent of 1865 the kid fingers are separate one from another.

Lucretia Sallée, of the U.S.A., in 1865 had the idea of backing the leather heads with cement in order to strengthen them. Clarkson put a leather covering over dolls made of corkwood, and Lacman a covering over dolls of papier mâché. Many of the makers mention the kind of head which goes with these leather bodies, such as a porcelain head to Kintzbach's in 1869 and bisque or composition heads to those of Sarah Robinson.

By 1895 'Extra fine Kid Baby Dolls' were for sale in the U.S.A. with bisque turning heads, bisque hands, and hip, knee, and arm joints, for $2.35.

Hermann, in his patent for 1906, covered plastic heads with leather.

Patents

1840 Leather dolls with china heads made in Sonneberg
1857 Rohmer. Leather arms for dolls
1861 Chauvière. Kid dolls jointed and stuffed
1865 Blakesee. Patterns for arms cut from leather
Sallee. Leather heads backed by cement
1866 Clement. Leather dolls
Darrow. Dolls from raw-hide
1867 Clarkson. Leather covering over corkwood
1869 Kintzback. Fastening a leather arm to a porcelain head
1870 Chauvière. Kid dolls
1874 Lacman. Moulded dolls of papier mâché, covered with leather
1879 Bru. Leather dolls
Vogel. Heads and limbs covered with stretched leather
1882 Voirin. Cuir moulé or moulded leather
1883 Robinson. Stuffed and jointed leather dolls with bisque or composition heads
1890 Pulvermacher. Leather dolls
1903 Decker. Complete leather dolls with stained features
1906 Hermann. Unbreakable head of plastic material covered with the skin of an animal
1908 Scherf. Knee joints for leather or rag dolls

Wax

Plates 124–210, 337–9, 349

Sardis, the capital of Lydia, was an ancient town well known for its toys. Here wax was used as a coating over a wooden base in order to give a smooth effect to dolls, which in the Doric dialect were known as '*dagys*' and in the Ionic as '*dagynon*'.

Throughout medieval Europe full-sized figures, which were replicas of notable persons, were made of wax and placed in churches and chapels. Later, as wax was expensive as well as heavy, these figures had wax faces and hands only, the bodies being frameworks of canes and wood over which the clothes would be placed. Cellini, the sixteenth-century Italian craftsman, made wax figures, and the country of Spain also excelled in realistic effigies with natural colouring and with glass eyes.

During the seventeenth century there is mention of wax dolls in Germany, especially those made in Augsberg by Daniel Neuberger, which were of extra hard wax and coloured. It was the fashion for a rich lady whose baby had died to have it copied full-size in wax, and this would be dressed in baby clothes and kept in a cradle. Small votive figures and dolls were made of solid wax in moulds, but later the heads and limbs were hollow. The parts were joined to wooden bodies which eventually gave way to bodies of stuffed material.

Wax doll, given to a child born in 1835. Chestnut hair, elaborately plaited, painted grey eyebrows, inset hazel eyes with dark rims, carmine cheeks. Dressed in a pale blue cloak with blue ribbons, a cream silk bonnet with whale bones, the clothes being made near Banbury, the stockings woven nearby at Middleton Cheney, where stockings used to be woven. The outfit is intended to represent that worn by Queen Victoria at the Christening of the Prince of Wales. *Haslemere Museum*

Wax was also used as a thin layer on wood or on composition, usually being spread over the head and yoke and then tinted, but with the passing of time the wax often cracked.

Dolls were still alluded to as 'babies' during the eighteenth century. In 1701, Dr. Claver Morris of Wells visited London, and while there he purchased a doll for his baby daughter Molly, 'a Wax Baby with an invention to make it cry and turn its eyes'. The entry definitely states 'turn', which is interesting.[1]

In 1712 a doll $2\frac{1}{2}$ ft. high with head, arms, and hands of wax, could have human hair set into the wax head, each hair being put in separately.

[1] *Somerset and Dorset Notes and Queries*, June 1938.

Daniel Defoe, writing from Paris in 1722, reported this item in the *Daily Post*: 'the Duchess of Orleans made a present to the Infant Queen of a wax Baby, Three Foot High, with diamond earrings, a necklace of pearls, and diamond cross, with a Furniture of Plate for a toilet, and Two Indian chests full of linen, and several sorts of cloaths for the Baby, the whole for that Princess to play with'.

Wax doll, 1849. Brown wig, inset eyes, blue leather arms. Wearing a muslin dress trimmed with lace. This doll was purchased at Ascot Races for the late Mrs. Mardell, when a child. She was born in 1840. *Cuming Museum, Southwark, London*

In 1755, many dolls had wax heads on wooden bodies, but by 1761 many had stuffed bodies. Some of these were stuffed with very coarse straw, the stems being pushed well down into the limbs. Wax over composition was used in 1784 for many dolls with stuffed bodies. Madame Tussaud made her models of solid wax which was poured into moulds, and there were modellers who made wax heads and limbs for use in hospitals. These had inset hair and glass eyes similar to the models of Madame Tussaud, who during her training had made studies of some of the victims of the guillotine.

A. Loriot of New Bond Street, London, sold dolls, clowns, and soldiers, and from this shop about 1797 was purchased a wax doll as a present for the year-old daughter of George IV. This was a dressed wax doll and cost 8*s*. Many wax dolls had kid arms in 1815, and in Germany Madame Wunder's highly-painted dolls were on show at Christmas time. Small wax dolls were very light and dainty to hold, with round brown eyes and painted features, very fragile, and with clothes sewn so that they would not come off.

Portrait dolls of Queen Victoria in her coronation robes had heads and arms of wax, stuffed leather bodies and wooden legs. Others of 1840 show her in her wedding gown, and many dolls of this period could have been made as souvenirs.

Pedlar dolls had wax faces which were either 'white' or black, some with wooden legs, some with mere sticks—for the wares on the trays were the main attraction—the doll itself often wearing a long red cloak.

Wax dolls were not so popular in the U.S.A. as in England, partly owing to the climate, but they could be purchased in 1837, and by 1840 there was a toy store in almost every town. James Parmilee of Connecticut advertised wax dolls for sale in 1845, and others were imported by Louis Bauersach, who claimed them as 'the handsomest and best-made imported dolls' of 1850.

England excelled in making wax dolls and quite a few were based on portraits of Royal children, for Queen Victoria's family was large. Vicky was born in 1840, Edward in 1841, Alice in 1843, Alfred 1844, Helena 1846, and Louise in 1847. Madame Montanari was said to have made a portrait of this princess when she was a few years old. The other royal children were Arthur, born in 1850, Leopold in 1853, and Beatrice in 1857.

Small wax dolls about 9½ in. high were hawked at Ascot races in 1849. These dolls had wax heads, inset eyes, hair wigs, and arms of blue leather. Dressed in muslin trimmed with lace and ribbons, one of these dolls is now in the Cuming Museum at Southwark. She has blue shoes with pink rosettes and carries a bouquet. Other little wax dolls of the cheaper variety may be discovered in the Folk Museums of English country towns—for instance, at Honiton in Devon there is one which was sold for 1*s*. 6*d*. Marked size 3, she has a wax head, inset eyes, a wig, stuffed body and legs, and arms of red leather. She wears a mauve dress with a small blue apron.

Wax doll, fair wig, inset enamel eyes blue with black pupils, pink cheeks, red lips. Cloth body, stuffed, red leather arms. She wears a mauve dress, trimmed with braid, and a blue silk apron. *Honiton Museum, Devon*

The majority of larger wax dolls had their bodies made of calico and stuffed; to this would be added hollow arms and legs of wax. The two or three holes in the legs, which usually ended just above the knee, were bored in the wax, and in some eyelets were inserted. Through these holes the tape was threaded and the limbs tied to the body. In like manner the hollow arms usually ended just above the elbow. The wax yoke fitted over the linen torso and was kept in place by having two holes pierced at the front and the back, the tape threaded through and tied around the body. The linen, calico, and tapes were usually white in colour and although these bodies were strong they were mere bags of straw when compared with the careful detail which went into the making of the heads.

Sometimes a 'fringe' of hair on a strip of braid was wound around the wax head, some had hair inserted in to a 'slit' along the top from crown to forehead, whereas others had real hair inserted in groups or singly. Many had fair hair and eyebrows, and eyelashes were

Wax doll of about 1882. Inset fair hair and eyebrows, cobalt blue eyes with white lines, painted mouth. White calico body, wax forearms and lower legs. Dressed as a baby doll in long clothes. Mark on body in a purply blue. (From fold in skin at back of neck, and the slight turn of head, this doll is similar to a Pierotti.) *Bethnal Green Museum*

carefully inserted or painted, cheeks and mouth tinted, and eyes painted or inset. Eyes were of the paperweight variety, or of dark brown glass with pupils, or like the one in the Hove Museum which has pale blue eyes with no pupils.

The dolls of Richard Montanari had muslin stretched across the wax faces, with small holes pierced so that the eyes might show through. A doll of this type in Mrs. Graham Greene's collection is marked 'A. Montanari' on the label awarding it a prize medal at the 1851 Exhibition, which indicates that Augusta also used this method.

The Montanaris, Bazzoni, Barton, Pierotti, and Santy all showed dolls at International Exhibitions between 1849 and 1859. These beautiful dolls were sold by agents or in bazaars or shops; their creations were stamped by the shop owners, usually on the stuffed body and were rarely signed. Those doll bodies which were machine-stitched must be well after 1855, for the sewing-machine was not universally used until several years after its invention, when it could be hired by the week.

The Anglo-American author, Mrs. Frances Hodgson Burnett, describes dolls in her books. In *The One I Knew The Best of All*, which is about her own childhood, she mentions a black gutta-percha doll and a wax one. 'At night this doll had her wire pulled and her wax eyelids drawn down.' She also describes the wax dolls of her youth as having black or brown rows

AU NAIN BLEU
E. CHAUVIERE
Boul' des Capucines, 27
• PARIS •

Mark found on Wax Doll. Mrs. Henessy. Photo No. 201

1880, Bethnal Green

Mark in purple on front of doll's body. Mrs. Grahame Greene. Photo No. 209.

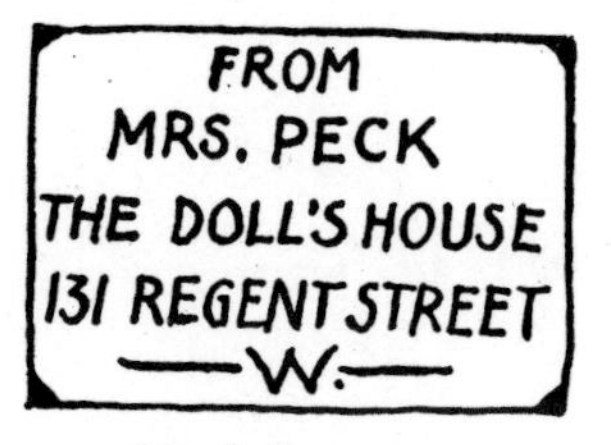

Mark in mauve. Mrs. Fox. Photo No. 207

SHOP MARKS FOUND ON WAX DOLLS

of dangling curls sewn on a little black scull cap, or stuck on with mucilage. The face and neck only were of wax, with smooth round face, a dab of wax for a nose, red paint for a mouth, eyebrows were two arches of brown paint, the eyes to open or shut were of black or blue glass with no pupil, and the wax lid pulled down over them by means of a wire which came out of the side. The calico body was stuffed with sawdust, the arms and legs dangled, the lower arms being covered with pink, blue, yellow, or green kid.

Mrs. Burnett was born in 1849, and is writing of the time when she was about three years old, so this dates these wax dolls to 1852. When she wrote the book, published in 1893, she said the dolls of that day had expression instead of vacant faces, proper noses, cheeks, and brows, parted lips with pearly teeth, and could stand upright on their own feet.

Many unmarked wax dolls have a peculiar family likeness, the little drooping mouth on the

Montanari dolls, the happier Pierottis, sometimes with head slightly turned towards the side (both families coming from the west end of London), and the rather gay Marsh's, lower in the social scale and hailing from the Fulham Road.

Towards the end of the 1870s, wax dolls in the U.S.A. could still be bought with muslin-covered faces; others had turning heads, pierced ears and composition arms and legs. Some had heads of papier mâché with a coating of wax, and many of the soft bodies were still being sewn by hand and stuffed. By 1883 some dolls had flirting eyes and a few had weighted eyes for closing, the best English eyes being bought for a guinea a pair.

Between 1868 and 1880, well-known doll makers were Edwards of the Waterloo Road, Marsh and Bartenstein. In the latter's patent of 1880, where he made a doll with two faces, this was of wax over composition. In 1891, the Meech Brothers of 50 Kennington Road, London, were wax doll makers to the Royal Family in 1891, and by 1895 Mary Anne Marsh was selling and mending dolls of bisque, and wigs and heads for French jointed dolls. In Mally's patent for 1896 his wax doll opened and shut the eyes by means of a gadget which came out of the side of the head, or it could be worked by pulling a cord.

Montanari
180 Soho Bazaar
London.

Doll belonging to Mrs. Heather Fox. Photo No. 193

Pierotti

Back of wax doll's neck. Photo No. 199

Santy. Inventor
340 Long Room
Soho. Bazaar
London

Doll at Bethnal Green, 1860. Photo No. 165

SIGNATURES FOUND ON WAX DOLLS

About 1901, Lucy Peck advertised 131 Regent Street as 'The Dolls' Home' and stated that she was a maker of best English Model Wax Dolls, real hair inserted, and dolls' repairs a speciality. By 1911 her address is changed to Kensington High Street. Thomas Betts made dolls between 1900 and 1906 and Mrs. Marian Betts continued from 1906 to 1912.

Gradually wax dolls were replaced by those which could survive the hot summers of India, where so many people went during the reign of Queen Victoria. Apparently to-day, if wax dolls travel by air, their faces may sometimes become covered with minute cracks caused by air pressure. It has been suggested that the hollow heads be stuffed with cotton-wool, but as this would involve taking the doll apart, it seems advisable that the ardent collector should go by sea when travelling with companions such as these.

The Wax Doll, 1804, from 'Original Poems for Infant Minds', published in America

Mamma now brought her home a doll of Wax,
Its hair in ringlets white and soft as flax;
Its eyes could open and its eyes could shut,
And on it with much taste its clothes were put.

. . .

She plac'd it in the sun,—misfortune dire;
The wax ran down as if before the fire!
Each beauteous feature quickly disappeared,
And melting left a blank all soiled and smeared.

From 'Dollys Own Picture Book', 1860, published in England

Now Lucy was a charming child
And never said 'I won't!'
When little Dick her plaything spoiled
She said 'Pray Dicky don't!'

He took her waxen doll one day
And turned it round and round,
And tore its arms and legs away
And flung them to the ground.

From the crude drawing it seems that the arms and legs were made of wood, and the two eyes have come out.

Rag

Plates 211–23

A bundle of rags tied around with string towards one end made a crude head on a crude body. Tied around again, there was a waist, and if arms were added and a long skirt, then here was a doll which had existed for years and years. All over the world rag dolls have been made in homes, loved beyond recognition, and then have vanished.

Faces have been indicated with stitches, paint or even tar, but although rag dolls are usually such jolly things they have a curious history, for some of their ancestors were used by witches! In seventeenth-century America, some rag dolls were found which belonged to a woman who was supposed to have bewitched some Boston children. This unfortunate 'witch' was a half-witted laundress who was later executed, for by ill-treating the dolls she was supposed to have ill-treated the children.[1] There are a few horrid rag dolls in English museums, some of which have been found stuffed up chimneys; apparently they were used to stick pins into, as were many of the old wax effigies.

By the eighteenth century most children had some kind of home-made doll and rag dolls were some of the easiest to make. Wealthy children played with beautiful cloth dolls with carefully embroidered features and elaborate dresses made from the material of their own gowns. There are pictures of children carrying such dolls. Rag dolls were also made by some of the well-known makers of wax dolls such as Augusta Montanari and John Edwards.

The Hawkins doll of 1868 is not strictly a rag doll as the textile was stiffened with glue and pressed between heated dies, so it comes under the heading of Composition, but the Hawkins method was used for making doll masks which could be purchased ready made and fitted to home-made rag dolls.

The U.S.A. dolls of Izannah Walker also had the material pressed with glue. A cloth form and the external webbing had stuffing between, in addition to the inner stuffing, and the whole doll was covered with cream-coloured sateen. The patent taken out in 1873 is one of the earliest for dolls of this kind.

Steuber patented a method of stuffing a doll's leg—he sewed the stocking B to the leg A, and the shoe C to the stocking B—then the back seams were sewn up in one operation and the resulting leg was then stuffed. This can be seen in the diagram.

Martha Wellington's dolls were of stockinette, stuffed, painted, and sewed with a wire frame inside, and Lucinda Wishard used twisted wires forming loops and knots which enabled the dolls to bend. Rebecca Johnson used waxed cloth over what she termed a supporting shell, and Wolf Flechter invented a device for stuffing rag dolls—for they had to be well stuffed in order to make them firm.

[1] Marshall and Inez McClintock, *Toys in America*, 1961.

In 1888 Phillip Samhammer, listed as a doll manufacturer in London, patented an improvement on rag dolls: 'such dolls of the cheaper kind usually have a stuffed head in one with the body upon which a wax or other face is applied, and more expensive kinds of dolls have the entire head of wax or porcelain and separate from the body and affixed thereon. It is only in the latter class of dolls, having hollow heads made separate from the body, that the motion of opening and closing the eyes automatically by a change in the position of the doll has heretofore been practicable, and the heads of such dolls are liable to become easily detached from the body. My invention enables moveable eyes to be applied to dolls of the cheaper and stronger kind. The head and neck are made of a flattened cardboard tube.'

About 1890, Mrs. Martha Chase of Pawtucket, Rhode Island, made dolls from stockinette for her own family and friends' children. One day they were seen by the keeper of a store where she had gone to buy some doll's shoes and he asked her to make some for him. Eventually they proved so popular that a company was formed to make these dolls, a factory was built behind her home, and in 1896 the Chase Stockinet Doll Company was turning them out by the thousand.

In 1893, Ida Gutsell made patterns for rag dolls which were printed on a sheet, to be cut out, sewn together and stuffed. Neubart printed a doll which was made with a front half and a back half which were sewn up the sides and round over the head, and fitted on a circular base. Louise Bowden's was a flat doll with 'darts' in the head, thus forming a rounded head when seamed; the patterns of Smith and of Schab were of two flat pieces with darts and gussets and stuffed with cotton.

This was the period when the flat printed cotton sheets became so popular: many were put out by the Arnold Print Works in the U.S.A., and by the Dean's Rag Company in England. A French rag doll called '*Poupée Satin*' was made by Marignac in 1894, but rag dolls were commercially produced mainly in England and the U.S.A.

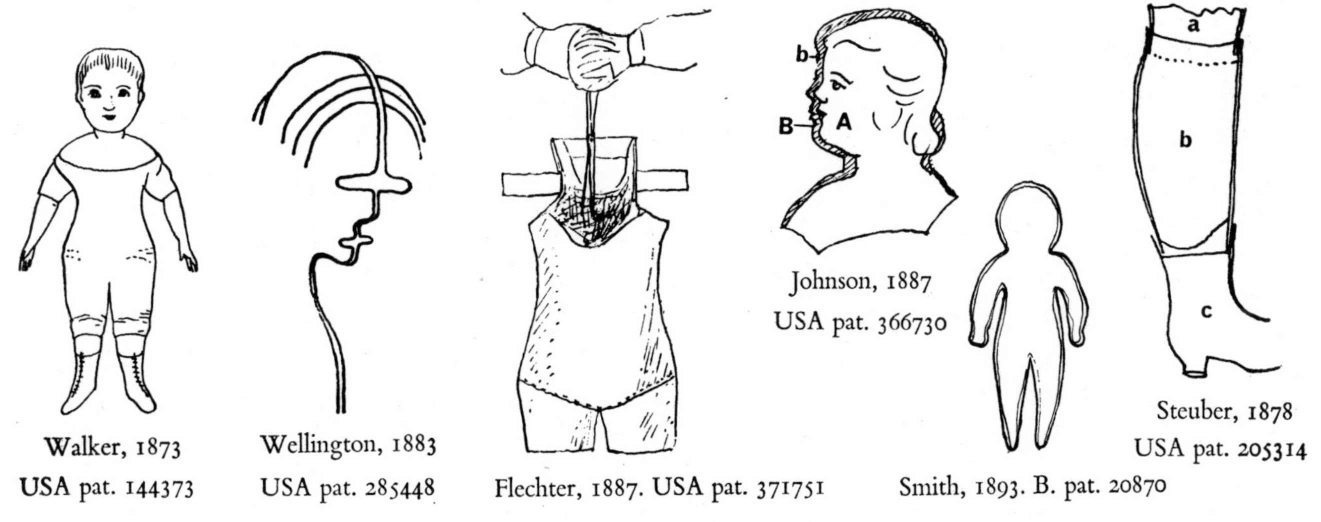

Walker, 1873 USA pat. 144373

Wellington, 1883 USA pat. 285448

Flechter, 1887. USA pat. 371751

Johnson, 1887 USA pat. 366730

Smith, 1893. B. pat. 20870

Steuber, 1878 USA pat. 205314

PATENTS CONCERNING RAG DOLLS

PATENTS CONCERNING RAG DOLLS

Eisenmann moulded cardboard for the faces of his rag dolls, which was then covered with a layer of coloured gauze, and a coating of colour. Eye sockets were cut in the moulded cardboard for inset eyes. Hockey's rag dolls could bend and sit down, and Florence Barker's were stuffed with 'pungent herbs'.

Mademoiselle Renée de Veraine made a rag doll with two faces, one smiling and one crying. The doll was made of two fronts only and the unwanted face was covered with a little cap.

In 1908 Dean's made dolls from six pieces of fabric, two front, two back, and two for the soles of the feet, and in 1909 Margarete Steiff of Wurtemberg registered marks for rag dolls. It is interesting to notice that there are many more women than men patenting these dolls of cloth and rag, and also that many of the sheets were printed in different languages, proving the popularity of the rag doll throughout the world.

Patents

1854 Quinquadon. Cork powder for stuffing dolls
1868 Edwards. Rag dolls
1873 Walker. Dolls of cream-coloured sateen, stuffed
1878 Steuber. Method of making doll's legs
1883 Wishard. Rag doll, stiffened with wires
Wellington. Stockinette doll
1887 Flechter. Device for stuffing dolls
Johnson. Rag dolls of waxed cloth
Wolf. Rag dolls
1888 Samhammer. Rag dolls with eyes to open and shut
1890 Chase. Stockinette dolls
1893 Gutsell. Cut-out dolls of cloth
Neubart. Rag doll
Bowden. Cut-out doll of cloth
Smith. Rag doll with 'darts'
Schab. Rag doll
1893 Arnold Print Works. Rag dolls
1894 Marignac. The '*Poupée Satin*'
1898 Sheppard. Stockinette doll
1899 Browne. Fabric doll
1900 Mead. Rag doll printed on cloth
Newell. Rag doll printed on cloth
1903 Gay. Rag doll
Dean. Rag doll on cloth
1905 Eisenmann. Rag dolls with cardboard faces
1906 Hockey
Barker
Véraine
1908 Dean
Bach Bros.
Scherf. Knee joints for leather or rag dolls
1909 Steiff. Cloth dolls
1910 Gibson. Rag doll

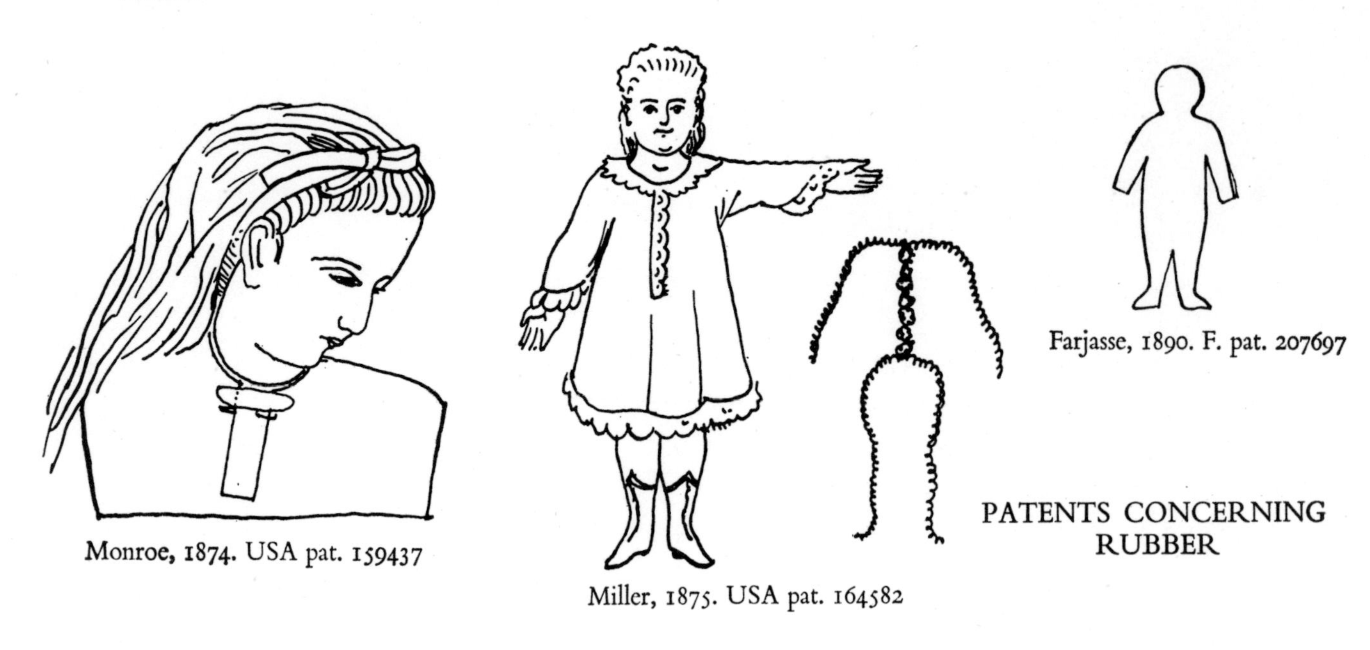

Monroe, 1874. USA pat. 159437

Miller, 1875. USA pat. 164582

Farjasse, 1890. F. pat. 207697

PATENTS CONCERNING RUBBER

Rubber

Plates 241–3

Dolls were made of gutta-percha in 1823, this material being soft and pliable, but although similar to Indiarubber, it was not of an elastic quality. Charles Goodyear, in the U.S.A., discovered his vulcanizing process in 1839.

Thomas Forster was one of the first to make rubber heads and other parts for dolls, taking out a patent in England in 1844. These were of Indiarubber and were made in moulds, and in 1849 Payne patented his hollow rubber dolls.

By 1850 some dolls had bodies of gutta-percha in place of the previously stuffed leather bags, and doll-heads of Indiarubber were advertised. A rubber doll made of vulcanized rubber, as in the Goodyear patent, appeared in the U.S.A. in 1851, but rubber dolls were not a great success—for after a while the rubber cracked—and for several years makers tried to discover new methods.

Mademoiselle Rohmer used gutta-percha or rubber for her stuffed dolls, which were jointed or unjointed, in 1857; and in England, Richard Brooman's rubber dolls were made with a top half and bottom half so that the join was at the waist, covered with a belt.

The year 1858 was a boom year for the use of rubber, and many patents were lodged. Hammond made a flesh-coloured rubber, D'Autremont made Indiarubber dolls, Tredoulat made doll-heads, Benda's dolls and those of Arnaud were jointed by means of Indiarubber, and the rubber heads made by Mademoiselle Rohmer had a cord running down through the doll's body. Stevens coated his rubber dolls with skin in 1861, and others placed wire inside the bodies in order to make them bend.

Gutta-percha heads were probably those which when squeezed and pressed could alter the expression on their faces. Bacılard made heads, Gerabon 'Grimacing dolls', and the dolls of Geradin had moving eyes. Briens put enamel eyes on his doll-heads in 1860, and in 1874 Monroe made a hard rubber doll with a turning head, and a wig made from the pelt of an Angora goat. Bru made a jointed rubber doll in 1878. Miller's flexible rubber dolls were strengthened with a wire frame which passed down the body, arms, and legs, thus enabling the hollow rubber doll to bend.

Some claimed that rubber dolls were good for infants as they assisted them when cutting their teeth, but when Hecht, in 1885, had the idea of fixing metal whistles into the rubber dolls, for years after mothers removed them from their children's toys. So where there should be a whistle one finds a hole, and the doll, if put in the bath, gradually filled with water.

Many rubber dolls were made in the 1890s: Hannoversche Caoutchouc, Warmuth, Dolffs & Helse, and the Rheinsche Gummi Fabrik all made dolls of this substance and entered trademarks. Statham made dolls of seamless rubber and Boult put hairs into the hard rubber heads by means of needles and adhesive material in 1893. F. M. Schilling, a well-known doll maker, made some rubber dolls stamped with his mark of a cherub with wings.

However, solid rubber dolls are very cumbersome and even those which are hollow are heavy to hold, and gradually their 'skins' turn to a dull grey colour which is not attractive. The best thing about rubber dolls is that they are unbreakable, but there is a faint smell pervading them and the feel of an empty hot-water bottle! But in spite of being unbreakable they must have led a very tough life compared with their more fragile sisters—for hardly any of them seem to have survived.

Patents

1839 Goodyear
1844 Forster. Heads and other parts of rubber
1849 Payne. Hollow Indiarubber dolls
1857 Rohmer. Rubber arms for stuffed dolls
1858 Brooman. Vulcanized choutchouc for dolls
Benda. Limbs joined by Indiarubber
Tredoulat. Heads
Hammond. Mechanical dolls of flesh-coloured rubber
D'Autremont. Indiarubber dolls
Rohmer. Rubber heads
1859 Rostaing. Gutta-percha dolls
1860 Baculard. Gutta-percha heads
Briens. Rubber heads with enamel eyes
1861 Stevens. Rubber dolls coated with glue and skin
1873 Hickisson. Doll-heads of choutchouc
1874 Monroe. Doll of hard rubber
Gerabon. Grimacing doll
Geradin. Rubber doll with moving eyes
1875 Miller. Rubber dolls with wire inside
1878 Bru. Jointed rubber doll
1885 Hecht. Dolls with whistles
1889 Boyer. Rubber heads with expressions
1890 Fargasse. Rubber doll
1893 Statham. Dolls of seamless rubber
Continental Caoutchouc & Gutta-percha Co.
Warmuth
Dolffs & Helse
Schilling
1894 Fayaud. Rubber doll
1899 Hannoversche Caoutchouc
1895 Wollcot & Ryder. Hollow rubber dolls
1905 New Eccles Rubber Works
1908 Indiarubber & Telegraph works

Metals

Plates 224, 351

In the Middle Ages dolls had been made of silver in Holland, and metal of all kinds was used for parts of dolls and later for doll-heads.

In 1861 Poulin made metal heads for dolls which had eyes of enamel, and Vervelle made doll-heads in 1876 and again in 1879; Péan Frères made metal heads in 1887—all of these makers taking out patents in France.

Schön, in 1886, took out a patent in Germany for doll-heads made from sheet metal which could be of brass, zinc, or tin-plate, and Schimansky in 1888 said 'in lieu of making dolls' heads and limbs of porcelain, paper pulp, or other fragile or undesirable substance, I produce these parts of cast metal, molten tin, or zinc, and the doll wears a pasted wig'.

May Brothers mention metal for their 'bébés, poupées, pantins', and for joints. Heinrich made dolls of lead and pewter, and Sommereissen used aluminium for doll-heads in 1898.

About 1899 there were many little metal dolls and dolls with metal heads. In 1901, Vischer registered the word 'Minerva' in New York for his metal doll-heads, a word which he had used since 1894. Some of the best metal heads for dolls were those marked DIANA and made by Alfred Heller of Meiningen in Germany. These heads were hollow and were joined to stuffed bodies. They were more or less indestructible, for should they become dented it was possible to remove the head and push out the dents. The hair was in one with the head,

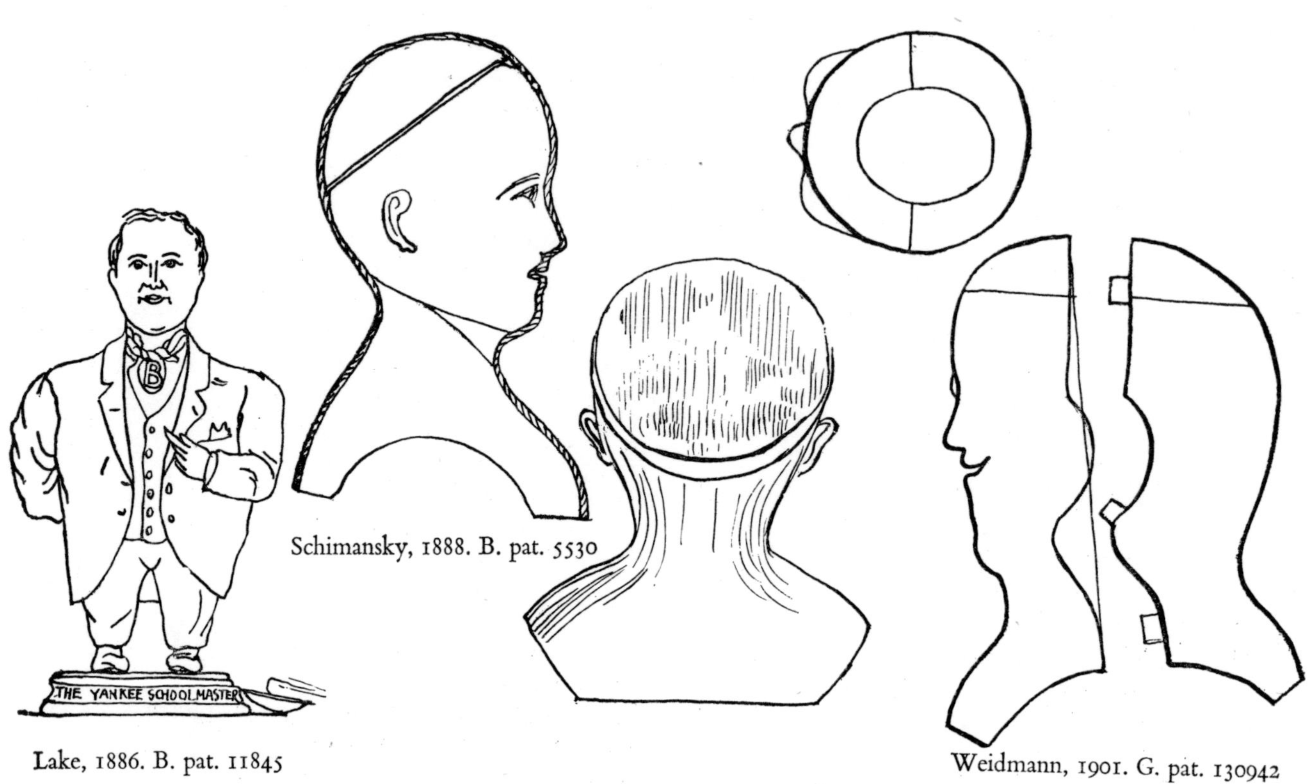

Schimansky, 1888. B. pat. 5530

Lake, 1886. B. pat. 11845

Weidmann, 1901. G. pat. 130942

PATENTS CONCERNING METAL

which was carefully painted, and except by tapping them one would not suspect that they were made of metal. These dolls could be bought in the U.S.A., about 1903, with stuffed bodies and kid forearms.

Metal was also used for parts of dolls, especially for hands. Dolls with porcelain heads made in 1860 by Reidemester and Huret were fitted with metal hands, and those of Ellis in 1871. Some dolls had magnetic hands so that they could pick up things, and some had metal feet. One of the earliest patents to mention metal was that of Breisson, in 1853, where he patented dolls' shoes of metal in France.

Patents

1853	Breisson. Metal shoes
1860	Reidemester. Metal joints
	Huret. Metal hands
1861	Poulin. Metal heads with enamel eyes
1871	Ellis. Metal hands
1876	Vervelle. Metal heads
1877	Atwood. Jointed doll of sheet metal
1879	Vervelle. Metal heads
1886	Lake. Iron figure
	Schön. Heads of sheet metal
	Péan frères. Heads of sheet metal
1888	Bull. Pewter
1888	Schimansky. Metal heads with pasted wigs
1890	May Bros. Metal dolls
1895	Heinrich. Metal dolls
1898	Sommereissen. Aluminium doll-heads
1899	Cohn. Dolls of sheet metal
	Bishoff
	Haffner
1901	Weidmann. Bodies with metal parts
	Vischer. Metal doll-heads
1903	Heller. Metal doll-heads
1906	Bing. Metal dolls
1909	Lehmann. Dolls of sheet metal

Celluloid

Celluloid as a material for dolls appears as early as 1862. This was a substance made to imitate ivory, china, etc., but as it contained camphor and gun-cotton it was highly inflammable and would burn even in water. Therefore it was not a suitable material for dolls, especially as it was easily dented, and like ivory, it turned yellow with time. However, it was used for about 60 years, at first only for the head or head and yoke, these being joined to stuffed bodies. Again it is a substance which requires moulds, whether for complete dolls or for doll parts.

Hyatt of the U.S.A. took out a doll patent in 1862 on behalf of the Celluloid Manufacturing Company, and Lefferts and Carpenter also belonged to the same firm. Carpenter's dolls of 1880 were carefully finished with pumice stone, the eyebrows being incised and coloured. Some were jointed at the neck and they all had wigs of real hair.

The heads and limbs were moulded in sections at first, Boitel's being joined to stuffed bodies, but about 1892 the doll-heads were made in one single piece, Schultz moulding his from a single tube of celluloid. In 1894, in England, the celluloid dolls of Nuttal & Maden were prepared in sheets and moulded while hot.

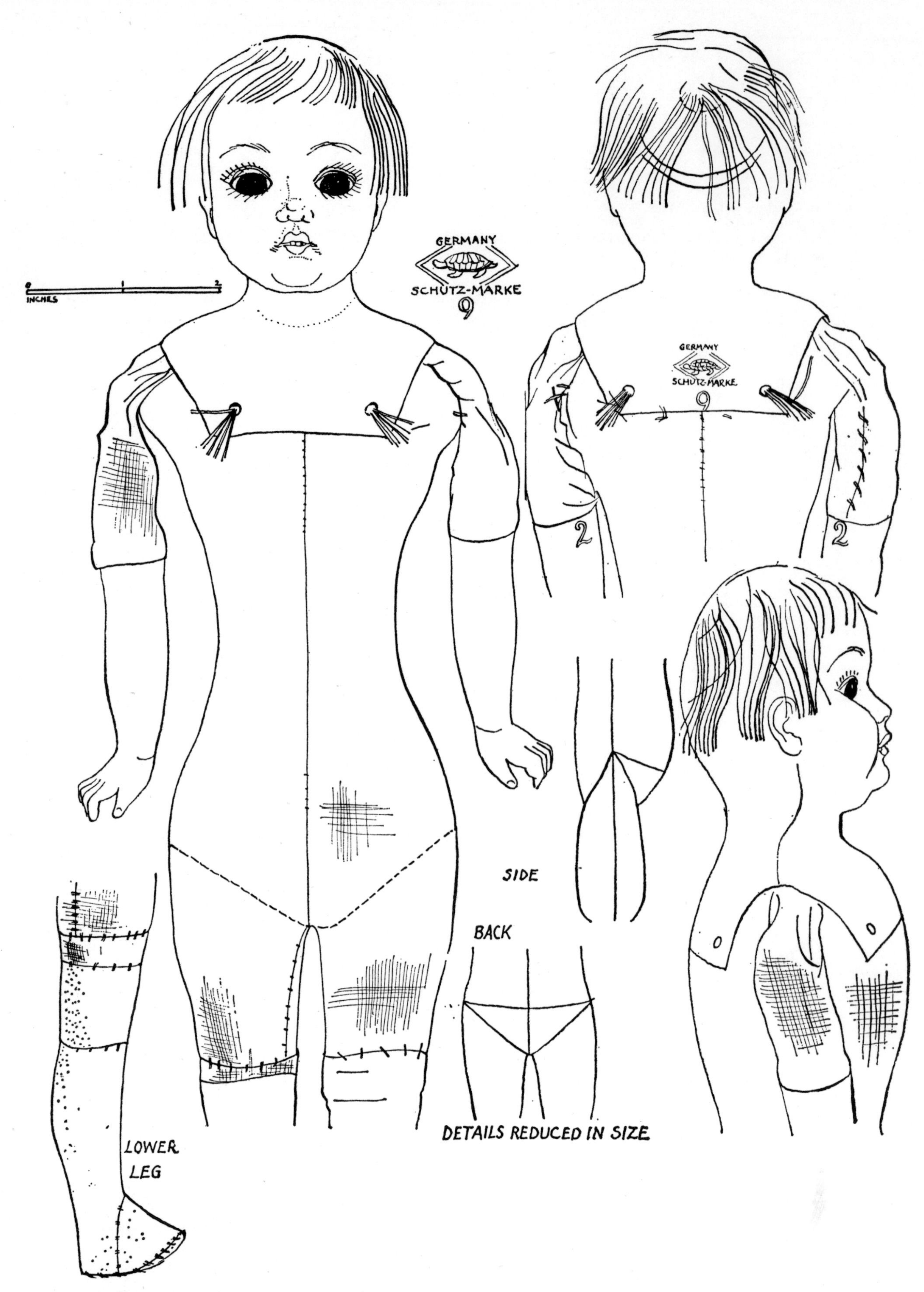

Celluloid doll, about 1899. 15 in. long. Hair wig, painted eyebrows and eyelashes, dark brown eyes to open and shut. Mould mark at side following curve of ear. Two teeth showing. Marked on the yoke with the sign of the Rheinische Gummi-und-Celluloid-Fabrik. Stuffed canvas body, bisque lower arms and kid lower legs. *Lent by Mrs. J. C. Cole*

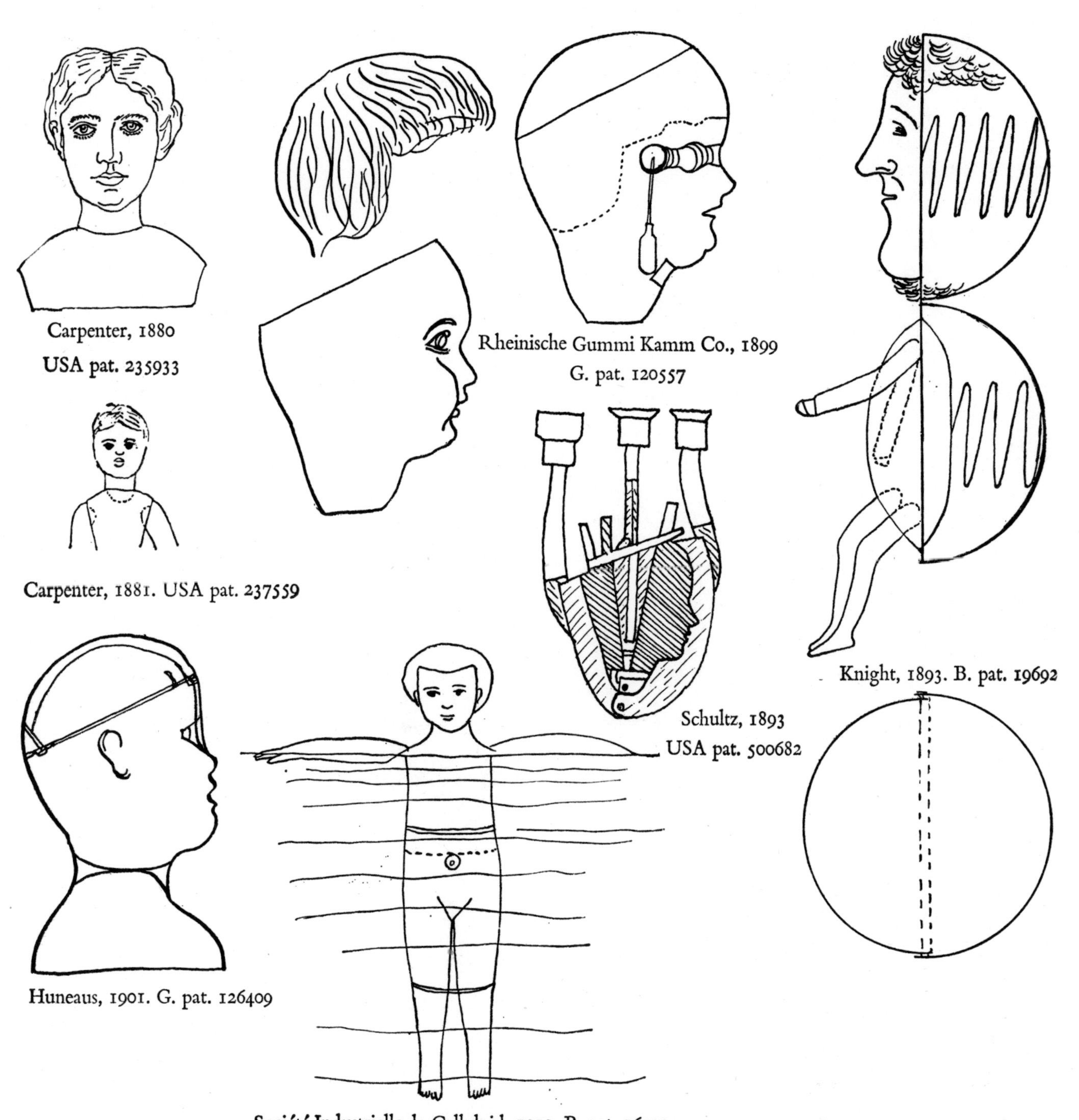

PATENTS CONCERNING CELLULOID

The first mark registered for a celluloid doll seems to be that of the Lenel Bensinger Co. of Mannheim, Germany, in 1895. This was the tortoise or turtle mark where the little animal is walking towards the left with the word SCHUTZMARKE stamped below. This is the German word for trademark.

In 1899, the Rheinische Gummi & Celluloid factory patented a doll where the modelled hair lifted off in order that the moving eyes could be easily repaired should they become broken. Their sign was the tortoise or turtle within a diamond, which in 1899 did not have *Schutzmarke* stamped underneath.

Closing eyes of pressed celluloid, made by Reinhardt in 1904, could be used in doll-heads of other material. In his patent the lids closed down over the eyeballs. Glass eyes were fixed into many of the little celluloid dolls. Dilute celluloid was used for painting doll-heads, giving an effect like that of china, just as wax had been put over the earlier wooden heads.

The Société Industrielle de Celluloid took out a British patent in 1910 for their celluloid swimming dolls, launched in Germany the year before. The joints had to fit particularly well, otherwise the dolls would sink.

Patents

1862 Hyatt. Celluloid Manufacturing Company
1880 Carpenter. Colouring celluloid heads
1881 Lefferts and Carpenter. Turning heads and complete dolls
1887 Boitel. Heads and limbs of celluloid
1892 Jourlait. Celluloid heads without soldering
Kratz-Boussac. Doll's heads made in one piece
1893 Mandel & Sichart. Celluloid doll-heads
Vallée & Schultz. All celluloid dolls
Schultz. Dolls from a single celluloid tube
1893 Knight. Doll face in celluloid ball
1894 Nuttal & Maden. Dolls from celluloid sheets
1895 Lenel Bensinger Co.
1899 Rheinische Gummi-Kamm-Companie
Hannoversche-Gummi-Kamm-Companie
1901 Hunaeus. Celluloid head
1904 Reinhardt. Closing eyes
S.F.B.J. Celluloid head
1905 Rheinishe Gummi, etc. Glass eyes in celluloid heads
1909 Société Industrielle, etc. Swimming dolls

II Details

Hair

In dating dolls the hair plays a very important part, and the drawings should help to show the various ways in which it could be dressed.

Human hair was used on the early wooden heads, sometimes just roughly glued on, the bonnet or cap keeping it in place. Later, hairs in groups were pasted to coarse muslin which was wound around the head as in a fringe, starting at the base. Alternatively, groups of hairs were sewn to muslin rather like a woven rug, as in the drawing for the doll of 1735.

At the end of the eighteenth century doll wigs were carefully made for the fashion dolls to show off their coiffures, and these were displayed and sent abroad as much for their style of hair as for their dresses, for even the wig would be changed from time to time.

Small wooden dolls merely had their heads painted a shiny black; better ones had grey curls painted in loops across their foreheads and in front of their ears. The period known as Biedermeyer in Germany simply meant a 'homely or early Victorian' style and was between 1820 and 1848 when most little dolls had a dab of black paint on top of their heads.

Papier mâché and porcelain dolls rely on their hair-dos for dating as these were usually in one with the head, and painted dark brown or black. The early bisque or Parian dolls, mostly fair, had 'hair' moulded also, but animals' hair was used for wigs, the skin itself being pasted to the bisque head in the manner of a tight leather bonnet with the hair facing outwards.

Wax dolls from about 1840 to 1850 had what were known as 'Slit Heads'. This horrid name is given to those dolls who have their hair inserted into a groove along the top. This groove follows a line of a centre parting, and the hairs, having been previously laid down and stitched flat, are then pressed firmly into the glued 'slit'. The result is a deep centre parting and the hair, though rather thick, is quite effective.

A more realistic way was to have the hair inserted into the wax. This was done on the expensive dolls, many makers inserting real hair. Advertisements showed that young ladies could have their own hair put on the doll's heads; the Montanaris, the Pierottis, and Marsh all did this, sometimes taking more than six hours to complete the doll's head, and all using slightly varied methods in their use of knives and needles.

Many materials have been tried for dolls' wigs, including flax or the hairs of some animal, even those of a mouse. Ansil Monroe, of the U.S.A., claimed that he was the first to use the pelt of an Angora goat.

WAYS OF DRESSING THE HAIR

WAYS OF DRESSING THE HAIR

The wigs were fixed to the heads with strong gum, often coming rather low at the back of the head and obscuring the name of the maker, for it is here that so many makers of bisque heads signed their names. Where the bottom of the mark still shows, it may be possible to recognize it from the signs given here, for it is a pity to pull up a wig which has been securely put in place.

Pollak in 1884, and Kubelka in 1889, took out patents for making recesses of plastic material in the hard heads of dolls, such as porcelain, rubber, or vulcanite, into which the locks of hair were inserted. Boult took out a patent in which the hairs were pricked in by means of needles. When the heads were of porcelain or of another hard substance, recesses were made and filled in with plastic material, but if the heads were of rubber or papier mâché, then the hairs were pricked in direct.

In France, Pecclet had a method of pasting hair to the doll-heads, and in 1890 he had what he termed a 'wig machine'.

Eyelashes also received attention and for a long time these were painted around the eyes or eye sockets with strokes coming away from the direction of the nose, except for those wax dolls which had real hair inserted. Amongst the patents for eyes the eyelashes are sometimes on the edge of the closing lid which gives a natural effect, whereas in others the painted lashes stay around the eye socket while the lid closes without them.

In 1905, Madame Müller had the idea of attaching hairs to a strip of elastic material, or of clipping the edges of feathers and cutting the quills in two. These were secured by glue or wax.

Eyebrows, like eyelashes, were usually painted direct on the foreheads of the dolls and the way in which these were done varies considerably. Some heads had raised eyebrows made in the mould, which indicated exactly where the brush-strokes should be applied. Kammer & Reinhardt were one of the firms to do this. Wax dolls also had painted eyebrows, though the more expensive had hairs inserted.

In 1910, Louis Steiner of Sonneberg placed haired strips behind perforations in some of the bisque heads, in such a manner as to produce the appearance of hair growing where the eyebrows should be.

Patents

1874 Monroe. Wigs for rubber dolls
1884 Pollak. Curls direct into readymade heads
Kubelka. Curls direct into readymade heads
1887 Pecclet. Wigs for poupées and bébés
1889 Kubelka. Plastic recesses for inserting hairs
1890 Pecclet. A wig machine
1893 Boult. Hairs put in with needles
1905 Müller. Eyelashes
Bergner. Detachable wigs
1910 Steiner. Eyebrows

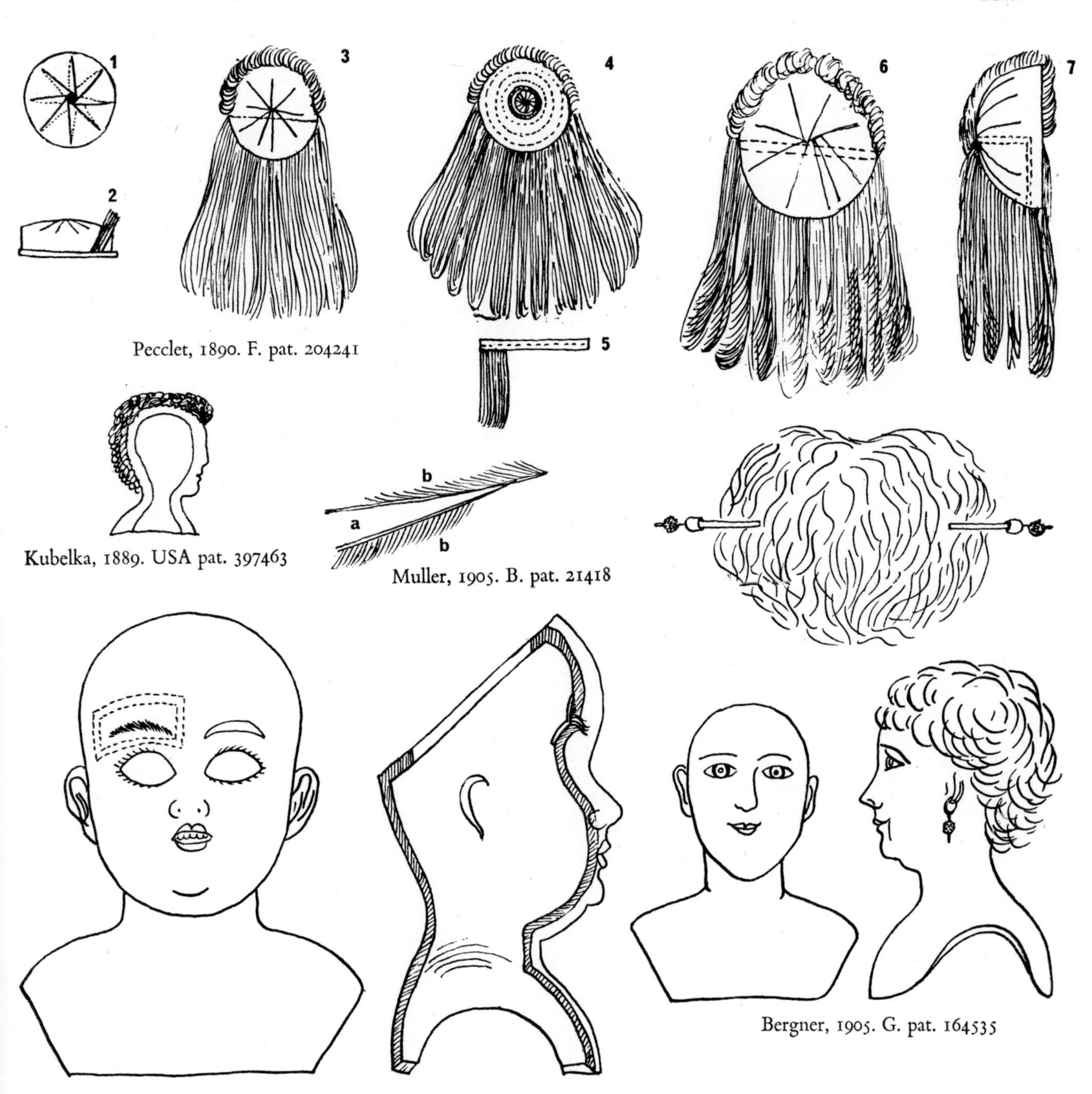

L. Steiner, 1910. USA pat. 952716

PATENTS CONCERNING HAIR

Hair Styles

1691 A few hairs would be gummed to the heads to peep under the caps, or the tops of heads could be painted black

1692 When hair was tied up with ribbon and a bow in front, it was known as a 'fontage'

1694 A 'commode' was a frame of wire, two or three stories high, and covered with tiffany or thin silk

1690–1700 Hair attached to heads with gum, often only in the front, and peeping below muslin caps

1735 Hair could be sewn in groups to coarse muslin and then gummed to the head

1750 Hair dressed close to the head

1760 Hair combed smoothly back, and a small bun twisted on top of head
1764 Front hair raised on rolls of horsehair, or on wool and frizzed
1768 Front hair dressed very high off the forehead
1776 Hair drawn up over a wire frame, and crowned with flowers or fruit
1777 Hair piled up, often three times as high as the face, and topped with flowers and ribbons
1780 Hair made to stand out around the face, broad instead of high, or there could be loose ringlets all over the head
1784 Hair piled up equal to the height of the face
1795 Short hair was the fashion
1800 Hair to the neck, about chin-level and perhaps a short fringe
1817 Smooth with centre parting and dressed high at top back
1825 Tiers of curls at sides, with high bun on top
1827 Rows of curls high at sides, and arranged high on top with bows
1833 Curls a little lower at sides, centre parting, bows on top
1834 Hair swept upwards in high puffs and loops, some having ringlets drooping over either cheek
1834–40 Hair very smooth with large flat bun at back
1839 Loose curls down side of face, plait at back twisted into a bun
1840 The high knots and loops have disappeared, and ears show
Hair very flat, drawn back from a central parting, and ringlets over the ears
1848 Three curls on each side of the face, rest of hair piled high at back
1850 Very smooth with centre parting, draped around the ears with a bun, or twist, or plait at back of head
1859 Centre parting, with curls at sides to about chin-level. Small girls have two plaits tied at the back with a large bow
1863 Princess Alexandra was married in 1863 and many copied her style of hairdressing
1864 Central parting and plaits wound across top of head, low back. All this smooth hair is worn under bonnets, which gradually become smaller, and are put farther back on the head
With the coming of 'pork-pie' hats perched on top of the head, the buns became larger and lower down, and the heavy chignon was covered with a net. Nets could be of silk embroidered with jet
1867 Large bun low at nape of neck
1868 Hair off the face and dressed high at the back
1873 Hair could be low with bow at back, or dressed high with flowers and net
1875 Hair drawn off the face with large buns and coils
1880 A little coil at the back and a ribbon across the front
1891 Hair dressed on top of head, and a fringe over the forehead
1896 Hair softly drawn towards the back
1899 Soft hair piled loosely into bun on top of head, soft thick fringe
1903 Hair swept loosely up on top of head

Eyes

The eyes of dolls have always received attention for they give expression to the whole face—one has only to enter a room in which there are dolls to feel that the place is already occupied. Such great care is taken with the painting and fixing that it is rare to find a doll with even a squint, and cross-eyes are quite unheard of, though recently dolls have been provided with spectacles, and many a fashionable bisque doll had a lorgnette among her belongings.

In Holland some of the better dolls had moving eyes as early as 1636, and an entry[1] in an English diary for 1701 states that wax dolls with turning eyes could be purchased in London. This may mean turning sideways or it could mean turning downwards.

[1] By Dr. Claver Morris. *Somerset and Dorset Notes and Queries*, June 1938.

In England the aim was to make eyes appear as natural as possible. In France the idea was to make them larger than life-size, and the dolls coming from the Jumeau factory are noted for their extra big eyes, which in profile can be recognized protruding slightly.

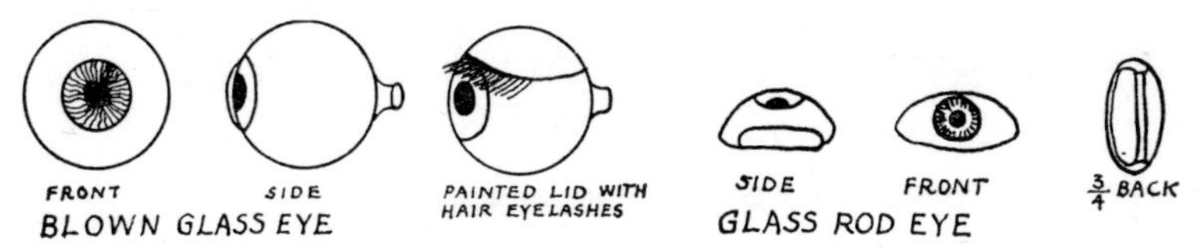

Types of glass eyes used on Pierotti dolls

In the human face, the distance between the eyes is normally the width of an eye from corner to corner, but the distance varies, and in dolls the eyes are usually placed farther apart than this. Widely spaced eyes give breadth to the baby-faced dolls and a serene beauty to the older ones. Although the Jumeau eyes were very large, the distance between them was not increased, so that a Jumeau head is recognizable by this owl-like peculiarity. When the eyes are large and the distance between them also increased, then the face has an added beauty, a modern human example being the face of Mrs. Jacqueline Kennedy.

Early dolls had painted eyes, though in fact they may be found on dolls of any date—the wooden 'Dutch' dolls always have painted eyes, mostly blue—but eyes of blown glass were inserted into the larger wooden doll-heads at the end of the seventeenth century. The English ones had no pupils, and in the Continental ones the iris is so dark a brown that the pupil is difficult to see.

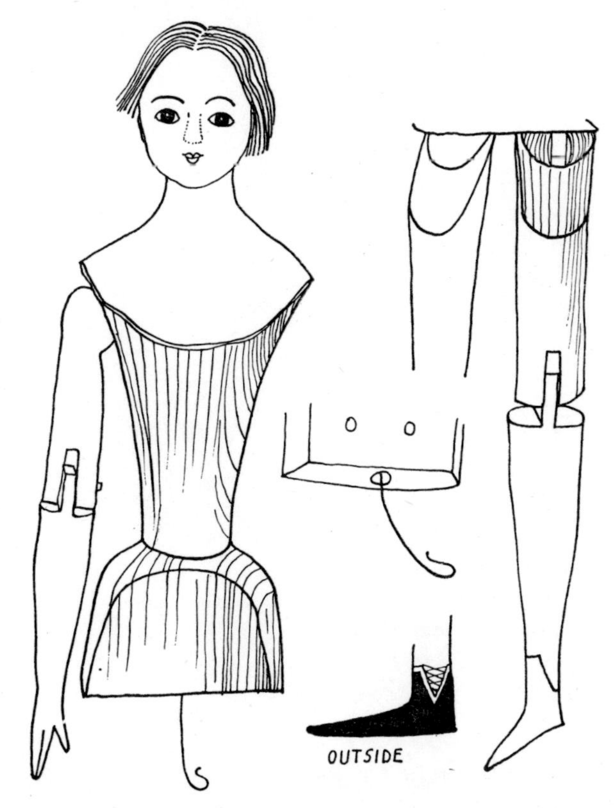

Wooden doll. Nineteenth century. 15 in. long. Wax over composition for the head, wax over wood for the yoke. The lid and eyes are in one, and close by pulling the wire down through the body. *Luton Museum*

Enamel eyes are mentioned in early French patents. Rousselot, Blampoix, Briens, and Poulin all used enamel eyes in heads of various materials between 1845 and 1862. Hollows were formed in the face when glass eyes were inserted from the back—in wooden, waxen, and china heads—and were fixed with wax or gum. The flat, diamond-shaped enamel eyes were put on the face into diamond-shaped grooves deep enough to take the piece of glass.

Wires down through the body and coming out between the legs enabled the eyes to turn downwards giving the effect of closing, and in 1850 this idea, which previously had been used on dolls with wooden bodies, was also applied to wax dolls. Later on the wire in the stuffed bodies projected at the side. Théroude's patent in 1854 was one of the first French patents to mention closing eyes. In some the lid was painted on the eyeball, while in others separate wax lids would come down over the eye, and later the wire down through the body was replaced by a gadget concealed under the hair.

Wax baby doll. 1807. The dark eyes in the hollow sockets open and shut by means of a wire through the body. Presented by a lady in 1873, who had received it 66 years before. *Bethnal Green Museum*

Wax doll. 1850. The inset eyes close by pulling a wire through the body. She wears a straw hat and a muslin and lace dress. *Bethnal Green Museum*

In 1880, Steiner made eyes move by giving two turns on a bending rod or bar; the gadget protruded just above one of the ears. In 1881 he took out a patent for manufacturing artificial eyes for dolls, which incidently were made similar to glass eyes for humans. Jumeau's patent in 1887, where the lids came down over the eyes, had a gadget at the back of the neck just under the hair, the eyes themselves being hemispherical.

According to Samhammer's patent, by 1888 it was the usual thing on both wax and porcelain heads for dolls' eyes to close when the doll was laid in a recumbent position.

In 1890, Carl Halbig took out three patents concerning dolls' eyes. In the first, the eyeballs and eyelids were on a sphere, which when worked by a gadget from under the back hair,

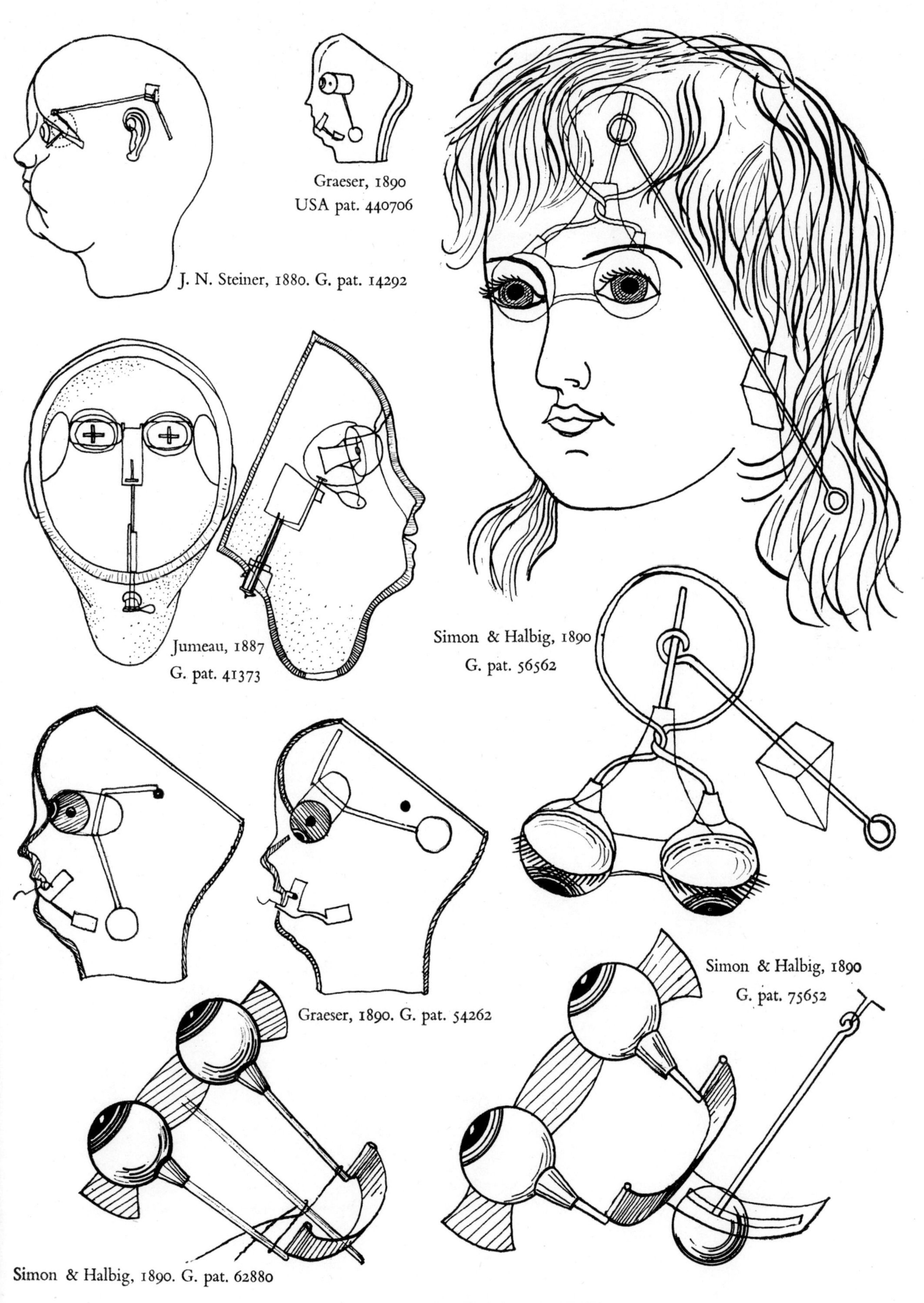

PATENTS CONCERNING EYES

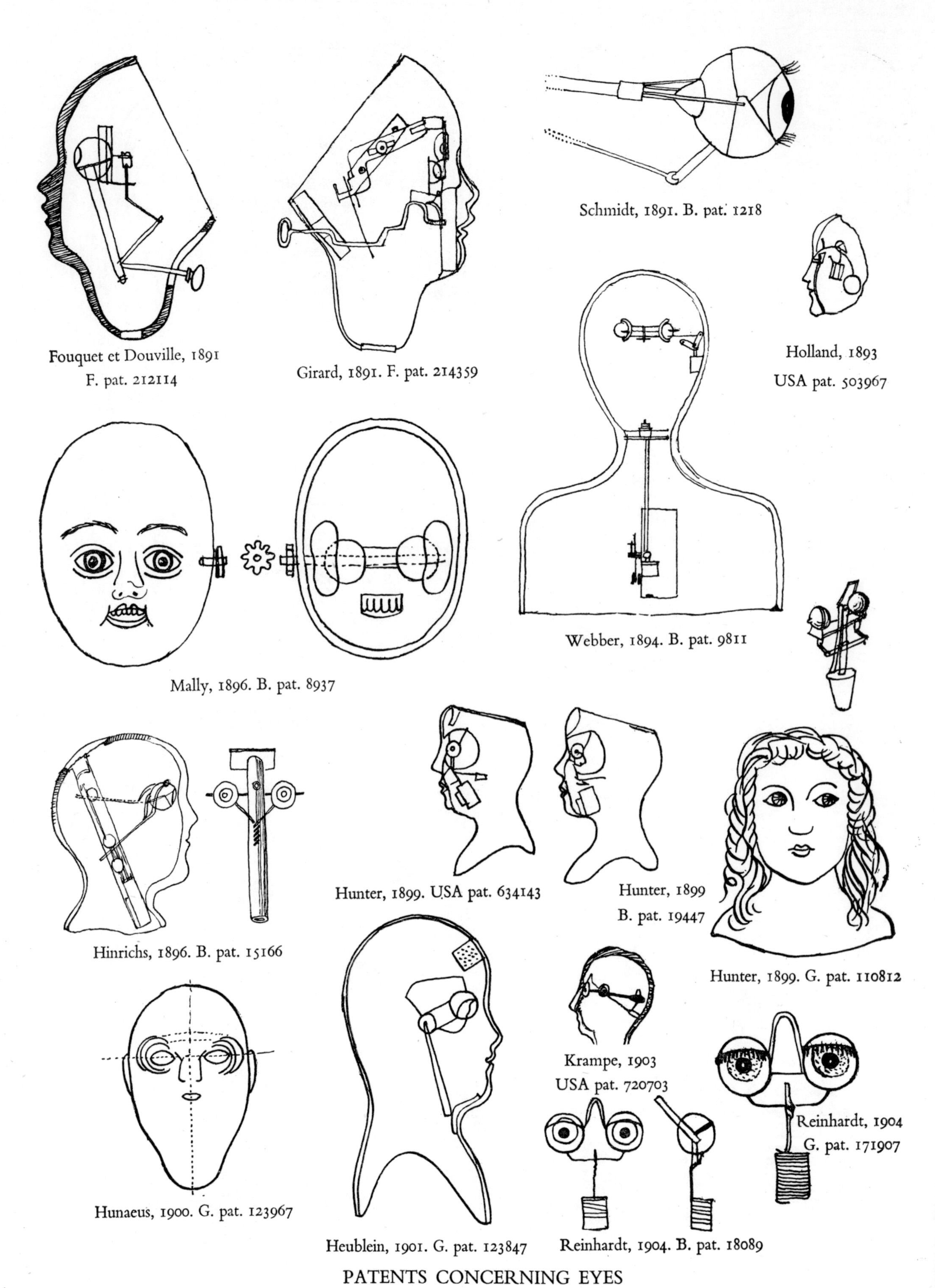

PATENTS CONCERNING EYES

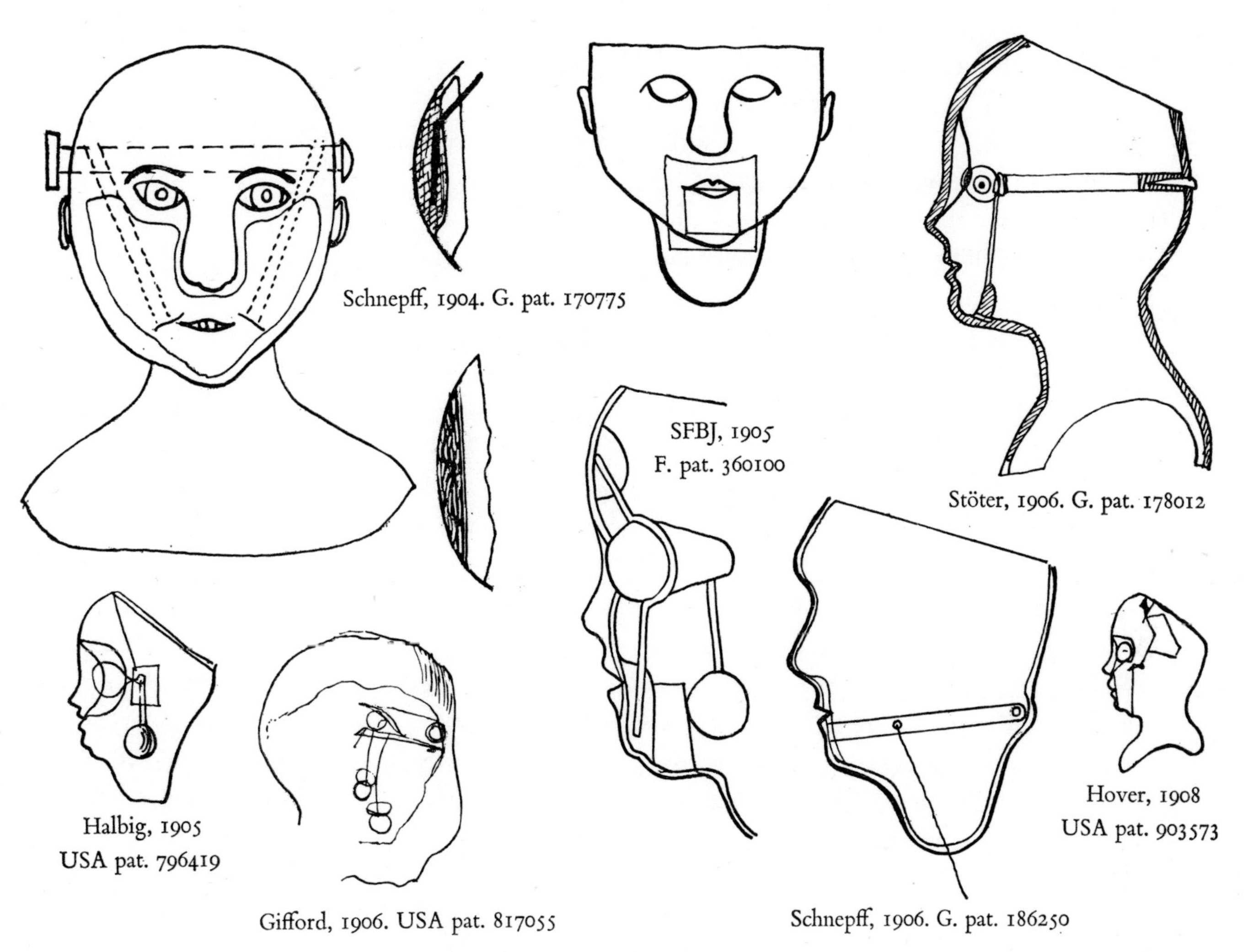

PATENTS CONCERNING EYES

turned the spheres and gave the appearance of the eyes closing. In addition there were eyelashes fixed to the rim of the 'lid', one of the first sleeping dolls to be so complete. In the second patent the eyes were made to move from side to side according to which cord was pulled, while in the third patent the eyes could do both, that is 'flirt' or close by means of the gadget protruding at the base of the head.

Graeser, also in 1890, made a talking and sleeping doll, in which not only could the eyes close, but the bottom lip came down while the doll said the words Papa-Maman. Again the gadget was worked from outside the head, this time just above the ear. In 1891, Girard, probably referring to a Bru doll, patented a method combining the eyes and lids, and in 1892 he patented a doll which not only talked and slept, but could also 'breathe'.

Legrand patented enamel eyes in 1891, and Schmidt took out a peculiar patent for sleeping eyes, where an upper and lower lid both closed at a point lower down than the middle of the eyeball. In this patent was found the first mention of a weight, though Holland's patent in

1893 is the first where the drawing shows a weight bringing down the lids when the doll is laid in a recumbent position.

Fouquet & Douville patented eyes which could move in all directions (1891); in 1893 these worked by weights which swung to and fro as in a see-saw. Lafosse also used weights for closing eyes. The method of Bemis was to use weighted balls which moved along in a tube; when the doll was laid down these rolled along causing the eyeball to rotate downwards, thus bringing down the lid. Fleischmann & Bloedel also made a sleeping doll at this time, and Jumeau again in 1896.

Mally's patent describes eyes thus: 'To an ordinary wax face opposite the orbits, I insert a rocking spindle or shaft, and in this I fix by means of wax, two glass eyes. In the wax at the back of each of the eyeballs or thereabouts, I insert a stop-pin, one projecting upwards, the other downwards. The stop-pins are set in such a manner so as to permit the spindle and eyeballs turning sufficiently to let the eye disappear. The rocking spindle may be worked by means of a knob or button on the outside of the face, or by the pull of one or more cords, the ends of which are attached to the inside of the face.'

In Hunter's patent the eyes moved from left to right and could also close. In 1903, Simon & Halbig's patent was lodged by Carl Halbig, stating that he was the sole owner of the firm. S.F.B.J. perfected moving eyes in 1904, and Reinhardt made celluloid eyes with closing lids complete with eyelashes, working by weights. This sleeping movement was used for several years to follow, and can be seen in Halbig's drawing for 1905. And so, by means of weights, dolls, like good children, shut their eyes and went straight to sleep when laid down in their wickerwork cradles and their barcelonnettes.

Patents

1845 Rousselot. Enamel eyes and teeth
1854 Théroude. Closing eyes
1855 Blampoix. Enamel eyes
1860 Briens. Rubber heads with enamel eyes
1861 Poulin. Metal heads with enamel eyes
1862 Briens. Turning head with enamel eyes
1874 Geradin. Rubber doll with moving eyes
1880 Steiner. Moving eyes, with two turns on a bending rod or bar
1881 Steiner. Manufacture of artificial eyes
1886 Schmitt. Moving eyes
1887 Jumeau. Moving hemispherical eyes with eyelashes for sleeping dolls
1890 Simon & Halbig
    Closing eyes
    'Flirting' eyes
    Eyes to move and close
1890 Graeser. Closing eyes and moving bottom lips
1891 Girard. Method of combining eyes and eyelids
    Fouqet et Douville. Moving eyes in all directions
    Legrand. Enamel eyes to move
    Schmidt. Sleeping eyes by means of weight
1892 Girard. Closing eyes to talking and breathing doll
    Meyer. Closing eyes
    Ring. Closing eyes
1893 Lafosse. Weighted eyes
    Fouquet. Weights to and fro as with a see-saw
    Holland. Lids come down over eyes
1894 Webber. Head and eyes move in a 'natural manner'
    Fleischmann & Bloedel. Movement of lids and lashes

1895 Nube. Moving lids
1896 Hinrichs & Bemis. Eyes close when lying down
Jumeau. Moving eyes
Mally
1897 Ring. Closing eyes
1899 Hunter. Eyes turn with or without shutting
Rheinische Gummi, etc. Moving eyes for celluloid heads
1900 Huneaus. Eyes close when lying down
1901 Heublein. Closing eyes
1903 Krampe. Oscillating eye-lever
Halbig. Moving eyes
1904 Reinhardt. Celluloid eyes
1905 Müller. Eyelashes
Rheinische Gummi, etc. Glass eyes for celluloid dolls
S.F.B.J. Moving eyes
Halbig. Weighted eyes
1906 Gifford. Weighted eyes
Stöter. Moving eyes
1908 Hover. Moving eyes
1909 Fitch. Eyes
Wear. Closing eyes
1910 Lemon & Page. Doll with tears falling from eyes

Joints

Wooden dolls, known as Dutch dolls, were jointed at the shoulders and thighs, and the arms and legs could move forwards or backwards. In these 'Peg' dolls, the joint was a crude hinge fastened with a wooden peg, which later was also used at the elbows and knees. This method was used for the large wooden dolls, many having the legs covered with silk, and some having leather forearms in place of wood.

Gradually ball-joints replaced the peg joints and by 1828 many of the larger dolls were jointed by this method. Actually, ball-joints had been used in lay figures for artists since the days of Dürer, and small lay figures had been given to children to play with. Some of these had a wax coating over the wooden head, reaching down over the yoke.

With the coming of porcelain heads, yokes were joined to leather bodies, some white, some pink, and at first stitched by hand and with no joints. When arms were attached separately they could move at the shoulders and makers tried various darts and gussets to enable the dolls to sit—first at the thighs, later at the elbows and knees. The cutaway grooves were of curious shape, for the stuffed leather sausages were extremely stiff, and the results were far removed from anything found on the human body.

One of the first dolls to raise its arms was that of Jean Rousselot in 1845. The wire arms were covered with kid, and by winding up the doll it could raise or lower them. This doll had a German head, enamel eyes and teeth.

In the early 1850s, rubber was used for jointing dolls, but dolls with kid bodies and limbs lasted throughout the nineteenth century with various methods of construction. Later the lower arms and lower legs were of composition, and later still the complete arm jointed at wrist, elbow, and shoulder was fastened through the upper part of the kid body.

When studying the stuffed kid bodies, look carefully to see if the stitches are by hand or by machine, and also the various ways in which the sections are joined. Heads and yokes can be of porcelain, bisque or pipe-clay, usually unmarked but often with ears pierced for earrings. A few have turning heads known as swivel necks; Briens made his doll with a turning head in 1862.

The Martin sitting doll of 1863 had swivel joints enabling the doll to take a sitting position.

A Small Version of an Artist's Lay Figure, 13 in. high. Possibly 1750. Dressed in cream coloured gown of later date, machine-stitched, and pale blue overdress with brown markings. *Lent by Mrs. de Clifford*

Ball-and-socket joints are those resembling the way in which the human femur bone joins the pelvis, that is a convex portion fitting into a concave piece. The upper arms of dolls are rounded with a ball-shaped joint fitting into a hollow, or the rounded end fitting into a hollow portion on the body. Thigh joints were also made in this manner, especially with the coming of the hollow composition bodies and the bisque arms and legs.

Just as in Victorian furniture and buildings the constructions were hidden, so in dolls their joints were concealed in various ways. Clothes were firmly stitched on or were part of the doll: in 1876 a patent was taken out in which the clothes were made especially to conceal the joints.

Joel Ellis, a wagon maker in the U.S.A., turned his attention to doll making about 1873, using mortise-and-tenon joints for wooden dolls. The wood was of rock maple, the hands and feet were of metal, and only those parts of the body which showed were painted. These dolls were made in three sizes and as only a few of them were manufactured they have become collector's pieces. The French dolls by Simonne about the same time have similar wooden joints but hers are covered with kid.

Later, in the U.S.A., the Ellis dolls were improved upon and jointed wooden dolls were made by Sanders, Martin, Johnson & Taylor, the firm of Mason & Taylor producing jointed dolls at Springfield from 1879 onwards; in 1881 they patented a wooden device for turning a composition head on a wooden body.

Much thought was expended on the turning and tipping of heads, swivel necks, etc. Often the hollow head was fixed to the body by means of a hook, and elastic would enable it to turn, but many a threaded doll now has wobbling limbs and a nodding head. These cords can be replaced by doll menders, but before this is done, it is interesting to study the method used for attaching the limbs and inserting the eyes, for by so doing it is easier to pinpoint a date for the construction. Mason & Taylor, Mothereau, Ring, and Fleischmann & Bloedel all had turning heads on their dolls, and the drawing of Kestner's patent shows how a new head may be substituted for a broken one.

New heads to old bodies, new wigs to old heads, all these things make it more difficult for a collector of the present day to ascertain a date.

The Sarah Robinson joints are very similar to those used by Armand Marseille, in fact many dolls with kid bodies are jointed like this between the 1870s and 1890s. They are beautifully made and very strong, moving both forwards and backwards, and Théroude's doll of 1890 could put the arms and legs out towards the side also.

Many dolls had the lower arms and lower legs attached to their kid bodies by rivets which passed through a thick band of kid and then into the composition limb. Others, including those by Jumeau, could have threaded arms and legs with ball-joints at the humerus and femur.

Universal joints, that is those which can move in any direction, were used in the U.S.A. by Charles Fausel in 1896.

By studying the patent drawings, which are arranged in chronological order, it is possible to see when hooks were used to fasten a head to a body or the various methods of knee joints, etc., and it would seem that the dolls of Handwerck, Eisenstadt and Verpillier could move their hands at the wrists, and those of Schultz and of Purvis could move at the ankles also.

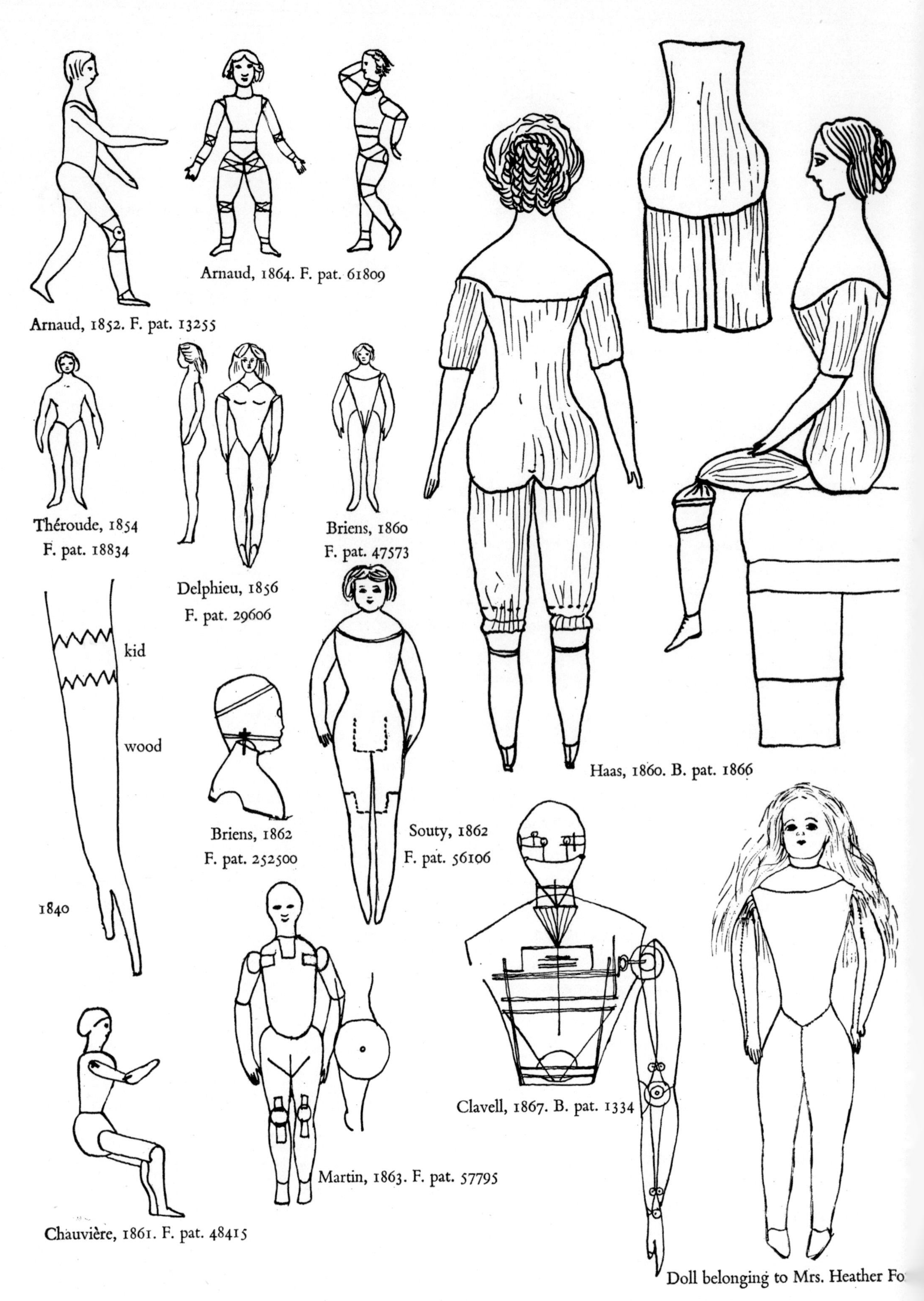

PATENTS CONCERNING JOINTS, 1852–67

PATENTS CONCERNING JOINTS, 1873–83

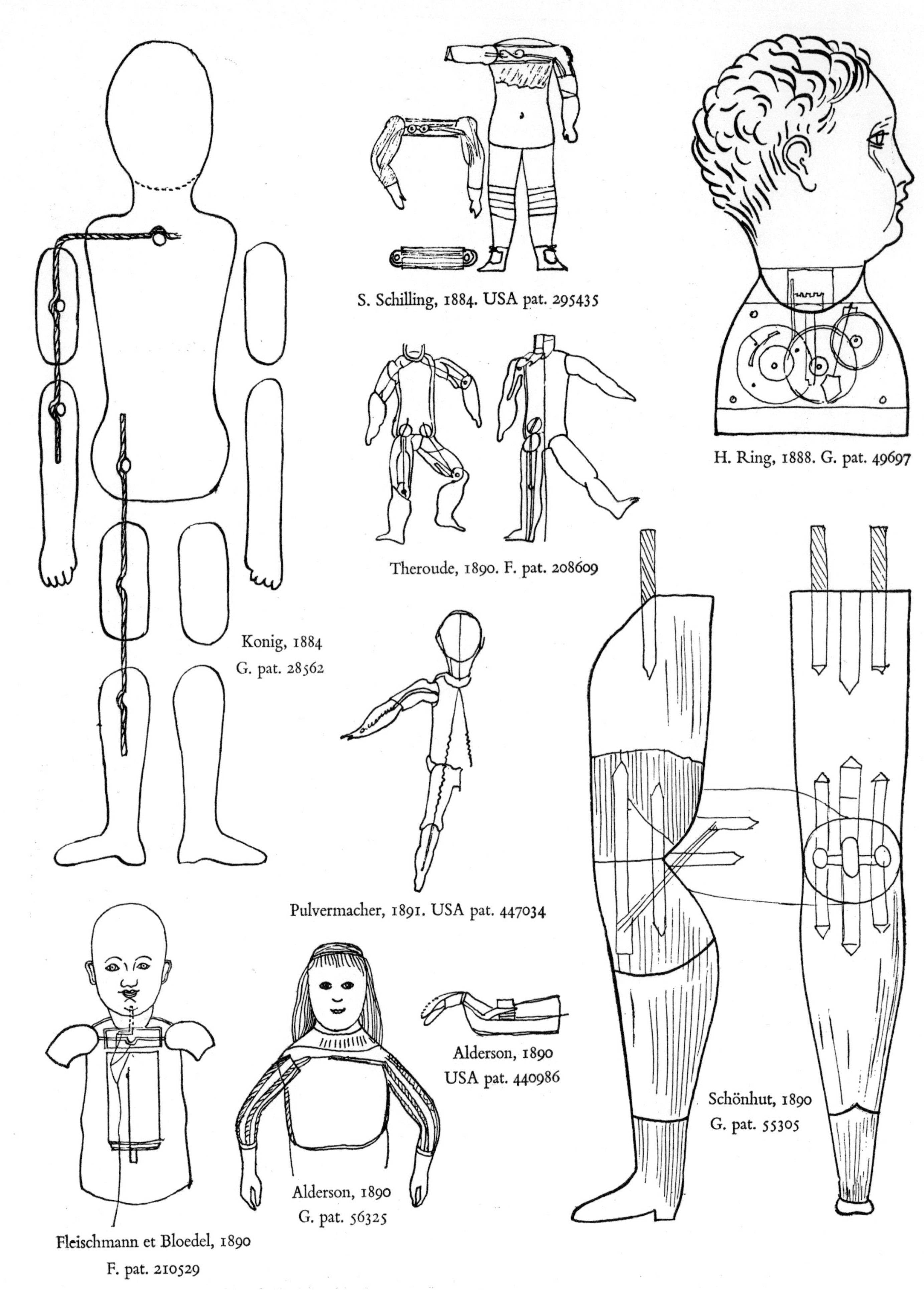

PATENTS CONCERNING JOINTS, 1884–90

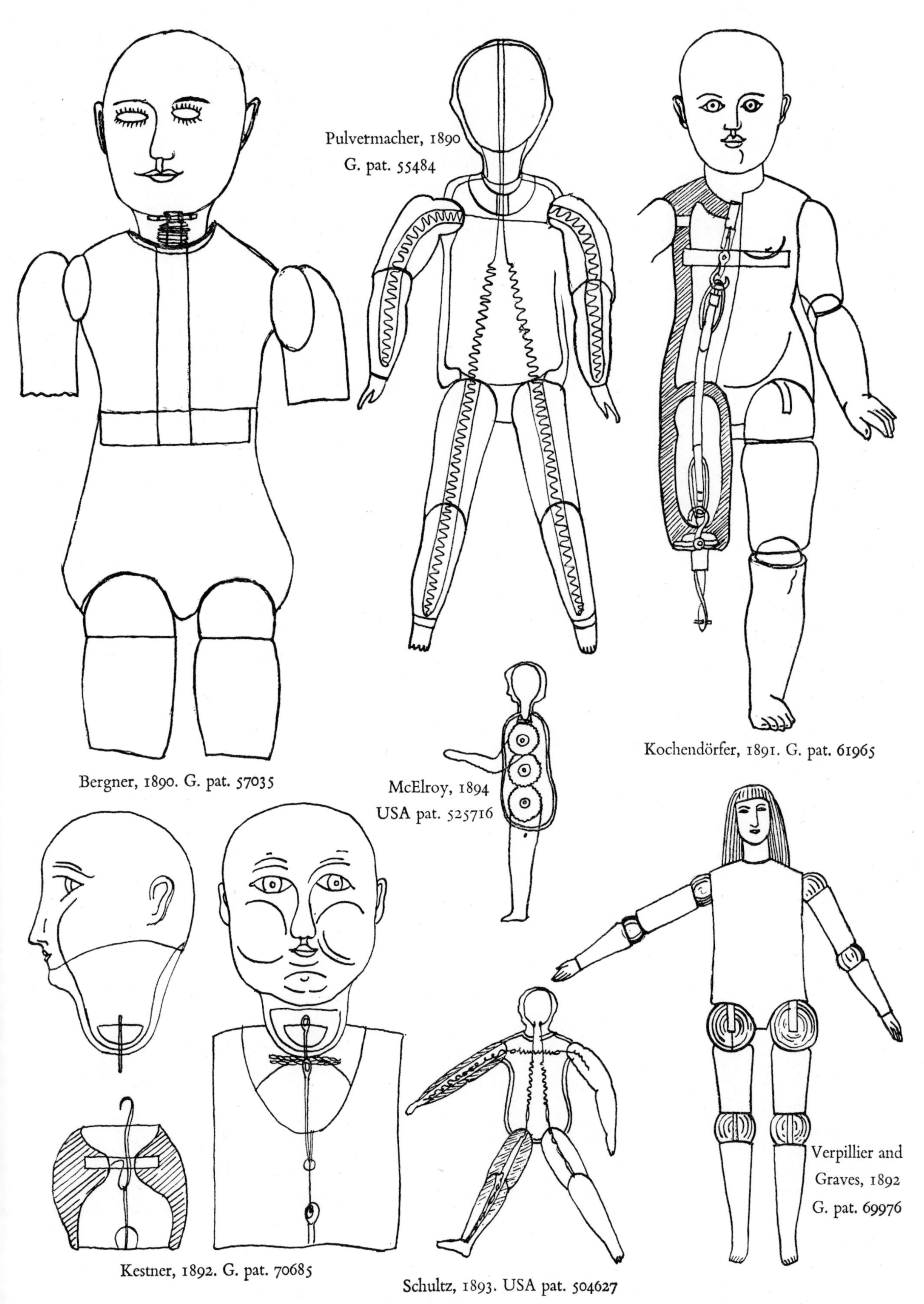

PATENTS CONCERNING JOINTS, 1890–4

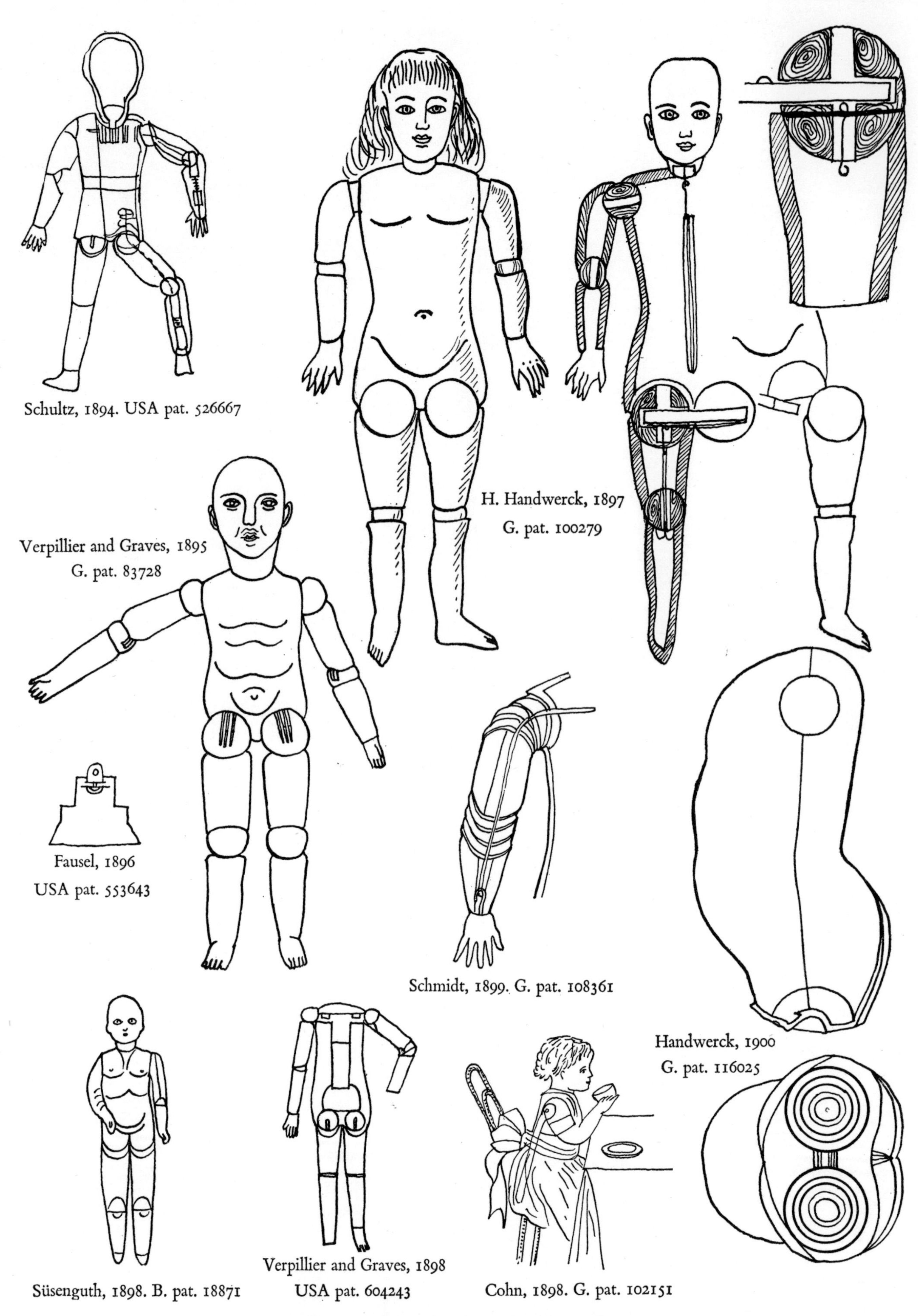

PATENTS CONCERNING JOINTS, 1894–1900

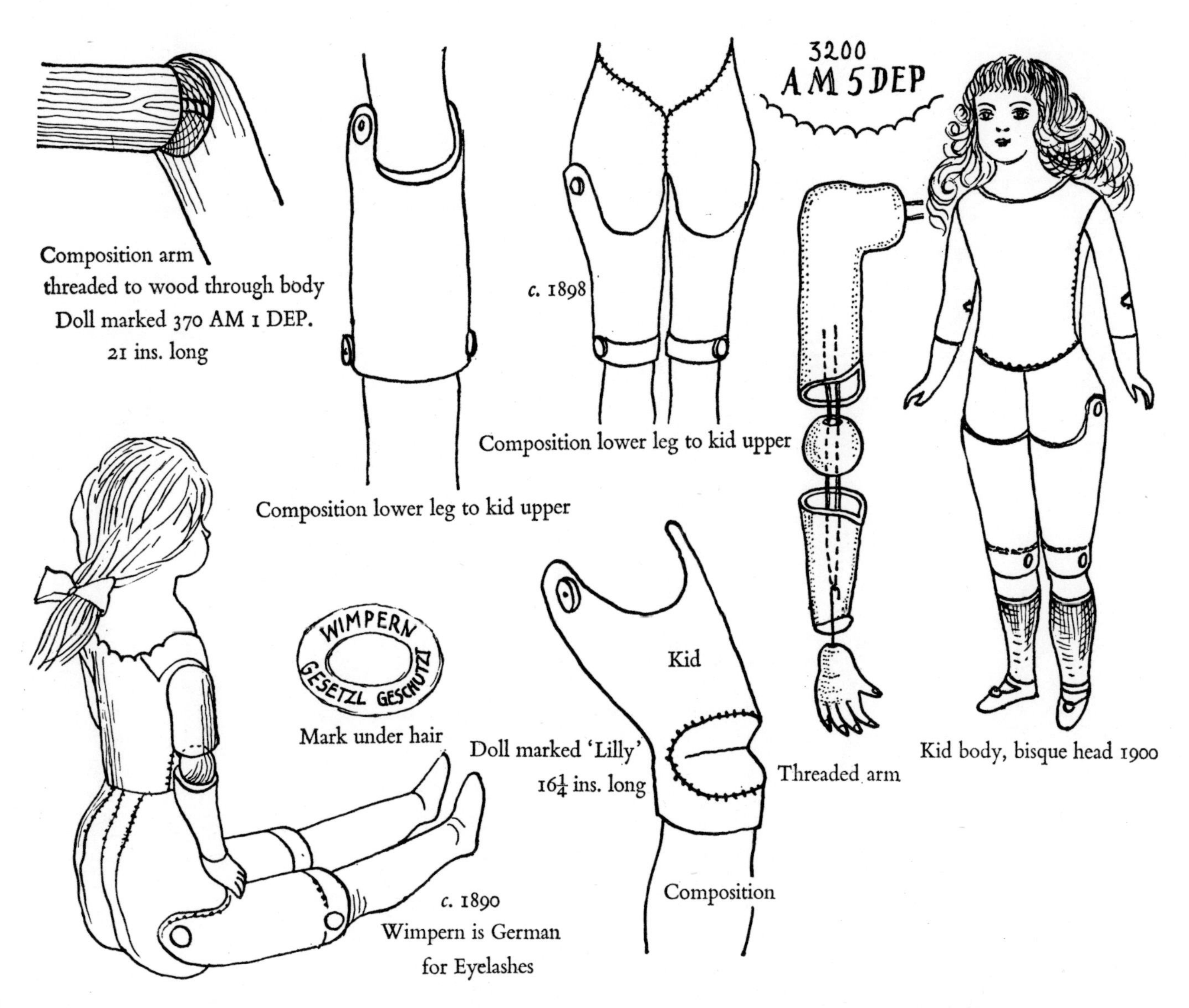

JOINTS FOUND ON DOLLS WITH BISQUE HEADS AND KID BODIES

Patents

1845 Rousselot. Wire arms covered with kid
1848 Dumerey. Jointed feet for dolls
1850 Huret. Jointed doll with moulded body
1852 Bruchet. Jointed doll
1852 Arnaud. Joints held by elastic
1857 Rohmer. Joints for kid dolls
Roy. Bust joints
1860 Haas. Sitting doll with porcelain head, legs and arms
1860 Galibert. Jointed doll
Reidemester. Metal joints on doll with head and lower arms of porcelain
1861 Chauvière. Jointed kid doll, stuffed
1862 Souty. Jointed dolls of pumice stone, coated with glue. Heads and arms of porcelain
Jumeau. Swivel head
Briens. Jointed doll with turning head
1863 Martin. A sitting doll with swivel joints

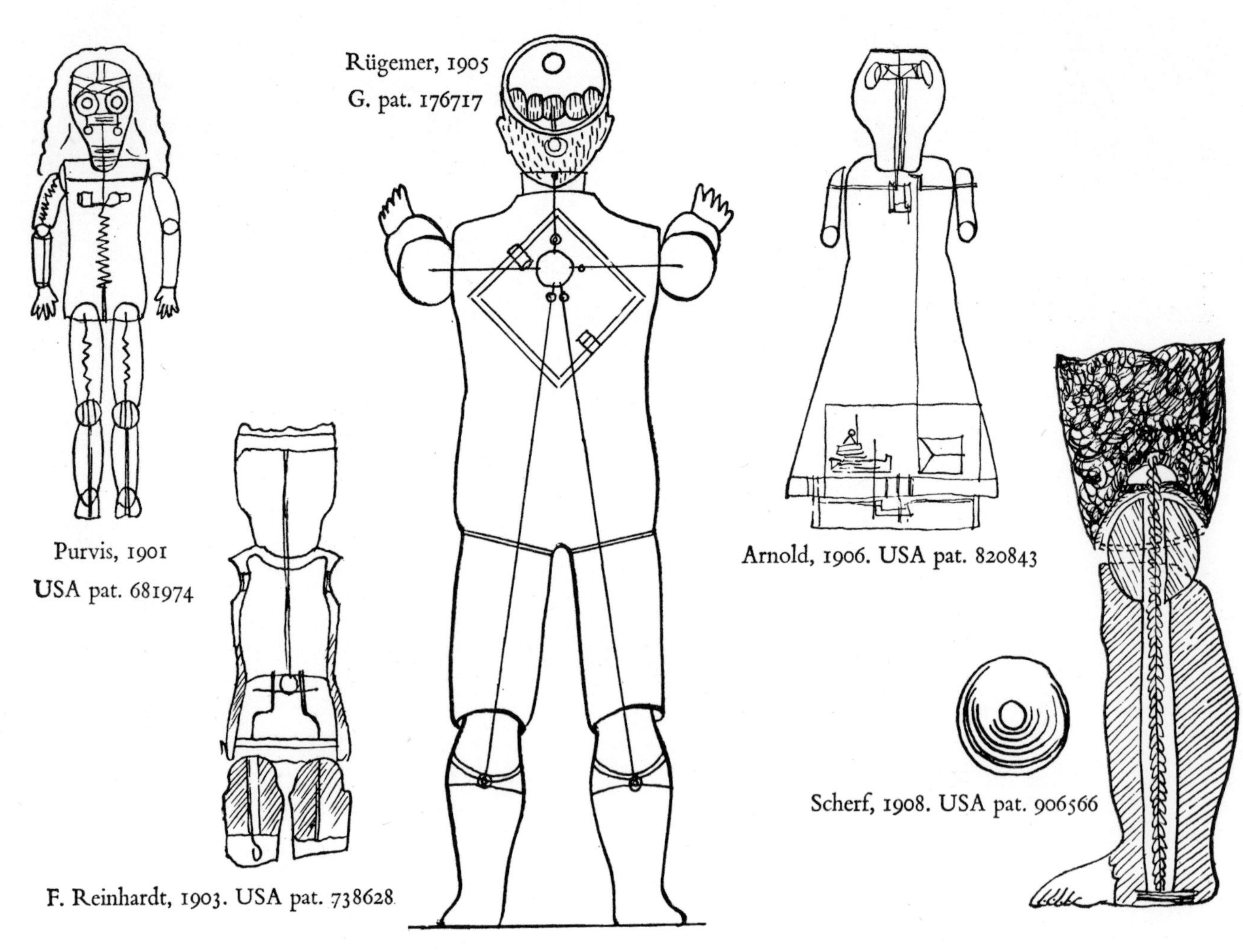

PATENTS CONCERNING JOINTS, 1901–8

1864 Arnaud. Doll with concave and convex parts held together with rubber

1865 Lee. Ball-and-socket principle connected by springs
Dehors. Bust joints
Lecomte-Alliot. Jointed doll

1867 Joliet. Jointed doll
Clavell. Jointed doll

1869 Leverd et cie. Jointed doll
Restignat. Jointed doll made of cork

1870 Chauvière. Kid doll, stuffed and jointed

1871 Lacman. Movable hands

1873 Ellis. Joints for dolls usually made of wood

1877 Atwood. Jointed doll of sheet metal

1878 Bru. Jointed rubber doll
Jumeau. Jointed doll body of papier mâché

1879 Martin. Wooden dolls with ball-and-socket joints

1879 Vogel. Jointed doll

1880 Mothereau. Unbreakable jointed bébé
Sanders. Tenon-and-mortise joints

1881 Mason & Taylor. Wooden device for turning a composition head on a wooden body
Bartenstein. Head to lean backwards

1884 Robinson. Joints for kid dolls

1884 Schilling. A fixed transverse tube at the shoulder portion with elastic cords secured to the arms, and a means for connecting the cords within the said tube

1888 Blay. Joints
Ring. Joints

1889 Bergmann. A turning head which could also move down and up
Cordier. Jointed doll

1889 Bien. Jointed doll
1890 Alderson. Jointed arm and hand
Pulvermacher. Springs for joints
Bergner. Turn at waist
Fleischmann & Bloedel. Joints
Pintel. Jointed dolls 'en pâté'
Schönhut. Wooden joints
Théroude, père. Joints for dolls
1891 Kochendörfer. Jointed doll
Pulvermacher. Doll with springs
1892 Simonot. Jointed dolls
Bour. Jointed dolls
Behu. Jointed dolls
Fleischmann & Bloedel. Jointed dolls
Kestner. Jointed dolls
Verpillier. Ball-and-socket joints
Kestner. Doll limbs attached by hooks
Falck Roussel. Joints
Graves. Spherical joints
1893 Ascher. Joints
Schultz. Springs within the body
1894 Schultz. Tubular jointed members
Lambert. Jointed doll
Bouchet. Turning head
McElroy. Movable arms and legs
Verpillier & Graves. Joints
1894 Webber. Joints
1896 Fausel. Universal joints
1897 Ohlenschlägen. Jointed doll like an acrobat
Handwerck. Jointed doll
1898 Thompson & Freeman. Jointed doll
Cohn. Doll with moving arm
Lafosse. Jointed doll
1899 Schmitt. Joints
Eisenstadt. Joints
Horstmayer. Joints
Verdier. Joints
1900 Handwerck. Joints (for Bébé Cosmopolite)
1901 Eckert. Ball-and-socket joints
Weidmann. Doll with metal parts
Purvis. Doll with wire interior
Wislizenus. Jointed dolls
Eisenstadt. Jointed dolls
Steifel. Jointed dolls
1902 Eckert. Ball-and-socket joints
Treude & Metz. Joints
1903 Consterdine. Jointed doll
Schoenhut. Jointed doll
Reinhardt. Jointed doll
Liebermann. Doll's head
1905 Rügemer. Jointed doll
Young. Jointed doll
1906 Arnold. Doll with turning head, etc.
Horne. Doll's head
Meier. Jointed dolls
Schnepff. Movable features
1907 Hincks. Joints
Fiedeler. Turning and bowing of heads
1908 Scherf. Doll's knee joint

Dress

In the middle of the fifteenth century 'charming and attractively dressed' dolls were for sale on stalls outside the Palais de Justice, Paris, and by the sixteenth century the French capital played an important part in doll dressing. Dressed dolls were given as presents to Royalty, and others displaying clothes were sent to the principal courts of Europe.

From about 1700 to 1750, dolls had low-cut square necks to the fronts of their bodices which terminated with a V at the low waist. The elbow sleeves ended with a muslin frill cut from a circle of material. A frill edged the neckline and the V front was often tucked or laced across. Skirts were long and full, and were sometimes worn over a hooped petticoat edged with a fringe, the little hoops being made of cane. Some dolls wore corsets made of brown canvas in 1750 and had their bodices stiffened with whalebone.

The aprons reached to the ground in 1744, but were short in 1752. Shoes could be pointed with two bands across the instep, and the square heels were sometimes painted red.

By 1780 the muslin caps had larger crowns, and some dolls wore straw hats above the mob cap. The neckline had a fichu, and looped panniers came from the slightly higher waist, and some wore stays.

In Philadelphia, as early as 1785, one could purchase 'Drest dolls, Naked ditto, Lilliputian dolls, and Wigs for dolls'.

Dolls on which clothes were displayed were used in France and in England. These were not playthings as such, and were redressed and recoiffured many times in order to show the latest fashion. The 'fashion doll' was welcomed in the U.S.A., India, and Italy; it was exhibited in Venice at certain times of the year. Rose Bertin, dressmaker to Marie Antoinette, would travel across Europe in her coach, within which was a collection of carefully dressed

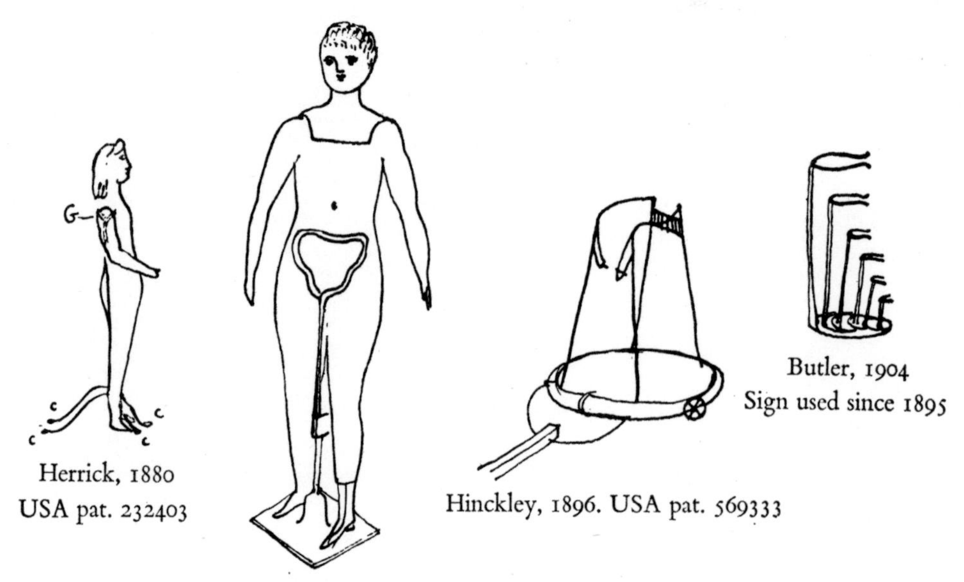

Herrick, 1880
USA pat. 232403

Staples, 1886. USA pat. 352161

Hinckley, 1896. USA pat. 569333

Butler, 1904
Sign used since 1895

DOLL SUPPORTS

dolls, so that the fashions of France were sent abroad before the days of mannequins and catalogues.

At one time Marie Antoinette ordered a doll to be dressed in the garb of a Carmelite nun. She requested Madame Campan to clothe this doll for the little Marie Thérèse so that the child would be familiar with this kind of dress. She did not want her daughter to stare or be frightened when later she took her to the convent of Carmelites at St. Denis, to visit an aunt who had taken a veil of this order.[1]

White stockings were worn up till 1778; the first female to wear black silk stockings in England was said to be Mrs. Damer, a sculptress, who lived between 1749 and 1828.

During the eighteenth century wooden dolls were introduced by a Spitalfields merchant in order to display his silk fabrics, some of which were woven with metal threads. About

[1] Joan Evans, *Madame Royale.*

10 in. high, these dolls were known as 'bagman's dolls' and were carried around to the larger towns. They had wooden hands carved with separate fingers, well-spaced eyes, small top lips, protruding noses and nicely proportioned bodies. In 1788, a boatload of these 'mannequins' was dispatched to India, where the ladies could see the English fashions. Natalis Rondot reported[1] in 1849 that until the fashion doll arrived in Calcutta the little cloaks had been worn on the ladies' heads instead of around their shoulders.

Gradually the fashion doll disappeared as wares began to be shown in catalogues. In 1827, a French patent was taken out for a torso, called a mannequin. This torso was seamed and stuffed and was similar to the dummies seen in shop windows well into the early twentieth century. Although not at all lifelike, so modest were the window dressers that the shop blinds would be pulled down whilst the dummy was being dressed for display.

In 1830 a sewing machine had been invented in France which did a chain stitch, but the French thought the invention would throw people out of work, and the factory was destroyed by an infuriated mob. About 1850, a machine was made to make a stitch as we know it to-day, and far from putting people out of work, many more were employed, and gradually multitudes of frills and rows and rows of tucks became the fashion.

When undressing dolls, I began to wonder when it was that they first wore 'drawers', as they were called. Apparently, in Italy, they were worn by women early in the seventeenth century, and later were introduced into France. Mrs. Pepys was French and may have worn some, but English ladies did not wear them until about 1806.

At first the drawers reached just below the knee, and by 1820 the gathered legs had a band fastened with one button. A pair at Platt Hall, Manchester, worn by the Duchess of Kent, had a wide waistband with back lacing. Pantelettes had separate legs and after about 1830 were worn by little girls only. By 1834, the drawers were joined and had a back fastening at the waist, the legs being finished off with four tucks. By 1840, they had become elaborate affairs trimmed with Broderie Anglaise.

Under-petticoats were lined with horsehair or corded, and a straw plait was inserted in the hem, and many other petticoats were worn. Over one of flannel was one padded with horse-hair, then one of stiffened Indian calico, and above this one of starched muslin. Some dolls had hoops in the hem of the flannel petticoat, which could be made of red woollen material.

By looking at the patent drawings, it is quite easy to see that the 'Clothes Maketh the Doll'; manufacturers were quick to realize that the way in which their dolls were dressed mattered a great deal. Medals were given at Exhibitions, Jumeau winning one in 1851 for the meticulous manner in which his dolls were dressed. Madame Montanari, also, was noted for the beautiful way in which she attired her dolls for the Great Exhibition, with their waxen shoulders showing above their low-necked gowns.

In 1852, Augusta Montanari made a drawing which she called 'an Ornamental design for a Doll'. This watercolour was entered in the Earthenware Class of the Design Registry, and

[1] *Report on the French Exhibition*, 1849.

was probably for a porcelain doll. The clothes were long and full, and the bonnet was trimmed with looped ribbons in alternate colours of blue and white, with ruchings around the face and hair.

Dolls gradually began to have better-made lower legs and feet, and makers of footwear registered their marks upon the soles. In 1855 a doll with a trousseau was among the presents given to Queen Victoria for her children when she was staying with the Emperor and Empress of France. The Empress Eugénie was said to choose her gown from a doll dressed in duplicate, instead of going to her wardrobe.

In 1856, long drawers trimmed with lace were worn, over these a flannel petticoat, often red, then a wide under-petticoat, then a padded petticoat stiffened with whale-bone, a white starched petticoat with frills, two muslin petticoats, and finally the dress. Sometimes to save the bulk around the waist, two or three of the petticoats would be sewn into the same band.

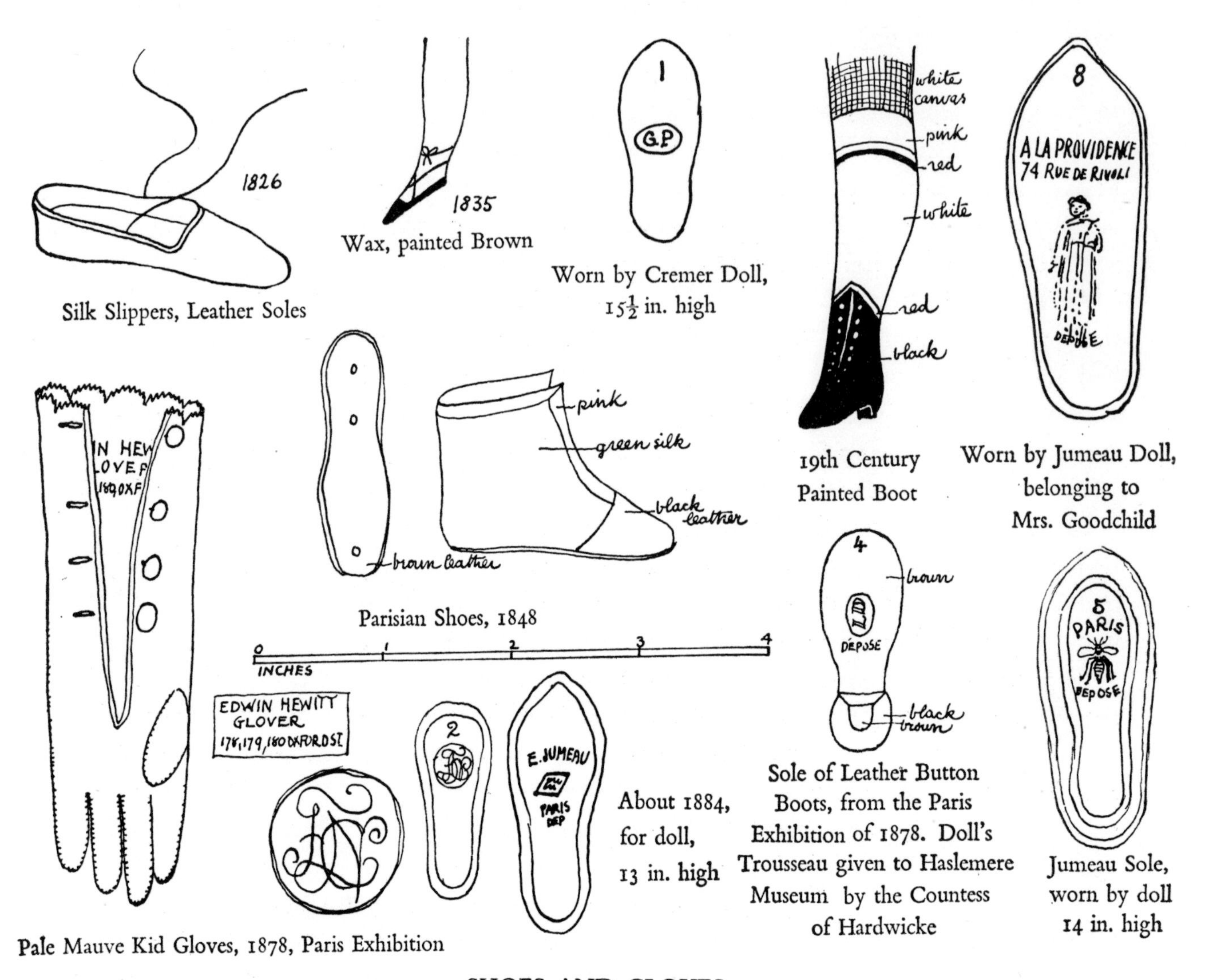

Silk Slippers, Leather Soles

Wax, painted Brown

Worn by Cremer Doll, 15½ in. high

19th Century Painted Boot

Worn by Jumeau Doll, belonging to Mrs. Goodchild

Parisian Shoes, 1848

About 1884, for doll, 13 in. high

Sole of Leather Button Boots, from the Paris Exhibition of 1878. Doll's Trousseau given to Haslemere Museum by the Countess of Hardwicke

Jumeau Sole, worn by doll 14 in. high

Pale Mauve Kid Gloves, 1878, Paris Exhibition

SHOES AND GLOVES

The crinoline, weft of horsehair, warp of linen, held the enlarged skirts correctly, but the weight was enormous. To replace the bulk of all the petticoats the 'cage' was made, at first of split cane, later of ribbon steel. Queen Victoria wore one of these in 1858 and commented on the fact that it was so much lighter in weight.

In this same year fashionable dolls could replace their crinolines by wearing drawers threaded with wires, an idea patented by Luis. Small girls dressed like the grown-ups and wore miniature crinolines which were shorter, showing their underclothes beneath. This led to the wearing of pantelettes, an odd idea where tubes of laces and frills were tied on around the knees to show beneath the dresses. Others might wear long pants with a back slit.

About this time the first successful sewing-machine was made by Isaac Singer, and some years later these could be hired for 1*s*. 6*d*. a week. In 1858, a cutting machine enabled a knife to cut through two dozen double thicknesses of cloth to the same pattern in one operation.

ALL DRESSED UP

Wide dresses worn over the 'cage' had become even wider, but in 1859 the Empress Eugénie was said to have appeared at a Court ball without a crinoline, and at the fashionable Longchamps races in 1860 not a crinoline was to be seen. So, as France was the leader of fashion, in a few years the crinoline had disappeared, and its place taken by many-flounced petticoats and the little crinolette.

In 1864, the dye works at Hoechst, near Frankfurt, produced the hitherto unknown 'aldehyde green'. When the Empress appeared at the opera wearing a gown made from silk dyed to the new shade, this brilliant green known as Hoechst Green became the fashion.

Lazarus & Rosenfeld of 4 Houndsditch, London, a noted district for doll makers, registered a design in 1867 in the Earthenware Class for an ornamental doll's hat. This appears to be in one with the head, and if so, would be one of those known in the U.S.A. as a 'Bonnet Doll'.

Wide skirts, which had been the fashion for about 15 years, were now flatter in the front, with the folds of the dress looped up towards the back in the manner of a milkmaid, and thus forming the bustle of 1870.

Patterns could be purchased for making dolls' clothes, and Charlotte Slade, in 1874, patented a trousseau for dolls consisting of a package of miniature patterns, and one in 1877 for a doll's hat trimmed with flowers. In her drawings the little knickers have a back fastening. Small parasols were made to open and shut, Pannier patenting one for dolls in 1872 and Gorguet in 1875.

In *The Little Princess* (adapted from her story of 1887) Mrs. Hodgson Burnett describes a doll costing £100, with clothes from a Parisian modiste. She is dressed for the theatre with an ermine-lined cloak, and has a blue and gold opera glass. She has black velvet hats with ostrich feathers, coats, lace-frilled petticoats, and a trunk with a key, within which were trays of 'lace collars and silk stockings and handkerchiefs, there was a case containing a necklace and a tiara which looked quite as if it were made of real diamonds; there was a long sealskin and a muff; there were ball dresses and walking dresses and visiting dresses; there were hats and tea-gowns and fans'.

Gold label on trunk containing trousseau. *Bethnal Green Museum*

Another kind of trousseau was sold by Henry Cremer, the Regent Street Toyman, who advertised eggs containing a 'Dolly and a Dolly's Trousseaux' in 1874; and a British patent had wearing apparel for dolls printed on fabric ready for cutting out.

Dolls were being noticed more and more for their wonderfully made accessories, so much so that they were put on as a Charity Exhibition in New York City in 1880. Advertised as 'The Dolls' Reception' it may have been the forerunner of such exhibitions in which dolls have been the means of collecting money both in the U.S.A. and in Europe.

The dolls at this exhibition would have been both baby dolls and grown-up ones, the latter wearing bustles. Between 1884 and 1890, a little bustle was tied on at the back with loops around the waist, or on some not so well dressed, a wad of tissue paper would be stuffed up under the folds so that they hung correctly. People wore bustles to replace the weight of the back folds, and by 1890 all that was left of the bustle was a small pad of horse-hair worn at the back waist.

As in real clothes, so in dolls' clothes, and many makers marked these with their special label. Madame Alexandrine Deropkine put her sign on the doll clothes in 1886, Emile Jumeau put his on little boots and shoes in 1891. Danel also marked his shoes on the soles in 1889, and Rose Lisner of New York was noted for her dressed dolls in 1890.

A way of finding how dolls should be clothed is by studying the many paper dolls of the period; rag dolls, where the sheets were sold in the flat, often have underclothes printed on them in addition to the dresses. It would seem that at the beginning of the twentieth century, the little drawers were buttoned at the sides instead of at the back, and as they were stepped into rather than drawn on, the name 'knicker' gradually came into use.

From 1905 onwards, fine white embroidery was done on white organdie muslin, and baby dolls wore gowns of madapollam bought for sixpence a yard. Boys' knickerbockers and velveteen suits, and their sisters' voluminous petticoats had all disappeared completely, long before the time of the First World War; but when undressing an Edwardian doll, it is amazing to find the amount of clothes which were worn well into the twentieth century.

The details given below are often painted in one with the legs, sometimes on the little wax dolls and often on the porcelain and bisque lower legs—those of bisque might have details added in lustre. Usually these legs are small in comparison to the doll's head.

1820–30 Cloth boots just above the ankle, no heel, side lacing
1830 Silk slippers with no heel, with crossing ribbons tied above ankle
1835 Wax legs have little brown painted slippers with brown crossing ribbons tied in a bow above ankle. With these the doll wears long pantalettes
1840 Flat heeled slippers, large rosette low down, near toes, later a huge bow replaces the rosette
1847 Gaiters, buttoned on the outside
1848 Buttoned boots, high in the front. Long pantalettes were on their way out
1850 Elastic sided boots, square toes, toe cap and front seam
1857 Two colour cloth boots with straight tops, often maroon above and black beneath
1858 In May of this year, the eldest daughter of Queen Victoria, and future mother of the Kaiser, wore high-heeled shoes and may have sprained her foot for this reason
1859 Cloth boots just above ankle, black toe-caps, front or side buttoning. Ribbed stockings
1860 Heel-less sandals continue to be worn with summer dresses
1860–75 Elastic-sided boots, rosettes, square heels. A slightly higher boot with front lacing and straight top
1868 Boots to a point in front, shaped heel. The pantalettes or knickers show just below the knee
1870 Round toes with low front and bow, higher shaped heels. Kid boots, white satin or coloured reaching just above the ankle, laced on inner side
1871 Cloth top boots, buttoned on outside, small heel, straight tops. Worn with white stockings
1873 Long white socks worn with black slippers, low heels, square toes with bows
1874 Cloth top boots, laced, slightly high in front
1885 Black boots with red edging, high in front to a point, square heels. White socks with red band at top
1888 Button boots could be of two colours, leather toe cap and slipper of a dark colour, with lighter top usually finished straight.
Other boots high point in front, pointed toes, square heels. Boots were worn with both summer and winter clothes
1895 Black boots, long white socks, blue ribbon and bow tied under the knee

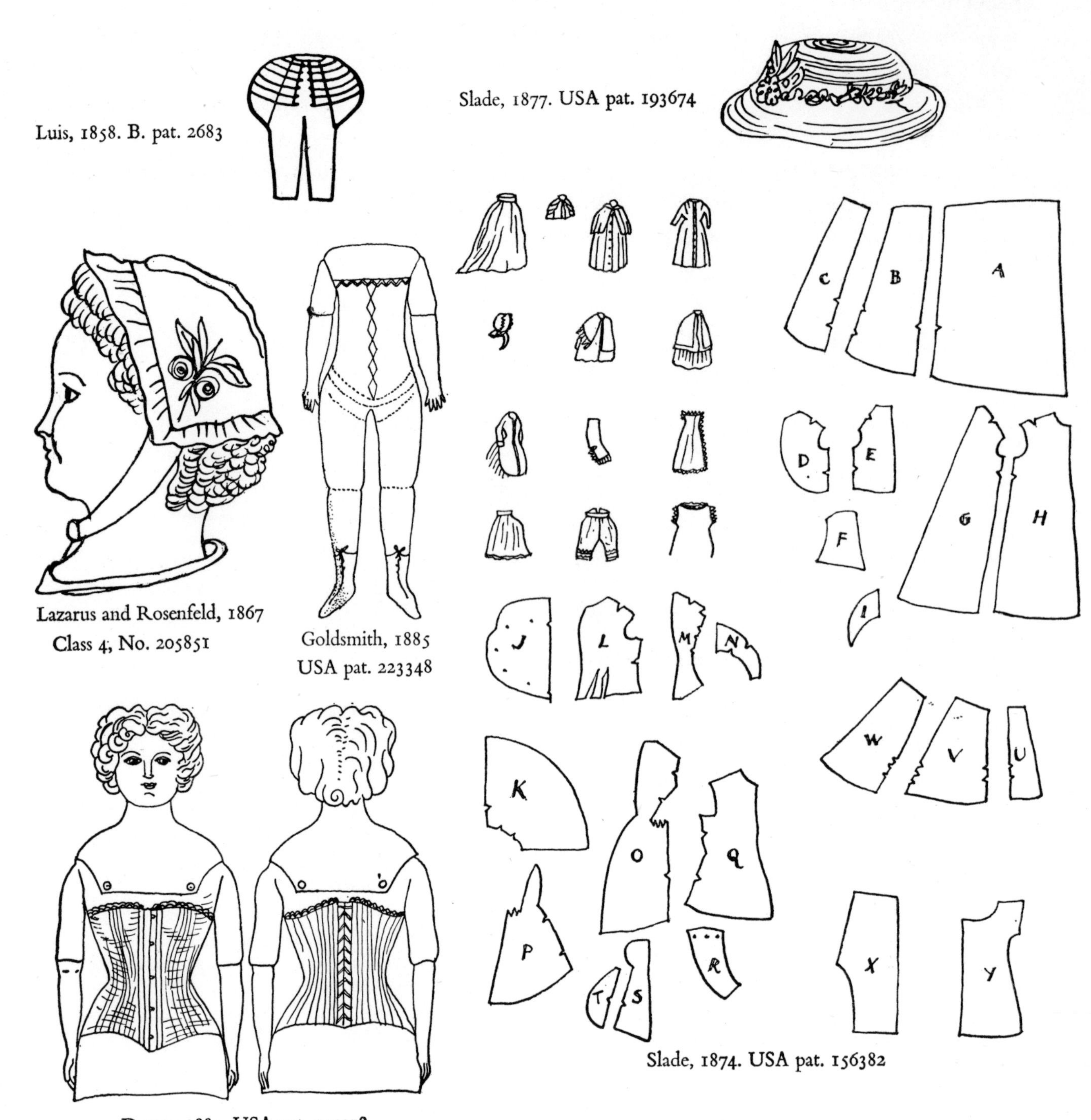

Luis, 1858. B. pat. 2683

Slade, 1877. USA pat. 193674

Lazarus and Rosenfeld, 1867
Class 4, No. 205851

Goldsmith, 1885
USA pat. 223348

Slade, 1874. USA pat. 156382

Dotter, 1880. USA pat. 235218

PATENTS CONCERNING DRESS

Patents

1853 Breisson. Metal shoes
1858 Luis. Dolls' drawers with wires
1872 Pannier. Parasol
1874 Slade. Trousseau
1875 Gorguet. Parasol
1876 Newton. Clothes to conceal joints
1877 Slade. Hat
1879 Wheeler. Dresses
1880 Dotter. Printed corset
1883 Maillard. Dolls' sleeves
1885 Goldsmith. Printed corset
1886 Deropkine. Clothes marked
1887 Isaacs. Clothes
1894 Maden. Printed pictures on dolls' dresses
Mason. Wearing apparel
Fell. Detachable garments
Mally. Clothes for dolls to facilitate dressing and undressing
1897 Wolf. Clothes
1889 Danel. Shoes marked
1891 Jumeau. Shoes marked
1904 Reilly, Kate. Fashion dolls
1903 Bosworth, Frederick. Fashion dolls

White work

Unmarked dolls are sometimes found to be dressed in white clothes embroidered in white. This was known as 'white work' or 'Broderie Anglaise', and consisted of a series of cut holes worked in buttonhole stitch. Designs for these patterns were given in the periodicals of the period and usually consisted of daisy-like flowers with sprays of leaves, holes being cut in the petals and leaves, while the stem would be worked in 'stem-stitch'.

Broderie Anglaise was popular in America, where it was used for babyclothes, dolls' clothes and underwear in 1842, and between 1840 and 1850 little sprigs of flowers were worked on coarse muslin or net.

By 1850, about the same time as the coming of baby dolls, mass-produced trimmings and insertions were made by machine in Switzerland. These were imported in great numbers and took the place of the Broderie Anglaise which, until now, had been done by hand. In order to tell the difference the reverse side of the material should be carefully studied.

Between 1866 and 1870 the small cut holes were grouped much closer together so that hardly any of the material showed between, and by 1870 the holes had become as much as ½ in. across and these were filled in with threads in spider's-web fashion.

In England, about 1863, the scalloped edges were also done by machinery, but were not cut into scallops; this was done at home with scissors after the material had been purchased by the yard from a shop. As late as 1908, this cutting of the scallops was done at home.

Machinery for various types of openwork was invented, and by 1868 eyelet holes were also done by machine, and by 1870 much of this work was used on Christening robes. Many baby dolls are dressed in what is known as long clothes; 'tucking' a baby, or putting it into short clothes was quite an event, while at a later date a boy would be 'breeched'.

Off-white embroidery was the fashion about 1876, and was known as Ecru. Broderie Anglaise, working in various widths, was also done on narrow bands of fine muslin known as zephir.[1]

Small square holes were the fashion between 1886 and 1896 and larger square holes between 1895 and 1904, so that the little bonnet shown on the unmarked baby doll could be dated about this later time.

[1] E. Iklé, *La Broderie Mécanique*, Paris, 1931.

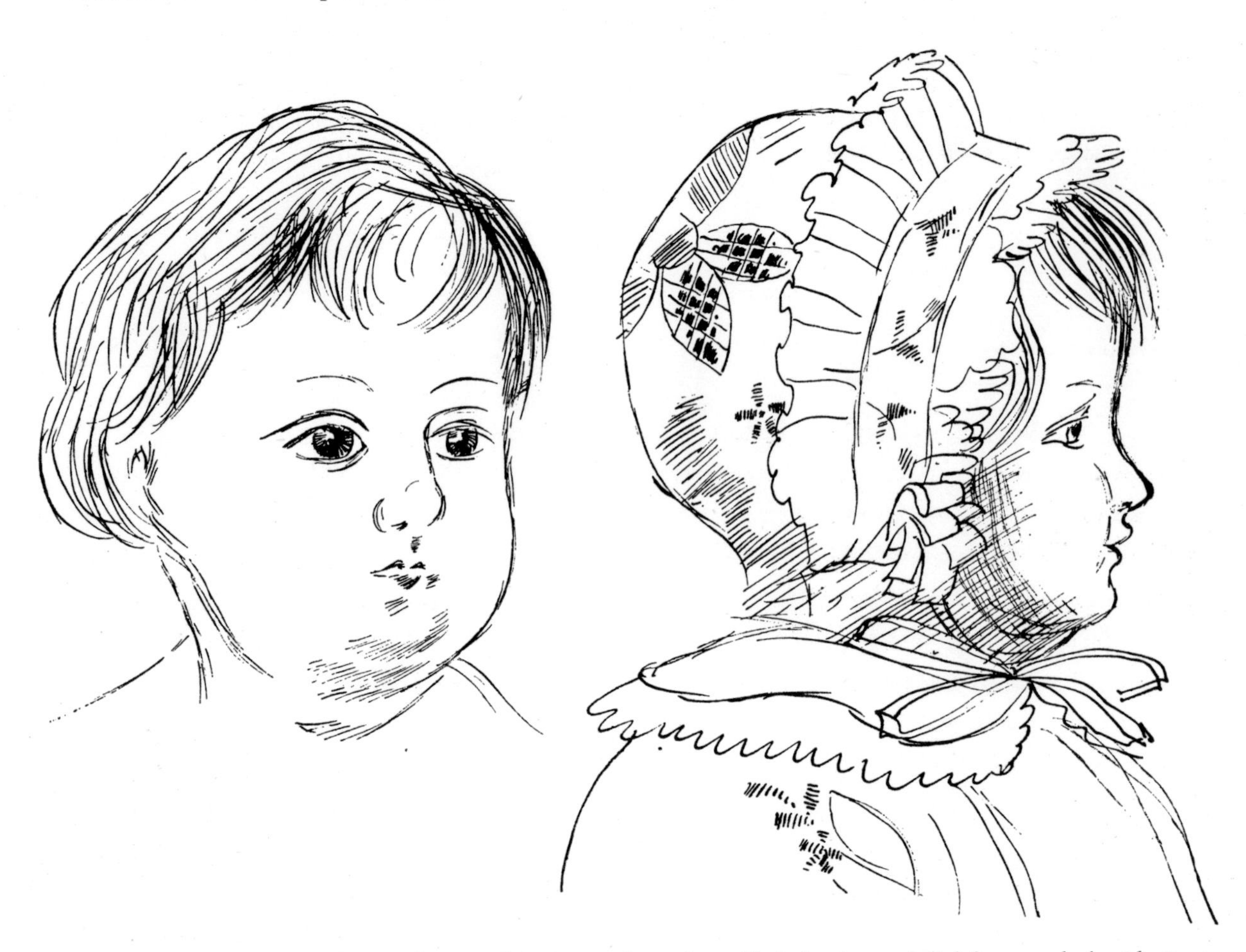

An unmarked wax doll, dressed in Broderie Anglaise. Inset ochre-coloured hair, head turned slightly towards the side. Inset blue eyes with white streaks, pink lips, ochre skin, no tint on cheeks. Canvas body, wax lower arms and lower legs. 8 in. to waist, 16 in. to knee. Dressed in a white short sleeved dress, knee length, short loose coat with collar tied at neck, long sleeves. Pink ribbon around waist, knickers, short white flannel petticoat, and muslin petticoat with top. All muslin machined embroidered in white. *Lent by Mrs. Mitchenor, and now in Bethnal Green Museum*

1 Child with a stump doll. Detail from the painting 'Charity' by Lucas Cranach the Elder (1472–1553, School of Saxony). German. *The National Gallery, London.* 2 Detail from the painting 'The daughters of Sir Matthew Decker' by Jan de Meyer. Signed and dated 1718. English. *The Fitzwilliam Museum, Cambridge.* 3 Child with a wooden doll, and leading strings on the child's gown. Detail from the painting 'A Family Group' by Michiel Nouts, 1636. Dutch. *The National Gallery, London.* 4 Wooden doll. English, 17th century. *Height* 6 in. *City Museum, Leeds.*

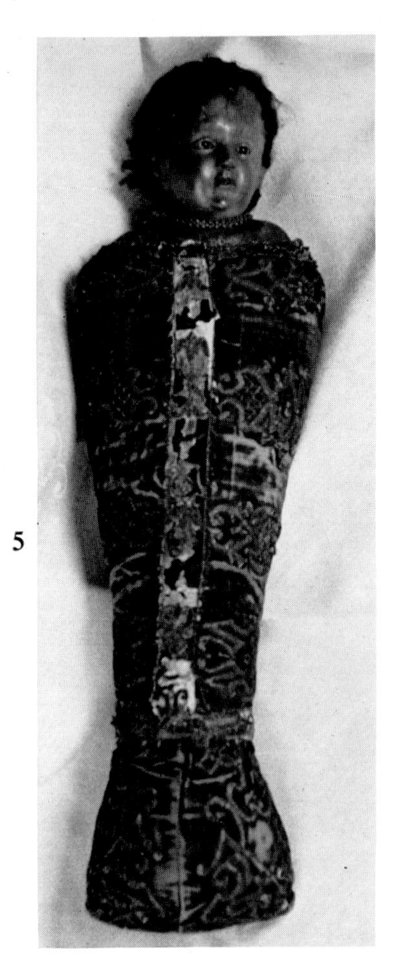

5

6

7

8

5 Neapolitan swaddle doll. Head of gesso over wood, body covered with red velvet embroidered in gold. The coral necklace is original. Naples, *c.* 1650. *Height* 18 in. *Brooklyn Children's Museum.* These dolls were used at Christmas for the elaborate creches for which Naples was famous. **6** Wood. Clothes of red silk with white lace front and collar, a net apron and metal bodice. Nuremberg, early 18th century. *Height* 14½ in. *Landesgewerbeamt Baden-Württemberg, Stuttgart.* **7** Wood. Head and hands of carved wood, painted. Jointed limbs. Brocade dress, with a lining of brown silk printed with text of *c.* 1728. Italian, 1730. *Height* 19¾ in. *Landesgewerbeamt Baden-Württemberg, Stuttgart.* **8** Wood. Turned birchwood. Nas Dalecarlia, Sweden, 18th century. *Height* 9½ in. *Nordiska Museet, Stockholm.*

9

10

11

12

9 Wood. Real hair knotted on cord stitched on linen. Fawn silk brocaded dress, the bodice stiffened with whale-bone and laced to form a corset. White lawn shift and sleeves edged with lace. Two white linen quilted pockets tied round the waist under the dress. English, early 18th century. *Height* 18 in. *The London Museum.* **10** Wood. Dress of coloured silk and cream voile. English, 18th century. *Height* 20 in. *Hove Museum.* **11** Wood. Blue silk robe with beige silk petticoat. English, mid 18th century. *Height* 16 in. *Blaise Castle House Folk Museum, Bristol.* **12** Wood. Brown blown glass eyes. Jointed arms with fairly large hands and carved upturned palms. Silk dress over a hooped underskirt, two other petticoats and brown canvas corsets. English, *c.* 1750. *Height* 20 in. The doll was given by Princess Louisa, daughter of George II, to Elizabeth Sampson, and was presented by her descendant, Mrs. Bell, to Queen Mary. *The London Museum.*

13

14

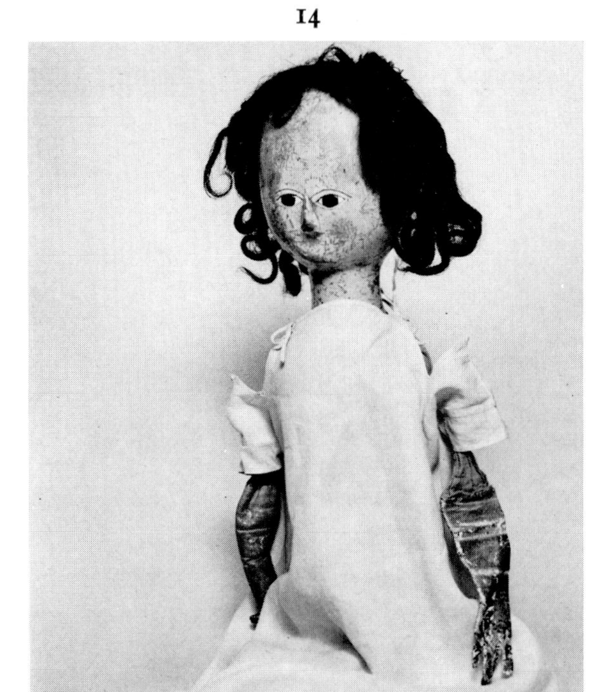

15

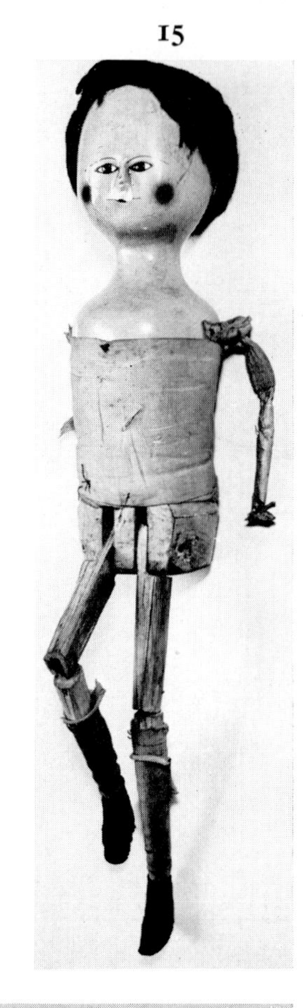

16

17

13, 14 Wood. Enamel eyes, brown with no pupils. No ears. The 'kid glove' arms are slightly stuffed. Wearing a chemise and stockings—note the 'slits' at shoulders. Probably English, second half of 18th century. *Height* 25 in. *Bethnal Green Museum, London.* **15** Wood. Wig added later. Painted head, kid forearms and stockinet uppers. Silk covering to lower legs. Probably English, second half of 18th century. *Height* 22 in.; head $4\frac{1}{2}$ in. *The London Museum.* **16, 17** Wood. The hair is sewn to black material which is nailed to the head, a tress possibly hanging down the back. The enamel eyes are nearly black, with no pupils. Flat wooden hands, carved. Legs covered with muslin, sewn up the back. Dressed *c.* 1800, a blue and white muslin bonnet is worn over the cap, a muslin over-dress open at the back with inset sleeves. Muslin cape, three chemises, a white petticoat and a longer petticoat. Tie-on pocket with handkerchief. Silk boots sewn up the front. English, late 18th century. *Height* 19 in. *Bethnal Green Museum, London.*

18 19 20 21

18 Wood. Kid hands. White muslin gown, two petticoats, stays, bodice, hoop of cane. Mob cap and knitted stockings. Probably English, 1770–80. *Height* 12 in. *The London Museum.* **19** Wood. Arms and legs missing. Cotton dress and bonnet. Bought at Bishop's Castle in 1815. English. *Height* 8 in. from head to end of trunk. *Hove Museum.* **20** Wood. High carved comb. Spade hands with fingers slightly carved. Dress fastens at the back with buttons made of small knobs, covered, and fastened with a loop. A row of bows covers the buttons. Hand-sewn yellow kid boots, piped with blue. English, 1812–30. *Height* 12 in. *Bethnal Green Museum, London.* **21** Wood. Belonging to Peace Page, Danvers. American, *c.* 1800. *Height* approx. 12 in. *Essex Institute, Salem.*

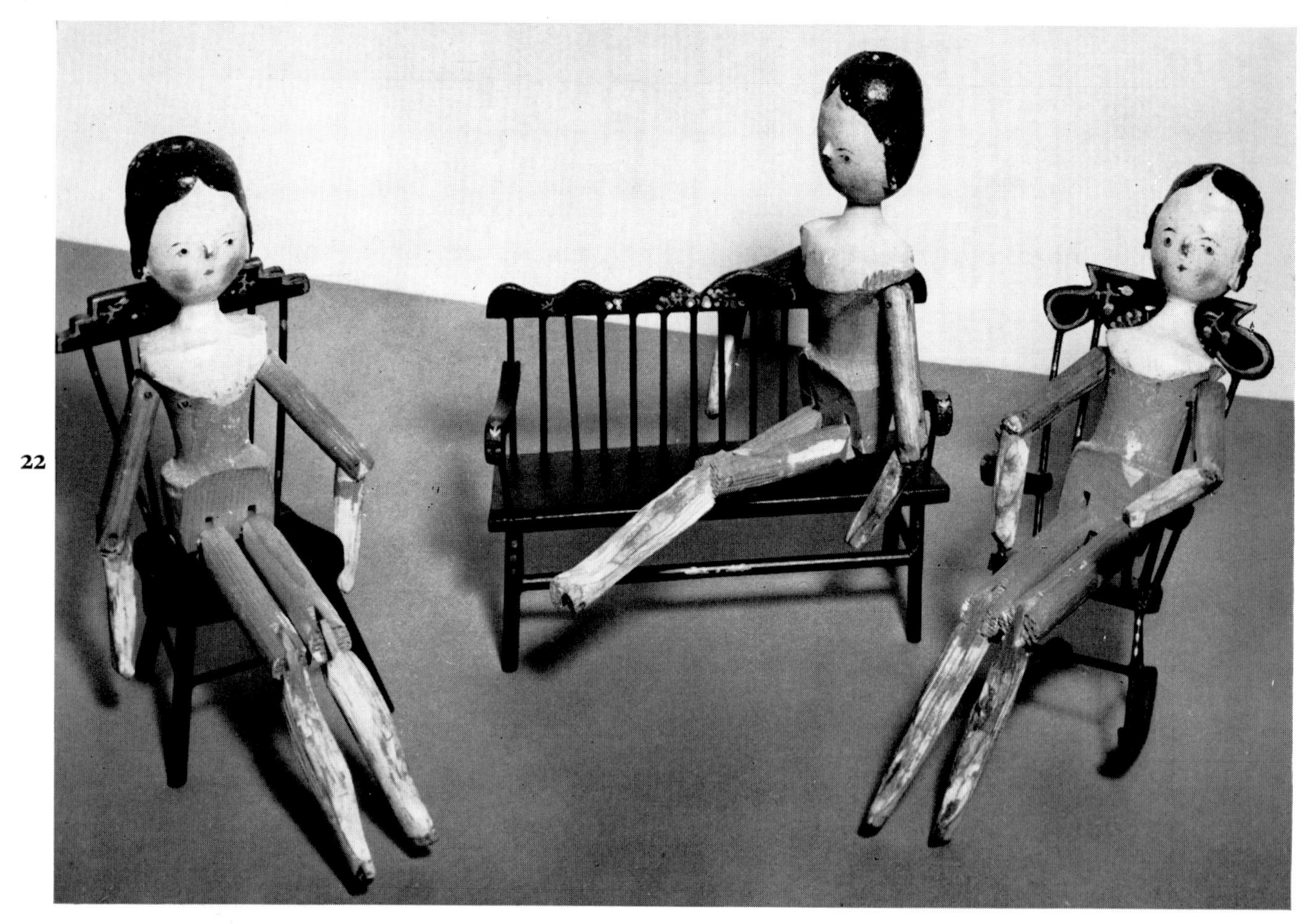

22

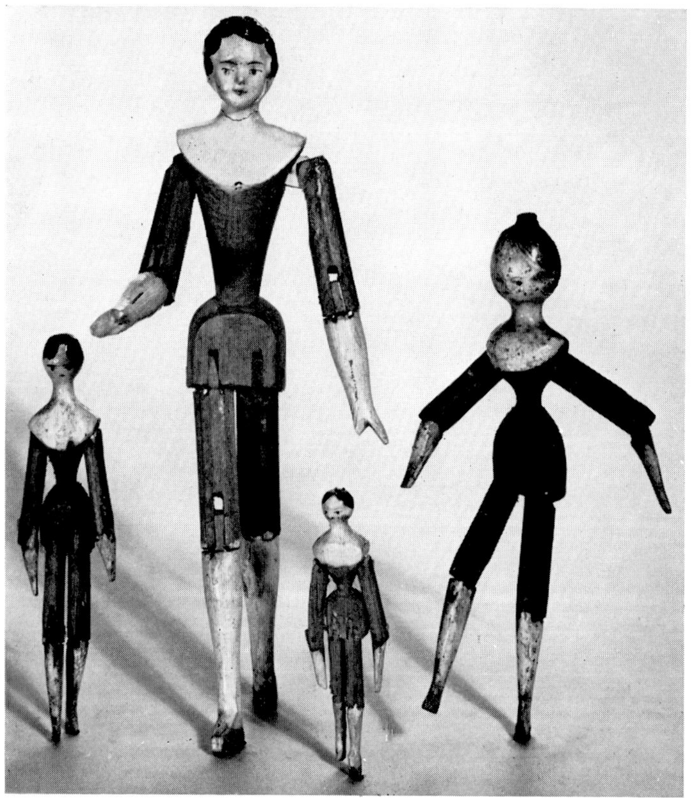

23

24

22 Peg-woodens. Painted hair, faces and yokes. Hinged joints. ? Central European, early 19th century. *Height* 9 in. *Children's Museum, Detroit.* **23** Peg dolls. Joints at shoulders, elbows, thighs and knees. Painted hair, one with top-knot, deep painted yokes and lower arms and legs. ? Central European. 1820–30. *Heights* $3\frac{1}{4}$, 6, $2\frac{1}{4}$ and $4\frac{1}{4}$ in. *City Museum, St. Albans.* **24** Peg dolls. Various hair styles carved and painted. The smallest doll has no joints at elbow or knee. All have deep painted yokes, and flat painted shoes with pointed toes. ? Central European, 1830–40. *Heights* $3\frac{1}{2}$, 1, $5\frac{1}{2}$, 3 and $4\frac{3}{4}$ in. *City Museum, St. Albans.*

25 Wood. Carved coloured head, body covered with leather. Biedermeier doll with 'turban' top-knot, delicately tinted clothes with lace and white net. Sonneberg, Germany, 1820–30. *Height* 13 in. *Deutsches Spielzeugmuseum, Sonneberg.* **26** Wood. Red and brown silk dress, trimmed with gold lace, and a string of tiny blue beads around her neck. 1854. *Height* 22 in. *American National Red Cross Museum, Washington.* One of two dolls which were made by a wounded soldier of the Crimean War and presented by him to Florence Nightingale, in grateful appreciation of her ministrations to the sick and wounded. The other he presented to Queen Victoria. When Miss Nightingale was a child, she treated her dolls as patients, bandaging their limbs and pretending they were ill. **27** Wood. Carved wooden head with glass eyes. Carved loops show where the painted hair should begin. Stuffed body. Black trousers, red waistcoat and white shirt. South Germany, 1830. *Height* $12\frac{1}{4}$ in. *Landesgewerbeamt Baden-Württemberg, Stuttgart.*

28 Wood, painted. From the surroundings of Hlinsko, Austria, beginning of 20th century. *Heights* 6 and $7\frac{1}{2}$ in. *National Museum, Prague.* **29** Wood. Carved and painted. Russian, *c.* 1800. *Heights* $13\frac{3}{4}$, $14\frac{1}{4}$ in. *Deutsches Spielzeugmuseum, Sonneberg.* **30, 32** Wood. Large, very heavy 'Dutch' doll, jointed. Painted features, hair, lower arms, and lower legs with shoes. Slightly carved head with ears and nose. Probably Dutch, *c.* 1830. *Height* $22\frac{1}{2}$ in. Given by Miss Gatesman in 1900. *Saffron Walden Museum.* **31** Wood and paste. Pribram, Austria, beginning of 20th century. *Height* $5\frac{3}{4}$ in. *National Museum, Prague.*

33 34 35 36 37

33 Papier mâché. Head painted, body covered with leather. Biedermeier period. Sonneberg, Germany, 1820–30. *Height* 26½ in. *Deutsches Spielzeugmuseum, Sonneberg.* **34** Papier mâché. Stuffed body. Black dress, red kerchief and pinafore. South German, *c.* 1830. *Height* 13 in. *Landesgewerbeamt Baden-Württemberg, Stuttgart.* **35** Composition. Composition hair, inset glass eyes, holes for nostrils. Unjointed kid body, small waist. Lower arms and legs of painted wood, one foot replaced with one of cloth. Extensive wardrobe, with many clothes made by former owner, the mother of the Misses Sally and Joanna Williams. ? American, *c.* 1830. *Height* 17 in. *Plymouth Antiquarian Society, Massachusetts.* **36** Papier mâché. ? European, *c.* 1830. *Height* 30 in. *New Milford Historical Society, Connecticut.* **37** Papier mâché. Fixed glass eyes, chemise and trousers of white cotton. Swedish, *c.* 1830. *Height* 12¼ in. *Nordiska Museet, Stockholm.*

38 Composition. Hair wig, painted features. Soft muslin body, kid forearms and flat kid hands. Green dress, muslin pantelettes edged with frill, and hand-made slippers. English, 1830–7. *Height* 16 in. *Bethnal Green Museum, London.* **39** Papier mâché. Dressed as the wife of Biberacher peasant. Kirchenanzug, Germany, *c.* 1840. *Height* $27\frac{1}{2}$ in. *Landesgewerbeamt Baden-Württemberg, Stuttgart.* **40** Papier mâché. ? English, *c.* 1840. *Height* 26 in. *City Museum, Leeds.* **41** Composition. Painted black hair, brown eyes. Unjointed kid body, small waist. Lower arms and lower legs of wood, feet missing. ? American, 1840. *Height* 17 in. Given by Mrs. Charles O. Strong. *Plymouth Antiquarian Society, Massachusetts.* **42** Composition head and hair. The looped hair shows the ears. Painted features. Muslin dress, three petticoats, long pants tied at waist, back slit. English, *c.* 1840. *Height* 10 in. *Bethnal Green Museum, London.*

43 Doll head with hair top-knot. Possibly made to display the latest coiffeur. Sonneberg, Germany, *c.* 1833. *Height* $9\frac{7}{8}$ in.
Deutsches Spielzeugmuseum, Sonneberg.

44, 45 Composition. Deep yoke edged with blue paint. Painted hair and features. Kid body, wooden lower arms and legs. Pink kid band above elbows and knees. Brown dress trimmed with lace. Probably English (similar dolls were also made in America), *c.* 1840. *Height* $16\frac{1}{4}$ in. Given by Miss J. Bennetts. *Saffron Walden Museum.* **46** Composition. Wooden body and limbs. The donor stated that this doll was handed down in her family in Nova Scotia from 1830. The dress, which is original, is somewhat earlier in style. English, 1830. *Height* 12 in. *Brooklyn Children's Museum.* **47** Costume figure of a man in Biberacher peasant clothes of *c.* 1840. Kirchenanzug, Germany. *Height* $26\frac{1}{2}$ in. *Landesgewerbeamt Baden-Württemberg, Stuttgart.* **48** Papier mâché. 'Flirting' eyes. Probably German, from 1843. *Height* $19\frac{3}{4}$ in. *National Museum of Finland, Helsinki.*

49 Composition. Hair wig, fixed glass eyes. Shows teeth and tongue. Kid body. Various additional clothes, including four dresses. Holding a pelerine. English, 1840. *Height* 18 in. *Bethnal Green Museum, London.* **50** Composition. Cream dress. Powell collection. Probably English, 1842. *Height* approx. 8 in. *Victoria and Albert Museum, London.* **51** Papier mâché. Cloth body, stuffed with hair; brown leather arms 16 in. long. Blue leather boots about 5 in. long. Black Forest, Germany, 1840. *Height* 30 in. *Kidders Trading Post and Doll Museum, Apache Junction.* **52** Papier mâché. Head coloured and varnished. Stuffed leather body. Dressed in Schwabian costume. German, mid 19th century. *Height* 20 in. *Landesgewerbeamt Baden-Württemberg, Stuttgart.*

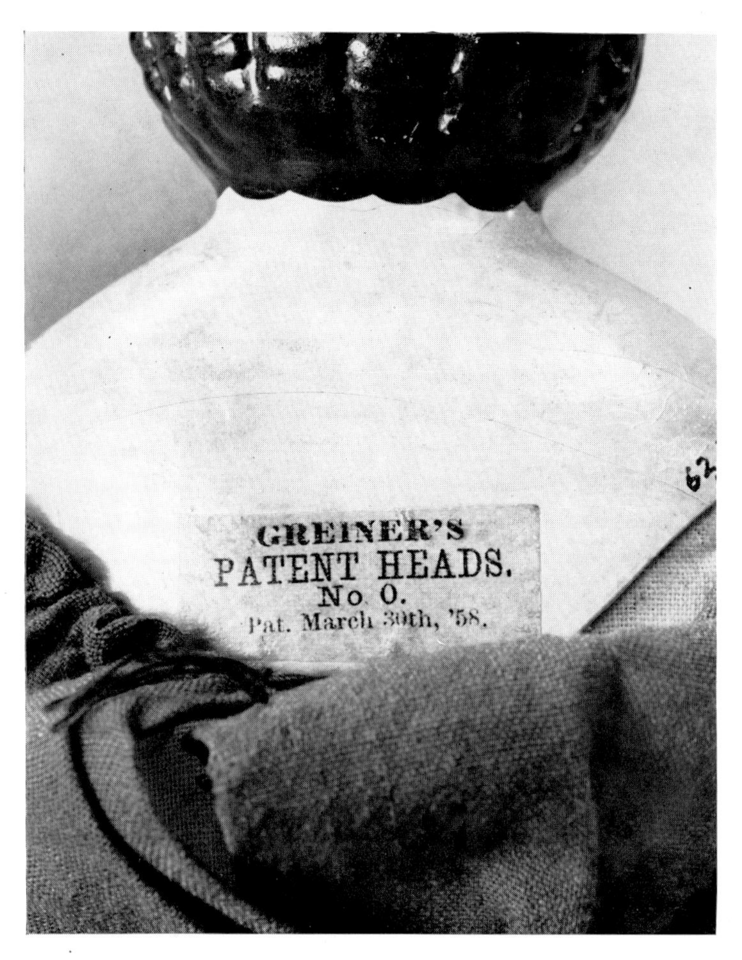

53

53, 54 Papier mâché. Papier mâché head and yoke on cloth body with leather arms. Label on back of shoulders shows this to be one of Ludwig Greiner's early heads. Philadelphia, 1858 onwards. Gift of Mrs. J. R. Devereaux. *Height* 13 in. *Smithsonian Institution, Washington.*

54

55 Papier mâché. Greiner patent mark on back of shoulder. Painted blue eyes. Hand-made cloth body. Dress trimmed with lace and braid. Philadelphia, 1858. *Height* 17½ in. *McCully House Toy Museum, Jacksonville.*

56 Papier mâché. A later Greiner doll with blonde hair and blue eyes. Arms and hands of leather, rest of body cloth. Dress of tan and white striped lawn, trimmed with black ribbon. Label stuck on back reads 'Greiner's Patent Doll Heads, No. 6. Pat. Mar. 30, '58, Ext. '72 Factory, 414 N. 4th St., Phila.' Philadelphia, *c.* 1872. *Height* 23 in. *Children's Museum, Detroit.*

57

58

59

60

57 Papier mâché. Dressed as the wife of a wealthy burgomaster of Biberach. German, *c.* 1860. *Height* 17¾ in. *Landesgewerbeamt Baden-Württemberg, Stuttgart.* **58** Papier mâché head and hair. Wooden legs and arms. Padded kid body. English, mid 19th century. *Height* 12½ in. *The Toy Museum, Rottingdean.* **59** Papier mâché. Blue glass eyes. Mid nineteenth century. *Height* 30¼ in. *National Museum of Finland, Helsinki.* **60** Composition. Composition lower arms and legs, stuffed body. *c.* 1890. *Height* 20 in. *Mrs. Graham Greene.*

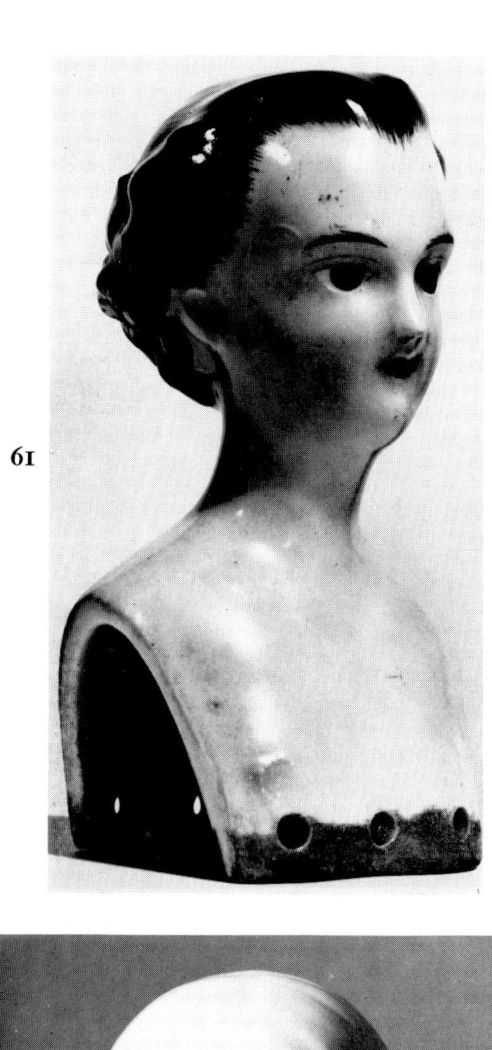

61

62

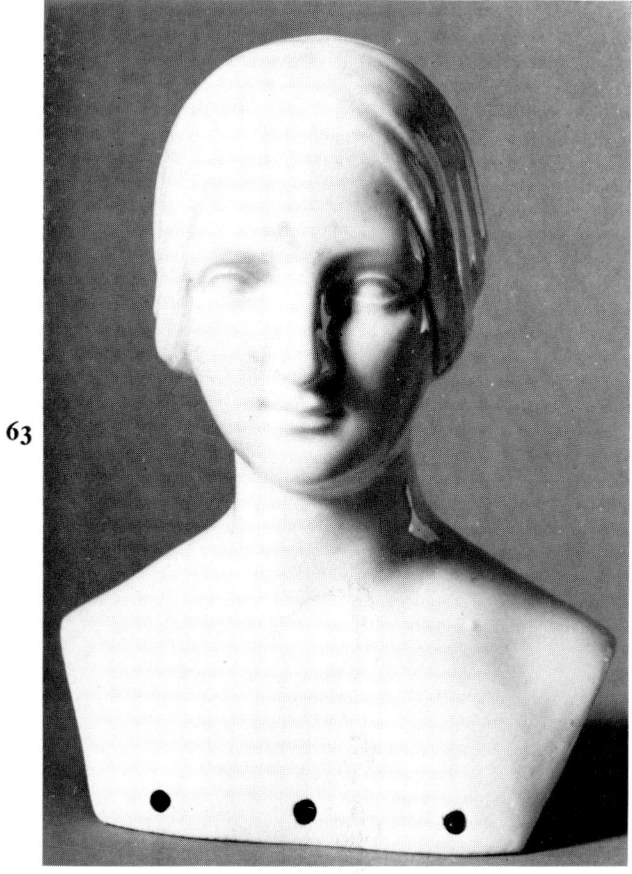

63

64

61 Porcelain doll-head. Painted features, highly glazed, with brown hair decorated with green leaves and blue and pink flowers. Yoke has three holes, front and back (earlier than yokes with only two holes). Probably European, early 19th century. *Height* 4 in. *The London Museum*. **62** Porcelain. Probably English, *c.* 1835. *Height* 14 in. *City Museum, Leeds*. **63** Porcelain head. Marked with the Meissen mark of the blue crossed swords under the glaze. The hair is drawn towards the back in a carefully arranged plait. German, first half of 19th century. *Height* $4\frac{3}{4}$ in. *Germanisches National-museum, Nuremberg*. **64** Porcelain. Berlin-headed doll. Marked under glaze with a sceptre in green. German, 1838–40. *Fru Estrid Faurholt*.

65 Porcelain. Porcelain head with black hair. Dressed in student uniform. Probably German, from *c.* 1850. *Height* $14\frac{1}{4}$ in. *National Museum of Finland, Helsinki.*

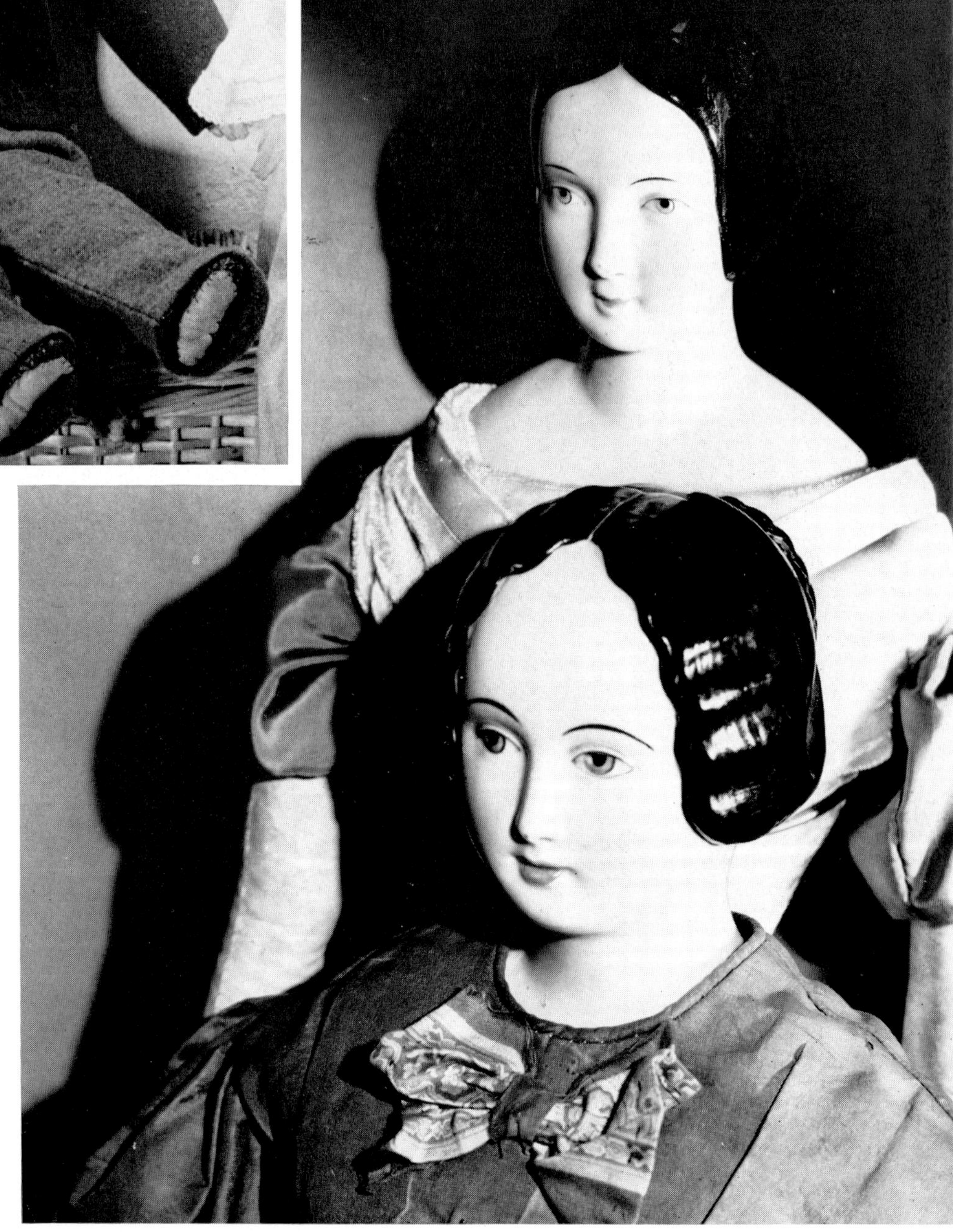

66 Porcelain. Portrait dolls of Biedermeier period, heads finely painted, hair modelled. Leather-covered bodies. Sonneberg, Germany, *c.* 1840. *Heights* $24\frac{1}{2}$, $27\frac{1}{2}$ in. *Deutsches Spielzeugmuseum, Sonneberg.*

67

68

69

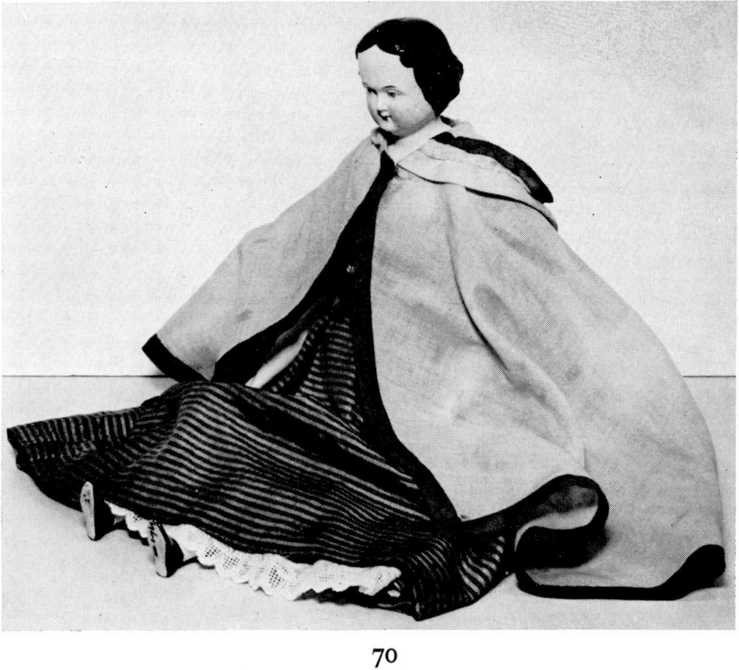

70

67 Porcelain. Forearms and lower legs of porcelain, stuffed body. Probably English, early 19th century. *Height* 16 in. *City Museum, St. Albans.* **68** Porcelain. Probably German, *c.* 1850. *Fru Estrid Faurholt.* **69, 70** Porcelain. Lustre head, pale blue eyes, yoke with three holes front and back. Lustre legs with bows beneath knees. Red laces on the black shoes, with brown soles. Porcelain forearms. Possibly German, mid 19th century. *Height* 20 in. *Bethnal Green Museum, London.*

71

72

73

74

71 Porcelain. Lustre head with coloured detail. Stuffed body, forearms of blue kid. Said to represent Princess Alexandra about the time of her marriage in 1863. Probably English. *Height* 12 in. *The London Museum.* **72** Porcelain. Known as the 'Fair Quaker', this doll was given to the late Margaret Armour by Eliza Wigham, an Edinburgh Quaker. It was dressed for her in 1865 in replica of and from materials belonging to her mother's wedding gown. Probably English. *Height* 24 in. *Museum of Childhood, Edinburgh.* **73, 74** Porcelain. Lustre head with coloured details, parian face and hair. Stuffed body, bisque forearms and legs. Mauve silk dress. Carrying a bouquet of white flowers. White blouse, cerise velvet jacket with white embroidery. Combinations, crocheted silk petticoat, embroidered silk petticoat, pink silk crocheted crinoline, lace-edged muslin petticoat with lace and pink ribbons. Said to represent Princess Alexandra about the time of her marriage in 1863. Probably English, *c.* 1863. *Height* 16½ in. Given by Queen Mary. *The London Museum.*

75

76

77

78

79

80

75 Porcelain. Pink lustre. Stuffed body. Probably English, mid 19th century. *Height* 15 in. *Mrs. Heather Fox.* **76** Porcelain. Two little 'Frozen Charlottes'. Porcelain throughout with no joints. Could either use a swing or play the piano. Probably English, *c.* 1850. *Height* $2\frac{3}{8}$ in. *Luton Museum.* The name 'Frozen Charlotte' comes from a New England ballad in which a maiden went for a sleigh ride in her evening gown and no wrap, and was frozen stiff. The term is now used for all little china dolls without joints. **77** Porcelain. Probably German, *c.* 1870. *Height* $5\frac{1}{2}$ in. *Fru Estrid Faurholt.* **78** Porcelain. 'Frozen Charlottes'. These are white, but there are also those completely black. Probably English, mid 19th century. *Height* (average) $\frac{1}{2}$ in. *Museum of Childhood, Edinburgh.* **79** Porcelain. Probably German, 1870. *Height* 15 in. *Fru Estrid Faurholt.* **80** Porcelain. Probably German, *c.* 1875. *Fru Estrid Faurholt.*

81 Porcelain. Head, yoke, arms, and legs of porcelain, with cloth body. Probably German, *c.* 1880. *Height* 9½ in. Gift of Miss Marie Estelle DeRonceray. *Smithsonian Institution, Washington.*

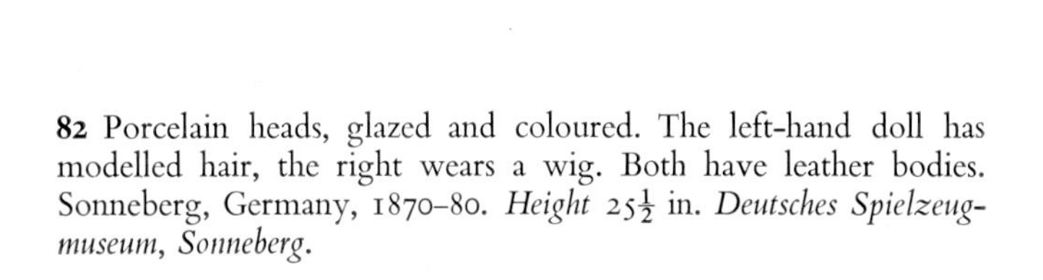

82 Porcelain heads, glazed and coloured. The left-hand doll has modelled hair, the right wears a wig. Both have leather bodies. Sonneberg, Germany, 1870–80. *Height* 25½ in. *Deutsches Spielzeugmuseum, Sonneberg.*

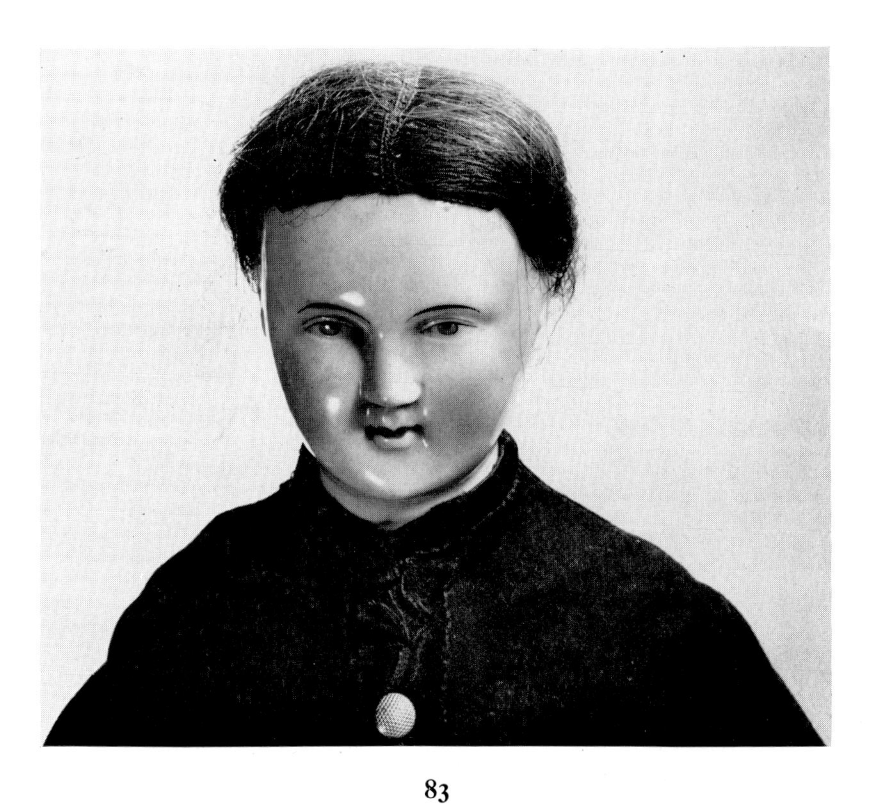

83

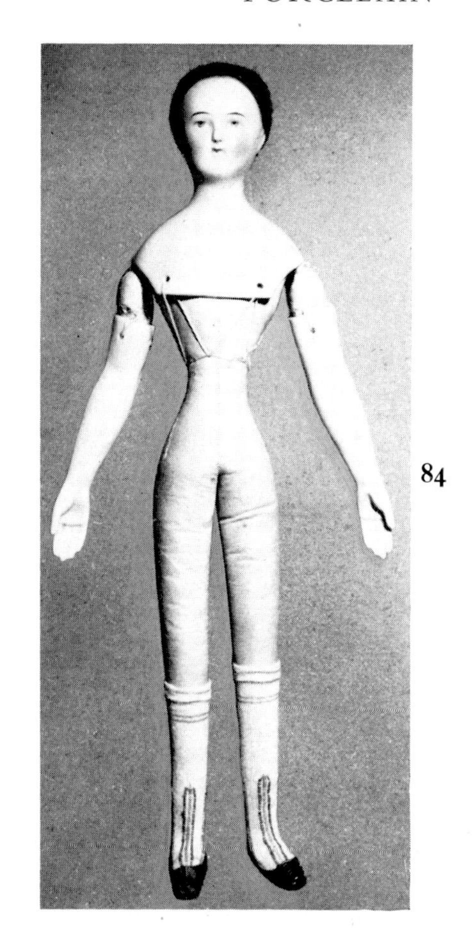

84

85

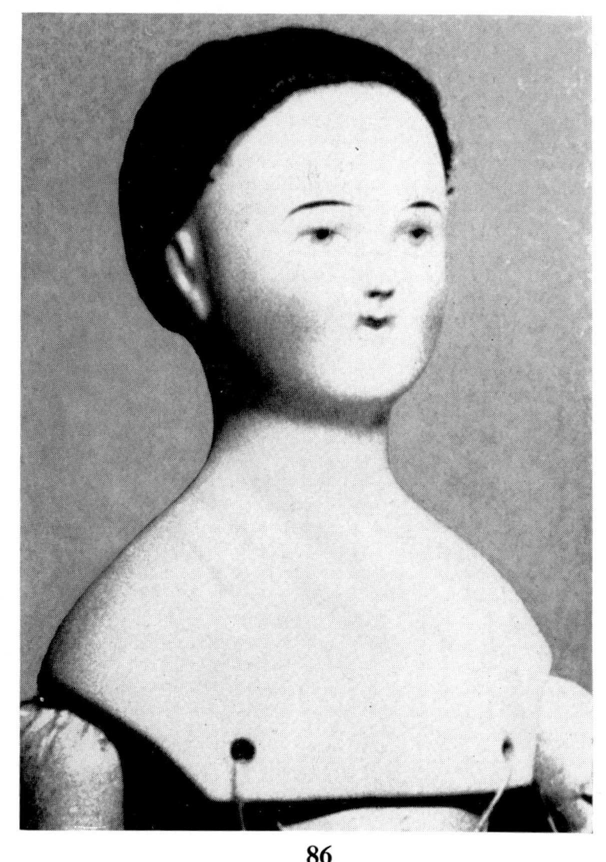

86

83 Porcelain. Hair wig, leather arms, stuffed body. Probably German, *c.* 1860. *Height* 22 in. *City Museum, St. Albans.* **84, 86** Porcelain. Hair wig, arranged in large plaited bun at back. Painted features, blue eyes. Kid body hand-sewn. Probably German, *c.* 1880. *Height* 17 in. *Miss Ruth Wainwright.* **85** Porcelain. Hair wig, fixed to head in which are holes, one on top, one at base of skull, one over each ear. Painted features, stuffed body, legs fastened with metal buttons at side of knee. English, late 19th century. *Height* 17 in. *Bethnal Green Museum, London.*

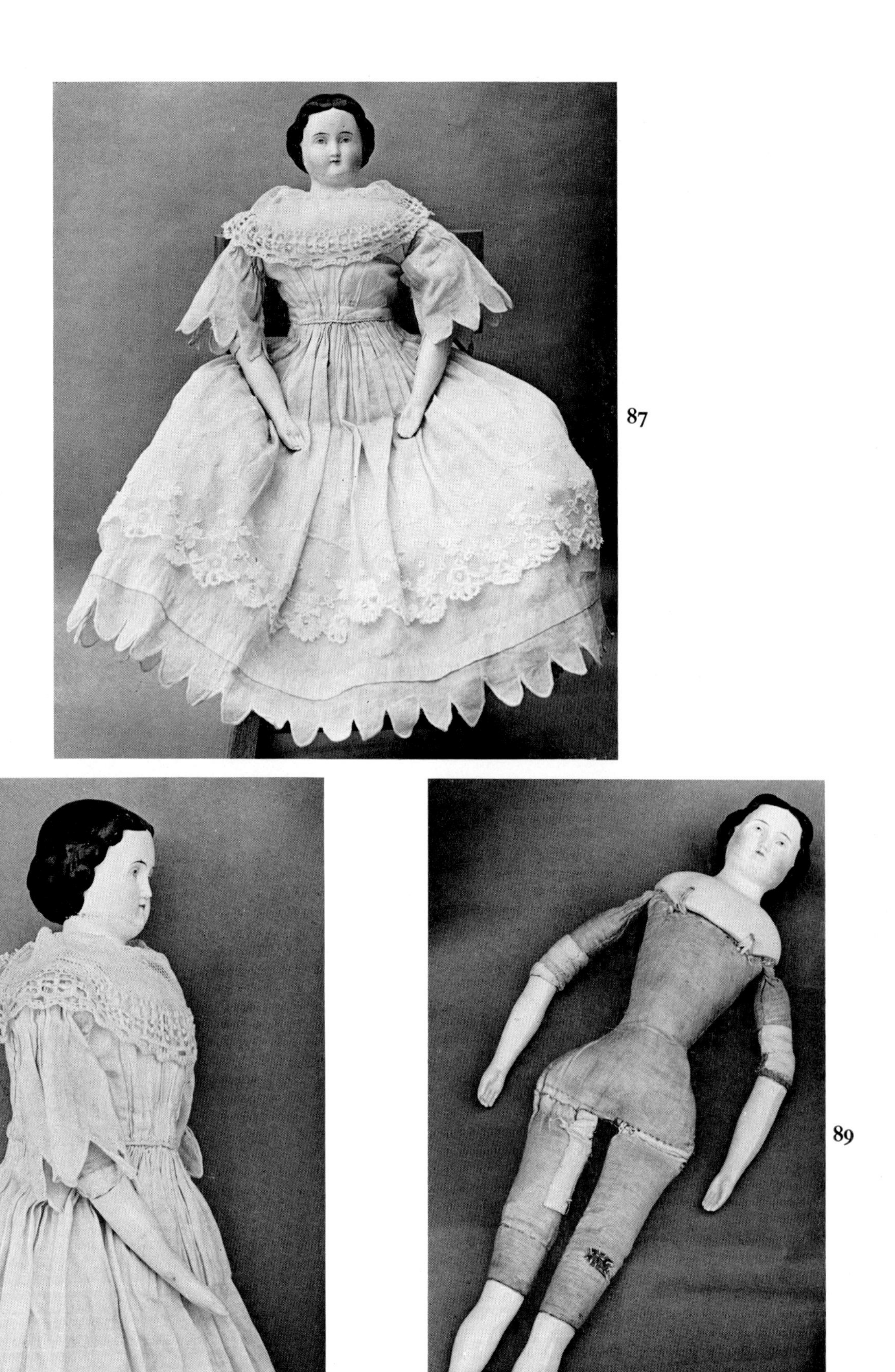

87–9 Parian. Glazed hair. Flat-heeled boot with red front lacing. Probably English, mid 19th century. *Height* 15½ in. *Mrs. Lorna Hennessy.*

90

91

92

93

90 Parian. Biedermeier period. Fair hair, leather body. Black taffeta dress trimmed with braid, petticoat and knickers, white socks and black leather shoes. Stuttgart, Germany, early 19th century. *Height* 27½ in. *Landesgewerbeamt Baden-Württemberg, Stuttgart.* **91** Parian. Marked on back yoke 10 B. Dressed in white lawn, lace trimmed. ? French, early 19th century. *Height* 10 in. *The London Museum.* **92** Parian. Bisque fair hair. Raw Sienna canvas body, bisque forearms, parian legs decorated with bow of pink lustre, black boots with straight top and brown soles, the whole covered with knitted stockings. Brown dress of the St. Marylebone Charity School, and blue ribbons. English, 1860. *Height* 14 in. *Bethnal Green Museum, London.* **93** Parian. Bisque arms and legs, black painted boots. Black and blue striped dress, with velvet top. Spare dress in cardboard box. French, *c.* 1860–70. *Height* 10½ in. *Mrs. Graham Greene.*

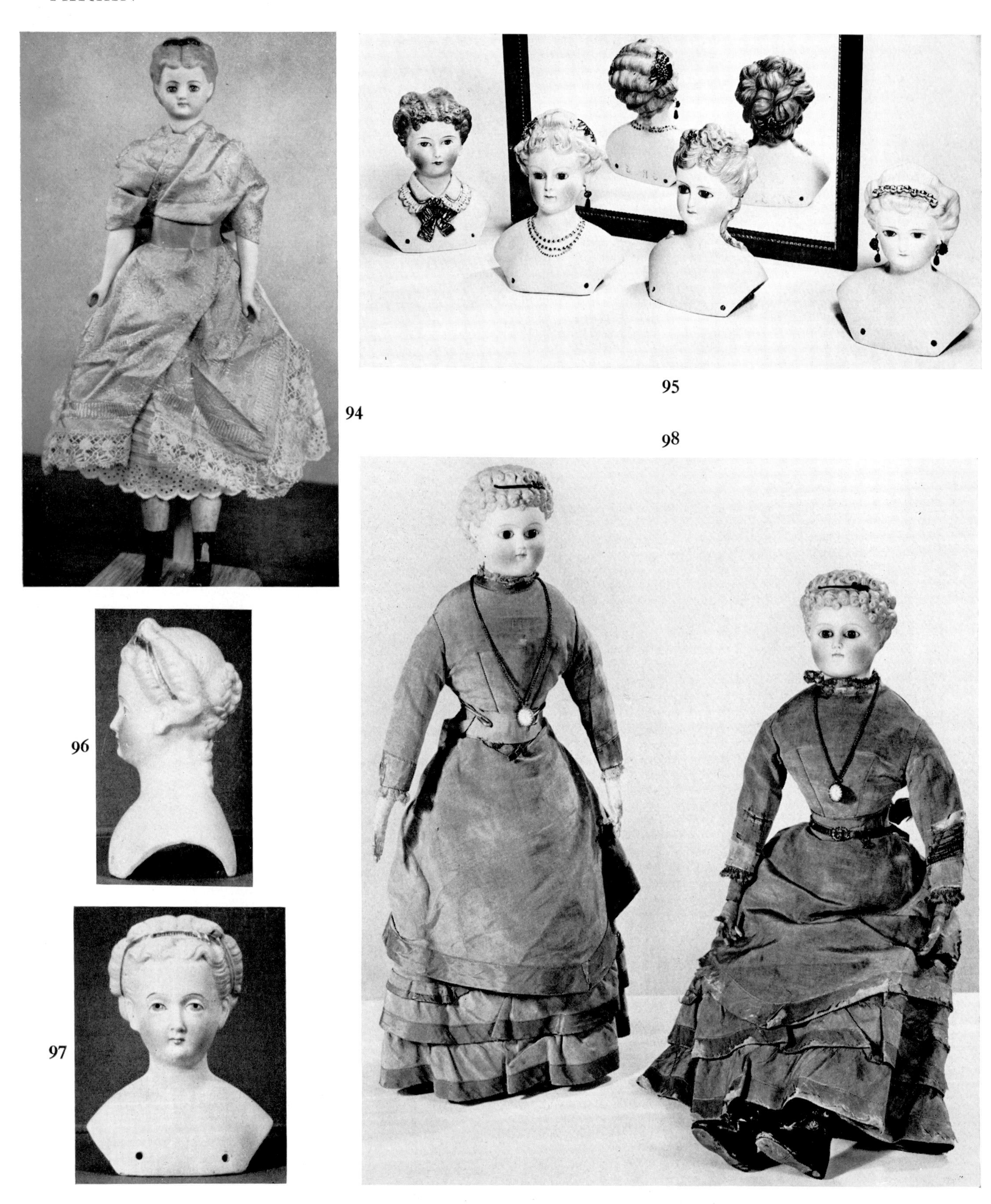

94 Parian. Swivel neck, stuffed body, wooden legs with blue painted boots and gold buttons. ? English, 1860–70. *Height* 12 in. *Mrs. Heather Fox.* **95** Parian heads. European, *c.* 1870. in. *Museum of the City of New York.* **96, 97** Parian head. With golden band in hair. ? French, 1870. *Height* 4 in. *Fru Estrid Faurholt.* **98** Parian. Twins with identical heads, beribboned coiffures and dresses. ? French, *c.* 1870. *Museum of the City of New York.*

99

100

101

99 Parian. Blue inset eyes, cloth body, bisque arms and legs. Marked on back yoke '31' with '3' underneath. Lower leg marked '12'. Probably English, 1860–70. *Height* 12 in. *Mrs. Lorna Hennessy.* **100** Parian. Probably English, *c.* 1870. *Height* 15 in. *City Museum, Leeds.* **101** Parian. Hair modelled in green net with gold lustre band and feathers. Stuffed body, parian forearms and legs. White muslin dress, fullness at back with rows of muslin frilling, trimmed with red bows. Known as 'Lucy'. Probably English, 1860–70. *Height* 16 in. *Red House Museum and Art Gallery, Christchurch.*

102

103

104

105

106

102 Bisque. Mohair wig, fixed glass eyes, leather body. A Parisian doll carrying a dog and lorgnette. Frankreich, 1850–60. *Height* 15 in. *Deutsches Spielzeugmuseum, Sonneberg.* **103** Bisque. Jumeau type. Hair wig, fixed eyes. Kid body, kid arms with separate fingers on hands. Green taffeta dress, embroidered with real lace and white beads. All clothes firmly stitched on. The doll wears earrings and carries a lorgnette. The dress may be the Hoehst green made fashionable in Paris by the Empress Eugénie. French, *c.* 1868. *Height* 18 in. Given by Mrs. Charles Barnes of Dulwich in 1930. *The London Museum.* **104** Bisque. Bisque head and yoke, swivel neck, fair wig, fixed blue glass eyes, pink dot at inner edge and at nostrils. Painted lashes and eyebrows, holes for earrings. Jointed kid body and limbs, hands with separate fingers, toes indicated by stitching. French, *c.* 1870. *Height* 16 in. Given by Miss Mary H. Russell, born in Plymouth in 1860. *Plymouth Antiquarian Society, Massachusetts.* **105** Bisque. Swivel neck, kid body. Dressed in fashionable walking costume of blue-grey serge of *c.* 1870. French. *Height* 17 in. *The London Museum.* **106** Bisque head and yoke. Fair hair wig, blue eyes, pink dot at inner edge. Painted lashes, pierced ears, swivel neck. Yoke attached by four holes to cloth body. Kid hands. Original dress of grey mohair, trimmed with narrow purple velvet ribbon; present dress copied in mid 19th century silk. ? English, *c.* 1868. *Height* $16\frac{1}{2}$ in. Given by Miss Emily Hussey of New Bedford, born *c.* 1860–5. *Plymouth Antiquarian Society, Massachusetts.*

107

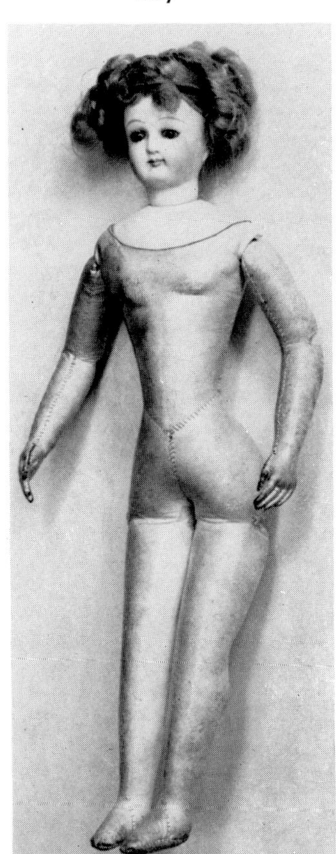

108

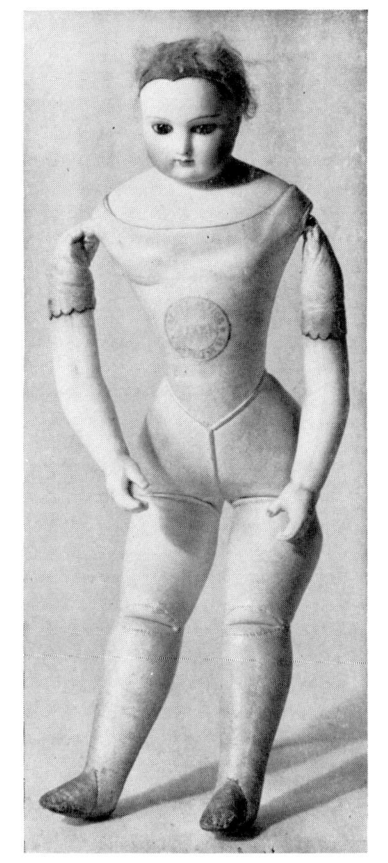

109

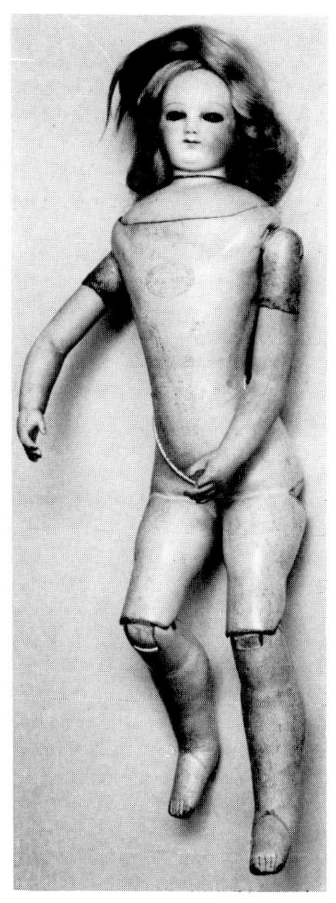

110

111

107 Bisque. Hair wig, fixed eyes of ultramarine, unpierced ears, swivel neck. Hands with separate fingers, kid body all hand-sewn. Bought with no clothes as part of stock of shop at Minster Gate, York. French, 1870–80. *Height* 13 in. *Bethnal Green Museum, London.* **108, 110** Bisque. Wig of animal skin with light brown hair made like a tight bonnet. Fixed eyes of dark blue, flat ears unpierced. Hand-sewn kid body, bisque forearms. Body marked 'MAKER, CREMER, Junior. 210 Regent St.' Dress trimmed with braid and edging. Sole of shoes marked G P. The bisque head has a French appearance, with a tortoiseshell comb reaching from ear to ear. English, *c.* 1862. *Height* 15½ in. Given by Mrs. N. Barrett. *Saffron Walden Museum.* **109, 111** Bisque. Marked 'Simonne, Paris'. Very white bisque head and yoke, greyish hair wig, fixed eyes. Head turns at neck with no socket showing. Trunk with many additional clothes. French, *c.* 1870. *Height* 13 in. *Bethnal Green Museum, London.*

112

113

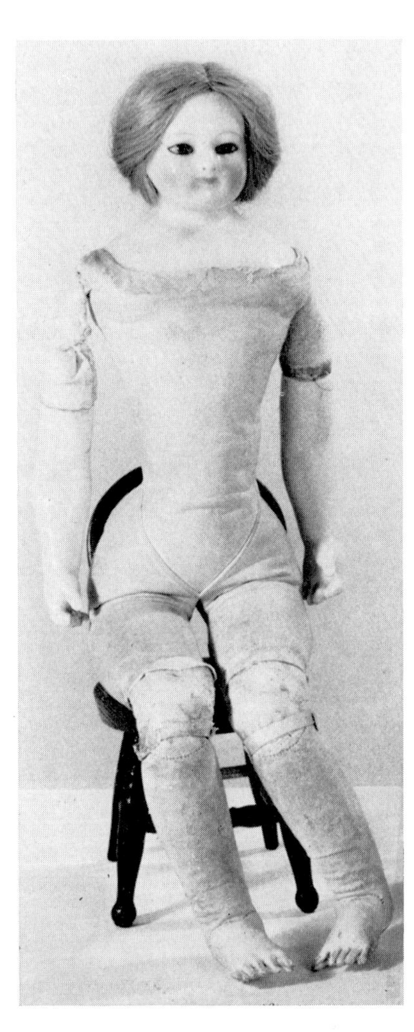

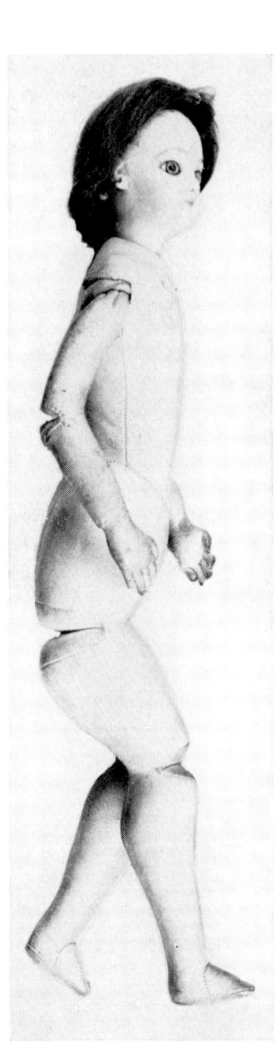

114 115 116

112, 114, 115 Bisque, glazed. Marked HURET. Fixed eyes, gutta-percha bodies. Extensive wardrobes. French. *Museum of the City of New York.* **113** Bisque. Fixed glass eyes. Dressed in a wedding gown of white ninon, veil of tulle, orange flowers. Bought in Paris in 1878. French. *Height* 19 in. *Nordiska Museet, Stockholm.* **116** Bisque. Hair wig, fixed eyes, pierced ears, swivel neck. Kid body, stamped on the back 'Jumeau, Medaille D'Or, Paris'. French, *c.* 1878. *Height* 17 in. *The London Museum.*

117

118

119

117 Bisque. Rohmer mark stamped on upper chest. Fine quality bisque, almost translucent. Deep blue eyes, painted. Swivel neck. Kid body and legs, bisque arms. Shoes of white satin. She holds a prayer book with gold cross and a rosary. French, mid 19th century. *Height* 16 in. *Mrs. Nina S. Davies.* **118** Bisque. Bought in Paris, made by Jumeau. French, *c.* 1870. *Height* 18 in. Gift of Mrs. Frank Brett Noyes. *Smithsonian Institution, Washington.* **119** Bisque (glazed, but not porcelain). Hair wig, dark blue inset eyes, swivel neck. Kid body, arms with hands with separate fingers. Earrings. Bought at the Paris Exhibition. French, 1878. *Height* 12 in. *Bethnal Green Museum, London.*

120

121

122

123

120 Bisque. Jointed gutta-percha body. French, *c.* 1878. *Museum of the City of New York.* **121** Bisque. Bisque arms, leather body. French, end of 19th century. *Height* 15¾ in. *Musée des Arts Décoratifs, Paris.* **122** Bisque. Bisque arms, leather body. French, end of 19th/beginning of 20th century. *Height* 14½ in. *Musée des Arts Décoratifs, Paris.* **123** Bisque. Papier mâché body. Blue dress with lace collar. French, 1880. *Height* 18½ in. *Musée des Arts Décoratifs, Paris.*

124 Wax creche figure. Wax head and hands, glass eyes, wire and hemp body, wooden feet. Outer skirt of frail silk, the petticoat a page of a hymnal with the notes showing more and more through the material as the skirt decays. Probably Italian, 17th century. *Height* 9 in. *McCully House Doll Museum, Jacksonville.*

125 126

127 128

125, 128 Waxen bust of a woman. Dutch, 1665. **126** Wax. *Left*, brown cloth with red velvet cuffs; *right*, beige cloth with silken cuffs. Dutch, second half of 17th century. *Height* $7\frac{1}{8}$ in. **127** Wax. Hair low at back of head, dressed with ribbons in the form of a fan, with two long curls in front. Silk dress with gold lace on the under-dress and many tiny bows. From the doll's house of Margaretha de Ruyter. Dutch, 1676. *Height* $7\frac{1}{2}$ in. *Rijksmuseum, Amsterdam* (**125-8**).

129 Wax. The man wears a close-fitting jacket, 'justaucorps' with row of buttons, jabot under chin, full wig, and many bows. The nurse is dressed in the manner of the lower class, and the children have ribbons dotted with bows, padded caps with velvet brims, and reins for learning to walk, i.e. leading strings. From the doll's house of Margaretha de Ruyter. Dutch, last quarter of 17th century. *Height* $4\frac{3}{4}$–$7\frac{7}{8}$ in. *Rijksmuseum, Amsterdam.*

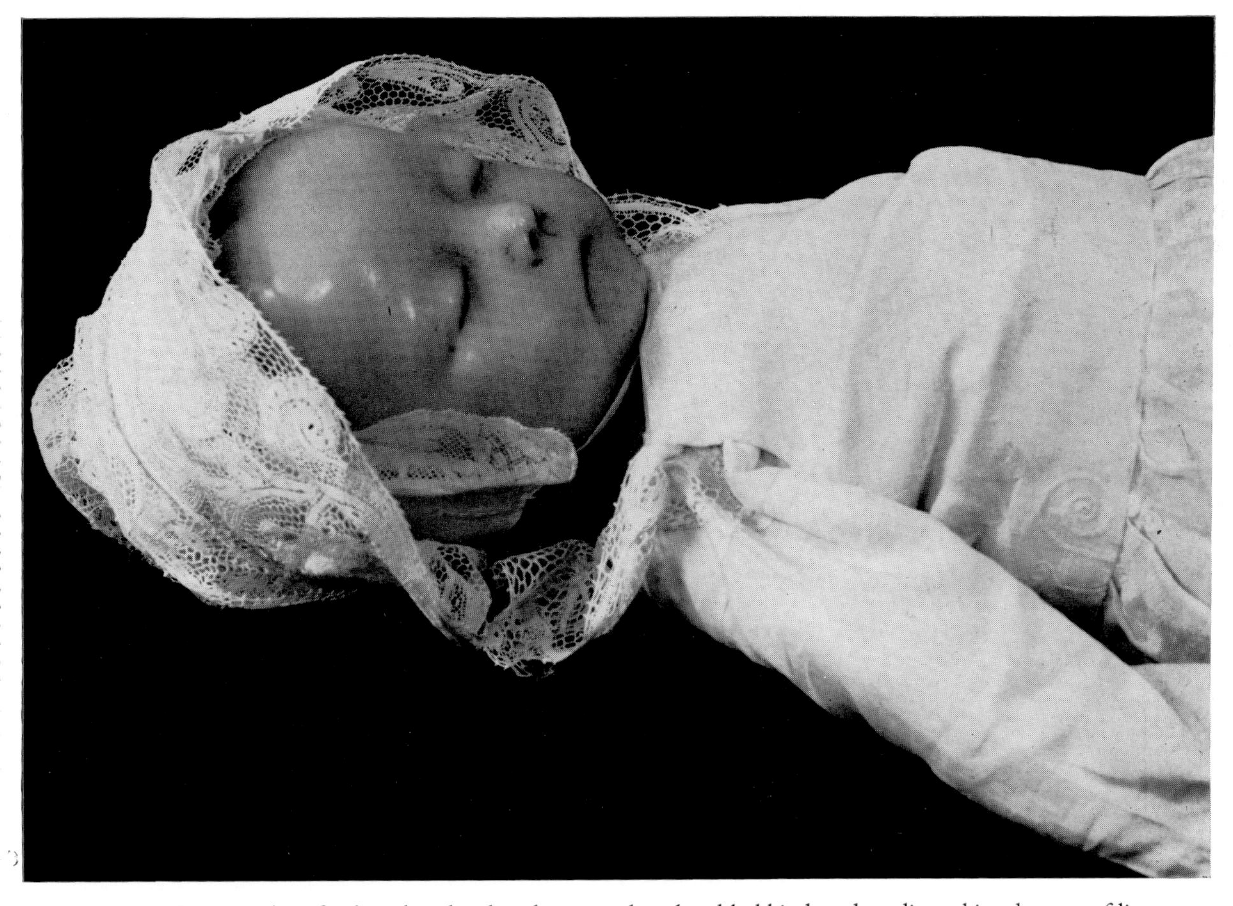

130 Wax infant. Cambric frock embroidered with cotton thread and bobbin lace, long linen shirt, drawers of linen damask. Hood-shaped outer cap, inner linen cap, triangular cap-piece with Valenciennes and Flemish bobbin laces, mittens of North Italian bobbin lace. Northern Spanish coat of arms embroidered on the robe. Spanish, *c.* 1690. *Height* 25 in. Frock $35\frac{1}{2}$ in. long, $27\frac{1}{2}$ in. wide; mittens $2\frac{3}{4}$ in. long, $2\frac{1}{4}$ in. wide. *Victoria and Albert Museum, London.* A custom is said to have been prevalent in the Spanish Peninsula of thus modelling the last member of a noble family. Lord Leighton said it was the most artistic specimen of its kind that he had ever seen.

131

132

131 Wax. Glass eyes, stuffed body and legs. Wide dress. English, 1759. *Height* 8 in. *Victoria and Albert Museum, London.*
132 Wax. Wax arms, stuffed body. Deep rose pink silk dress over panniers, trimmed with silver galon. Hair ornaments with lace and flowers, lace edged sleeve flounces, neck ruffle and lappets. Blue shoes. Known as 'Clarissa'. Probably English, 1760. *Height* 14½ in. *Red House Museum and Art Gallery, Christchurch.*

133 Wax. Lamb's wool hair, glass eyes, painted mouth open showing tongue and two teeth. Head and yoke, lower arms and lower legs of wax, the rest of the body wound cotton over padding. White satin dress, trimmed with gold braid, sequins and handmade lace. 18th century. *Height* 18 in. *Children's Museum, Detroit.* 134 Wax. Modelled and tinted wax, body of stuffed linen. Pink satin bodice, stomacher of cream-coloured satin, trimmed with Midland counties bobbin 'baby-lace'. Cream satin skirt, three petticoats, long stockings of knitted cotton, heelless shoes of white kid. Crêpe bonnet trimmed with lace, silk ribbons and gimp. Wig made in 1962 by Emile Ltd., Sloane Street, London. English, 1770–80. *Height* 27 in. *Victoria and Albert Museum, London.* 135 Wax. Brown painted hair, brown beady eyes. Dressed in cream satin with pink net and white flowers. Early 19th century. *Height* $5\frac{1}{2}$ in. *The London Museum.*

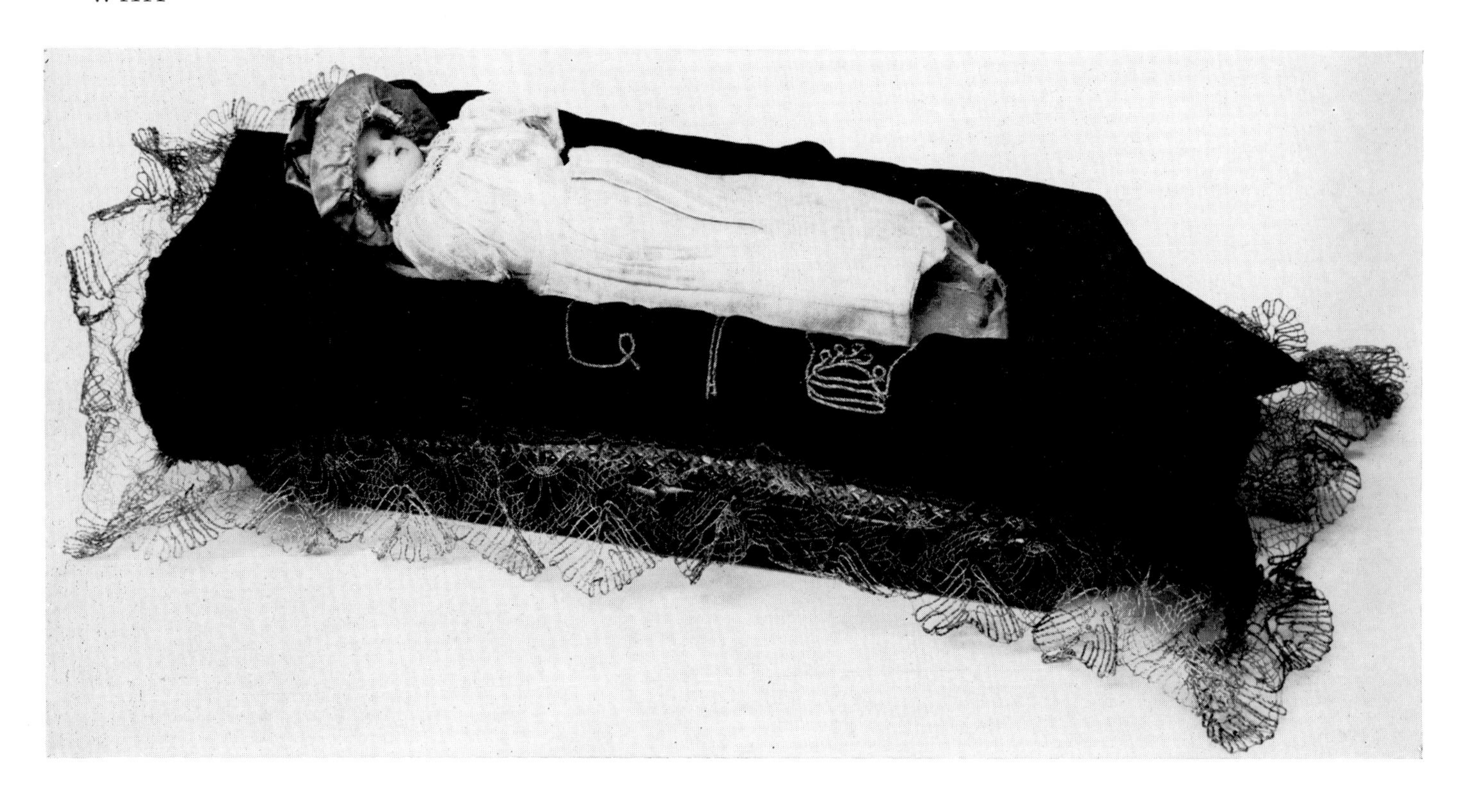

136 Wax. Very light in weight. White baby clothes and blue bonnet, in a velvet-lined box as a cradle. The velvet is fringed with gold lace and embroidered with a crown and the initial 'C', for Charlotte, Princess of Wales, to whom the doll belonged. She called it 'the great Doll's baby'. Probably English, *c.* 1800. *Height* 9 in. *The London Museum.*

137 Wax. Painted hair, brown beady eyes. Wax lower legs fitted with little pins, with painted brown slippers tied with small bows. White silk dress, short petticoat, long petticoat, and pants from the waist. Doll said to represent Princess Alexandrina Victoria (later Queen Victoria) at the age of 15. English, *c.* 1835. *Height* 8 in. Given by Queen Mary. *Bethnal Green Museum, London.*

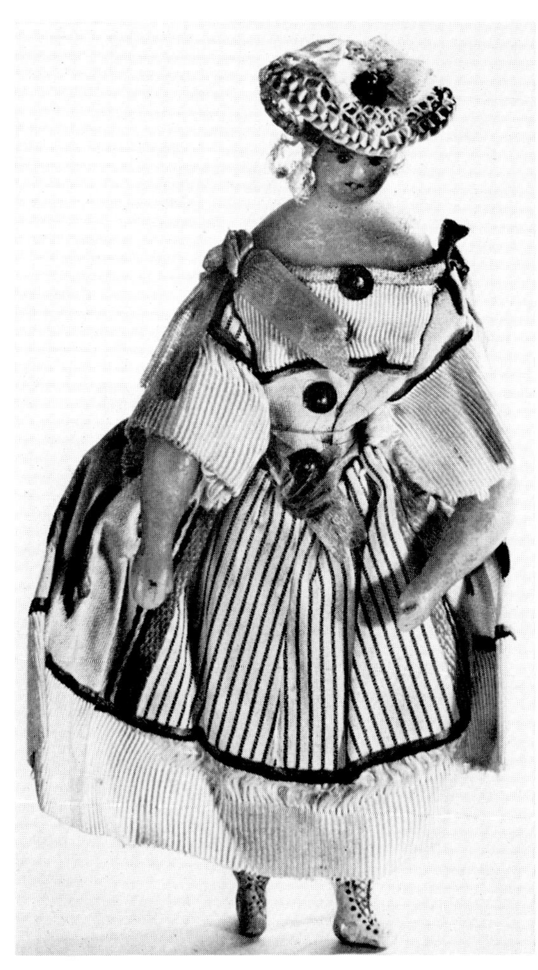

138

139

140

138 Wax. Black beady eyes and inset hair. Probably English, *c.* 1850 or earlier. *Height* $3\frac{3}{4}$ in. *City Museum, St. Albans.* **139** Wax. Painted hair. Probably English, *c.* 1850 or earlier. *Height* $5\frac{1}{4}$ in. *City Museum, St. Albans.* **140** Wax. Wax head and yoke, lower arms and legs, painted brown hair, brown beady eyes. Very light in weight. A perfect doll in a small box, on which is written 'Letitia Hawkins, Died 13th Dec. 1852 at 8 years. This doll was given the night before'. Probably English, 1852. *Height* $5\frac{3}{4}$ in. *The London Museum.*

141 Wax over composition. Hair wig, moving eyes with pull-wire. leather body. South German, 1830–40. *Height* 12⅝ in. *Deutsches Spielzeugmuseum, Sonneberg.*

142 Wax. Fixed eyes. Dressed in cream satin. Probably English, *c.* 1829. *Height* 29 in. *Mrs. Graham Greene.*

143 Wax over composition. Stuffed canvas body and legs. Kid arms. English dress of the time of William IV: purple silk coat over a muslin dress, and linen undergarments. There are also a pink dress, pink net dress, linen nightdress, two linen chemises, two linen petticoats, two linen handkerchiefs, and a linen bonnet. German, 1830–7. *Height* 17½ in. *Victoria and Albert Museum, London.*

144 Wax over composition. Fair wig. Eyes can be closed by pulling wire through body, wire coming out of side front. Blue leather arms with separate fingers, everything handsewn. English, *c.* 1830. *Height* 20 in. Known as 'Miss Emily', it was given by Miss I. Tremor to Queen Mary for disposal. *Bethnal Green Museum, London.*

145 Wax. Hair wig. Eyes close by means of wire coming out between legs, the eyes being spherical with wax lids attached. Tongue moves slightly. Stuffed body with wax lower arms and legs. Re-dressed in 1845. English, probably *c.* 1800 (described in 1874 as being 100 years old). *Height* 25 in. *Bethnal Green Museum, London.*

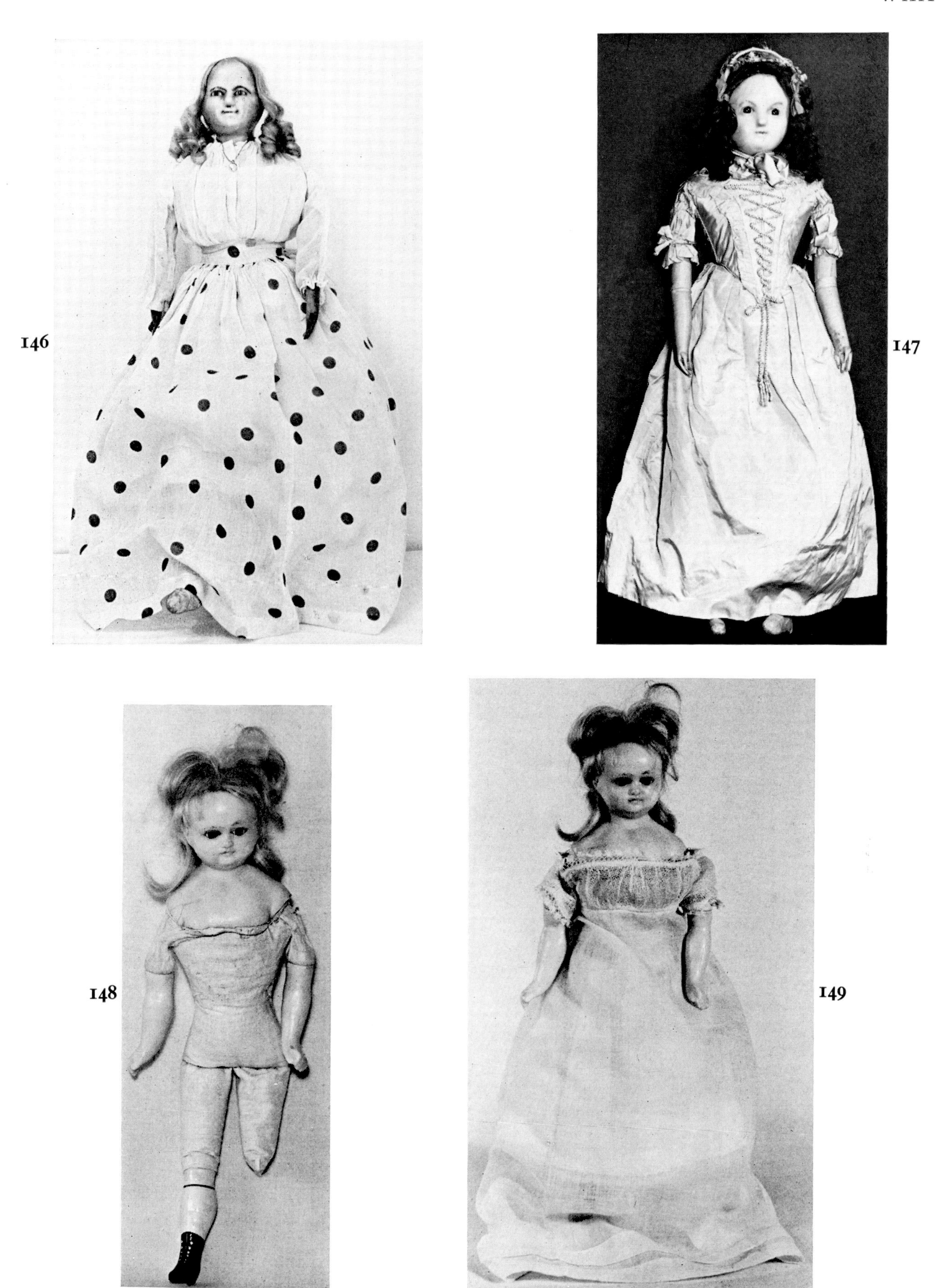

146 Wax. Probably English, *c.* 1840. *Fru Estrid Faurholt.* **147** Wax. Hair wig, tied with red ribbon. Glass eyes. Linen covered body and kid limbs. Pale blue taffeta period dress and bonnet. Probably English, 1845. *Height* 26 in. *Bowes Museum, Barnard Castle.* **148, 149** Wax. Head, yoke and lower arms of pink wax. Fair hair wig, blue fixed eyes. Stuffed body of white calico, painted china legs with black boots and white dots. Early 19th-century muslin dress. Probably English, *c.* 1840–50. Given by Mrs. A. E. King. *Height* 11½ in. *Saffron Walden Museum.*

150

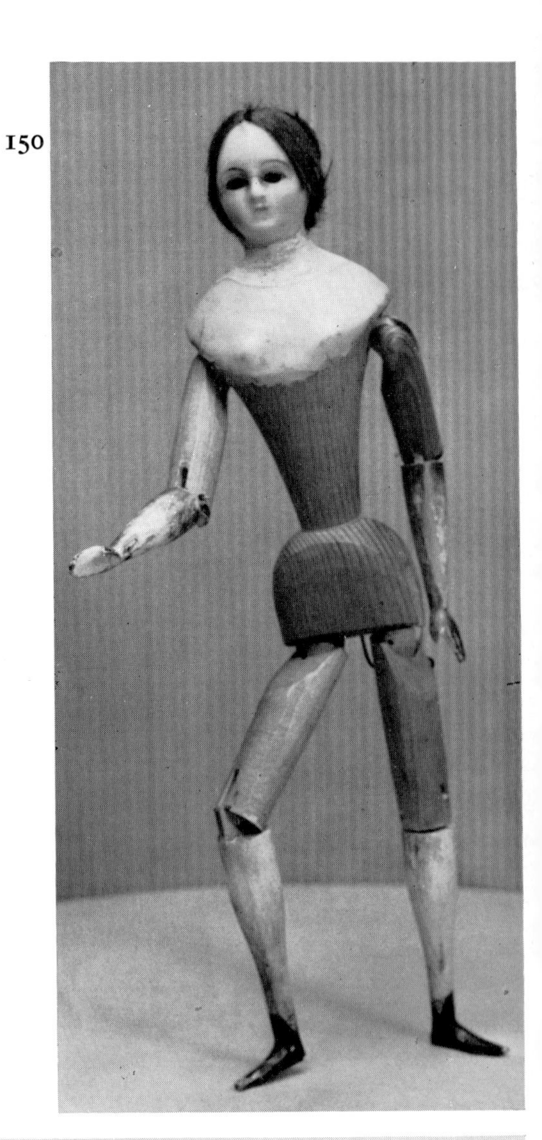

150 Wax-covered head, wooden doll. Real hair from 'slit-head'. Eyes move by wire at waist. Ball-joints at hips and shoulders, painted arms and legs jointed at elbow and knee. ? German, *c.* 1830. *Height* $15\frac{1}{2}$ in. *Red House Museum and Art Gallery, Christchurch.* **151, 152** Wax over composition. Deep wax yoke and wooden body. Hair set into a slit. Brown inset eyes controlled by wire down through body, lids painted on eyeball. Wooden-spade hands, wooden feet, the legs covered with red leather. Brown and white taffeta dress with red top. Red petticoat with hoop in the hem. *c.* 1843–6. *Height* 10 in. Owned by a daughter of Queen Victoria. *Bethnal Green Museum, London.*

151

152

153

154

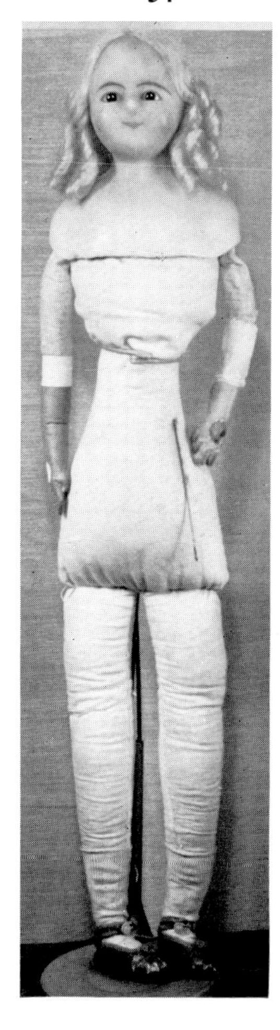

155

153 Wax over composition. Hair wigs, no ears, blue paperweight eyes which close by pulling a side wire, the wax lids being fixed to the eyeballs. Stuffed bodies with wax forearms and legs. Clothes almost identical, with face-cloth cloaks and velvet hoods with pink ostrich feathers. Everyday frocks of blue cotton with lined yokes, all hand-sewn. English, *c.* 1850–60. *Height* 30 in. *Bethnal Green Museum, London.* **154** Wax over composition. Slit-head for hair, stuffed body, thin pink leather arms, with lever at waist which closes the wax eye-lids. *c.* 1840. *Height* 24 in. *Mrs. Heather Fox.* **155** Wax over composition. Slit-head for hair. Very dark brown eyes, closing by means of wire. Stuffed cloth body and legs, wax forearms. English, *c.* 1840. *Height* 19 in. *Bethnal Green Museum, London.*

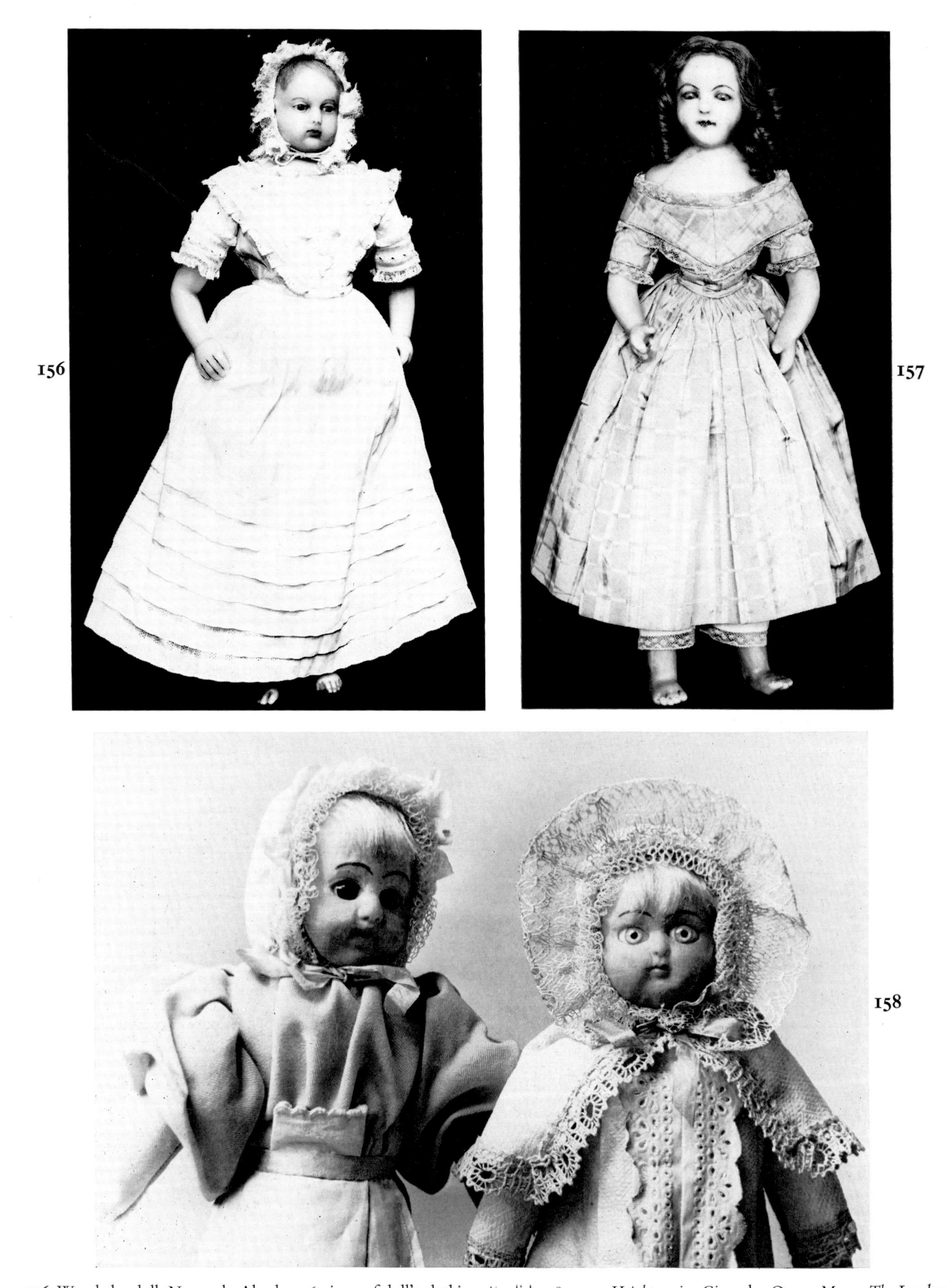

156 157 158

156 Wax baby doll. No mark. Also has 16 pieces of doll's clothing. English, 1840–50. *Height* 19 in. Given by Queen Mary. *The London Museum.* **157** Wax. Stuffed body. Original taffeta dress. English, 1845. *Height* 19½ in. Formerly belonged to the Princess Royal, born 1840, eldest child of Queen Victoria. *Tunbridge Wells Museum.* **158** Wax. The little 'Täuflinge' dolls from Sonneberg. The masks are coated with wax, and have inset glass eyes. 1851–2. *Height* 14¼ in. *Deutsches Spielzeugmuseum, Sonneberg.*

159

160

161

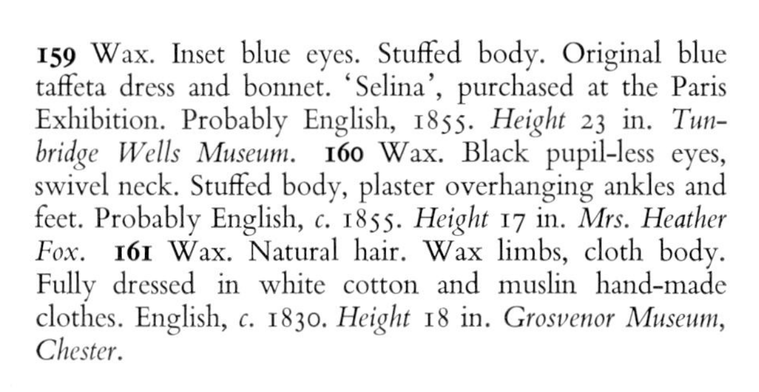

159 Wax. Inset blue eyes. Stuffed body. Original blue taffeta dress and bonnet. 'Selina', purchased at the Paris Exhibition. Probably English, 1855. *Height* 23 in. *Tunbridge Wells Museum.* **160** Wax. Black pupil-less eyes, swivel neck. Stuffed body, plaster overhanging ankles and feet. Probably English, *c.* 1855. *Height* 17 in. *Mrs. Heather Fox.* **161** Wax. Natural hair. Wax limbs, cloth body. Fully dressed in white cotton and muslin hand-made clothes. English, *c.* 1830. *Height* 18 in. *Grosvenor Museum, Chester.*

162

163

164

165

162 Wax doll in Highland dress belonging to the Duchess of Connaught. English, *c.* 1865. *Height* 26 in. *Windsor Castle.* **163** Wax. Very good quality wax, inset blue eyes, inset hair. Called 'Victoria', she was dressed by a ten-year-old girl and her governess on the Isle of Mull in 1860. Scottish, *c.* 1860. *Height* 17 in. *Bethnal Green Museum, London.* **164** Wax. Pink wax with deep yoke, inset hair, pierced ears, two deep creases where the arm meets the yoke. Beautifully dressed in white satin, embroidered with mauve sprigs. Boned 'Liberty' bodice, knickers with side openings, short flannel petticoat, long chemise, short lawn petticoat, long lawn petticoat edged with two frills. English, late 19th century. *Height* 26 in. Given by H.M. Queen Mary. *Bethnal Green Museum, London.* **165** Wax. Hair wig, fixed eyes. Body marked SANTY, etc. Named 'Rosa Mary', she has additional clothes. English, 1850–60. *Height* 32 in. *Bethnal Green Museum, London.*

166 Wax. Hair wig, fixed blue eyes, cloth body, arms and feet wax, all in perfect condition. Known as 'Rose Percy', this doll with her wonderful wardrobe was raffled at the great bazaar of the Sanitary Commission in New York during the Civil War, raising the sum of $1200. Dressed by the girls of Mrs. Hoffman's fashionable boarding school in New York, everything being sewn by hand. Among the dresses are a blue velvet gown with point-lace bertha, and one of solferino, the colour now known as magenta. A Dr. Peters bought the winning lottery ticket and 'Rose' was given to his daughter Bertha, who still let the doll go round earning money. Given to the Red Cross Museum in 1919. Probably English, 1862. *Height* 24 in. *American National Red Cross Museum, Washington.*

167 Composition. Hair in one with head, the whole covered with a thin coating of wax. Fixed eyes. Stuffed cotton body, wooden arms, lower legs and feet. Stiff gauze petticoat and long drawers under dress. ? English, *c.* 1860. *Height* 23 in. *Harris Museum and Art Gallery, Preston.* These dolls are sometimes known as 'pumpkin heads'.

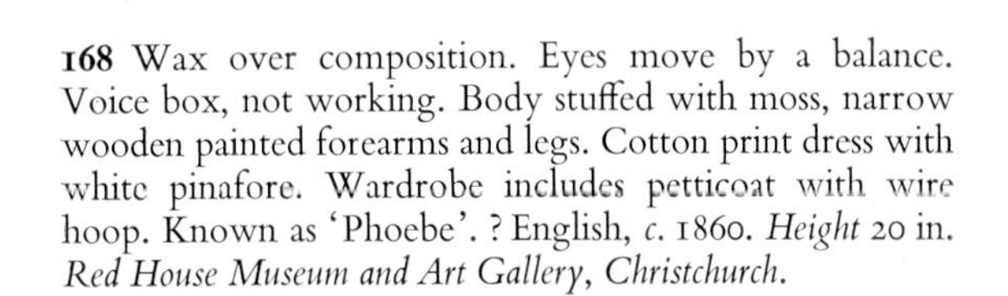

168 Wax over composition. Eyes move by a balance. Voice box, not working. Body stuffed with moss, narrow wooden painted forearms and legs. Cotton print dress with white pinafore. Wardrobe includes petticoat with wire hoop. Known as 'Phoebe'. ? English, *c.* 1860. *Height* 20 in. *Red House Museum and Art Gallery, Christchurch.*

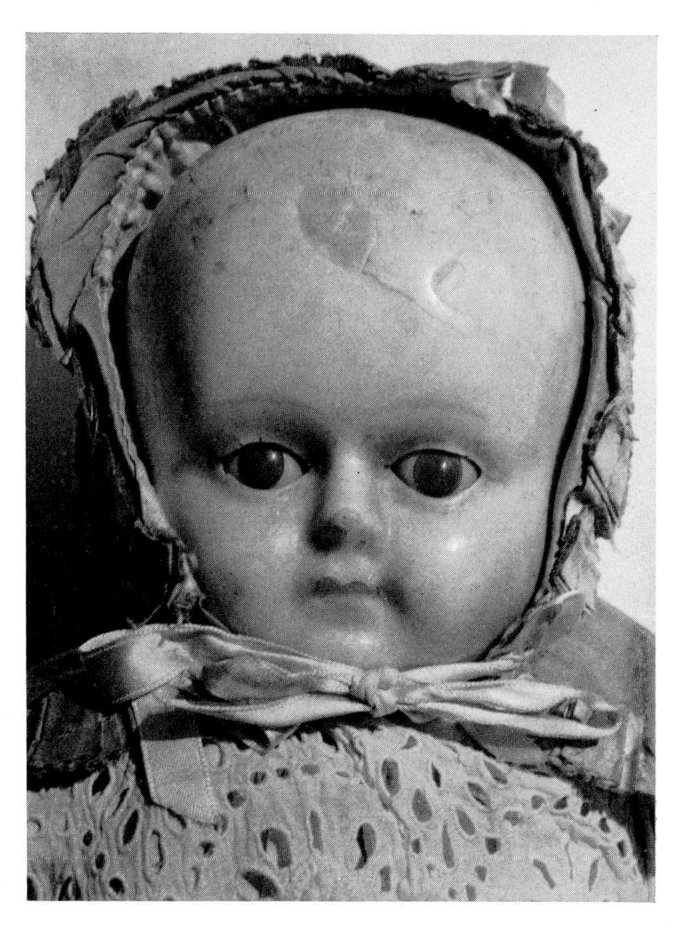

169 Wax over composition. Sleeping eyes with no pupils. Stuffed body with limbs of composition. Dressed in baby clothes of linen and nunsveiling. English, 1877. *Height* 22½ in.; head 4 in. *Hove Museum.*

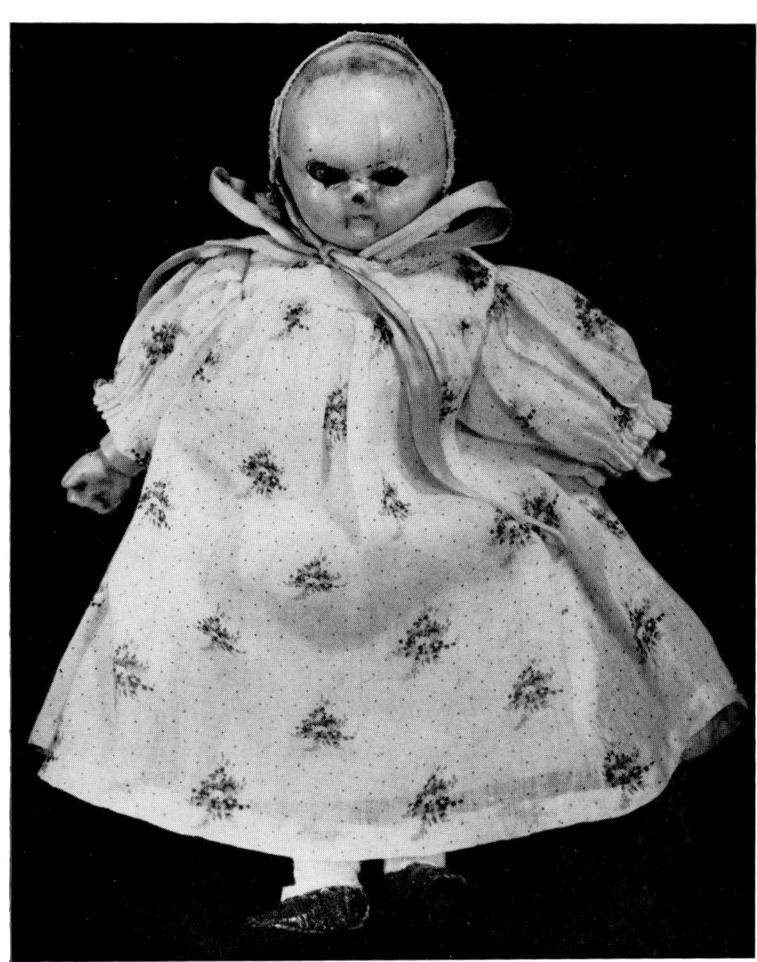

170 Wax on composition or wood. Closing glass eyes. ? English, 1880–90. *Height* 9 in. *National Museum of Finland, Helsinki.*

171 Wax over composition. Rococo doll with coloured wax head and leather body. Powdered hair. German, *c.* 1870. *Height* $20\frac{3}{8}$ in. *Deutsches Spielzeugmuseum, Sonneberg.*

172 Wax. Painted eyes. Wax wrists and cupped hands $2\frac{1}{2}$ in. long, wax legs 4 in. long. Depicting the Empress Josephine. French, *c.* 1800. *Height* 17 in. *Kidders Trading Post and Doll Museum, Apache Junction.*

173 174 175 176

173 Wax. Inset hair and eyebrows, inset eyelashes, head looks slightly towards the left. Dressed in 1900 by Lady Cave to represent her grandmother, Sarah Penfold, who died in 1856. English. *Height* 22 in. Given by H.M. The Queen. *Bethnal Green Museum, London.* **174** Wax. Inset hair, blue fixed eyes, wax lower arms and legs. Dressed in 'Dolly Varden' costume pseudo 18th-century style, after Dickens's heroine of Barnaby Rudge, fashionable *c.* 1871. English, 1869. *Height* 11 in. *Bethnal Green Museum, London.* **175** Wax. Inset eyes. Wired petticoat and bustle. English, 1873. *Height* 11 in. *Bethnal Green Museum, London.* **176** Wax. Woollen dress trimmed with lace and gathered into a bustle at the back, characteristic of the clothes in which ladies played croquet. English, *c.* 1875. *Height* 24 in. *The London Museum.*

177 178 179

180 181

177 Wax over composition. Bought at the Philadelphia World Fair, 1878. ? English or German. *Height* 14 in. *Kidders Trading Post and Doll Museum, Apache Junction.* **178** Wax. ? English, *c.* 1880. *Fru Estrid Faurholt.* **179** Wax-coated head. Fixed blue glass eyes. Probably English, 1880–90. *Height* 13¾ in. *National Museum of Finland, Helsinki.* **180** Wax. Sheepskin wig, fixed blue eyes. Stuffed body of coarse canvas, calico from the waist down, composition arms and lower legs. Chemise of coarse muslin, marked WASHABLE in mauve on front. French or English, *c.* 1875. *Height* 28 in. *Luton Museum.* **181** Wax. Elaborate hair wig, fixed glass eyes. Jointed leather body. *Height* 18½ in. *Deutsches Spielzeugmuseum, Sonneberg.*

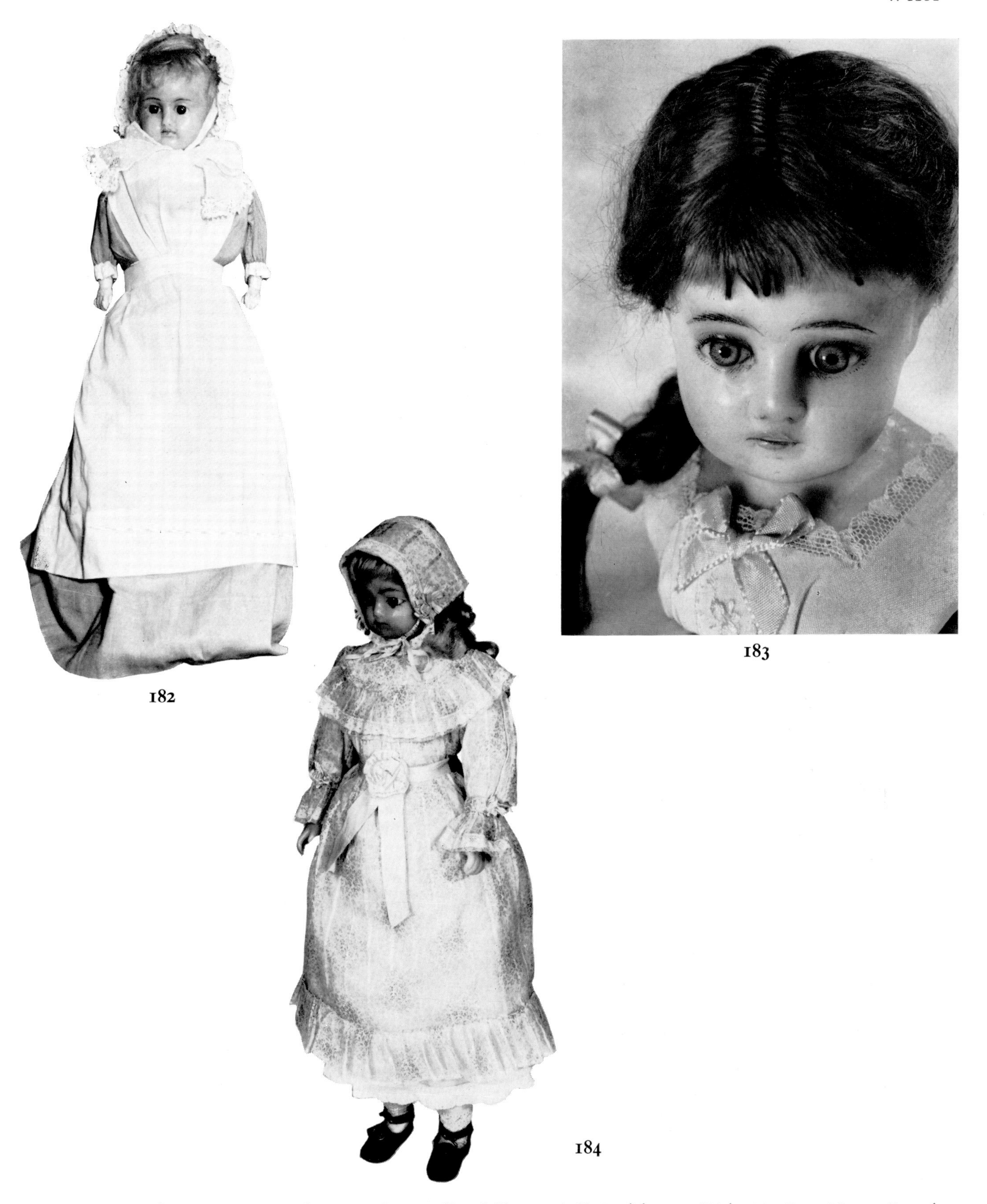

182

183

184

182 Wax. Dressed as a maternity nurse by a nurse for one of her children. Probably English, 1889. *Height* 18 in. *Bowes Museum, Barnard Castle.* **183** Wax. Natural hair with parting and pigtail. Fixed eyes. Probably English, 1880. *Height* 19¾ in. *Deutsches Spielzeugmuseum, Sonneberg.* **184** Wax. Pink dress. Has other clothes, including a pinafore marked 'Franklin'. Given by Miss Langdon. English, *c.* 1871. *Height* 25 in. *The London Museum.*

185 Wax. Elaborate hair wig, fixed glass eyes. Court dress. Probably German, 1885. *Height* $29\frac{1}{2}$ in. *Deutsches Spielzeugmuseum, Sonneberg.*

186 Papier mâché, wax-coated doll's head. Mohair wig, glass eyes. Exhibited in Chicago. German, 1893. *Height* $8\frac{1}{4}$ in. *Deutsches Spielzeugmuseum, Sonneberg.*

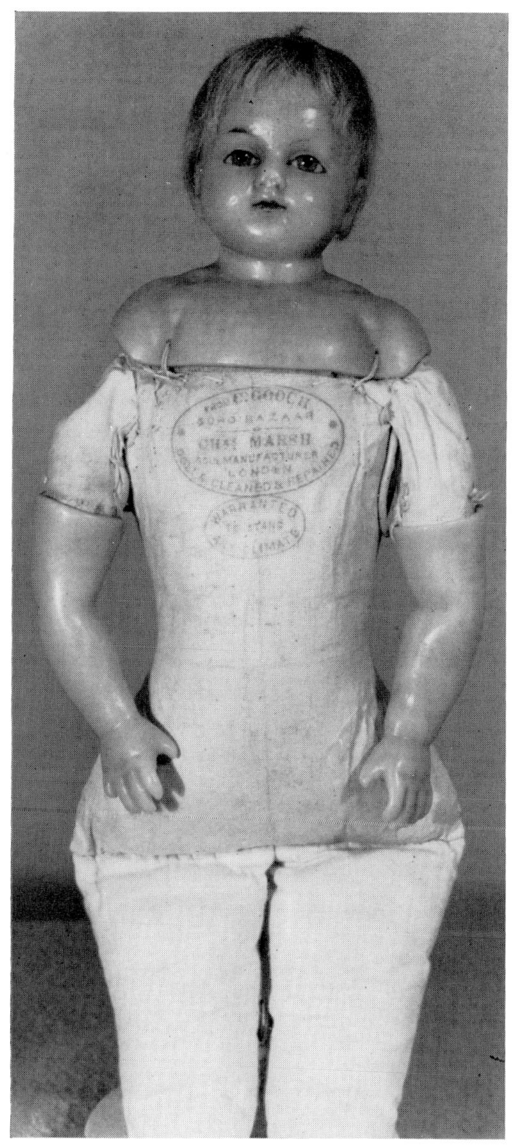

187

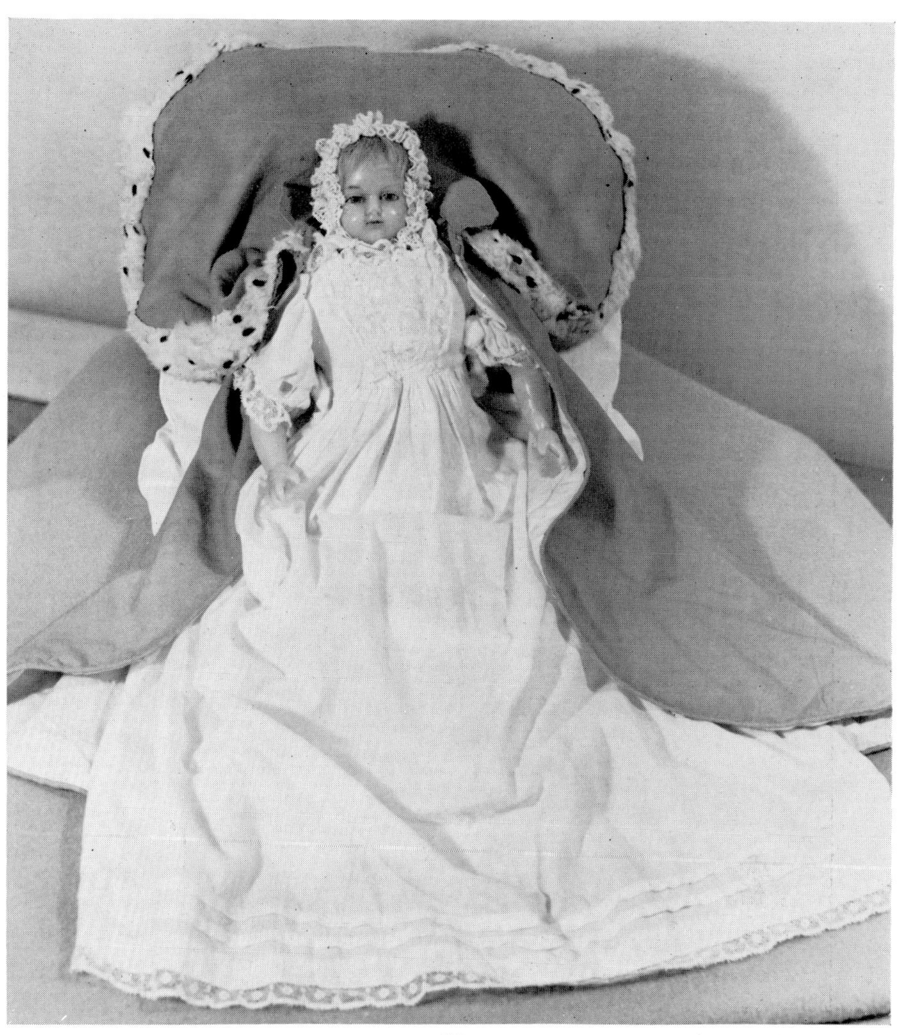

188

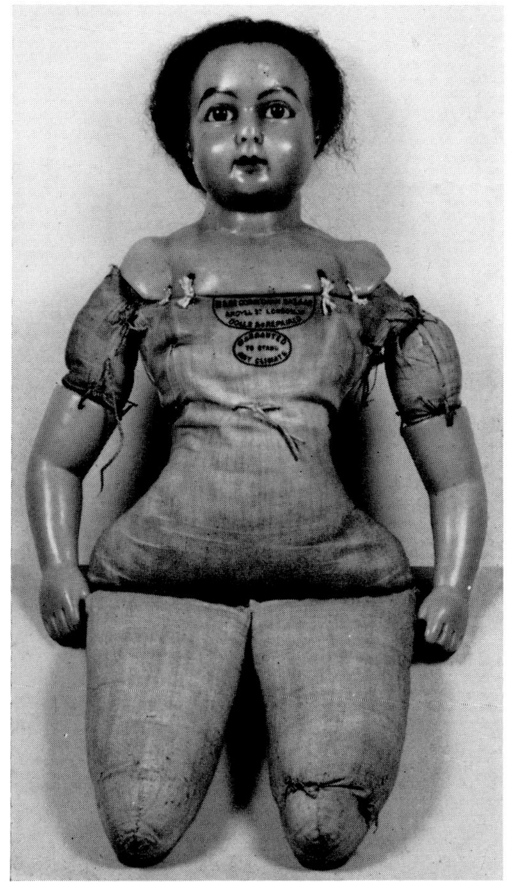

189

187, 188 Wax. Marked 'CHAS. MARSH. From C. Gooch', etc. English, early 1880s. *Height* 21 in. *Flax Home Industry, Grasmere.* **189** Wax. Marked with the sign of CHAS. MARSH. The lower legs of wax are missing, but the illustration shows how the stuffed calico body is made to fit into the hollow wax limbs. English, *c.* 1880–90. *Height* $17\frac{1}{2}$ in. to bottom of stuffed leg; total height probably $21\frac{1}{2}$ in. *Honiton and Allhallows Museum.*

190 Wax. Fair hair set in head with small tufts, deep blue inset eyes with hair eyelashes. Pink cheeks, stuffed body, wax lower arms and legs. Marked in front under the yoke 'From C. Gooch, Soho Bazaar, CHAS. MARSH,' etc. English, late 19th century (before 1895). *Height* 20 in. *Mrs. Nina S. Davies.*

191

192

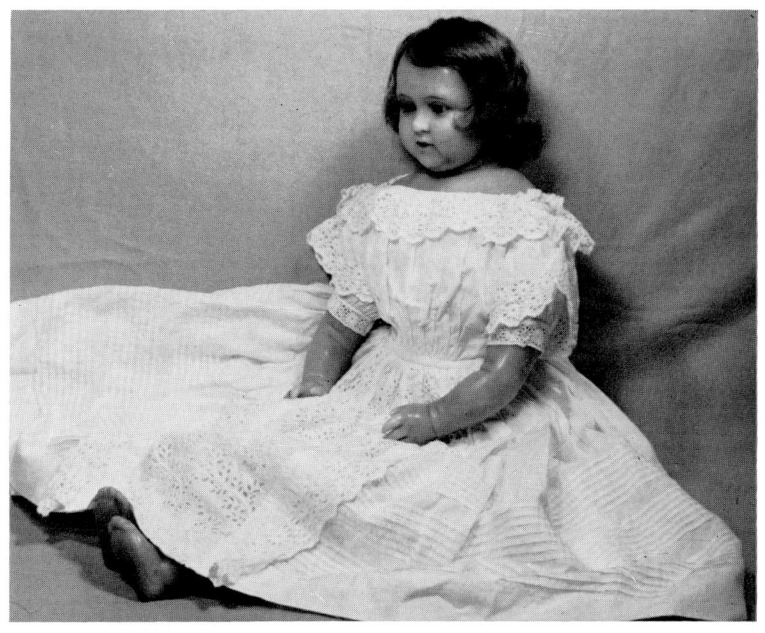

193

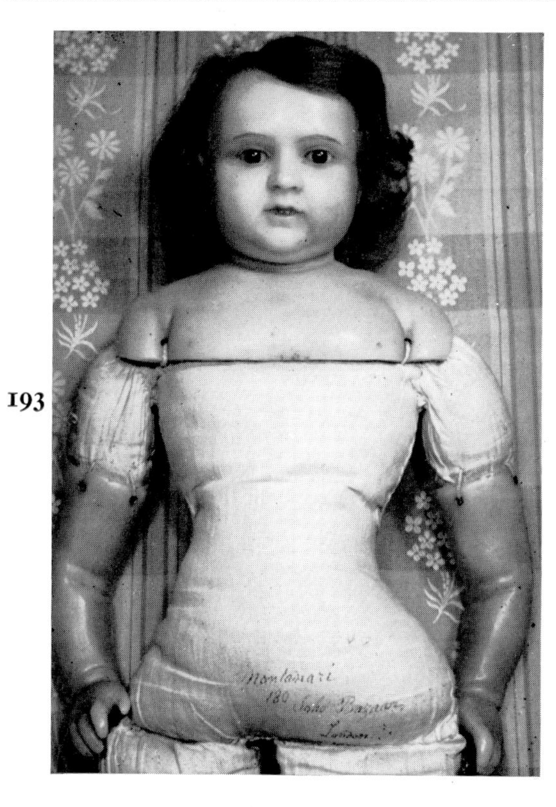

194

191 'Ornamental Design for a Doll', from the Earthenware Class of the Design Register, 4 August 1852. A watercolour drawing by Augusta Montanari, 29 Upper Charlotte Street, Fitzroy Square, London. *Victoria and Albert Museum, London.* **192, 193** Wax. Marked MONTANARI. The showing teeth are unusual for a doll by Augusta Montanari, whose dolls usually have a slightly drooping mouth with closed lips. English, *c.* 1870. *Height* 29½ in. *Mrs. Heather Fox.* **194** As illustration **190**.

195

196

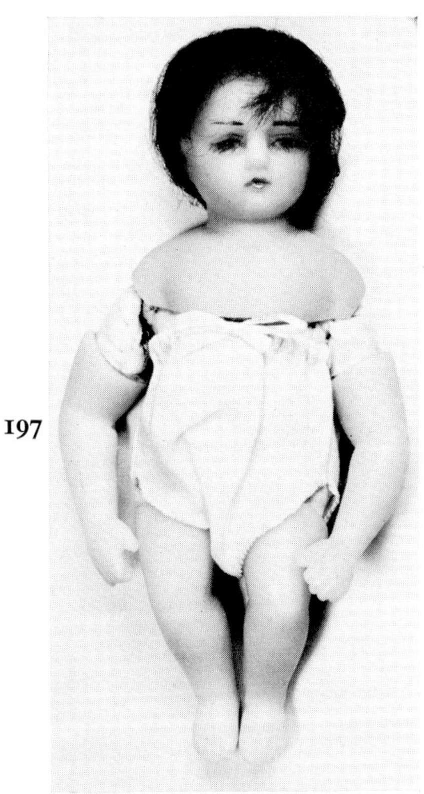

197

198

195 Wax. Stuffed body stamped on the front CHAS. MARSH, SOLE MANUFACTURER, LONDON. FROM E. MOODY, SOHO BAZAAR. DOLLS CLEANED & REPAIRED. WARRANTED TO STAND ANY CLIMATE. White baby clothes, blue cape. Early doll by Charles Marsh (Marsh is listed in the London P.O. Directory between 1879 and 1895; E. Moody is mentioned in 1891). English. ? 1870. *Height* 24 in. *The London Museum.* **196** Wax. Back of left leg stamped H. J. MEECH, DOLL MAKER, OLD DOLLS CLEANED AND REPAIRED. 50 KENNINGTON ROAD, LONDON S.E. White dress trimmed with pink velvet, flannel and calico petticoats, pearls and pink beads round her neck. English. ? 1845. *Height* 14 in. *The London Museum.* Meech was Doll Maker to the Royal Family in 1891. **197** Wax. Made by Pierotti. English, *c.* 1910. *Height* 6¾ in. *Miss Muriel Pierotti.* **198** Wax. Made by Pierotti. Wax head with inset blue eyes. Stuffed body, wax lower arms and lower legs. English, *c.* 1880. *Height* 21½ in. *Tunbridge Wells Museum.*

199

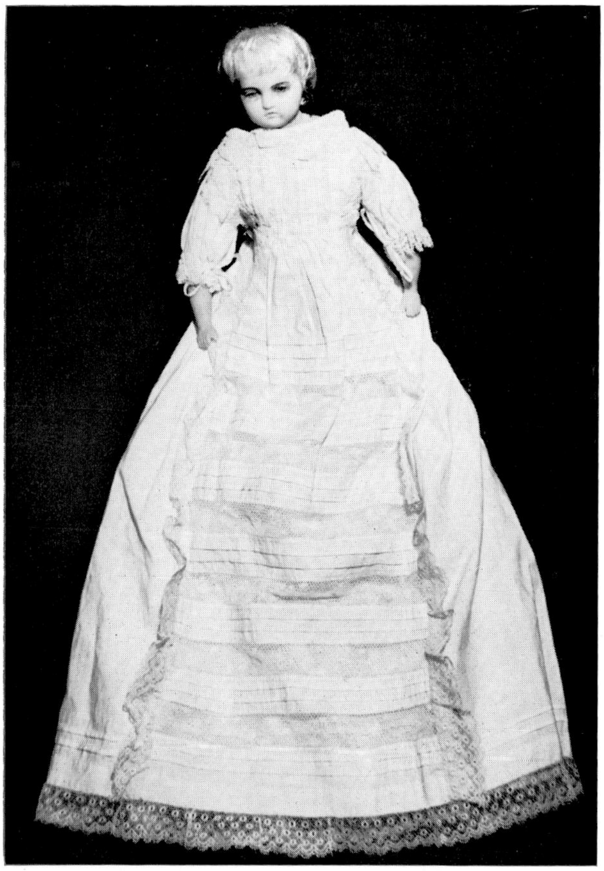

200

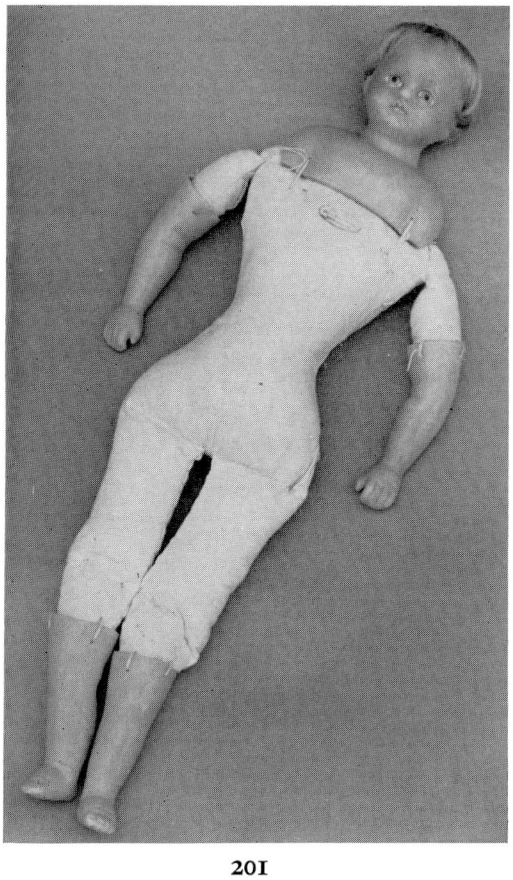

201

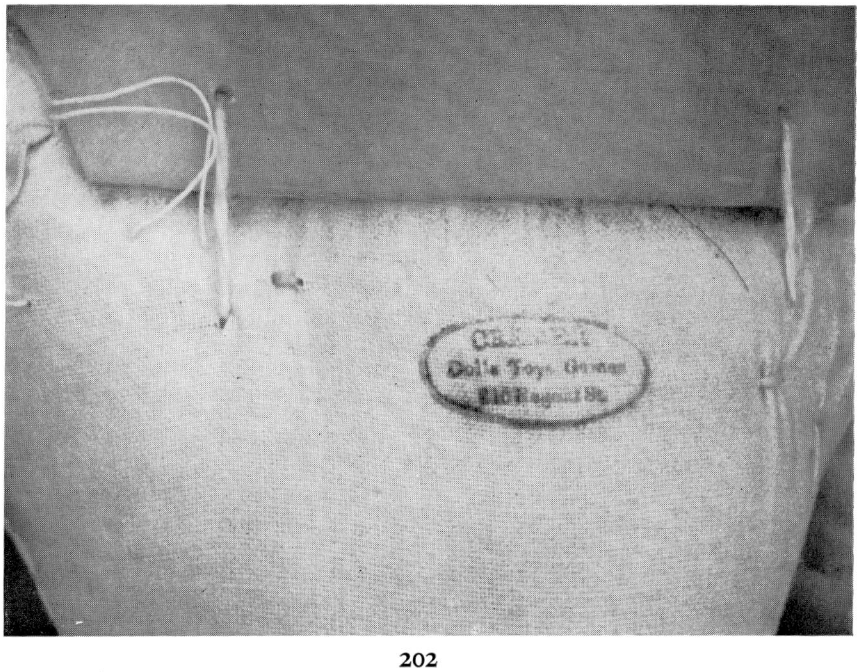

202

199 Wax. Baby doll made by Pierotti, name stamped under the hair. Goat hair, stuffed body, wax lower arms and lower legs. English, 1887. *Height* $15\frac{1}{2}$ in. *Tunbridge Wells Museum.* **200–2** Wax. Fair hair, blue inset eyes. Soft body, stuffed with hair, legs still sewn together. A faint mark PIEROTTI on back of head under the hair. English, *c.* 1880. *Height* 15 in. *Mrs. Lorna Hennessy.*

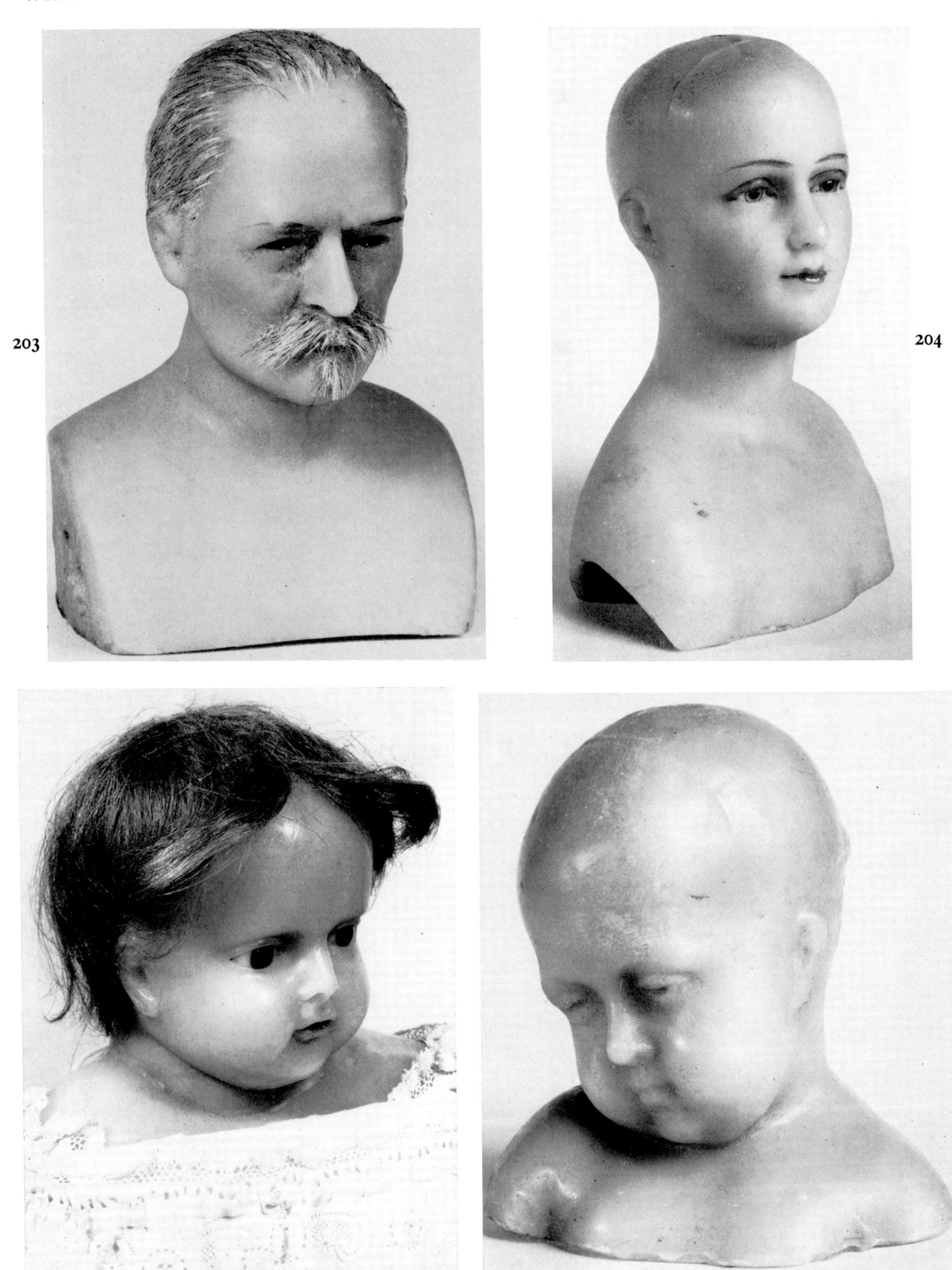

203

204

205

206

203 Wax head of a man, portrait of General Roberts, later Lord Roberts. Made by Pierotti. Inset hairs. English, *c.* 1870–80. *Height* $3\frac{1}{4}$ in. *Miss Muriel Pierotti.* **204** Wax head, by Pierotti, before hair is fixed. English. *c.* 1910. *Height* $6\frac{3}{4}$ in. *Miss Muriel Pierotti.* **205** Wax baby doll. Confirmed by Miss Muriel Pierotti as a Pierotti type. Inset hair, fixed eyes, thick folds in neck. English. Late 19th century. *Height* $23\frac{1}{2}$ in. *The London Museum.* **206** Wax baby doll-head by Pierotti. Shows the part which is lifted off in order to fix the glass eyes, and the hair is later inserted. English, 1860–80. *Height* $4\frac{1}{2}$ in. *Miss Muriel Pierotti.*

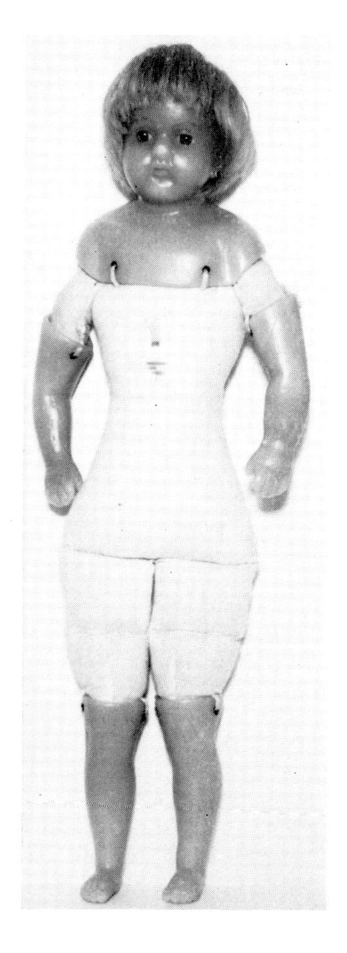

207, 208 Wax. Marked LUCY PECK. Known as 'Griselda'. English, *c.* 1902. *Height* 20 in. *Mrs. Heather Fox.*

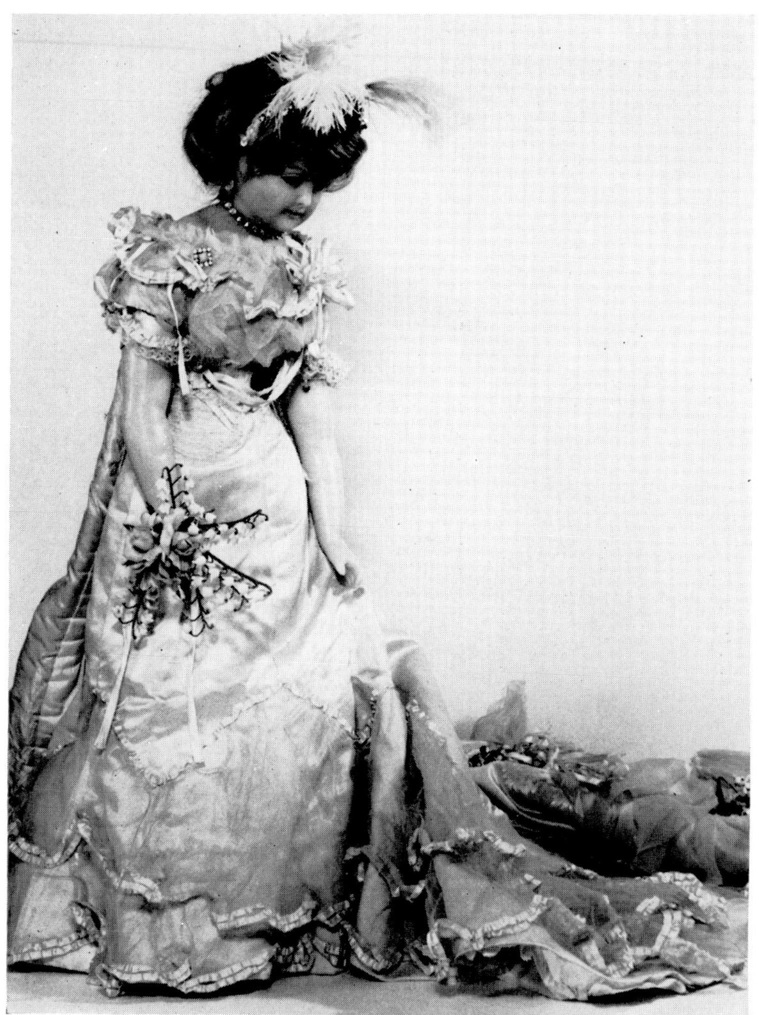

209 Wax. Marked in purple ink with the LUCY PECK sign. Dressed in chiffon and satin, with stiffeners in the bodice. English, beginning of twentieth century. *Height* $27\frac{1}{2}$ in. *Mrs. Graham Greene.*

210 Wax. Blue crêpe de Chine dress, trimmed with velvet. Cambric undergarments trimmed with machine-made lace, knitted stockings and cream satin shoes. Steel hatpin with ball top. Dressed by Frederick Bosworth, 9 New Burlington Street, London, W. English, 1903–4. *Height* 22½ in. *Victoria and Albert Museum, London.*

211–13 Rag. Bodies of wire spun with white silk, stuffed heads covered with silk. Hair of light brown silk; eyes, noses and mouth painted black. Swedish, *c.* 1660. **211** White silk dress with small black ribbons and white rosettes. White silk rosette in hair, pillow-made lace as a collarette, necklace and eardrops of white pearls. *Height* 3½ in. **212** Dress and cap of yellow silk with lace collar. Sleeves and apron of aerial silk weaving, the apron with border points. *Height* 2⅞ in. **213** Dress of white silk trimmed with green and white ribbons. *Height* 3⅜ in. *Nordiska Museet, Stockholm.*

214 Rag. Two negroes, dressed in evening dress. English, *c.* 1840. *Height* 7 in. *The London Museum.* **215** Rag. *Left*, head of woven material, features lost. *Height* 3½ in. Found under the floor of the Prinsens Palais, Copenhagen, built in 1744. *Right*, West Indian nurse, with head of black material, silk hair, embroidered eyes. Carrying a child made from embroidered material, *c.* 1860. *Height* 9 in. *Danish Folk Museum, Copenhagen.*

216, 217 Rag. Patented by Izannah Walker in the 1870s, but invented in the 1850s. American. *Museum of the City of New York.* **218** Rag. The Chase-Stockinette doll by M. J. Chase Co., Pawtucket, R.I. Heavy oilcloth body, painted flesh colour, stuffed with hair or cotton. The Chase mark is found under the right arm. American. *Height* 24 in. *Kidders Trading Post and Toy Museum, Apache Junction.* **219** Known as the 'Philadelphian doll'. American. *Museum of the City of New York.* **220** Rag. In the costume of the surroundings of Brno, Austria, beginning of 20th century. *Height* 10½ in. *National Museum, Prague.*

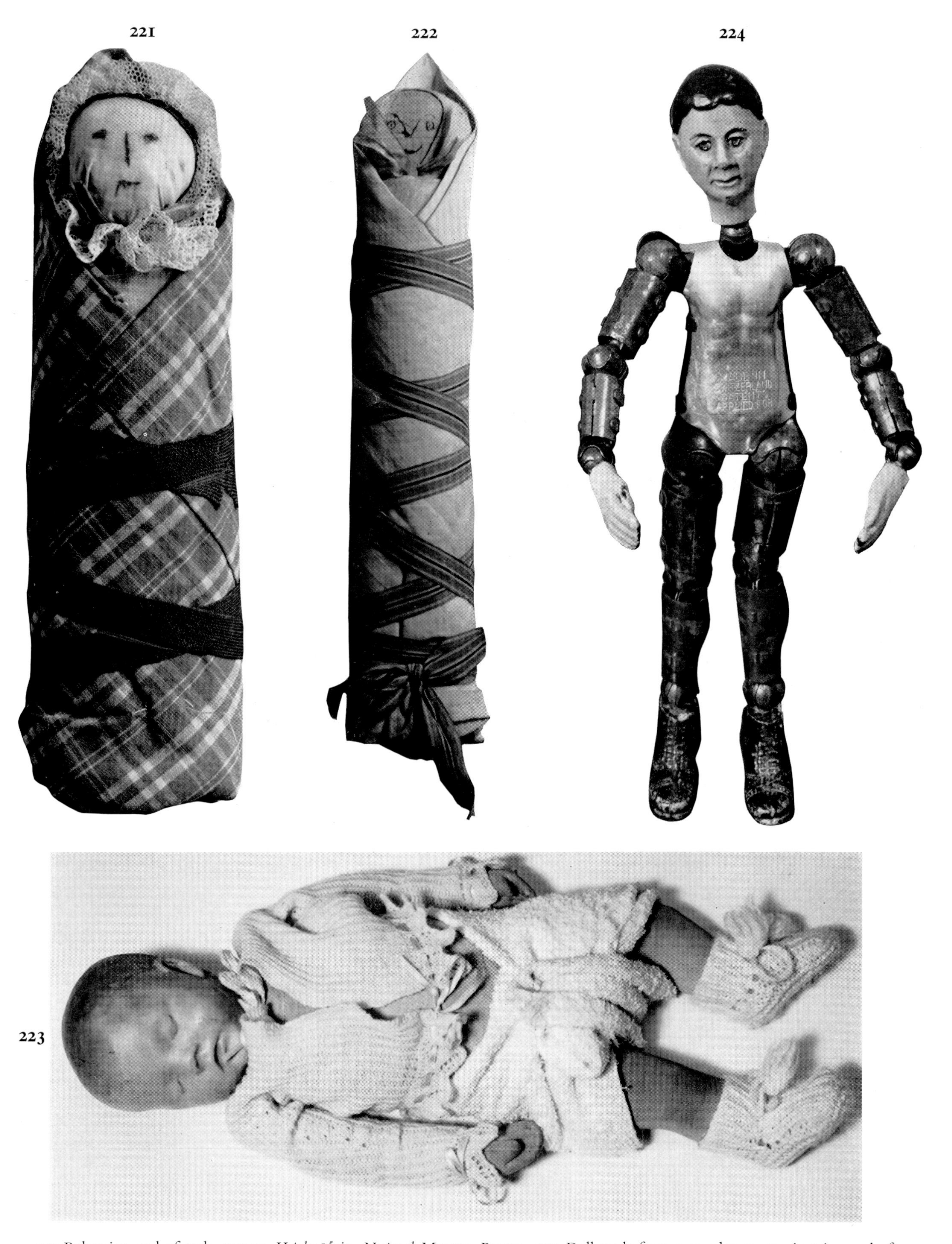

221 Bohemian, end of 19th century. *Height* $8\frac{5}{8}$ in. *National Museum, Prague.* **222** Doll made from a wooden spoon. Austrian, end of 19th century. *Height* 13 in. *National Museum, Prague.* **223** Stockinette. A life-size new baby, stuffed and weighted with sand to give an illusion of reality. Bought in Switzerland, and designed by Kathe Kruse, who at one time filled her dolls with sand. German, *c.* 1911. *Height* 18 in. *Bethnal Green Museum, London.* **224** Metal. A lay figure from Switzerland. *Height* $7\frac{1}{2}$ in. *Flax Home Industry, Grasmere.*

225

226

227

225 Miniature in oil on copper. A portrait of Queen Christina of Sweden—a 'dressing doll', with 12 different dresses painted on sheets of mica. Swedish, mid 17th century. *Height* 3⅛ in. *Nordiska Museet, Stockholm.* **226** Paper. A dressing doll, showing Jenny Lind with five out of the 60 dresses from different operas. English or German, *c.* 1840–50. *Height* 4 in. *Nordiska Museet, Stockholm.* **227** Paper. Figure of Jenny Lind with ten changes of costume and various hairstyles. Probably American, *c.* 1850, when the singer first visited the United States. *Height* 4 in. *Essex Institute, Salem.* Many paper dolls were marketed by Kimmel & Forster of New York.

228 Eugenie paper doll. The complete set consists of figure in petticoat, six dresses and mantles, two caps and four hats. The colours are rich. Titled in English, French and German. German, 1850–60. *Height* 10 in. *Museum of Childhood, Edinburgh.*

229 Paper. Printed in colour. With set of dresses made of material flatly arranged on cardboard, each with a hand behind the sleeve. Probably English, *c.* 1870. *Height* 9 in. *Mr. John Noble Pollock's Toy Museum.*

230

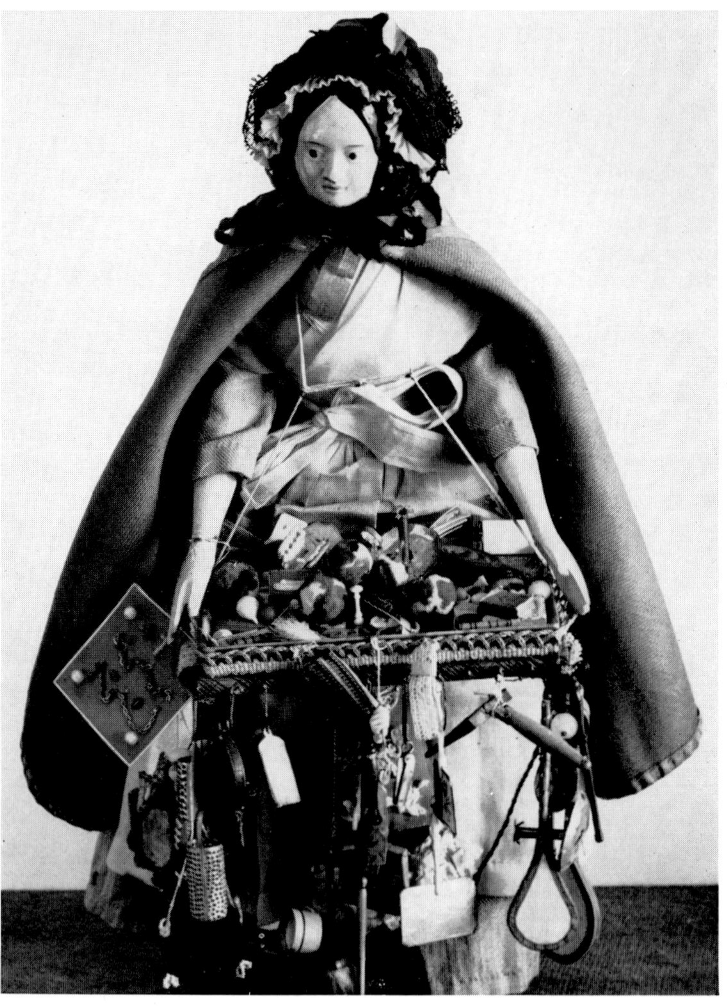

231

232

230 Leather. Face of white leather, stuffed body. Dressed as a pedlar with red cape, brown bonnet, white apron. Carrying a tray with miniature books and other domestic items, and a lantern. Similar to the pedlar dolls made by C. & H. White in the New Forest. English, *c.* 1820. *Height* 8 in. *The London Museum.* **231** Pedlar (young woman). Composition head, wooden hands. English, *c.* 1840–50. *Height* $11\frac{1}{4}$ in. *Colchester and Essex Museum.* **232** Pedlar. Wooden doll with fish stall. The crabs and shrimps are natural, the chicken is composed of shells. English, 1820. *Height* with stall 14 in. *Tunbridge Wells Museum.*

233

234

235

236

233 Wood. Pedlar doll, said to have been made by the Dowager Queen Adelaide while staying at Witley Court, Worcestershire, in 1843. Red cloak, hand-made pins in tray. English, 1843. *Height* 11 in. *Mrs. M. E. Dickson.* **234** Pedlar (old woman). Composition head and hands. English, *c.* 1840–50. *Height* 12½ in. *Colchester and Essex Museum.* **235, 236** Man and woman pedlars. English, *c.* 1850. *Height* 9½ in. *City Museum, Leeds.*

237

238

239

240

237 'Old Woman in a Shoe'. Full of little dolls—parians, porcelains, bisques and jointed woods. Probably English, *c.* 1865. *Length of shoe* $8\frac{1}{4}$ in. Given by Mrs. Grey, Chelsea. *The London Museum.* **238** Peachstone doll, in walnut shell. Probably English, Victorian. *City Museum, Leeds.* **239** 'Old Woman in a Shoe'. Set of jointed wooden dolls, presented in 1860 to Fanny Maria Burton as a special school prize for needlework, at age 5. Probably English, 1860. *Height* $6\frac{1}{2}$ in. *Saffron Walden Museum.* **240** Mechanical doll with basket tray. Probably French, *c.* 1900. *Height* 16 in. Belonged to King George VI. *Windsor Castle.*

241 Rubber. Painted black eyes and hair which hangs in long curls down the back, with a centre parting. Purple silk dress, petticoat trimmed with tatting, knee-length pantelettes, black cotton stockings. Black leather slippers with one button on strap. American, before 1840. *Height* $29\frac{1}{4}$ in. *Essex Institute, Salem.* **242** Rubber. Goodyear patent, 1851. Paint retouched. American. *Height* 17 in. *McCully House Toy Museum, Jacksonville.* **243** Rubber. Figure of a child. This toy, which is completely crystalized, is moulded on a metal former and fixed by a pin and clumsy washer at the head. The bright colours are varnished. ? English, 1850. *Height* 4 in. *Museum of Childhood, Edinburgh.*

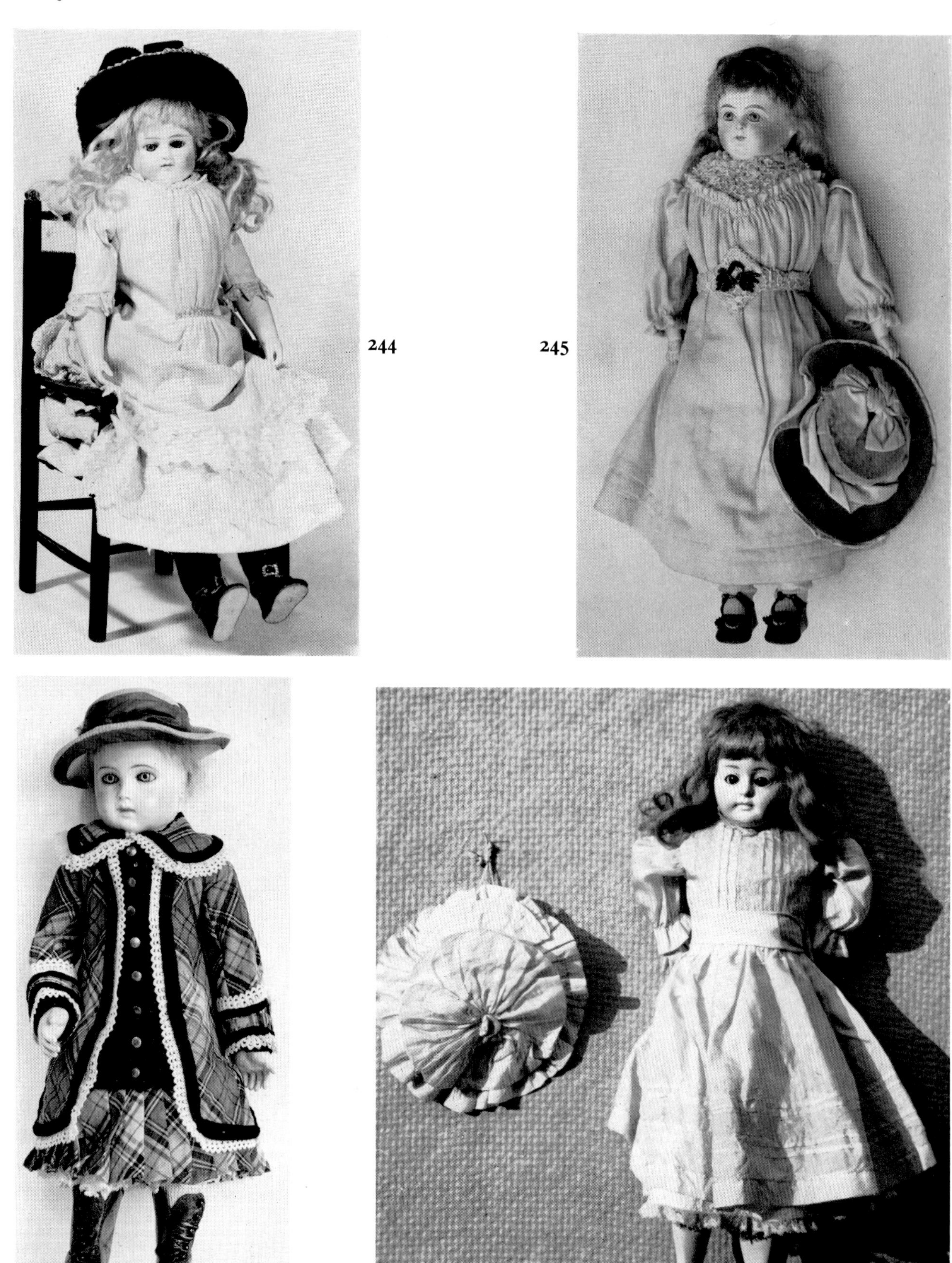

244 245 246 247

244 Bisque. White dress and red velvet hat. Probably French, *c.* 1882–84. *Height* 18 in. *Mrs. Graham Greene.* **245** Bisque. Purchased at the Paris Exhibition. White kid body, jointed arms and legs. Dressed in pink flannelette, with hat of turquoise velvet with pink silk trimming. Probably French, 1889. *Height* $20\frac{1}{2}$ in. *Grosvenor Museum, Chester.* **246** Bisque. Bisque arms, jointed body. Straw hat trimmed with red, coat bordered with guipure lace. French, early 20th century. *Height* $16\frac{1}{8}$ in. *Musée des Arts Décoratifs, Paris.* **247** Bisque. Light brown hair, bisque arms and lower legs, stuffed body. Probably French, 1890–1900. *Height* 19 in. *Grosvenor Museum, Chester.*

248

249

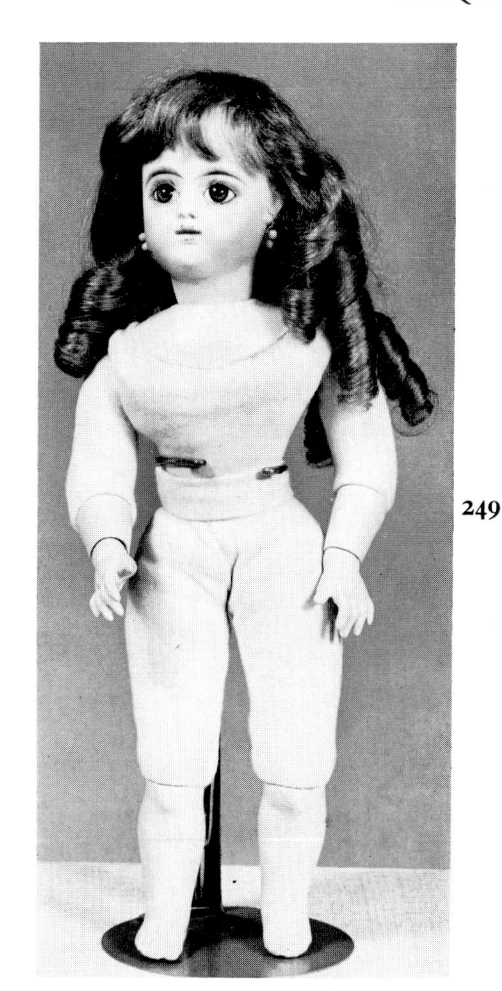

250

251

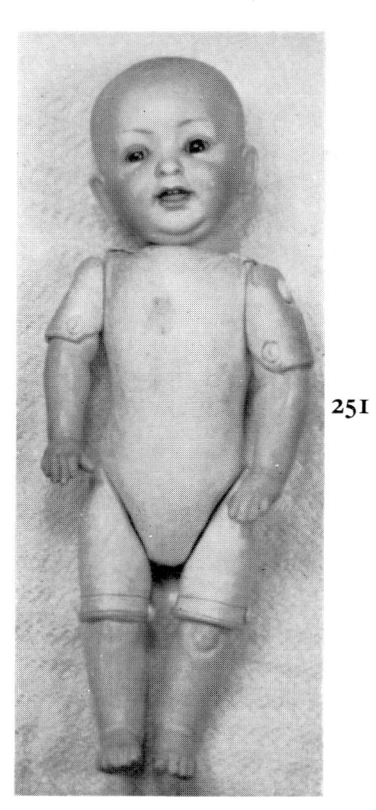

248 Bisque. Marked 'G.K 34–26'. Pierced ears. Wearing a nightdress. Given to former owner in 1885. Probably German. *Height* 14¾ in. *Mrs. Graham Greene.* **249** Bisque. Hair wig, blue paperweight eyes, pierced ears, closed mouth. Swivel neck incised 'F.G' on the back. Knit body, lower arm and lower leg of wood or composition, composition yoke, and swivel wrists. French, second half of 19th century. *Height* 15 in. *McCully House Toy Museum, Jacksonville.* It is interesting to see these child dolls with pierced ears, which had been the fashion for so long. Princess Beatrice, born in 1857, had her ears pierced when she was about four years old. **250** Bisque. Fair wig, fixed eyes. Marked '3093'. Probably German. *Height* 11¾ in. Former owner born in 1880. *National Museum of Finland, Helsinki.* **251** Bisque baby doll. Painted brush strokes for hair. Kid body, composition lower arms and legs. Back of body stamped 'DRGM 442919'. German, *c.* 1894. *Height* 12 in. *Mrs. Heather Fox.*

252

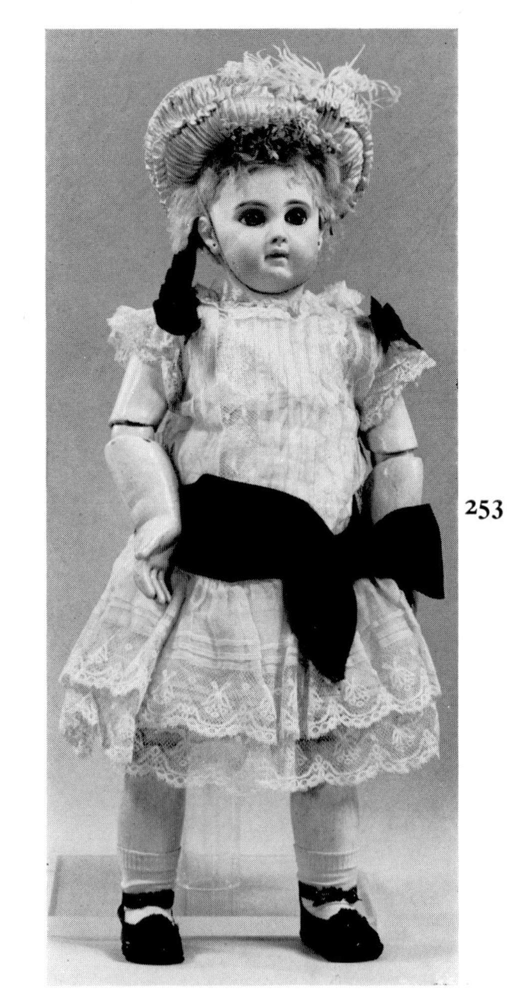

253

254

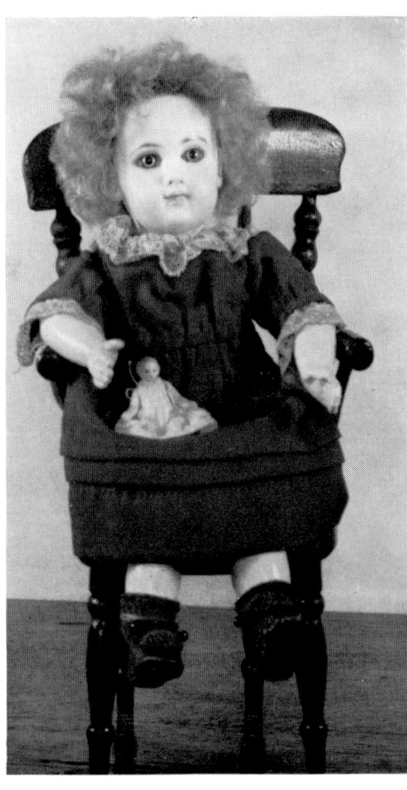

255

256

252 Bisque. Fair wig, very round paperweight eyes, pierced ears, swivel neck. Composition body. Marked 'E J'. Probably Jumeau, for she is beautifully dressed with the Jumeau mark stamped on the sole of her shoes. Bought in Paris in 1884. French. *Height* 14 in. *Bethnal Green Museum, London.* **253** Bisque. Jointed composition body. Mark impressed on the back of neck '8/ EJ' for Emile Jumeau. This and its companion (**258**), together with two similar but smaller dolls (8 in. high) by Jumeau, two baby dolls, and two trunks containing wardrobes for these dolls, were bought in Paris in the 1880s to 1890s for two sisters of the Batchelor family. Gift of Charles and Rosanna Batchelor Memorial Inc. French. *Height* 22 in. *Smithsonian Institution, Washington.* **254** Bisque. Wig, pierced ears, wooden body, threaded wooden limbs, painted. Size 4. Dressed in blue satin and lace, the shoes $1\frac{7}{8}$ in. long marked E. JUMEAU. French, *c.* 1880. *Height* 13 in. *Mr. John Noble/Pollock's Toy Museum.* **255, 256** Bisque. Lamb's fleece wig. Marked on body BEBE JUMEAU DEPOSEE, MEDAILLE D'OR PARIS. French, 1880–90. *Height* $11\frac{1}{2}$ in. *Mrs. Heather Fox.*

258

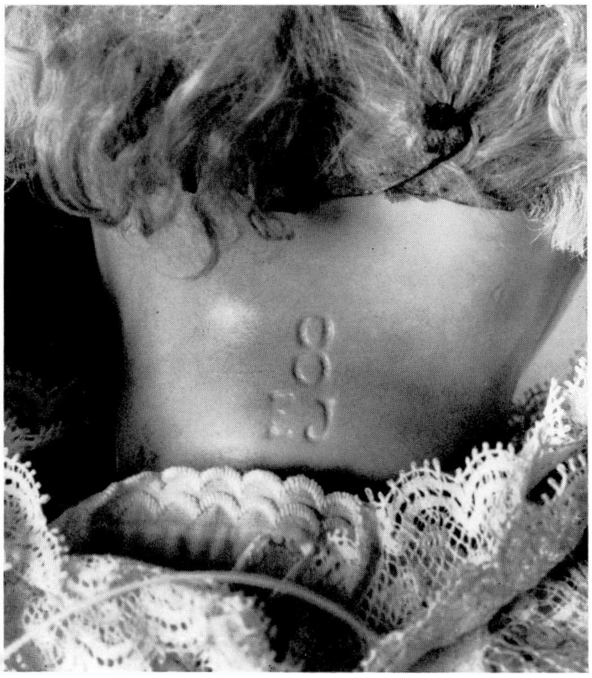

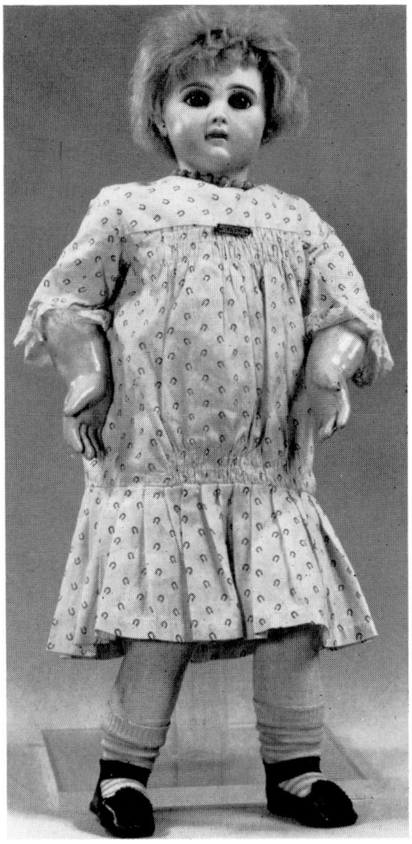

259

257

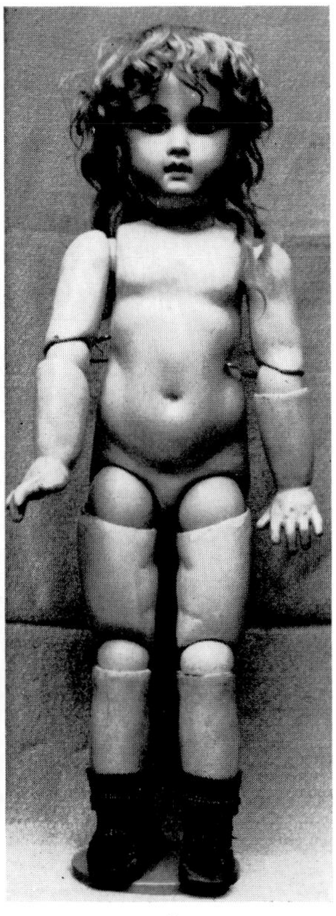

260

261

262

257 Mark impressed on back of necks of **253** and **258**. **258** Companion to **253**. *Height* 22 in. *Smithsonian Institution, Washington.* **259** Bisque. Doll by Jumeau with brown eyes, composition limbs, strung with elastic. Purchased at the Paris Exhibition. French, 1890. *Height* 22½ in. Lent by Sarah Beazley. *Tunbridge Wells Museum.* **260, 261** Bisque. Fair hair, blue eyes. Body marked JUMEAU MEDAILLE D'OR. French, *c.* 1890. *Height* 24 in. Known as 'Claudine'. *Miss Irene Blair Hickman.* **262** Bisque. Fair hair, brown eyes, jointed limbs. Marked on back of neck 'TETE JUMEAU DEPOSEE. B J SGDG 7', and on back of body 'Bébé Jumeau Deposée'. French, late 19th century. *Height* 16 in. *Mrs. Heather Fox.*

263

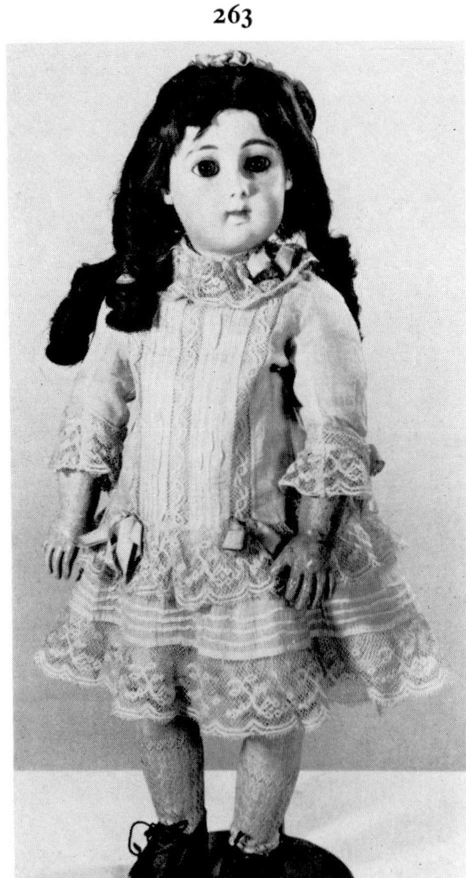

264

265

267

266

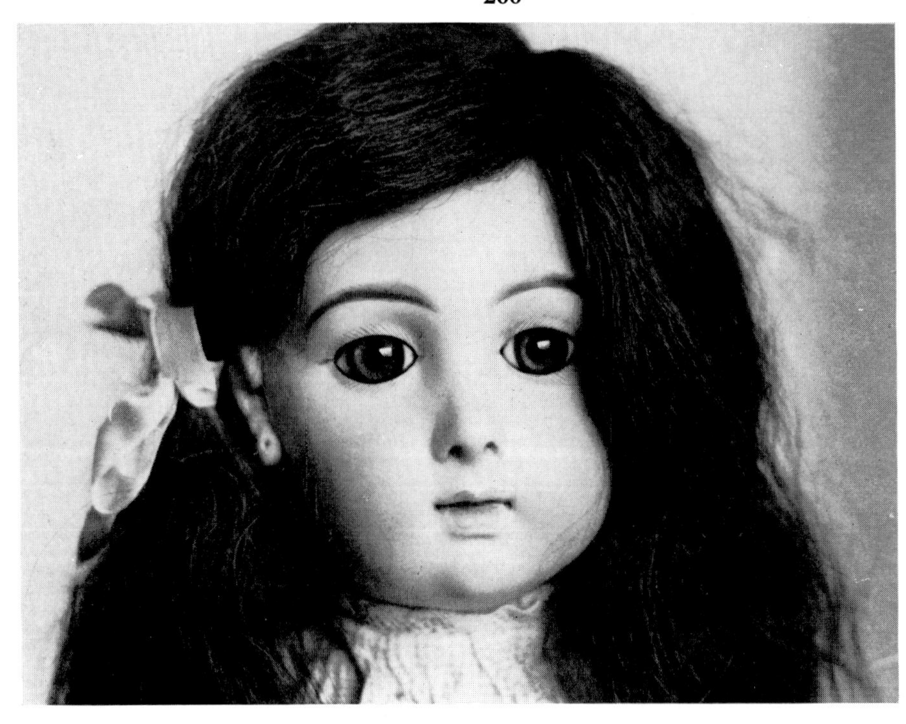

263 Bisque. 'Long-faced Jumeau'. French, late 19th century. *Museum of the City of New York.* **264, 266** Bisque. Real hair wig, golden brown. Blue eyes. Body marked JUMEAU. French, late 19th century. *Height* 26 in. *Mrs. Wigmore.* **265** Bisque. New hair wig, blue paperweight eyes, pierced ears, closed mouth. Back of head marked 'E 7 D' for Decamps. Composition body, ball-jointed legs, arms, elbows, stiff wrists. Body marked 'Jumeau, Medaille D'Or Paris'. French, 1880–90. *Height* 18 in. *McCully House Toy Museum, Jacksonville.* **267** Bisque. Brown paperweight eyes, pierced ears, closed mouth. Back of neck marked 'Paris Bebe' in red. French, late 19th century. *Height* 15 in. *McCully House Toy Museum, Jacksonville.*

268 269 270 271 272 273

268 Bisque. Bru twin babies, one with blue eyes, one with brown. Boy dressed in a Lord Fauntleroy suit. French, *c.* 1890. *Height* 7 in. *Museum of the City of New York.* **269** Bisque. Very dark eyes. Marked 'S F B J, BREVETE S G D G'. French, *c.* 1905. *Height* 14 in. *Mrs. Heather Fox.* **270** Bisque. Bru doll with brown inset eyes, jointed kid body, bisque lower arms, composition legs and feet. Named 'Francoise', she wears a dress which is not the original, but of the same date. French, 1890. *Height* $13\frac{1}{2}$ in. Lent by Sarah Beazley. *Tunbridge Wells Museum.* **271** Bisque. Jointed wooden body. French, *c.* 1891. *Height* 15 in. *Miss Irene Blair Hickman.* **272, 273** Bisque. All-wood body and limbs, pegged with wooden plugs. Ankle joints. Marked 'BRU JNE 5'. She has one dress and several dressy slips. French, *c.* 1891 or later. *Height* 17 in. *Miss Betsy Dean.*

274

275

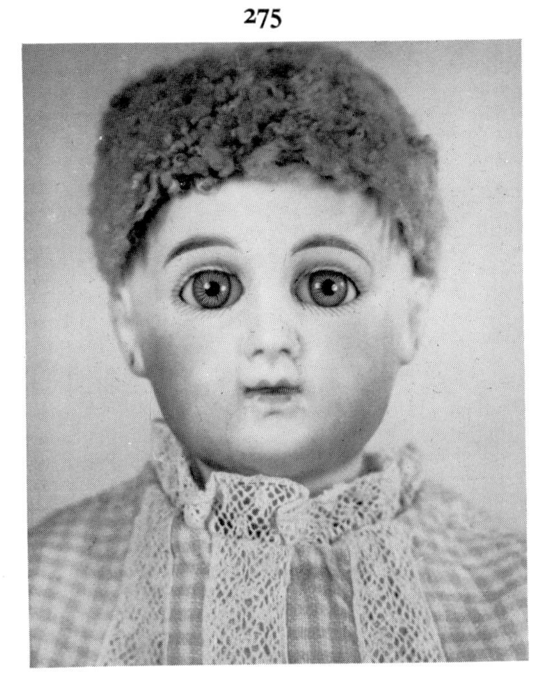

276

277

278

274 Bisque. Steiner. Hair wig fixed to cork, fixed brown eyes, pierced ears, closed mouth. Papier mâché double-jointed body. German, *c.* 1890. *Height* 14 in. *Miss Irene Blair Hickman.* **275** Bisque. Sheepskin wig, fixed blue eyes, closed mouth. Jointed body. Marked WD on back of neck. Probably German, *c.* 1881. *Height* 13 in. *Mrs. Heather Fox.* **276** Bisque. Marked '1295, F.S. &C, 28'. Not dressed in original clothes. Early 20th century. *Height* 13 in. *Miss Irene Blair Hickman.* **277** Bisque. Wig of short light fur. Composition body and bent limbs. Marked 'F S & Co 1272/32Z, deponiert'. Blue velvet suit with lace collar. Known as 'Paul'. German, early 20th century. *Height* 11½ in. *Red House Museum and Art Gallery, Christchurch.* **278** Bisque. Hair wig, brown sleeping eyes. Composition body with jointed limbs. Back of neck marked 'F S & C, 1253 39'. Dressed in mauve satin with cotton and flannel underskirts. German, *c.* 1910. *Height* 15 in. Given by Lady MacAllister, Hampstead. *The London Museum.*

279

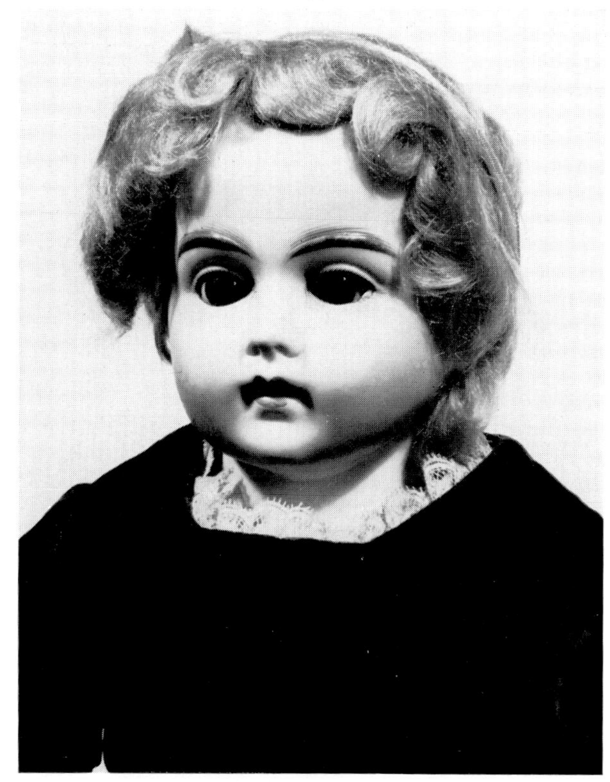

280

281

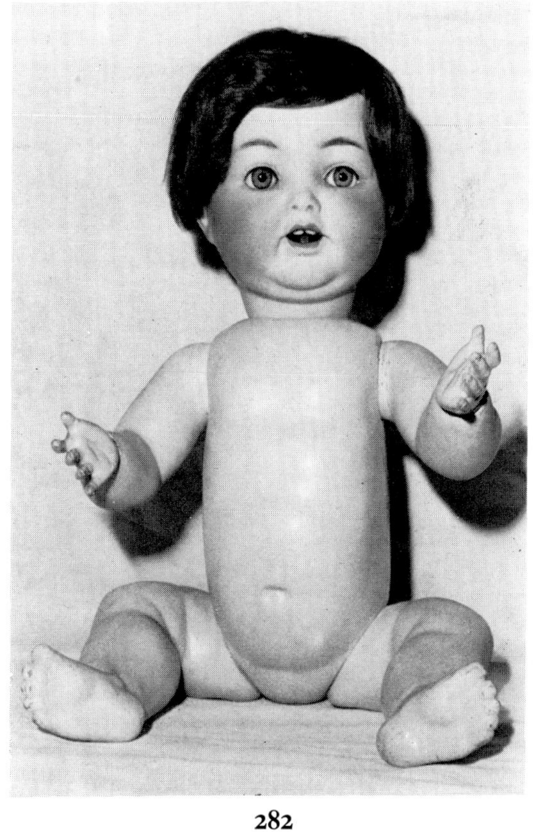

282

279, 280 Bisque. The head, marked with the Mercury sign of Cuno & Otto Dressel, and with fair wig and blue sleeping eyes, has been added to an earlier stuffed body with wax limbs. Red dress of velvet and silk, trimmed with lace, satin skirt with bustle, edged with red velvet. Underneath, three white linen petticoats, a pink woollen petticoat, white stockings and black leather shoes. There are also some spare clothes. *c.* 1885. *Height* 26 in. Given by Mrs. Glover of Barton-on-Sea. *The London Museum.* **281** Bisque. Sleeping eyes and jointed bodies. *Left*, marked 'C & O. Dressel'. 1900. *Height* 25¼ in. *Right*, moves by clockwork. *c.* 1910. *Height* 25¾ in. Sonneberg, Germany. *Deutsches Spielzeugmuseum, Sonneberg.* **282** Bisque. Marked CUNO & OTTO DRESSEL, GERMANY. Brown hair, blue-grey eyes. German, after 1910. *Height* 18 in. *Miss Faith Eaton.*

283

284

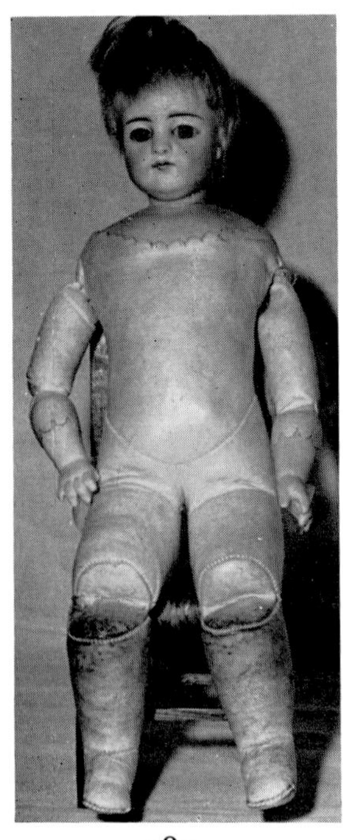

285

286

287

283 Bisque. Fair wig, brown closing eyes. Marked 'S & H 769 DEP'. Bought in Munich in 1891. German. *Height* 13 in. *National Museum of Finland, Helsinki.* **284** Bisque. Wig, closing eyes. Marked 'SH 1080 DEP. 7'. German. *Height* 19¾ in. The former owner born in 1894. *National Museum of Finland, Helsinki.* **285, 286** Bisque. Fair hair, blue eyes. Marked 'S H 4, 905' underneath. Pink kid body. Red flannel petticoat. German, *c.* 1888. *Height* 12 in. *Miss Faith Eaton.* **287** Bisque. Marked 'S & H, P B'. Dressed in indoor and outdoor clothes for the Home of Female Orphans, as worn in 1903. German, *c.* 1902. *Height* 15½ in. Given by Mrs. Dollar. *The London Museum.*

288 289 290 291 292

288 Mark of **289**. **289** Bisque. Jointed composition body. Mark impressed on back of head 'S 5 H 139 DEP'. German, *c.* 1900. *Height* 13¾ in. Gift of Miss Mable A. Barnes. *Smithsonian Institution, Washington.* **290** Bisque. Closing eyes, real eyelashes and eyebrows, composition body, jointed arms, wrists and legs. Marked 'Simon & Halbig'. Strung doll wearing a green satin dress trimmed with beige lace, and feathers in a green hat. German, early 20th century. *Height* 21 in. *Maryhill Museum of Fine Arts, Washington.* **291** Bisque. Marked 'S & H 939'. German, late 19th century. *Height* 16 in. *Miss Irene Blair Hickman.* **292** Bisque. Marked 'SH 1079–12 DEP'. German, late 19th century. *Height* 24 in. *Miss Irene Blair Hickman.*

293

294

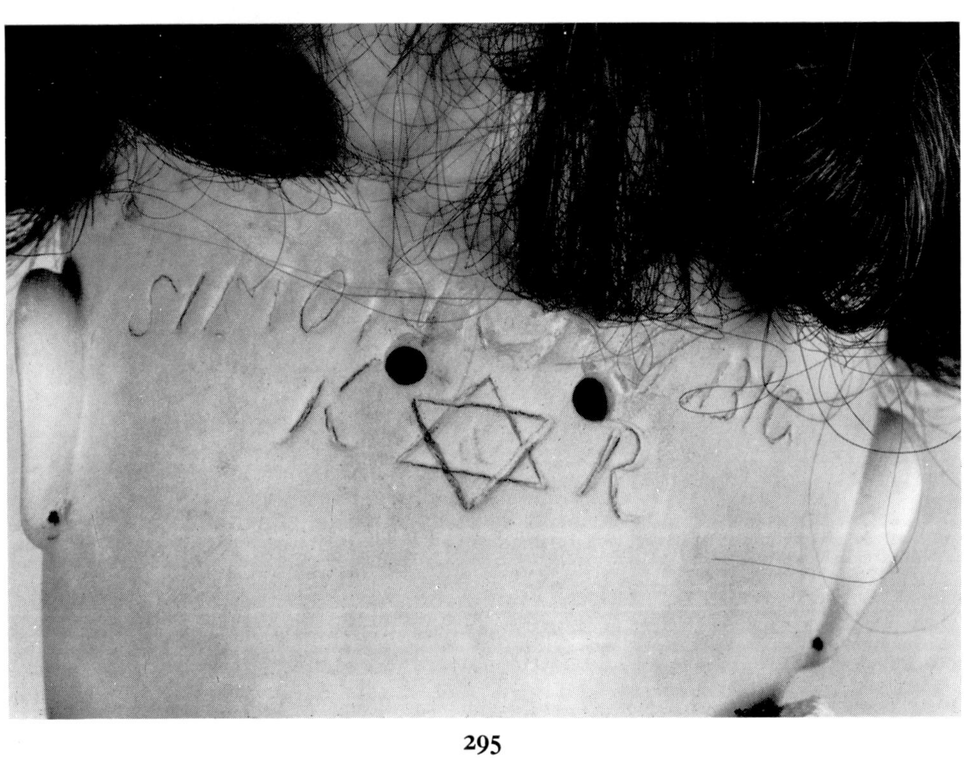

295

296

293 Bisque. Closing eyes, composition body, jointed arms, wrists and legs. Marked 'Simon & Halbig, K [star] R, 55'. Dressed as a bridesmaid in salmon pink and beige lace. German, *c.* 1900. *Height* 21 in. *Maryhill Museum of Fine Arts, Washington.* **294** Bisque. Sleeping eyes, jointed composition body. Marked 'Simon & Halbig' and 'K & R'. German, *c.* 1900. *Height* 28 in. Gift of Miss Mable A. Barnes. *Smithsonian Institution, Washington.* **295** Mark of **294**. **296** Bisque. Marked 'S & H, K [star] R'. German, *c.* 1904. *Height* 17 in. *Mrs. Heather Fox.*

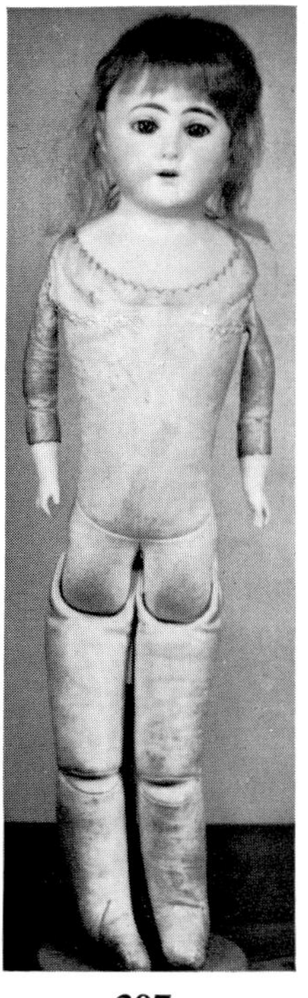

297

298

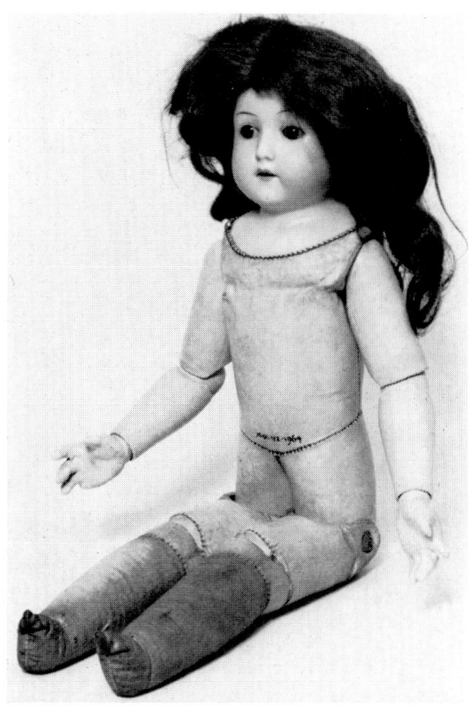

299

300

297, 298 Bisque. Bisque lower arms, kid body. Marked with horseshoe on back yoke and 'MADE IN GERMANY'. *c.* 1890. *Height* 20 in. *Mrs. Heather Fox.* **299** Bisque. Hair wig, bisque head with closing eyes, the lid being painted on the sphere. Unpierced ears, four teeth, hand-sewn fabric body of glazed calico, with composition arms. Marked 'Heubach'. German, end of nineteenth century. *Height* 18 in. *Bethnal Green Museum, London.* **300** Bisque. Heubach, Koppelsdorf. Jointed body. German, 1880–90. *Height* 24 in. *Mrs. Heather Fox.* **301, 302** Bisque. Marked with the Heubach sign. Head turned slightly towards right, wig made of bands of muslin sticking down the locks of hair—the rest comes out in a bunch from a hole at the top. Fixed eyes, unpierced ears. White buckram body, arms jointed by threaded cords, wooden ball knees fitting into hollow shell with cords, the buckram fitting tightly over. Composition lower legs. German, *c.* 1887. *Height* 16 in. Called 'Maggie', given by Miss N. M. Smith. *Saffron Walden Museum.*

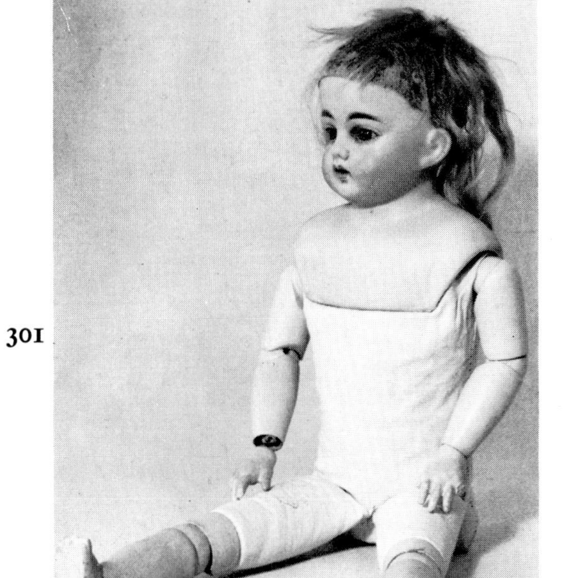

301

302

303 Bisque. Fixed eyes, kid body, threaded arms and legs. Marked with horseshoe and 'HCH 3'. White embroidered dress. German, *c.* 1890 (definitely after 1887). *Height* 20 in. *Maryhill Museum of Fine Arts, Washington.* **304, 305** Bisque. Brown hair, brown eyes. Marked HEUBACH-KOPPELSDORF, 300–3, GERMANY. *Height* 18 in. *Miss Faith Eaton.* **306** Bisque. Brown wig, weighted brown eyes, parted lips showing teeth. Kid body, bisque forearms, composition legs. Marked 'LILLY 8/0, Made in Germany'. Late 19th century. *Height* 16¼ in. *Luton Museum.* **307** Bisque. Hair wig, brown sleeping eyes. Marked '3/OX'. Complete with sets of clothes. Dressed *c.* 1898. German. *Height* 12 in. *The London Museum.*

308

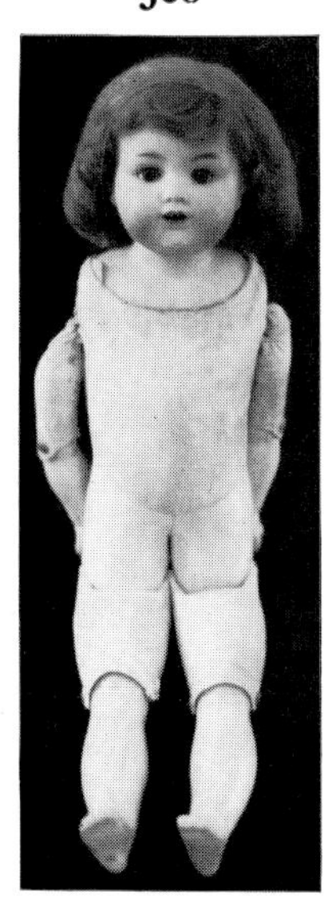

309

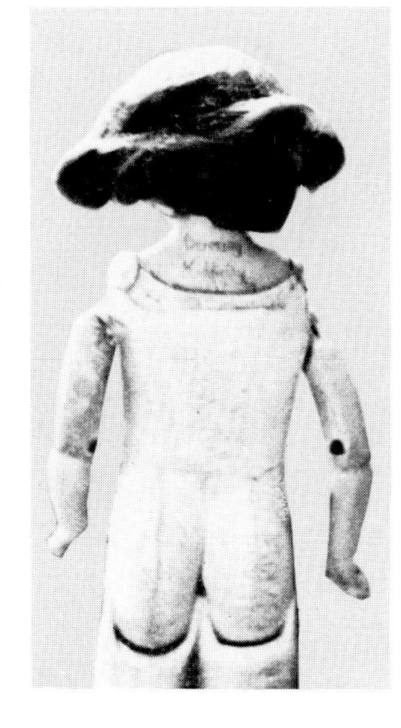

310

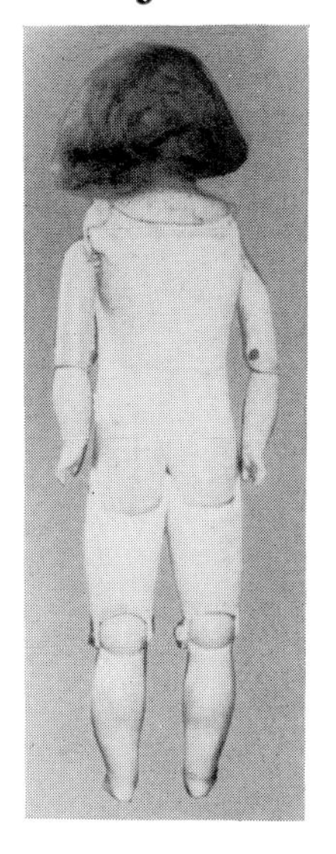

311

312

313

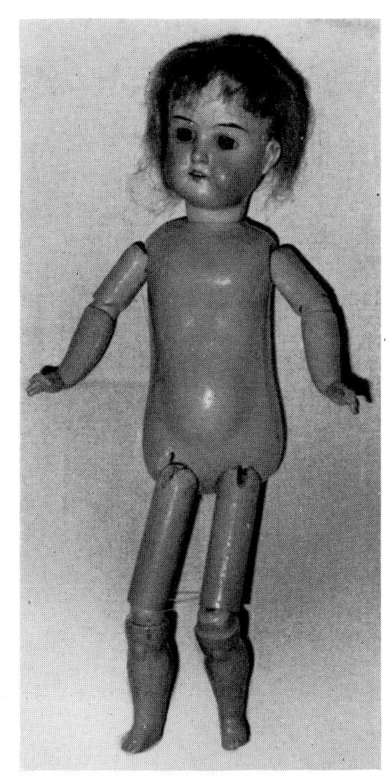

314

315

308–10 Bisque. Marked 'Kiddiejoy'. Kid body, composition forearms and lower legs. German, *c.* 1890. *Height* 18 in. *Miss Christine Smith.* **311** Bisque. Early 'A & M' head, red hair wig, kid body. Lavender-pink dress, white lace hem, trimmed with purple flowers, and yellow tatted medallions. German, late 19th century. *Height* 20 in. *Maryhill Museum of Fine Arts, Washington.* **312** Bisque. Blue closing eyes, jointed kid body, bisque lower arms. Lower legs of white cotton, small feet. Marked AM. Black mesh stockings and black shoes with buckles. German, *c.* 1902. *Height* 17 in. *Mrs. Heather Fox.* **313** Bisque. Fair hair, bisque arms, canvas body and legs. German, 1900. *Height* 18 in. *Grosvenor Museum, Chester.* **314, 315** Bisque. Marked 'FLORODORA, MADE IN GERMANY, A O M'. One of the trade names of Armand Marseille. German, 1901. *Height* 16 in. *Miss Faith Eaton.*

316

317

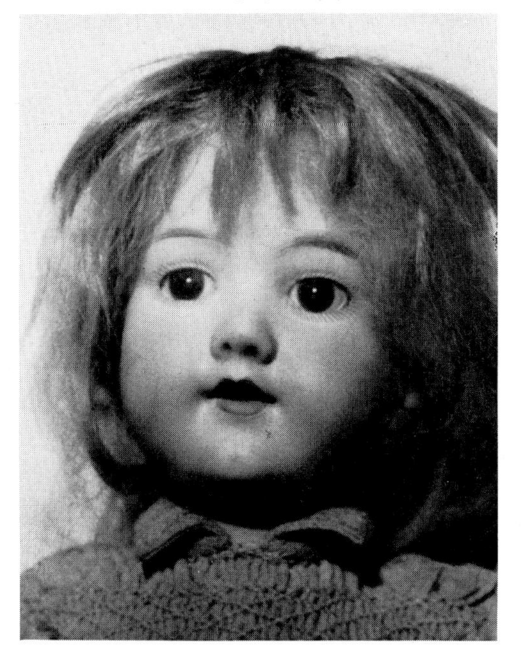

318

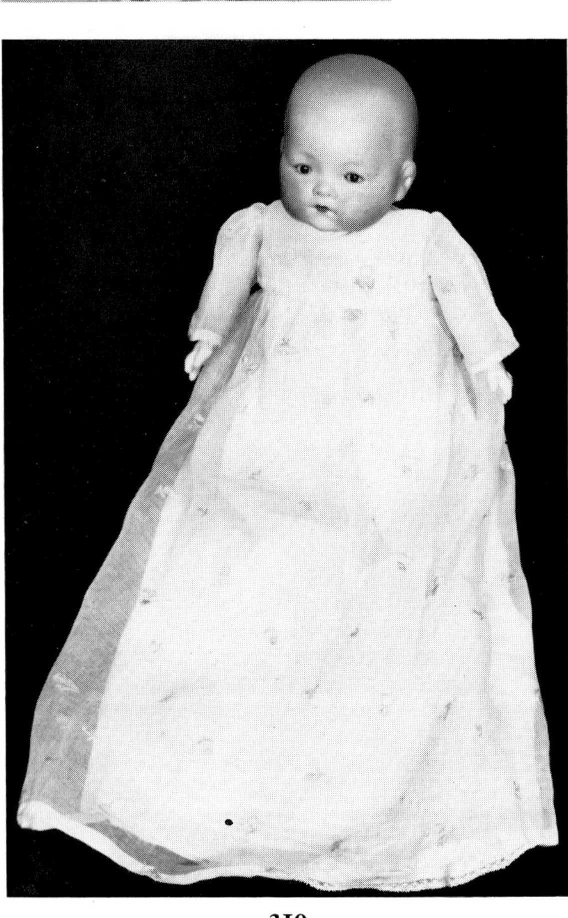

319

320

316 Bisque. Arms and upper legs of wood; composition body, lower legs and hands. Wearing a Christening robe with cape and cap. German, 1900–10. *Height* 18 in. *Grosvenor Museum, Chester.* **317** Bisque. Fair hair, brown eyes. Marked 'A 390 M'. Composition body, threaded wooden limbs and composition hands. German, early 20th century. *Height* 20 in. *Miss Alix Boyd.* **318** Bisque. Marked '3200, AM O DEP, MADE IN GERMANY'. Late 19th century. *Height* 4½ in. *Miss Moriarty.* **319** Bisque baby doll. Armand Marseille. Stuffed body and feet. Marked on back of neck 'A M Germany 341/3'. German, 1904. *Height* 13½ in. Lent by Penelope Cook. *Tunbridge Wells Museum.* **320** Bisque baby doll. Marked 'A.M. Germany 5/6/3/2K'. German, *c.* 1907. *Height* 15 in. *Bethnal Green Museum, London.*

321

322

323

324

321 Bisque. Marked 'Majestic 6 Germany'. Blonde wig, large blue eyes worked by balance. Composition body, jointed limbs of wood and composition. German, 1902. *Height* 21 in. *Red House Museum and Art Gallery, Christchurch.* **322** Bisque. Marked 'K & R 60'. Red hair, closing eyes. Kid body, jointed knees and arms. Embroidered dress, pantelettes and black shoes. German, late 19th century. *Height* 24 in. *Maryhill Museum of Fine Arts, Washington.* **323** Bisque. Marked 'K [star] R', with '53' lower down. Raised bisque eyebrows, painted. Pierced ears, wooden body and threaded limbs, painted. Dressed in white lawn, with Red Riding Hood cap and cape. German, *c.* 1900. *Height* 20½ in. *Mr. John Noble/Pollock's Toy Museum.* **324** Bisque. Fair wig, brown sleeping eyes, parted lips showing four top teeth. Head marked '390 A 11M.' Composition body stamped in red between the shoulders with the Dressel sign and the name JUTTA. German, 1907. *Height* 27½ in. Bought in 1908 for 9*s.* 6*d.*, and given by Miss Reeve. *Saffron Walden Museum.*

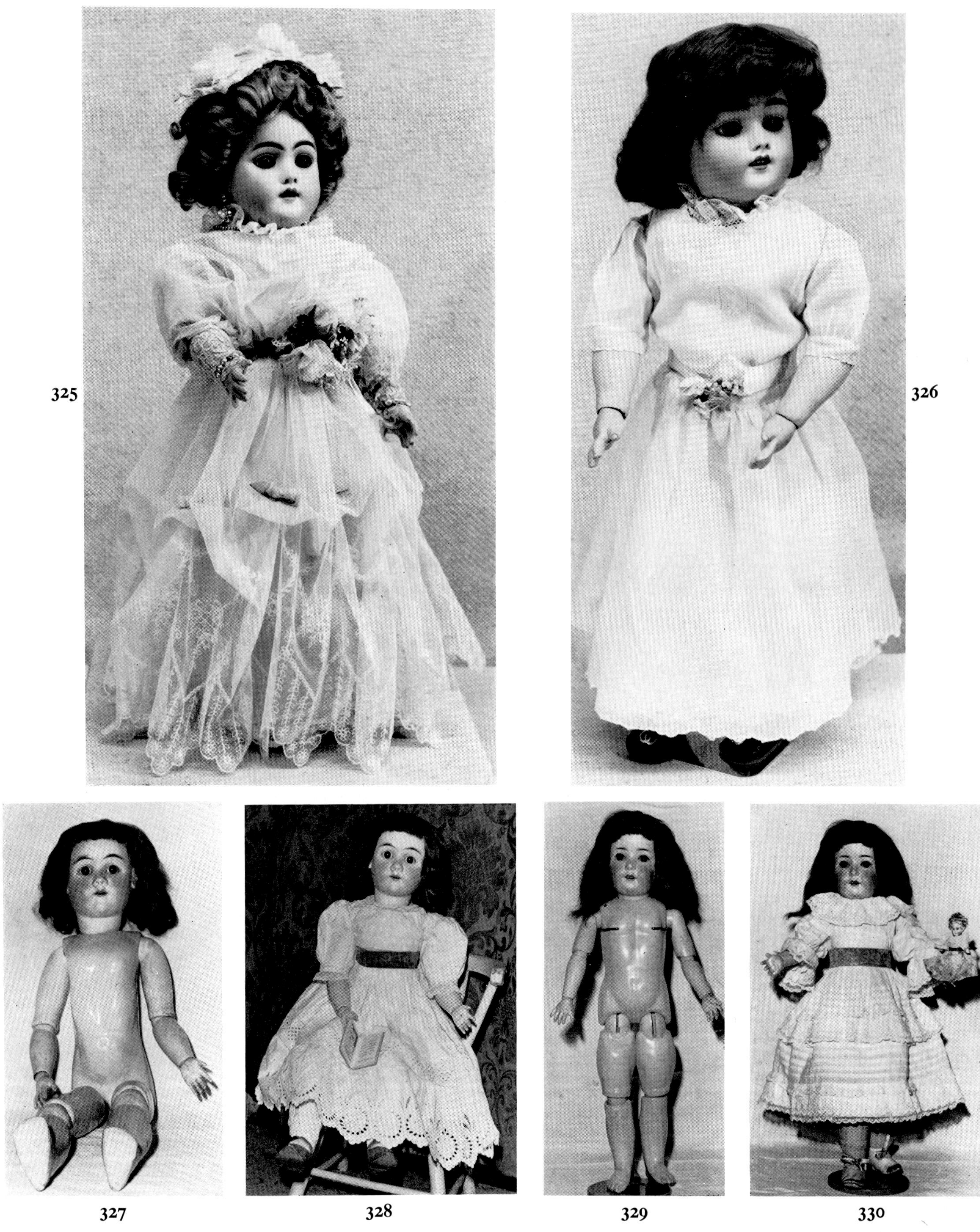

327 328 329 330

325 Bisque. Marked 'Handwerck—109-$11\frac{1}{2}$'. Fixed eyes, composition body, jointed arms and legs. Dressed as a bridesmaid in embroidered net over pink. German, *c.* 1900. *Height* 20 in. *Maryhill Museum of Fine Arts, Washington.* **326** Bisque. Marked 'D$\frac{1}{2}$-168-S$\frac{1}{2}$'. Composition body, jointed arms, wrists and legs. The 'D S' might be for Dreschsel & Stroebel, who made dolls in Germany in 1900. German, *c.* 1900. *Height* 18 in. *Maryhill Museum of Fine Arts, Washington.* **327, 328** Bisque. Marked 'MAX HANDWERCK, GERMANY 4'. Dark brown hair and eyes. German, after 1901. *Height* 27 in. *Miss Faith Eaton.* **329, 330** Bisque. Marked 'W G' with crown, '120 5 GERMANY'. Of later date, dressed in Edwardian clothes. Possibly by Strobel & Wilkin. German, after 1910. *Height* 20 in. *Miss Faith Eaton.*

331 Bisque. Marked 'Germany 13 Walkure'. Closing eyes, composition body, jointed arms, wrists and legs. Beaded lace dress. German, 1902. *Height* 28 in. *Maryhill Museum of Fine Arts, Washington.*

332 Bisque. Fixed blue eyes, cloth body. Forearms and lower legs bisque. Marked on back of shoulders '26' impressed, '22' stamped in green. Probably German, 1909–14. *Height* 14 in. *Plymouth Antiquarian Society, Massachusetts.*

333

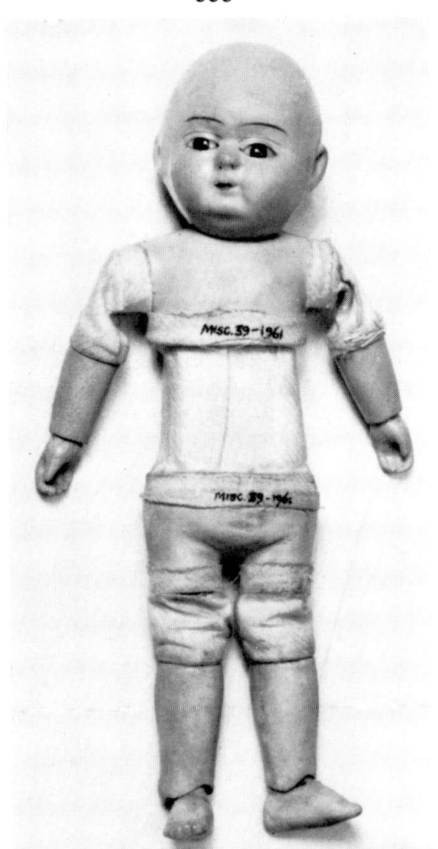

334

335

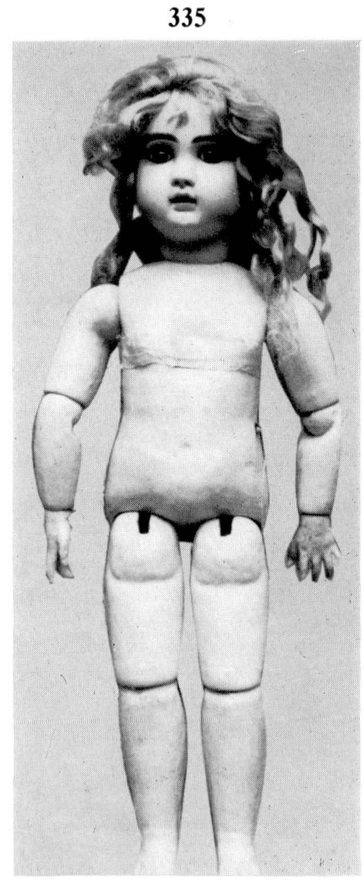

336

337

333, 334 Composition. Fitted with a squeaker worked by pressing the stomach. Probably English, 19th century. *Height* 8 in. *Bethnal Green Museum, London.* **335** Bisque. Two cords come out at side of body for 'Mama—Papa'. Marked in ink on body 'LE PETIT PARISIEN, BÉBÉ STEINER, MÉDAILLE D'OR, PARIS 1889'. *Height* 20 in. *Miss Irene Blair Hickman.* **336** Bisque. Very good quality bisque, hair wig, pale blue fixed paperweight eyes. Open mouth, showing six teeth at top, four at bottom, the teeth going round inside the mouth. Swivel neck. When wound up the doll moves forward on three wheels and says 'Papa—Mama' as it raises its arms. The skirt has been lifted to show the brake and key. In perfect working order. Probably French, 1870–80. *Height* 15 in. *Bethnal Green Museum, London.* **337** Wax. Sleeping eyes and talking mechanism (now broken) which operates by pulling a string. Purple velvet dress (faded to light brown) with cream silk overlay. Probably German, *c.* 1880. *Height* 17 in. *Blaise Castle House Folk Museum, Bristol.*

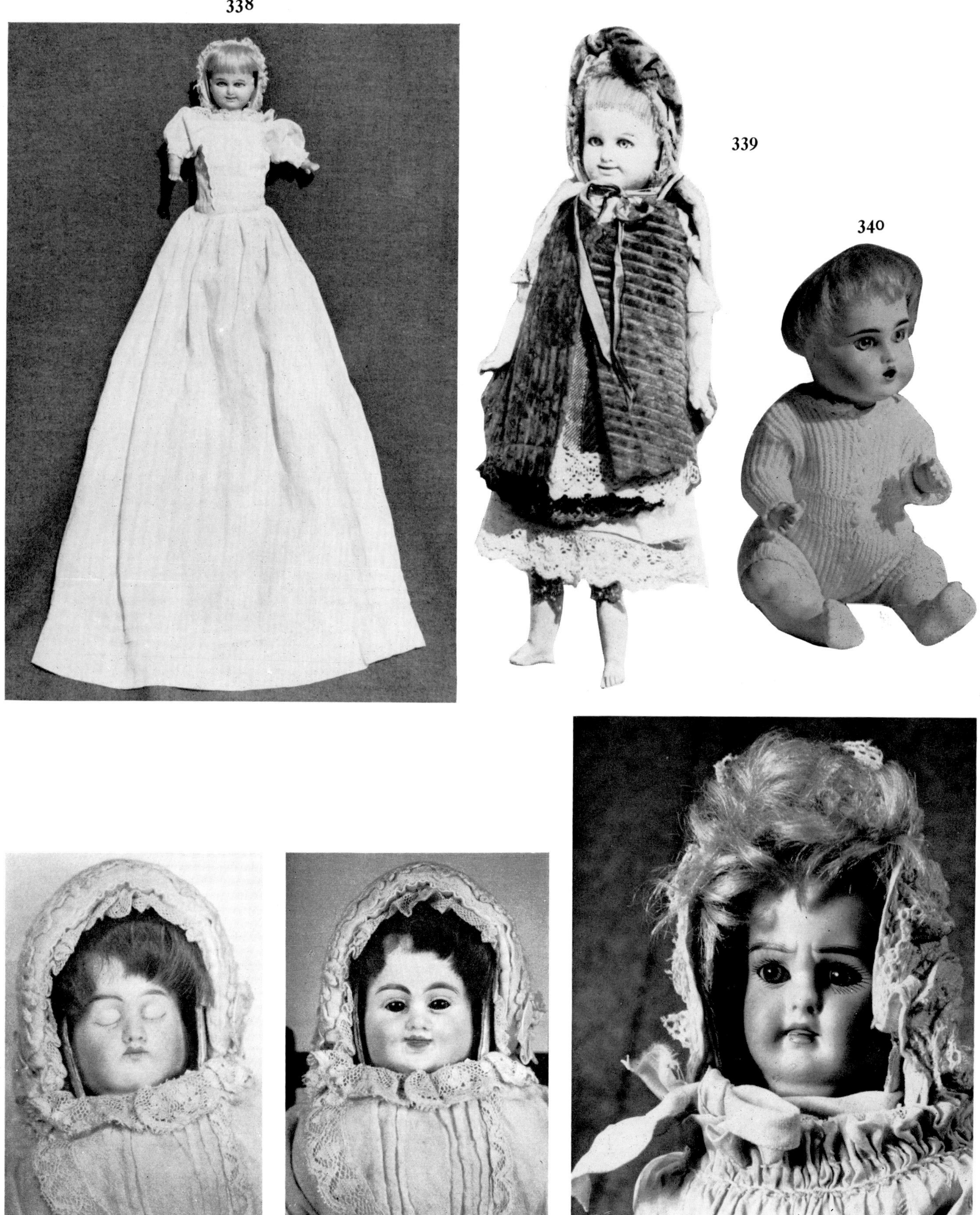

338 Two-faced baby doll. Wax head. Probably German, late 19th century. *Height* 14 in. *City Museum, Leeds.* **339** Two-face doll. Wax head. Probably German, late 19th century. *Height* 13 in. *City Museum, Leeds.* **340** Feeding baby. Bisque head, blue paperweight eyes, open mouth for feeding bottle, with hole in back of neck to drain out water. Composition body. Mady by Rudolf Steiner. German, 1889. *Height* 10 in. *McCully House Toy Museum, Jacksonville.* **341, 342** Three-face doll. Bisque head. Faces smiling, sleeping, and crying with tears. The head turns by means of a brass knob under the bonnet. Stuffed body, jointed limbs, plaster yoke. Marked 'CB' in a circle on yoke. German, late 19th century. *Height* 12 in. *Mrs. Heather Fox.* **343** Three-face doll. Bisque head made up of three faces, one smiling, one sleeping, and one frowning. A kind of cardboard hood covers the head to which the front hair is fixed, through which a knob pulls up in order to turn the faces, which move in one direction only, on a swivel neck. Composition body, threaded. Marked 'D.R.P.' in blue between shoulders at the back. Wears size 3 shoes. Probably German, 1905. *Height* $12\frac{1}{2}$ in. *Luton Museum.*

344

345

346

347

344, 345 Bisque doll with cart. Marked 'Limoges, FRANCE'. The walking mechanism is probably the one patented by Roullet & E. DeCamps in 1892. French. *Height* 12 in. *Brooklyn Children's Museum.* **346** Bisque. Flirting eyes, open mouth showing four glossy teeth. Marked 'S & H 10½', a talking and walking doll bought in 1911, but wearing Parisian clothes of 1912. German, *c.* 1910. *Height* 22 in. Given by Mrs. Scouloudi, Kensington. *The London Museum.* **347** Bisque. Two dolls riding on a tandem bicycle. Belonged to King George VI. Probably French, *c.* 1900. *Height* 10 in. *Windsor Castle.*

348

349

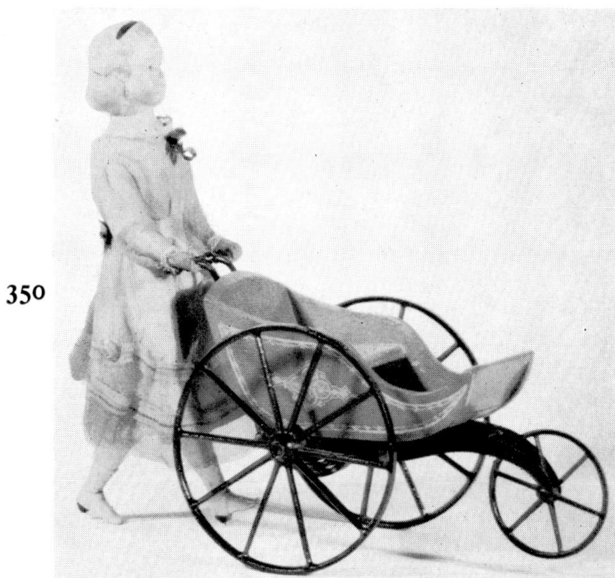

350

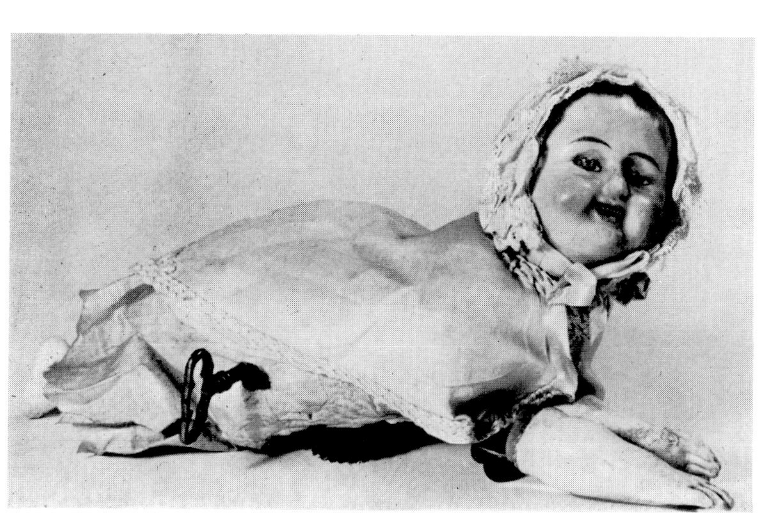

351

348 Mechanical male doll. Bought at the Paris Exhibition. Composition head and body. Original red velvet coat and black velvet breeches. Complete with key to wind for walking, by means of wooden roller under his boots. Probably French, 1855. *Height* 11 in. *Tunbridge Wells Museum.* **349** Wax. Sitting on a cart, 6 in. long, and holding a baby. Probably English, mid-Victorian. *Height* about 9 in. *City Museum, Leeds.* **350** Walking doll. Composition head marked 'X.L.C.R. Pat. Sept. 8, 1868'. Painted yellow hair, blue eyes. Upper torso wood, arms and legs of kid. High white boots with black heels and laces, white lisle stockings, white cotton petticoat with tucks, pantalettes with tucks and lace edge, green gauze dress trimmed with white lace and green ribbon. The carriage of red with gilt decoration, three black wheels, and marked 'Wm. F. Goodwins, Patents dated Jany 22d 1867 & Augt 25th 1868'. American. *Height* of doll 10¼ in.; carriage 5¼ in. *Essex Institute, Salem.* The walking doll was made in several forms by different manufacturers—it was invented by William F. Goodwin of New York. The legs of the doll lifted up and down when wound up, the carriage preventing the doll from falling. **351** Crawling baby doll. *c.* 1870. *Museum of the City of New York.* Both Clay in the U.S.A. and Newton in England patented their crawling dolls in 1871. They were sold for five dollars and were still popular in 1882. They were wound with a key and as they crawled along they could turn their heads slightly from side to side. Most were dressed as babies wearing bonnets, and cheaper ones were made entirely of tin.

352

353

352, 353 Bisque. Swimming doll, known as 'Ondine', French for 'water sprite'. Patented in 1876 by E. Martin. Cork body, arms, and legs of carved wood. Real hair. Clockwork movement in stomach enables her to swim in breast stroke, kicking her legs in the proper manner, and making progress in the water. French, *c.* 1878. *Height* 12 in. *McCully House Toy Museum, Jacksonville.*

III Novelties

Pedlar Dolls

Plates 230–6, 240

Pedlars carried their goods from door to door, either in baskets or on trays which hung from their necks with leather thongs or string. Hawkers travelled with a horse or other beast, and both pedlars and hawkers had to be of good character. They carried certificates to show this, which were usually signed by a clergyman.

In 1698, they were licensed in England. Early dolls depicting pedlars had wooden faces and mere stumps for bodies; they were dressed in cotton clothes similar to that seen in the 'Cries of London' series of engravings portraying the street hawkers of London by the famous eighteenth century artist Francis Wheatley (1747–1801). In their baskets were other little baskets, fans, combs, buckles, and suchlike.

In 1810, there were licensing commissioners and pedlars carried their licence with them in addition to their certificates of good character. Changerwife was the curious name given to them in the north of England, while others, especially those selling books, were known as Chapmen.

Between 1820 and 1840 dolls representing pedlars had carved wooden faces or heads of wax, either black or white. The young girls wore wide straw hats over their muslin caps, while the old women wore straw bonnets over theirs, or hoods the same colour as their capes. These were usually of dark brown serge or of red flannel, and all of them wore aprons. Some wore spectacles and had a glint in the eye, giving a curious know-all expression. But they were not for children; they were ornaments covered with a glass dome and graced the corner cupboards or occasional tables of the Victorian drawing-room.

It is from the minute contents on the trays of these dolls or in their brimming baskets that their date may be deduced. For instance, cotton stockings were made in 1730, ribbed stockings in 1759 and cotton sewing-thread was sold in hanks or skeins in 1812. About 1820 it was put on spools or reels, as they are called, and many little pedlars have these arranged in small boxes.

Pins were all handmade until 1824 and those mechanically made did not reach the country districts for a long time afterwards. The same guidance may be had from adhesive envelopes, which arrived in 1844, though sealing wax was used to the end of the nineteenth century by many people.

Inch-high Dutch dolls, little Bibles, penny-dreadfuls, or minute lithographs might also provide a date, for some of the latter commemorated some event, such as the opening of the Liverpool and Manchester Railway in 1830, or the new London Bridge in 1831.

The Pedlars Act was passed in 1871. In country districts people relied on the pedlar's visit in order to buy their boot and shoe laces, braid trimmings, linen and cotton lace, and many other items well into the Edwardian era.

Talking and singing dolls

Plates 333–7, 346

Jean Maelzel, a mechanic of Paris, in 1824 invented a doll which by means of bellows could say 'Papa' and 'Maman', in 1852 Théroude made mechanical dolls with voice and movement, in 1853 Guilliard a talking doll made of wood, and in 1854 Théroude made another doll which could raise its arms, open and shut its eyes, and also say 'Cou Cou'.

A crying doll in swaddling clothes was patented in 1858 by Robert, this being known as a 'Poupée-maillot'. Musical and jumping dolls were made by Herland in 1861, many of these patents coming from France.

Steiner, represented by Ricordeau of Paris, patented a speaking doll, known as the '*Bébé parlant automatique*', in 1862. Papa and Mama were words Victorian children used for their parents—which was fortunate, for the more usual words used to-day, such as Daddy and Mummy, would have required more complicated mechanism.

Madame Bru, in 1872, patented in England and in France a talking doll which sang various airs; this was sometimes alluded to as a 'Surprise doll'. Harwood's doll of 1877 had a reed mouthpiece fitted at the back through which one could talk. It was blown by the mouth to imitate vocal sounds and his patent stated that it was 'a new useful talking and crying doll'.

The Edison doll of 1878 was a phonograph doll where the lips of the mask moved, and in 1890 it was shown in a New York exhibition. This doll was about 30 in. tall and could recite nursery rhymes such as 'Jack and Jill', 'Mary had a little Lamb', etc., when it was wound up by a handle which protruded at the back about waist level. It will be seen that most sounds were made by working a gadget which came out of the side of the body, and not in the manner of a Teddy Bear, which growls as it is moved up and down.

The Lake doll, in England, was worked by means of bellows. The Hölbe doll was referred to as a singing doll, and the Webber doll when squeezed sang patriotic songs such as 'The Old Grey Goose is Dead'. William Lynd's doll was hardly a plaything as the speaker was concealed behind, under a cloth, while he spoke through a tube connected to the doll's mouth.

A musical doll by Sauerteig and Lutz (1888) had a box inside which was played by the jointed arm of the doll. Another phonograph doll was patented by Jacques of the U.S.A. and by Brookes in England, where the head of the doll had a hole at the top under the hair from which the sounds emitted.

A doll which cried out when put in a sitting position was patented by Ferdinand Max

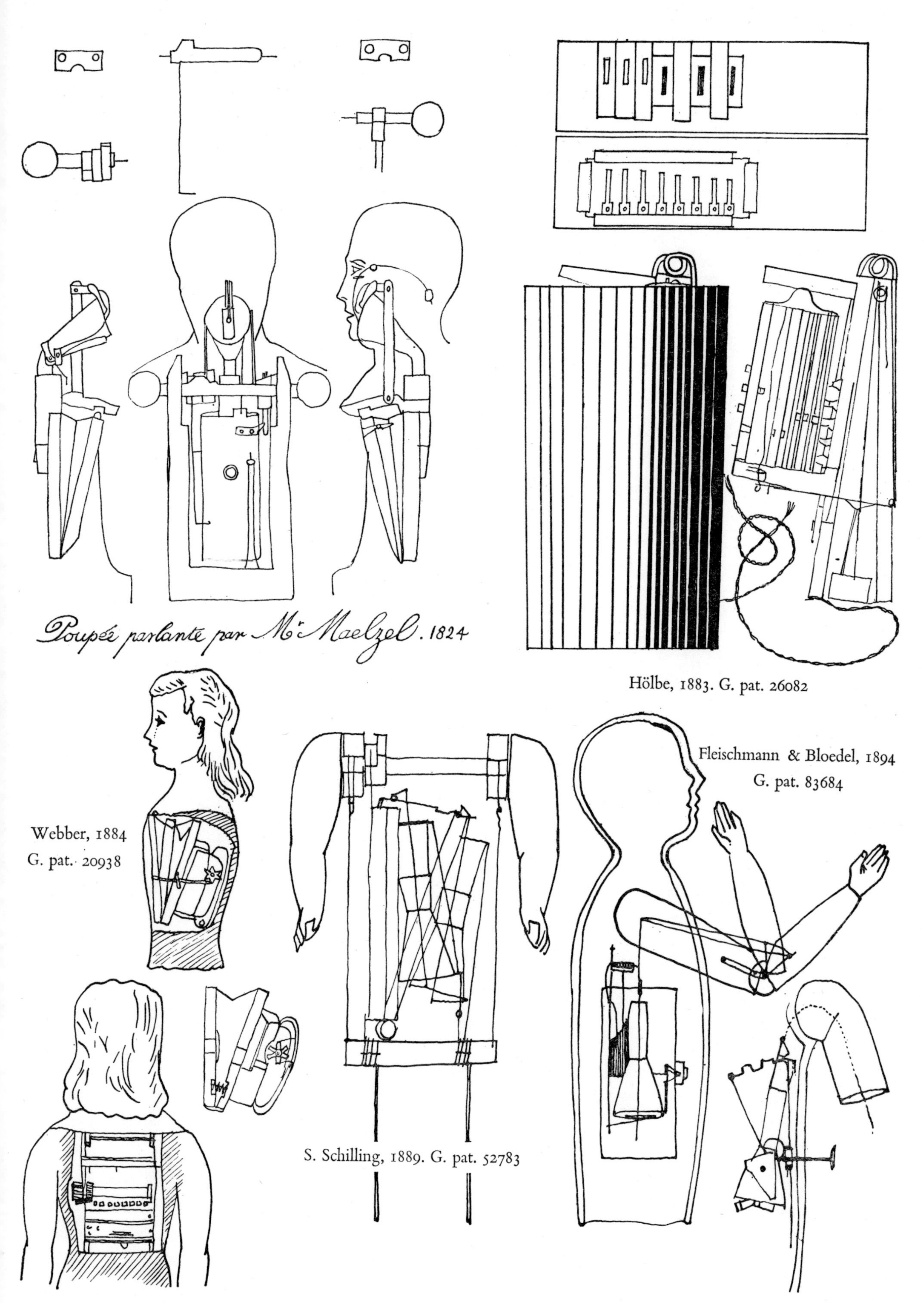

TALKING AND SINGING BY MEANS OF BELLOWS, PATENTS 1824–94

Schilling, who marks his dolls with a little cherub. Hölbe's doll in 1890 could say Papa-Mama or Mama-Papa by pressing a small rubber ball on the end of a string. Decoeur's also produced sounds by pressing a rubber ball with a sounding bell.

Madame Lafosse's doll of 1892 talked by means of bellows and in 1893 walked and talked simultaneously. She improved her dolls from time to time and in 1897 produced a doll which could cry, walk, and blow kisses.

Gay's musical doll worked by means of a rotating marble, and King made a crying doll; the working of both can be readily understood by looking at their patent drawings. In 1894, a doll by Fleischmann & Bloedel spoke by means of turning a knob which came out at the waist, and in 1896 some of their dolls could also imitate sending a kiss. In their French patent of 1897 the dolls could walk, talk, and blow kisses all at the same time. Girard's entry also mentions a doll able to do all this, and also Madame Lafosse, the former entry probably alluding to a doll made by Bru.

Other talking dolls were by S.F.B.J., Lambert, and Oscar Arnold who was represented by E. Marks. Some of these were phonograph dolls and some could turn their heads while speaking.

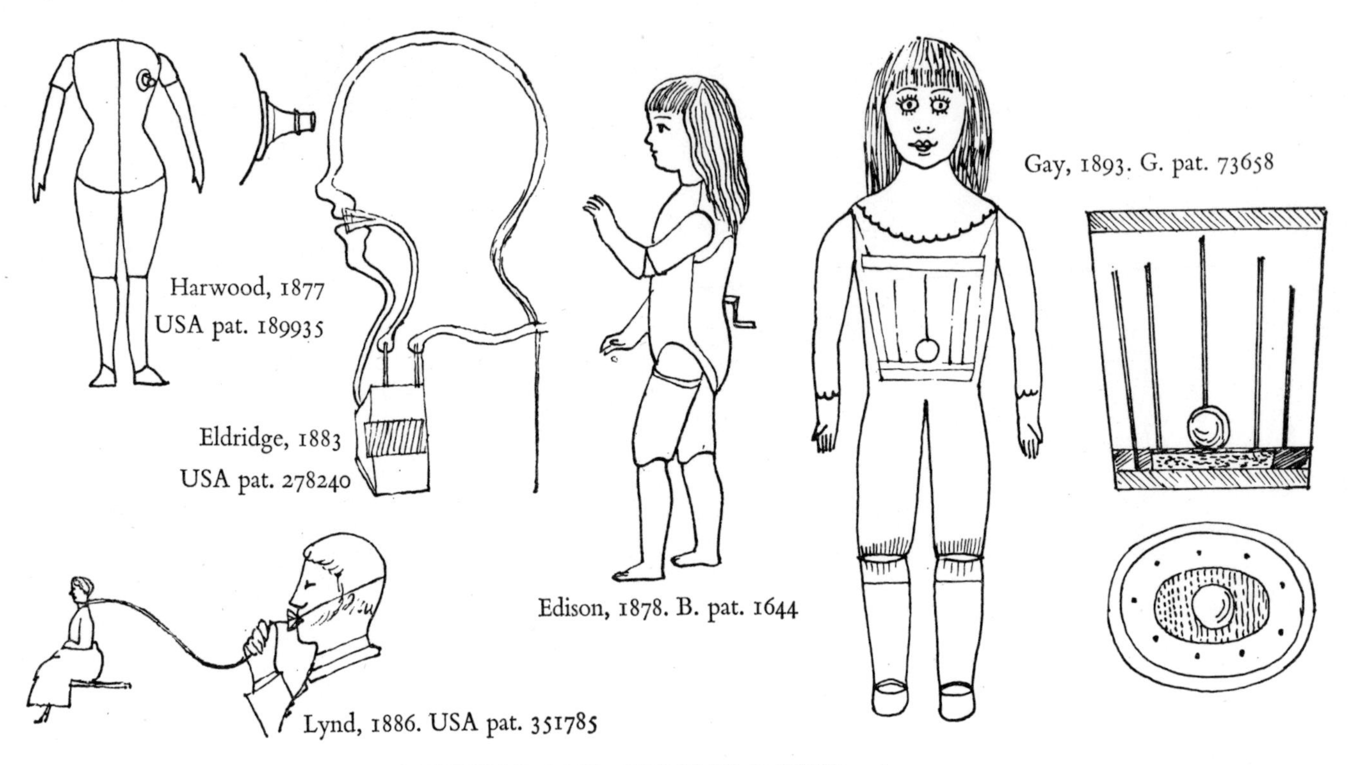

TALKING AND SINGING DOLLS, 1877–93

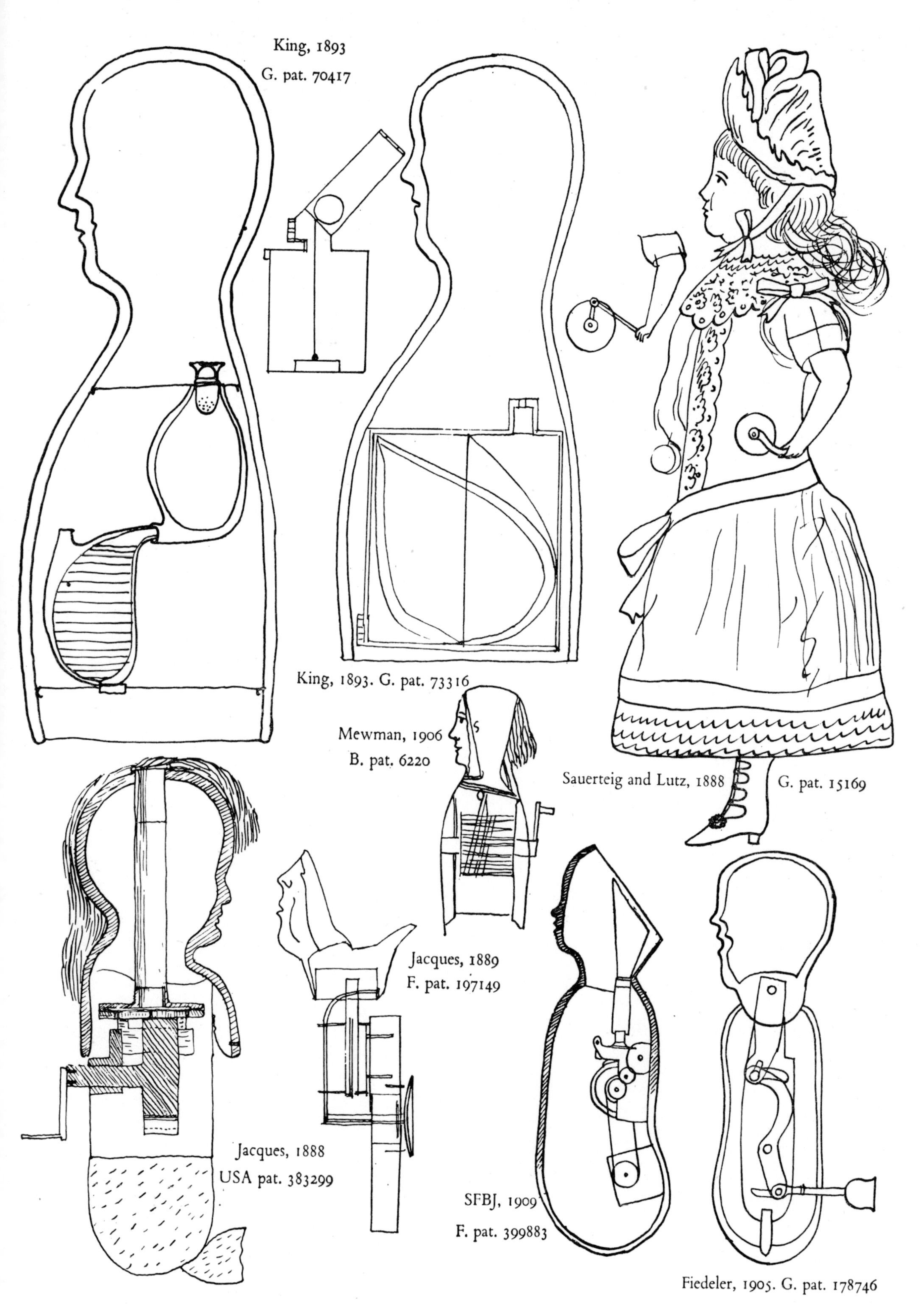

TALKING DOLLS, 1888–1909

Patents

1824 Maelzel. Talk
1852 Théroude. Talk
1853 Guilliard. Talk
1858 Robert. Crying baby
1861 Herland. Musical
1862 Steiner. Talk
1865 Herland. Musical and jumping
1870 Chauvière. Talk
1872 Madame Bru. Sing
1877 Harwood
1878 Edison. Recite
1879 Gregori-Olivier. Talk
1880 Hölbe. Musical
1882 Webber. Musical
Lake. Musical
1883 Eldridge
Hölbe. Singing
1884 Webber. Sing
1886 Lynd
1888 Sauerteig. Musical
Jacques. Musical
1889 Schilling. Cries when put down
1890 Graeser. Moving lips
Hölbe. Talk
Edison. Talk
Wolff. Talk
Decoeur. Talk
1890 Rayer. Musical
1891 Voigt. Musical
1892 Girard. Breathe, talk and sleep
Lafosse. Walk and talk
Ascher. Musical
1893 King. Crying
Boult. Musical
Gay. Musical
1894 Fleischmann & Bloedel. Musical
1896 Fleischmann & Bloedel. Musical
Lafosse. Talk and cry
Girard. Talk
Fleischmann & Bloedel. Blow kisses
1897 Fleischmann & Bloedel. Moving lips, walk, talk and blow kisses
Lafosse. Cry, walk and blow kisses
Girard. Talk, walk and blow kisses
1901 S.F.B.J. Talk
1902 Lambert. Talk and turn head
1904 Arnold. (Marks) Talk
1905 Fiedeler
S.F.B.J. Talk and blow kisses
1906 Mewman. Phone
Schnepff. Movable features
1908 Arnold. Talk
1909 S.F.B.J. Talk

Walking and crawling dolls

Plates 336, 344–6, 348, 350–1

The most popular walking doll was made in the U.S.A. by Joseph Lyon in 1862. This was known as the AUTOPERIPATETIKOS. Some had papier-mâché heads, composition bodies and kid arms, others had heads of bisque or porcelain. Their dresses varied; some were of yellow silk with black lace, others were dressed in royal blue or pale mauve, with ribbons. The dolls seem to have been treated with great care, for many of them are in perfect working order and even their boxes remain intact.

Other walking dolls of 1862 were fitted with porcelain or bisque heads of great variety, but as usual the porcelain had dark hair and the bisque fair, both moulded in one with the head, and some had the lower arms of leather, cloth, or of china.

A walking doll with step-by-step movement was patented in England by William Clark, also in 1862, and both Newton in this country and Robert Clay in the U.S.A. made crawling dolls, the latter having the arms and legs connected by a rod which was propelled by wheels.

Work's doll in 1873 had a multi-pedal wheel pivoted at the knee, which was worked by friction as the figure moved. The doll could raise its dress enough at the side to show but one pair of feet at once.

Peloubet's doll worked the feet automatically so that they came down alternately, first on the heel, then rocking over to the toe, then rising and moving forward by means of footed levers. The doll of Stranders and Perry crawled along the floor when pulled by a

The Autoperipatitikos Walking Doll, Martin & Runyon, 299 Broadway, New York. This version has a composition head, leather arms and metal feet. Wearing a dress of mauve, cream and black with green ribbons. *Bethnal Green Museum.* Another in the Victoria and Albert Museum has a porcelain head, and one in Kensington Palace wears a dress of Royal blue

string, and according to his patent this mechanism could also be adapted for rowing and swimming.

The '*Bébé Premier Pas*' was patented in France by Steiner in 1890. This walking doll moved when wound up at the side. Girard's doll, the '*Bébé Marcheur*' was probably one of Bru's, for Girard represented Bru at this time, stating that the doll was 'particularly remarkable', which indeed it was, for it walked and talked at the same time.

Roullet & Decamps' doll walked by means of weights, and in 1892 Thompson in England

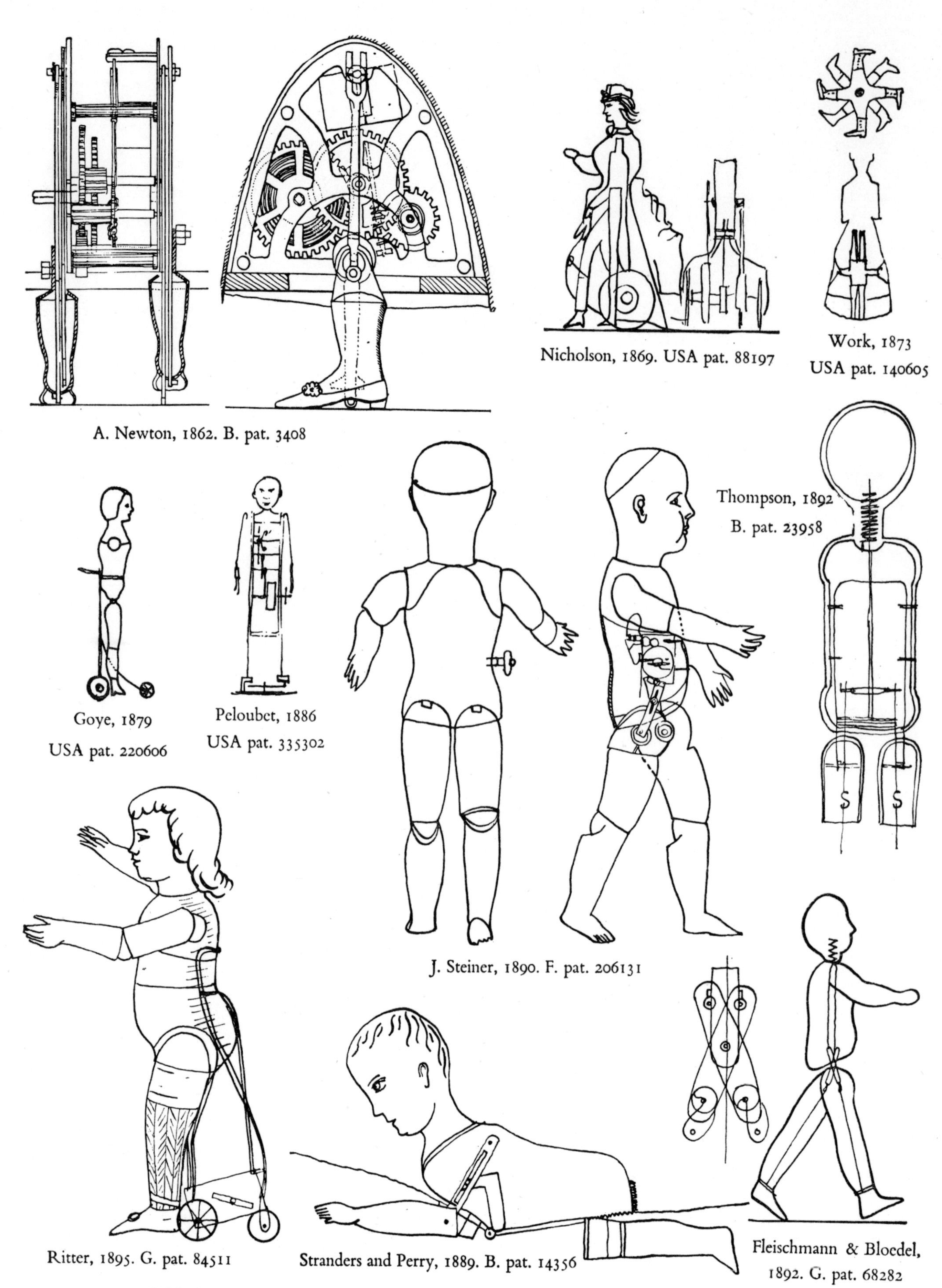

A. Newton, 1862. B. pat. 3408

Nicholson, 1869. USA pat. 88197

Work, 1873
USA pat. 140605

Goye, 1879
USA pat. 220606

Peloubet, 1886
USA pat. 335302

J. Steiner, 1890. F. pat. 206131

Thompson, 1892
B. pat. 23958

Ritter, 1895. G. pat. 84511

Stranders and Perry, 1889. B. pat. 14356

Fleischmann & Bloedel,
1892. G. pat. 68282

PATENTS CONCERNING WALKING AND CRAWLING DOLLS, 1862–92

patented a doll for Fleischmann & Bloedel, which could walk and turn its head from side to side while doing so. A doll by Cosman Frères walked, talked, and turned its head by pressing down on the shoulders; a doll by Rabery also walked and talked; therefore many of these walking-talking dolls may be dated around 1891–3.

Lloyd's walking doll moved when drawn along on a string, and Madame Soulard's doll, known as 'La Charlotte', moved along by means of springs.

Gedney's doll was made to run and then fall down, and Eisenstaedt's could take a 'striding movement'.

WALKING DOLLS, 1895–1904

Bromhead, trading as Treude & Metz, had a British patent for a walking doll in 1902, and Edmund Steiner, a citizen of the U.S.A., had a patent in which the child took the doll by the hands, gently drew it forward while standing on one foot, then the shank above the foot moved on the rod, and gradually the other leg moved forwards. Daspres' doll, in the same year, could also walk and talk.

Patents

1861	Clark
1862	Newton
	Vichy
1863	Autoperipatetikos. Munn and Cobb
	Autoperipatetikos. Martin and Runyon
1864	Brown Westhead
1869	Nicholson
1871	Clay. Creep
	Newton. Crawl
1873	Work
1875	Hotchkiss
1878	Jumeau
1879	Goye
1886	Peloubet
1889	Perry
1890	Steiner
1891	Malepart
	Girard
1892	Girard
	Roullet & Decamps
	Fleischmann & Bloedel
	Thompson. Heads from side to side
1893	Lafosse
	Cosman Frères
	Roullet & Decamps
	Rabery
1894	Lafosse
	Lloyd
	Fleischmann & Bloedel
1895	Ritter
1896	Fleischmann & Bloedel
	Gedney
	Imhof
1897	Fleischmann & Bloedel
	Girard
1898	Imhof
1899	Eisenstadt
	Imhof
1900	Imhof
	Martin
1901	Lehmann
	Eisenstaedt
1902	Charstone
	Bromhead
	Steiner
	Reinhardt
	Daspres
	Treude et Metz
1904	Fuchs
	Lehmann
	Arnold

Feeding dolls

Plate 340

Casimer Bru, Junior, of Paris took out a German patent in 1879 for a feeding doll, or '*Saugpuppe*'.

Rudolf Steiner made a feeding doll which sat in a chair, and Leidel's fed by means of a rubber ball. Schachne, also from Germany, made one in 1909.

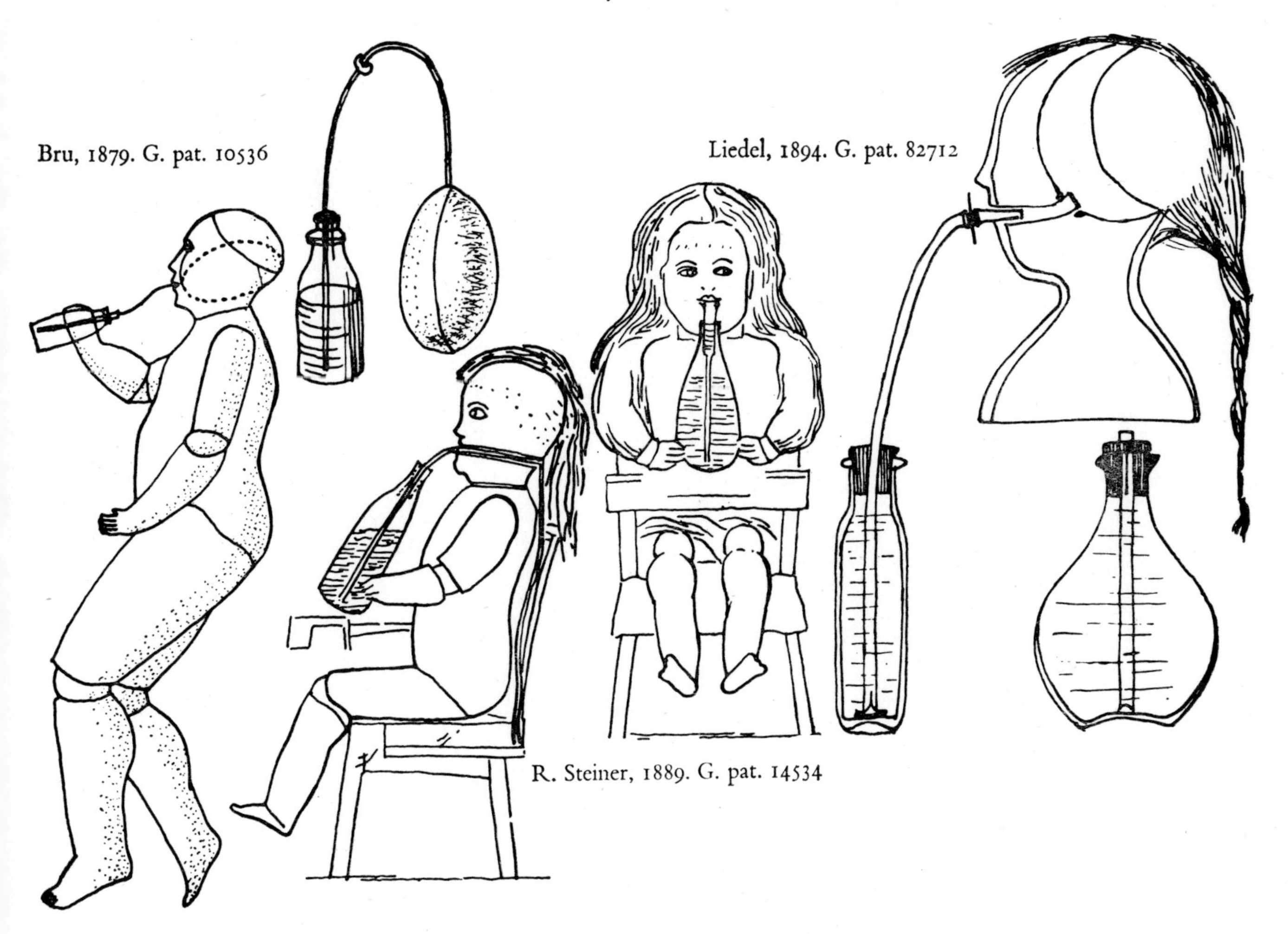

PATENTS CONCERNING FEEDING DOLLS

Patents

1879 Bru
1888 Steiner
1889 Steiner
1890 Steiner
1894 Leidel
1909 Schachne

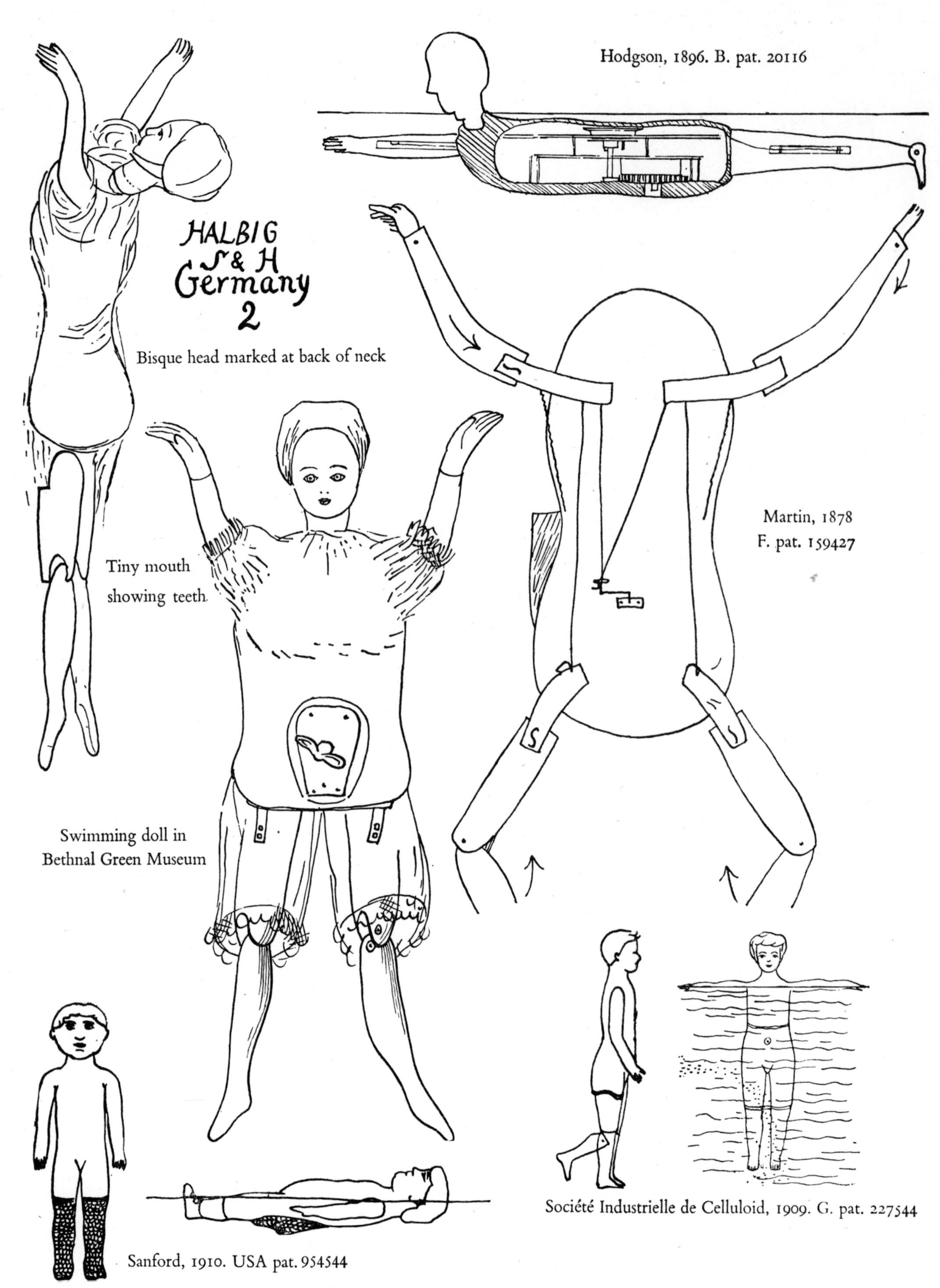

PATENTS CONCERNING SWIMMING DOLLS

Swimming dolls

Plates 352–3

In 1876, Martin took out a French patent for a swimming doll. Known as 'Ondine', this was manufactured by Charles Bertran.

Mrs. Hodgson, in Scotland, patented a swimming doll which worked with clockwork, the doll being of tin or other metal—and if of Indiarubber it could be inflated—in 1896.

A bathing doll was made by Standfusz of Dresden, and also by Arnold. But bathing dolls did not swim; the description merely meant that washing them did no harm.

The Société Industrielle de Celluloid made a swimming doll, known in France as '*Poupée Nageuse*', and in Germany as a '*Schwimmpuppe*', and later in 1910 they made what was termed 'an improved floating doll'. In the same year Sanford made a nautical doll.

Patents

1878	Martin
1896	Hodgson
1909	Soc. Ind. de Celluloid
1909	Standfusz
	Arnold
1910	Sanford

Oddities

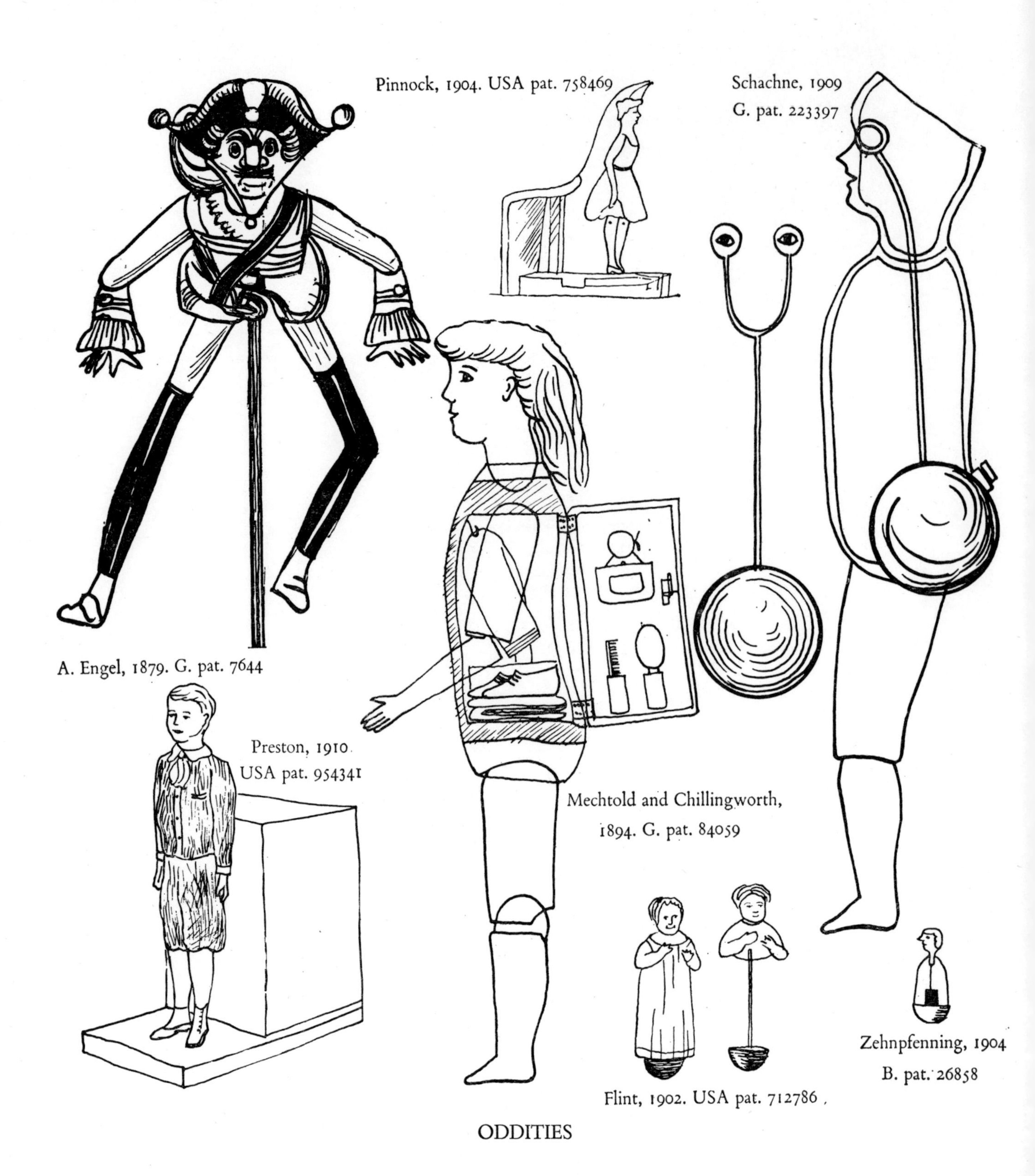

ODDITIES

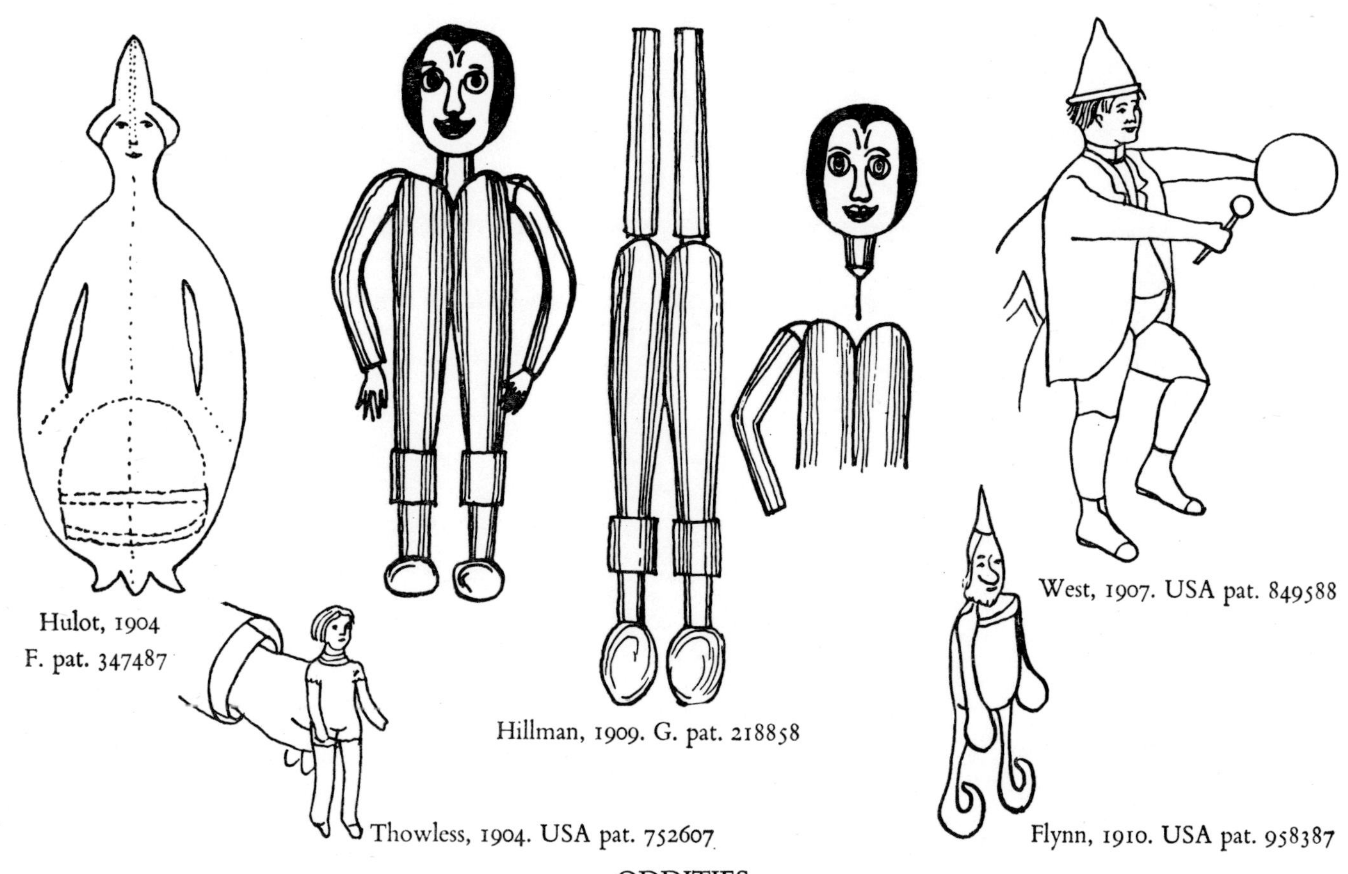

Hulot, 1904
F. pat. 347487

Thowless, 1904. USA pat. 752607

Hillman, 1909. G. pat. 218858

West, 1907. USA pat. 849588

Flynn, 1910. USA pat. 958387

ODDITIES

Patents

1859 Bresson. Flying doll
1865 Egrefeuil. Baptismal doll
1866 Pepper. Gymnastic
     Clavell. Dancing
1875 Schmetzer. Dancing
1876 Lutticke. Juggling
1879 Engel. Hampermann
     Boutard. Flying
1884 König. Polichinell
1887 Mora. Jumping
1888 Parquet. Dolls of blown glass
     Dehler. Telephone
1889 Grin. Jumping
1892 Bru. Talk, sleep and breathe
     Jaboulay. Dance
     Lehmann. Dancing doll on a top
1894 Mechtold. Wardrobe in body
     Sharples. Chocolate dolls
     Wilson. Doll in the shape of a hot-water bottle
1895 Wynne. Doll to blow soap bubbles
1896 Gray. Dancing doll
1897 Biddle. Smoking doll
     Wynne. Bubble-blower
1898 Gray. Dancing
     Bontempo. Jack-in-the-box dolls
     Berg. Bubble-blower
1899 Germain. Telephone
     Weigel. Hopping
1900 Reid. Tumbler doll
1901 Bousquet. 'Petit Pianiste'
1902 Flint. Tumbler doll
1903 Ulrig. Jumping
1904 Hulot. 'Poupée Jouet'
     Pinnock. Doll on a box
     Zehnpfennig. Tumbler doll
1905 Fiedeler. Nodding heads
     Budwig. Ornamental
1908 Hamburger & Coston. Dolls from distorted photographs
1901 Lemon & Page. Tears falling
1910 Preston. Dancing

Upside-down dolls

Patents

1894 Douglas
1909 Faugier

Skipping dolls

Patents

1887 Mora
1907 Köring
1909 Trautmann

Douglas, 1894. B. pat. 19850

Trautmann, 1909. B. pat. 5624

Köring, 1907. F. pat. 378721

Faugier, 1909. F. pat. 405786

Mora, 1887. G. pat. 42282

PATENTS CONCERNING SKIPPING DOLLS AND UPSIDE-DOWN DOLLS

Dolls with more than one face

Plates 338–9, 341–3

In 1866 Dominico Checkeni patented in the U.S.A. what he termed a 'Fancy Doll'. This was a doll with four faces, with a pivoted head, so that either face could be brought to the front, with a suitable wig covering the other three.

Leon Casimer Bru, in 1867, made a doll with a turning head to show two faces, one at a time; one was smiling, the other crying. Bartenstein's head of 1881 had two different expressions, the face not showing being covered with a bonnet. This was a revolving head, laughing on one side and crying on the other. Later he patented a head with three faces.

In 1887 double-faced dolls could be purchased in England and in the U.S.A. The faces were one laughing and one crying. A kind of cardboard hood covered the head, which was turned by means of a spring worked by a ring which came out of the top of the hood, which was then surrounded by a frilly bonnet. Some had faces of imitation wax and were washable and could be purchased in three sizes. By 1888 dolls not only had double faces but they could also cry Mama, Papa, by pulling at two cords which came out at the side of the body.

Joanny patented a Bébé with a double face, one talking and one crying, and Carl Bergner's patent was of a doll-head made in two parts so that several faces could be fixed to one body. Madame de Veriane's two-faced doll has been classed among the Rag Dolls, and Mlle. Eugénie Faugier, a resident of Belgium, patented her two-faced doll in France in 1909.

Checkeni, 1866
USA pat. 52782

Bartenstein, 1880. G. pat. 14429

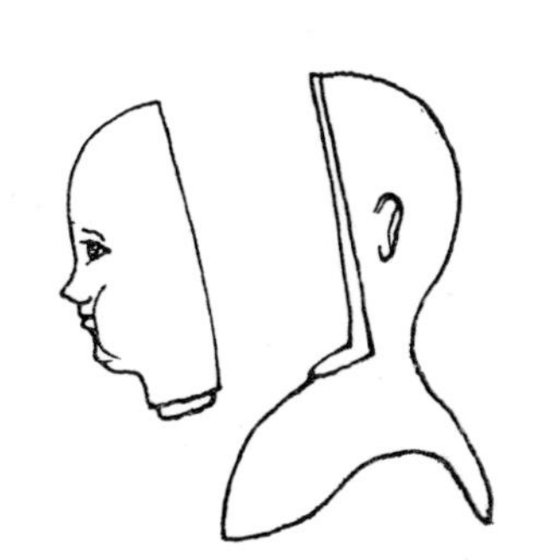

Bergner, 1904. B. pat. 27919

DOLLS WITH MORE THAN ONE FACE

Patents

1866 Checkeni. Four faces
1967 Bru. Two faces
1872 Benda. Changeable faces
1880 Bartenstein. Two faces
1889 Joanny. Two faces
1904 Bergner. Several faces
1909 Faugier. Two faces

D.R.P.

Doll 12½ in. long, with three bisque faces to one head. A kind of cardboard hood fits over the head, with a fringe of hair fixed to it. The knob at the top pulls up in order to turn the head around, which moves in one direction only to show one face at a time. The composition body is threaded and between the shoulders are the letters D.R.P. stamped in blue. Size 3 in. shoes. The three faces are smiling, cross and sleeping. *Luton Museum.*

Paper dolls

Plates 226–9

In 1780, in England, we find the word 'doll' being used instead of the word 'baby'. This was in the *Diary of a Country Parson*, by Parson Woodforde, where he mentions that he gave a child 'a very pretty doll cut out of paper, with several dresses to it'.

It is said that the English invented these one-sided figures made of stout paper or cardboard about 1790. They had changeable garments and not only do they provide clues to the dresses of the periods but also show the underclothes, for the doll usually wore some kind of petticoat over which the dresses would be put. A figure with six changes of dresses would be sold for 3*s*.

During the 1840s, paper dolls were exported from Europe to the U.S.A. and many of these figures were based on portraits of actual people. Some made their own figures as a pastime, and children would cut them out. One poor mite even paid for her own education by making and selling her dolls (McClintock). Some of the earliest in the U.S.A. were designed by John Greene Chandler in 1838.

Godey's Lady's Book for 1859 showed cut-outs where the dolls' costumes were printed in colour. Paper dolls were popular at this time, selling at a penny a sheet to 50 cents for hand-coloured; best-sellers were the Jenny Lind paper dolls showing the Swedish singer with several changes of gowns.

French patents were taken out by Madame Poncet and Lechertier Barbe, but by far the majority of paper dolls were made in the U.S.A. and in England.

John Lord Hinde, in 1888, made canvas-lined paper clothes for his English pressed pulp dolls. Made in halves and then joined, they differed slightly from the usual cut-outs. Bruno Voigt, in 1891, made what he termed an '*Orakelpuppe*'. This was a paper doll where the striped skirt consisted of several cards on which were sentences foretelling the future, in fact what we would call a 'fortune-telling' doll, of which the Victorians were so fond.

Tucks, a well-known British firm specializing in paper novelties, took out two patents in 1893. One was for a baby's face with the arms and a bottle printed in colour on a cardboard sheet. This could be taken apart and arranged with a robe and a cap of tissue paper. The

PATENTS FOR PAPER DOLLS

Tuck, 1893. B. pat. 11367

Tuck, 1893. B. pat. 23003

Betzig, 1894. B. pat. 25154

Gibson, 1895. B. pat. 14496

Trufant, 1895. USA pat. 537791

Gibson, 1897
USA pat. 585092

Wilmer, 1897
USA pat. 575749

Harrison, 1903. B. pat. 19348

PATENTS FOR PAPER DOLLS

other was for dolls printed in colours on cardboard, and provided with a number of changeable dresses. Often these novelties were slightly raised by the paper being stamped in a shallow mould.

Betzig, a designer of Fifth Avenue, New York, made paper figures with detachable paper garments, showing the kind of thing dolls wore in 1894; even the word 'garment' dated them. Edward Gibson, a physician of Minnesota, patented many of his both in France and in England. Paper loops gummed on the reverse side were patented by McCalmont in 1895.

Many novelties came from the U.S.A. Margaret Wilmer used discs inserted through slots, and Gibson made what he termed a 'roundabout doll'. Here the cardboard was doubled around to form the skirt, a simple way of making a flat printed doll to stand up.

Cohn's was a crude cardboard doll in which the tongue came out through a hole, and Wollheim made embossed cardboard heads for dolls, the kind which were pressed in a mould while the cardboard was damp and so could be used for the faces of rag-dolls.

In 1905, Gilbert made what were known as 'pantins', cardboard dolls which bounced up and down by means of strings. These had been popular in France for over 150 years—in fact they were named after their place of origin in France—and similar dolls had already been used by grown-ups in the classic times of Greece and Rome.

Patents

Year	Name
1859	Godey's Lady's Book
1860	Barbe
	Poncet
1868	Barbe
1874	Hart
1888	Hinde
1891	Voigt
1893	Tuck
	Dalimore
1894	Betzig
1895	Jefferson
	Gibson
	Trufant
	McCalmont
1897	Wilmer
	Gibson
1898	Furch
	Süszenguth
1899	Cohn
	Wollheim
	Robb
1901	Verdier & Gutmacher
	Gruss & Brückner
1902	Harrison
1905	Gilbert
	Eisenmann
1910	Gibson

IV Marks

As far as is known, the first recorded names of doll makers are those of Ott in 1413, and H. Mess in 1465, both in Nürnberg. Their dolls were most probably made of wood. Barbara Beuchin of Bamberg in 1600 had permission to display the dolls she had made in the market place of Nürnberg in order to sell them, and by 1700 there were six master doll makers living in this town.

Some of the makers supplied bazaars and shops with their wares and these might stamp their name and address on the bodies of the dolls, sometimes on the front, sometimes on the back, but unfortunately the bazaars seem to have kept no record of their stall-holders. Many of the ink signatures have faded brown with age, but where a genuine signature appears then there is no doubt of the doll's authenticity.

Early porcelain and china heads for dolls were rarely marked, though many potteries had trademarks. Sometimes the heads have been marked under the shoulder-piece, but as the yoke is usually joined firmly to the soft body of the doll, it is a pity to take it apart in order to discover a signature which may not be there. The better method of dating a head of this type is by the mode in which the hair is dressed. Many of the soft bodies will have been made at home and therefore will have no distinguishing mark on them.

Some makers give directions at the time of registration as to where their marks may be found; for instance, the little sign by Emile Jumeau, which is to be found on the sole of the doll's shoes.

Dolls' trademarks are like their birth certificates, for these register a definite date for their creation. These marks from Britain, France, Germany, and the U.S.A. date from when they were first deposited up to the year 1910. There are one or two marks from Japan, China, and Russia, and one from Belgium, but these have been registered in one of the four countries mentioned. Those from France are known as *Marques de Fabrique*, and those from Germany as *Waarenzeichenblatt.*

Marks incised into the china or bisque appear intaglio, that is sunken. On the bisque heads it is usual to find that the maker's mark has been scratched in the soft clay before firing, just where the hair wig would begin, or along the back of the yoke. When done in the mould the initials or name will be in reverse and this accounts for the rather sketchy manner in which they have been drawn. Very rarely is the date added, the numbers referring to the size or style of model or both.

When a doll has been made in a mould, and the initials cut in reverse in that mould, then of course they will appear raised or in relief upon the surface of the doll. This happens frequently when the doll is of celluloid or of rubber.

Where the dolls are marked with initials only, usually they are the first letters of the maker's name, though often the last letter signifies the place in which the maker worked. For instance, the initials B.S.W. stand for Bruno Schmidt of Waltershausen, and those of M.W.N. for Martin Winterbauer of Nürnberg. Others mark the dolls with the first letters of their firm, such as K. & H. for Klen & Hahn, and S. & H. for Simon & Halbig, the latter firm being owned by Carl Halbig. Marks of firms also vary in their detail, but in the main they follow the design registered, even if only a portion of it.

Bisque head of crying baby doll, about 1910. 11 in. long, painted hair, composition body. *Bethnal Green Museum*. The drawing shows where many marks are found

Where manufacturers made the heads only in their factories, the marks found on them will apply to that part only, and a doll with a broken head has often been taken to a 'hospital' to have a new one fitted, or a new body added to an old head.

Apart from maker's names, initials, or monograms, dolls have been given trade names, and these are marked on the dolls. By consulting the list of doll names, it is possible to find the exact year in which they were registered, and some of these appear among the designs for box labels. In 1901, there is a Max Handwerck who labels his doll the 'Original Bébé Elite'. This is possibly why Heinrich Handwerck adds the word 'genuine' in 1902 to the label which he has used since 1898, especially as both the Handwercks lived in Waltershausen.

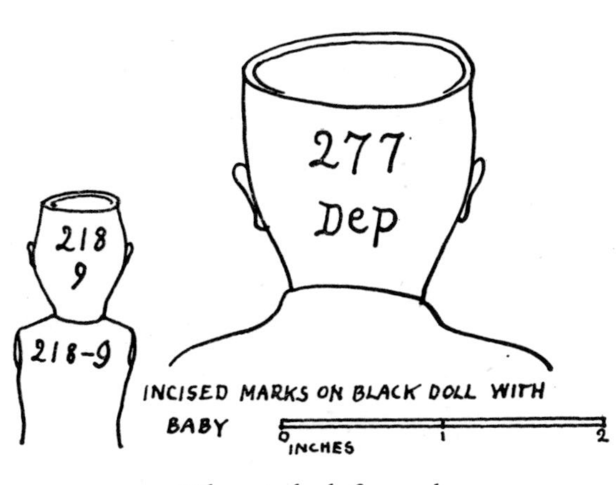

Where to look for marks

The three letters D E P are frequently incised on the back of a bisque doll's neck, and are found on both French and German dolls. In French, they stand for '*deposé*' a *Marque Deposée* being a registered trademark, and a *Marque de Fabrique* a trademark. In German, the word '*Deponiert*' or '*Deponirt*' comes from the German verb *Deponieren* which means to deposit, lay down or lodge the design at the time of registration.

The passing of the Trademarks Act in 1862 means that marks with the words Trademark, Schutzmarke, or Fabrikmarke are after this date, but they were rarely added before 1875. The first Schutzmarke added is found in 1875, Fabrikmarke 1876, and Trademark in 1881. The same applies to the letters D E P which are first found amongst the marks in 1884.

The words Brevet or Brevette simply mean patent, and other initials which may be found on dolls are those four cryptic letters S.G.D.G. When these letters appear it signifies that the patent or trademark has not yet received a guarantee from the French government. The actual initials stand for '*Sans Guarantie Du Gouvernement*', and apply to the country of France only.

Jumeau often uses these letters, and they are also incorporated in many signs, such as those of Watillaux, Morillot, etc., and the dolls of Mademoiselle Huret and Mademoiselle Rohmer. Many dolls are marked S.G.D.G. and have been erroneously considered to belong to a specific make.

Another set of four initials are S.F.B.J. These only occur on dolls made after 1905, the year when many firms formed the *Société Francaise de Fabrication de Bébés-Jouets*. On the sign the F is drawn in such a peculiar manner as to almost appear as a P, so that where a doll seems to be marked S.P.B.J. it is really one of those belonging to the S.F.B.J. group.

The country's name indicates a date after 1891, such as the single words Germany or France, etc. The words 'Made in Germany' seem to be of later date, and were used about the beginning of the twentieth century; for examples, see the Armand Marseille marks from the back yokes of the dolls with bisque heads (pp 230–1).

Other labels providing a clue to the date of a doll may sometimes be found stamped on the body. These may show when that particular firm gained some award, medal, or honour, usually at some exhibition, and naturally only appear after the date in which that firm received it. They may be stamped in one or more colours.

It is interesting to see the registered labels on the boxes in which the dolls were packed, for much information may be gleaned from a study of these. Sometimes the distributor is mentioned together with his address, sometimes whether the doll has a hair-wig or otherwise, and a space is left where details may be written such as the size, the colour of the eyes, etc., all showing that dolls with the same name may vary in their detail.

Some of the maker's names are incorporated in these box designs and often these are identical with those found on the actual dolls. Doll's trade-names are often found among these labels, and a few museums still have the actual boxes in which these dolls were sold.

„Aeolus"

1 Aeolus gesellschaft, 1910

Armand Marseille

2 Armand Marseille, Germany

3 Arnold Print Works, 1892

4 Martha Chase, 1896

5 Frank Darrow, 1866

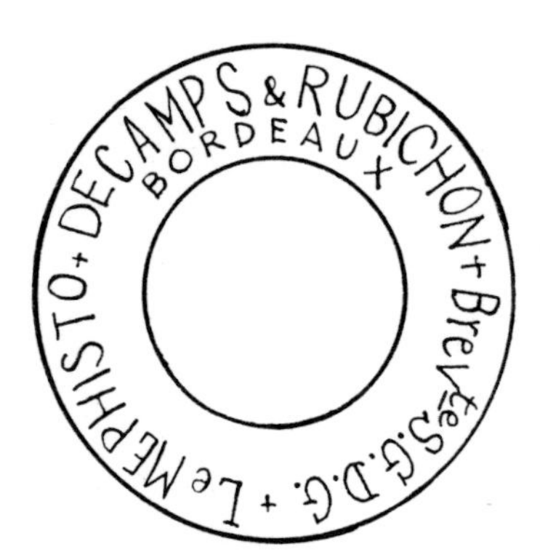

6 Décamps, 1908

Heinrich Handwerck

7 Heinrich Handwerck, 1898

8 Hannover Gummi Kamm, 1904

9 Jumeau, 1878

10 Jumeau, 1885

BÉBÉ JUMEAU

11 Jumeau, 1886

12 Jumeau, 1896

GeoM Kelsons

13 Kelson, 1904

14 Krausz, 1875

15 Krenkel, 1875

LES JEUX ET JOUETS FRANÇAIS

16 Soc. Levy, Perret, Simonin-Cuny, Alphonse and Alexandre Delhaye, 1909

17 Marsh, 1879

Montanari
Soho Bazaar.

18 Augusta Montanari

PFEIFER

19 Pfeifer, 1907

20 Salt, 1906

21 Simonne, 1863

Steiff

22 Steiff, 1907 German

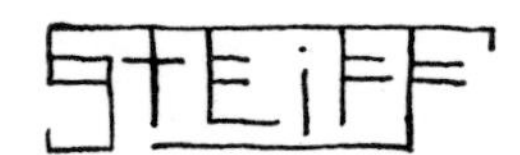

23 British, 1907

Steiffs
Prima Spielwaren.

24 German, 1908

25 USA, 1908

26 J. N. Steiner, 1889

27 Engelfred, 1889

28 Deropkine, 1886

29 Chambre, etc., 1886

30 Chambre, etc., 1897

31 Goblet, 1891

32 Giroux, 1888

33 Hannebelle, 1909

34 Landsberger, 1908

35 Armand Marseille

36 Potter called Armand Marseille, 1865

37 Auguste Martin, 1896

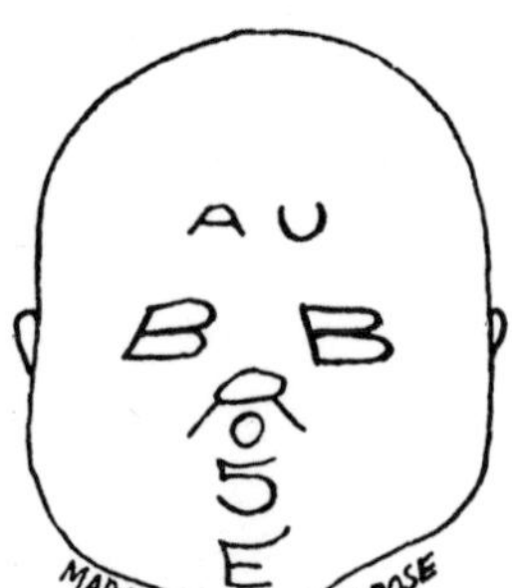

38 Au Bébé Rose, 1910

39 U. Wislizenus, 1910

40 Brentano, 1889

B B
MARQUE DÉPOSÉE

41 Boisson Berrod, 1895

42 Seligmann, 1892

43 Benoit fils et Romain, 1885

44 B. Schmidt, 1904

45 Barth and Wagner, 1877

46 Carl Adam, 1894

47 Chambon et Baye, 1889

48 Continental Caoutchouc, 1893

49 Merlin, 1897

C & S
PARIS

50 Sevette, 1884

C.R.

51 Rossignol, 1890

52 Dolffs & Helse, 1893

53 Dressel Kister, Passau, 1840

PARIS
DÉPOSÉ

54 Danel & Cie, 1889

D.P.

55 Hamburger, 1895

D ET P

56 Dannin et Paulet, 1908

Wittelsbach
CHINA
DeS
BAVARIA

57 Drechsel and Stroebel, 1900

EG

58 Eugène Gibon, 1895

59 Heubach, 1887

F.C.R

60 Rivaillon, 1900

61 Fischer Naumann, 1876

62 Falck, 1885

63 Schmit, 1902

64 Bing, 1906

G.C.&Co
N.

65 Carette, 1909

66 Gebrüder Fleischmann, 1903

G.F.

67 Gebaulet, 1910

68 Grieszmeyer, 1902

69 Lines, 1910

70 Ott, 1883

Puppe der Zukunft

71 Süszenguth, 1904

GS

72 Gans & Seyfarth, 1910

73 Alexandre, 1886

H&C
55

74 Hinrichs, 1890

75 H. Handwerck, 1891

76 H. Handwerck, 1891

77 H. Handwerck, 1895

78 Jewitt, 1870

79 Heinrichmeier & Wünsch, 1892

80 Ismenau Porcelain, 1786

81 Berner, 1888

82 Bishoff, 1899

83 Distler, 1910

J.D.K

84 Kestner, 1896

85 Kestner, 1896

86 Erdmann, 1891

87 Union des Fabs. de Jouets, 1884

88 Pflaumer, 1890

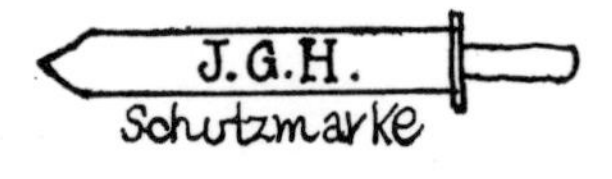

89 Heinrich, 1896

90 Haffner's Nachf, 1899

91 Jeanson, 1891

92 Joanny, 1907

93 Delhay, 1896

94 Du Val, 1890

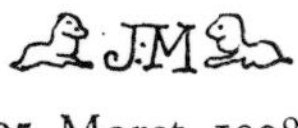

95 Moret, 1908

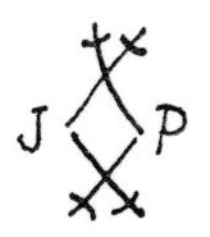

96 Petit, 1790

97 Petit, mark in blue, 1843

98 Le Jouet de Paris, 1902

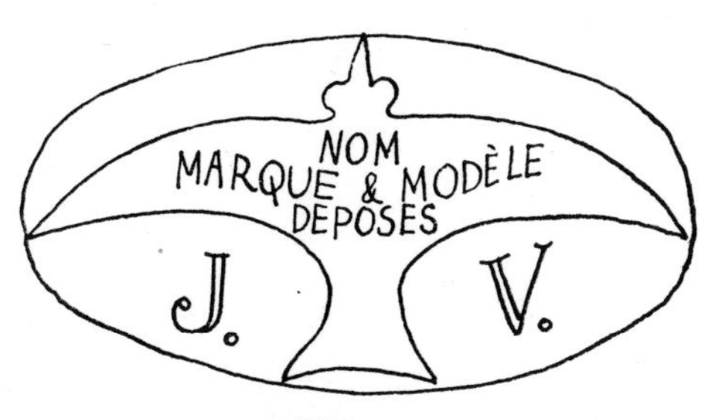

99 Viñes, 1909

100 Klen & Hahn, 1909

101 Bub, 1899

102 Bub, 1899

103 Kleinig & Blasberg, 1899

104 Klen & Hahn, 1902

105 Mohr, 1900

106 Meissen, 1720–30

107 Kämmer & Reinhardt, 1896

108 1903

109 1903

110 1904

111 1906

Kämmer & Reinhardt

112 Muller, 1907

113 Guhrauer, 1893

114 Limbach, 1772

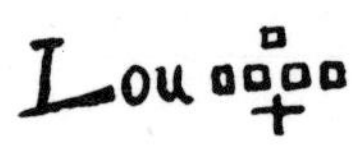

115 Limbach, 1855

116 Schmetzer, 1876

117 Legros, 1890

L. W. P.

118 Wessel, 1755

119 F. E. Marseille, 1888

120 Melchers, 1888

121 Dannhorn, 1895

122 Muller, 1907

123 Mermod Frères, 1887

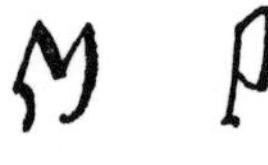

124 Migault et Papin, 1908

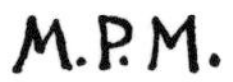

125 E. Muller, 1904

126 Leredde et Sonnet, 1888

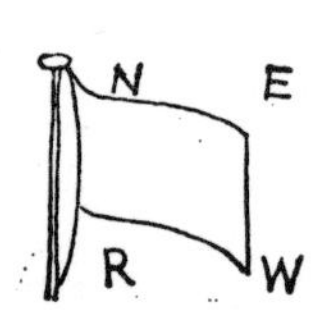

127 New Eccles Rubber Works, 1905

128 Denancy, 1891

P. F.

129 Fourot, 1909

130 Péan Frères, 1887

131 F. Richter, 1879

132 Ravenstein, 1760

133 Ravenstein, 1855

134 Ravenstein, 1855

RT & Co

135 Tschuschner, 1902

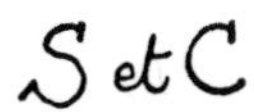

136 Saunier et Caux, 1889

137 Slevogt, 1889

138 Schneider fils, 1888

139 S.F.B.J. 1905

140 S.F.B.J. 1910

141 Godfrey, 1880

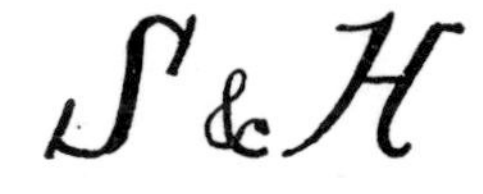

142 Simon & Halbig, 1905

143 Léve, 1909

144 Léve, 1909

145 Sauleau & Rouaud, 1910

146 Lanagnère, 1887

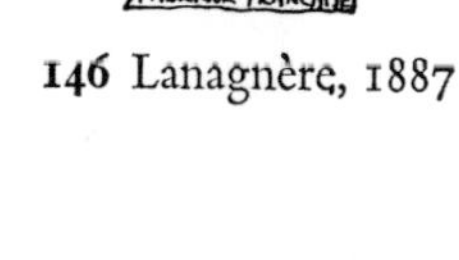

147 Rousseaux, 1891

148 Globe Supply Co., 1902

149 Dürfield, 1877

150 Reithoffer, 1897

151 Maillard, 1897

152 Warmuth, 1893

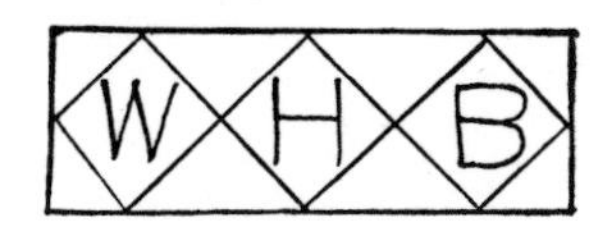

153 Baker, 1902

154 Whyte & Ridsdale, 1876

W. X. PARIS

155 Watilliaux, 1896

MAKERS' MONOGRAMS

156 Aubert & Papin, 1907

157 Siemroth, 1888

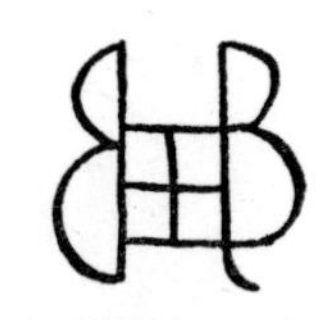
158 Harratsz, 1890

159 Hacker, 1875

160 Catterfelder, 1910

161 Dressel, 1875

162 Dressel, 1875

163 Rémignard, 1888

164 Pabst, 1900

165 Pabst, 1900

166 Sauer, 1908

167 Harratsz, 1894

168 Bretsch, 1878

169 Bretsch, 1878

170 Hende, 1910

171 Hager, 1875

172 Hager, 1876

173 Dorft, 1879

174 Dorft, 1879

175 Dorft

176 Dorft, 1907

177 Soc. de Jeux et Jouets Française, 1904

178 Dressel Kister, 1840

179 Neumann, 1887

180 E. & A. Muller, 1890

181 Muller, 1907

182 Fourot, 1909

183 Franken, 1893

184 Huneaus, 1901

185 Lehmann, 1902

186 Degen, 1908

187 Radde, 1876

188 Radde, 1876

189 Rogier, 1908

190 Pätzig, 1877

191 Schelhorn, 1909

192 E. Muller, 1890

193 Delcroix, 1887

PARIS

194 Delcroix, 1887

195 Winterbauer, 1910

196 Winterbauer, 1910

197 Winterbauer, 1910

198 Zierow, 1910

DECORATIVE ONLY

ANCHORS

199 F. Richter, 1879

200 Vincent Fils, 1888

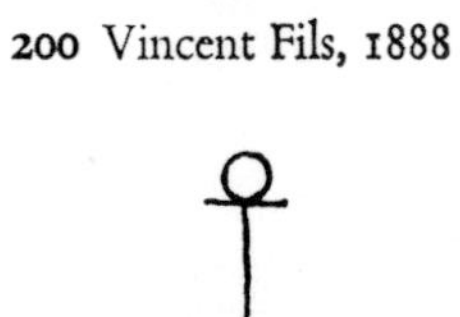

201 Wessel, 1755

ANIMALS, BIRDS AND INSECTS

202 Batt, 1883

203 Harmus, 1909

204 Jumeau, 1891

205 S.F.B.J., 1906

206 Kirn, 1888

207 Hannoversche Caoutchouc, 1893

208 Meier, 1892

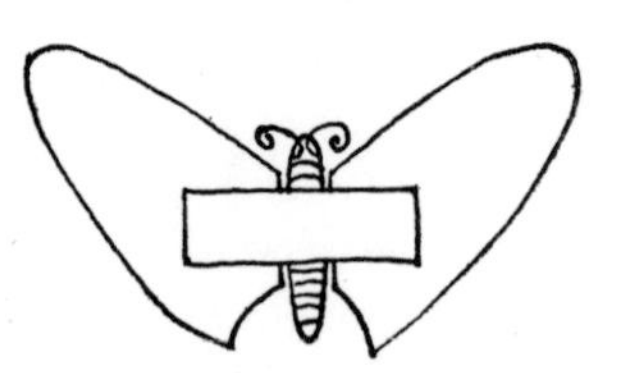

209 Eisenmann, 1908

210 Steiff, 1907

211 Steiff, 1908

212 Deans, 1909

213 Wedeses, 1892

214 Meyerstein, 1876

215 Bryan, 1877

216 Otte, 1891

217 Morillot, 1889

218 Weisz, 1895

219 Blank, 1891

220 Simon, 1875

221 Meissen, 1712–19

222 Hausmeister, 1909

223 F. Richter, 1886

224 Pencke & Rascher, 1892

225 Bensinger, 1895

226 Rheinische Gummi, 1899

CROWNS

227 Jacob, 1893

228 Kestner, 1896

229 A. Muller, 1896

230 Simms, 1887

231 Wheeler, 1879

FLOWERS AND LEAVES

232 Wedeses, 1892

233 Cayatte, 1909

234 Grosbrütenbach, 1855

235 Grosbrutenbach, 1770

236 Grosbrütenbach, 1770

237 Grosbrütenbach, 1770

238 Ismenau, 1786

239 Lonquet, 1908

240 Rösing, 1891

241 Fleischmann & Craemer, 1881

242 Clausthal, 1910

243 Bauersachs, 1895

GEOMETRIC SHAPES

244 F. Richter, 1907

245 Mohrhardt, 1897

246 Fehr, 1891

247 India rubber, gutta percha, etc., 1908

248 B. Schmidt, 1908

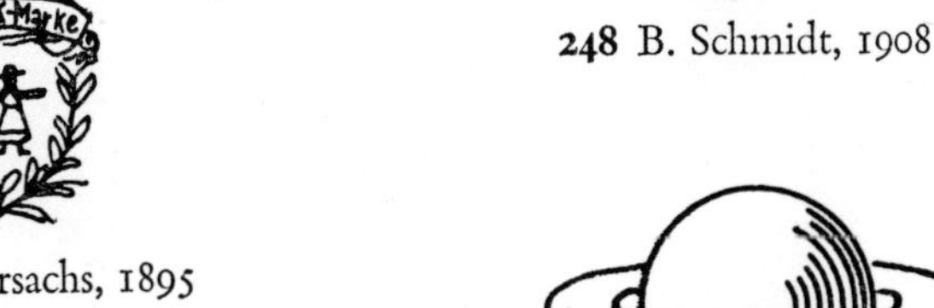

249 F. Richter, 1902

250 Taumeyer, 1890

251 Achenbach, 1891

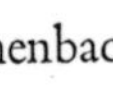

252 Achenbach, 1891

253 Achenbach, 1891

A1

254 Achenbach, 1891

255 Achenbach, 1891

256 Offene Handels, etc., 1908

257 Cayatte, 1909

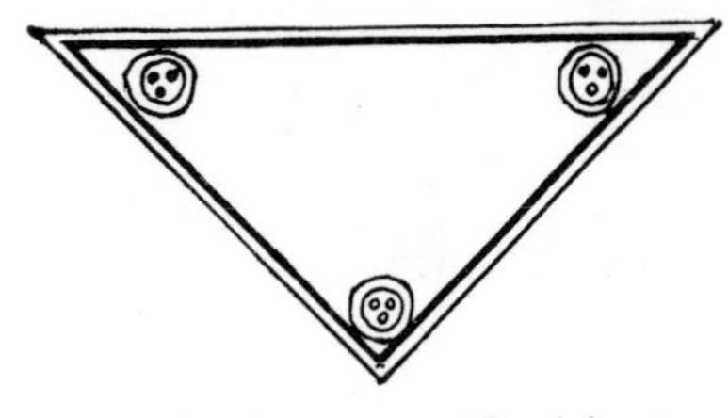

258 Fleischmann & Bloedel, 1895

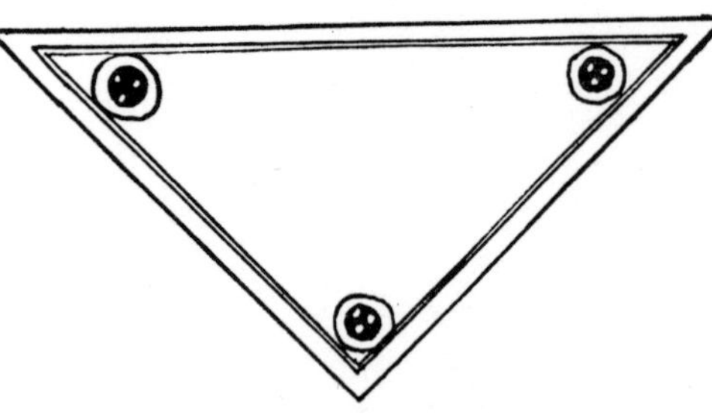

259 Fleischmann & Bloedel, 1903

260 Dressel Kister, 1840

HUMANS AND DOLLS

261 Dürfeld, 1888

262 F. Schilling, 1893

263 F. Schilling, 1895

264 L. Engel, 1898

265 Nörregaard, 1885

266 Scheller, 1877

267 Scheller, 1888

268 Hachmeister, 1908

269 Geyer, 1885

270 Haag, 1886

271 Sommer, 1886

272 Kestner, 1889

273 Tuchmann, 1891

274 Geyer, 1900

275 Fleischmann & Bloedel, 1909

276 B. Richter, 1902

277 Eisenmann, 1895

278 Bierer, 1908

279 Grimm, 1891

280 Perret, 1892

281 Bernard, 1894

282 Gobillot et Samson, 1891

283 Haüser, 1887

284 Müller & Froebel, 1884

285 Pfeiffer, 1904

SHIELDS

286 Warncke, 1887

287 Rauly, 1891

288 Zeuch & Lausmann, 1896

289 Eck, 1876

290 Eck, 1877

291 Krausz, 1875

292 Harratz, 1890

293 Harratz, 1894

294 Siemroth, 1888

295 Stein, 1888

296 Jumeau, 1888

SWORDS

297 1720–1730

298 1720–1730

299 1730–1733

300 1733–1763

301 1763–1774

302 1744–1814

303 1814–1875
Meissen Ware

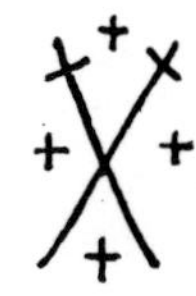

304 Tournay pottery 1750–1800
(included to compare with the above)

MISCELLANEOUS

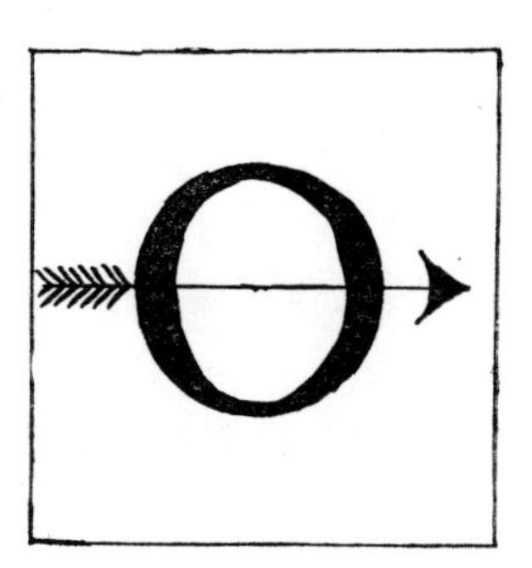

305 D. Peck, 1902

306 Rudd, 1905

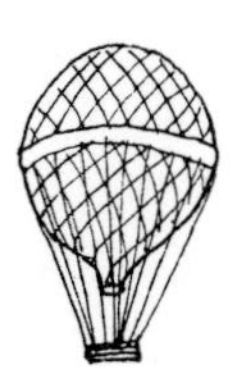

307 Grimm, 1889

308 Dressel Kister, 1840

309 Barker, 1906

310 Escher, 1881

311 Escher, 1896

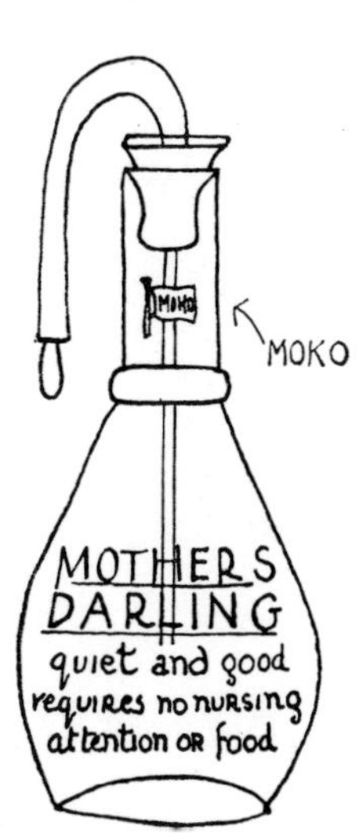

312 Kohnstam, 1910
British Mark

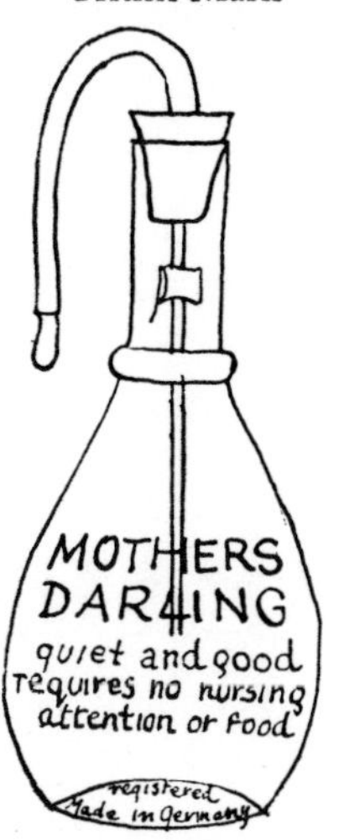

313 Kohnstam, 1910
German Mark

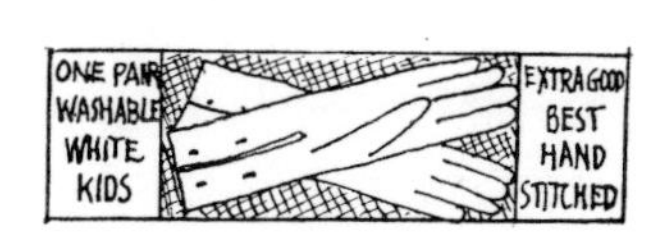

314 Christie, 1907

315 Soehlin & Bailliart, 1902

316 Dressel, 1895

317 Horne, 1890

318 Schultze, 1886

319 Clarke, 1870

320 Bull, 1888

321 Lipatoff, 1908

AABA

322 James, 1907

ADAMALIA

323 McAdam, 1909

A l'enfant sage

324 Fleischmann & Bloedel, 1897

ALMA

325 Borgfeldt, 1901

AMERICAN BEAUTY

326 Strobel & Wilkin, 1895

American Queen

327 Morgenroth, 1905

AMOUR-BÉBÉ

328 Guillet, 1896

Angelo

329 Gibbons, 1907

330 Richter, 1902

BABY

331 Philippart, 1907

332 Bawo & Dotter, 1910

333 Borgfeldt, 1908

BABYBUMPS

334 Horsman, 1910

335 Strawbridge & Clothier, 1906

BABY RUTH

336 Craemer & Heron, 1893

337 Abraham & Strauss, 1906

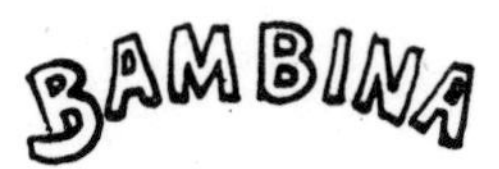

338 Dressel, 1909

BÉBÉ

339 Philippart, 1907

BÉBÉ ARTICULÉ

340 Winkler, 1899

BÉBÉ-BAISER

341 Girard, 1894

342 Girard, 1891

343 Girard, 1891

BÉBÉ COSMOPOLITE

344 H. Handwerck, 1895

BÉBÉ DE RÉCLAME

345 H. Handwerck, 1898

BÉBÉ ELITE

346 Max Handwerck, 1901

BÉBÉ EXCELSIOR.V.G.

347 Verdier, 1899

Bébé Favori

348 Cosman Frères, 1891

BÉBÉ FAVORI

349 Catusse, 1893

BÉBÉ FRANÇAIS

350 Danel, 1891

BÉBÉ FRANÇAIS

351 Jumeau, 1896

BÉBÉ JUMEAU

352 Jumeau, 1896

BÉBÉ HABILLÉ

353 Geyer, 1900

'Bébé l'Avenir'

354 Gutmann, 1907

Bébé le Favori

355 Cosman Frères, 1891

BÉBÉ LÉGER

356 Chalory, 1893

BÉBÉ LE GLORIEUX

357 Bonnal, 1904

BÉBÉ LE PARISIEN

358 J. Steiner, 1890

BÉBÉ LE PETIT FRANÇAIS

359 Bonnal, 1904

BÉBÉ LE RADIEUX

360 Bonnal, 1904

BÉBÉ LE SELECT.V.G.

361 Verdier, 1899

BÉBÉ LE SPÉCIAL

362 Bonnal, 1904

BÉBÉ L'UNIQUE

363 Bonnal, 1904

Bébé Loulou

364 Wannez & Rayer, 1891

BÉBÉ MASCOTTE

365 May Bros., 1890

BÉBÉ MÉTROPOLE.V.G.

366 Verdier, 1899

BÉBÉ MODÈLE

367 Rivaillon, 1900

"BÉBÉ MODÈLE"

368 Mettais, 1901

BÉBÉ MONDAIN

369 Bernheim & Kahn, 1906

BÉBÉ MODERNE

370 Schnitz, 1893

BÉBÉ MODERNE

371 S.F.B.J., 1903

BÉBÉ MONOPOLE.V.G.

372 Verdier, 1899

BÉBÉ MOUJIK

373 Bèrner, 1888

BÉBÉ NOUVEAU ARTICULÉ

374 Falck, 1885

BÉBÉ OLGA

375 Ballu, 1896

BÉBÉ ORACLE

376 Cayatte, 1909

BÉBÉ PARLANT

377 J. N. Steiner, 1862

BÉBÉ PARFAIT

378 S.F.B.J., 1904

"BÉBÉ PARISIANA"

379 S.F.B.J., 1902

Bébé Parisiana

380 Comptor General, 1905

BÉBÉ PETIT PAS

381 Girard, 1891
& Soc. Int. Inv. Mod.

BÉBÉ PHÉNIX

382 La Fosse, 1895

BÉBÉ PREMIER PAS

383 J. N. Steiner, 1890

BÉBÉ PRODIGE

384 Jumeau, 1896

BÉBÉ PROPHÈTE

385 Cayatte, 1909

BÉBÉ-SOLEIL

386 Guépratte, 1891

BÉBÉ TENTATION

387 Thalheimer, 1900

" BÉBÉ TRIOMPHE "

388 Fleischmann & Bloedel, 1898

„BI-BA-BO"

389 Jeidel, 1908

„Billydoll"

390 Steiff, 1909

BLUE BELL

391 Dawson, 1903

BOBBY BOBBYKINS

392 Hays, 1909

Bounceola

393 Süszkind, 1905

394 Hannoversche Gummi-Kamm, 1899

Bnporit

395 Baer, 1910

BUSTER BROWN

396 Bazley, 1904

BUSTER BROWN

397 Hamley, 1904

BYE BYE KIDS

398 Bach Bros., 1908

"CABINET PICKLE."

399 Coube, 1909

CELEBRATE

400 Borgfeldt, 1896

Cellulobrin,

401 B. Schmidt, 1910

CHANTECLER

402 Gamage, 1910

CHANTECLER

403 Aetna, 1910

Charakterpuppe

404 Kämmer & Reinhardt, 1910

CHERUB

405 Isaacs, 1887

'CHILD'S BENEFACTOR'

406 Crandall, 1878

Cinderella-

407 Wolf, 1892

Cinderella Baby

408 C. Bergmann, 1897

COQUET BÉBÉ

409 Gerbaulet, 1910

410 E. Muller, 1890

CUPID

411 Kohnstam, 1909

DAISY

412 E. U. Steiner, 1903

Dewey Doll

413 Süszenguth, 1900

DIANA

414 Heller, 1902 USA

Diana

415 Heller, 1903 Germany

Die Kokette:

416 Kämmer & Reinhardt, 1907

DOLLIE DIMPLE

417 Hinde, 1888

DOLLIT

418 Ivimey, 1906

Dolly Dimple

419 Hamburger, 1907

DOLLY DOLLYKINS

420 Hays, 1909

Dornröschen

421 Krampe, 1902

DRACHEN KAMM

422 New York Hamburger Gummi Waaren, 1899

DRAKE

423 Shepherd, 1909

EDEN-BÉBÉ

424 Fleischmann & Bloedel, 1890

Eden-Bébé

425 Fleischmann & Bloedel, 1896

EDEN-BÉBÉ

426 S.F.B.J., 1905

Eden-Puppe

427 Fleischmann & Bloedel, 1891

Eissen

428 Izon, 1906

Elsie

429 Borgfeldt, 1897

ETOILE BÉBÉ

430 Bernheim & Kahn, 1904

ENTENTE
CORDIALE

431 Kratz-Boussac, 1907

EUCHARY

432 Hughes, 1902

EUREKA

433 Kratz-Boussac, 1910

"Fairyland"

434 Foote, 1909

FIFTH AVE DOLLS

435 Dressel, 1903

Florodora

436 Borgfeldt, 1901

437 Borgfeldt, 1903

FLUFF-FLUFF

438 Cook & Solomon, 1902

FLUFFY RUFFLES

439 Schelhorn, 1908

GENTIL BÈBÉ

440 Naneau, 1905

GERMAN FAIR

441 Waite, 1856

Gip

442 Thurnauer, 1906

Globe Baby

443 Hartmann, 1899

GNOME

444 Moteurs Gnome, 1910

GOBLIN GOBBLERS.

445 Sherwood, 1910

grand Bazar National

446 Stein, 1888

GREEDY CHUGGY.

447 Sherwood, 1910

Gummoid

448 Nockler & Tittel, 1901

449 Deuerlein, 1908

Herz

450 F. Schmidt, 1910

"HUMPTYDUMPTY"

451 W. Peck, 1906

HUNGRY GILES.

452 Sherwood, 1910

IDÉAL BÉBÉ

453 Bortoli Frères, 1895

IMPERIAL

454 Hamburger, 1898

Jmperial H&Co.

455 Hamburger, 1901

International Doll

456 Borgfeldt, 1898

JEANNETTE
BrévetteSGDG
W.X. PARIS

457 Wattilliaux, 1891

JOLI BÉBÉ

458 Damerial, 1910

JUBILEE

459 Jenkins, 1875

„Jutta“

460 Dressel, 1907

KIDLYNE

461 Borgfeldt, 1907

Killiblues

462 Baker & Bennet, 1909

KISMI

463 Stallarde, 1905

464 Hughes, 1905

465 Snequireff, 1906

KRACKJACK

466 Hughes, 1910

LA CHARLOTTE

467 Soulard, 1896

LA FAVORITE-SURPRISE

468 Legros, 1890

L'AIGLON

469 Kratz-Boussac, 1906

"LA PARISIENNE"

470 S. Martin, 1900

LA PARISIENNE

471 Kratz-Boussac, 1910

LA POUPÉE QUI DESSINE
INVENTION DU BERGER NAVARRAIS

472 Gill'o, 1898

LA POUPÉE VOLANTE

473 Couturier, 1891

LE BEAU D'ABLE

474 Nicholas, 1907

LE GRACIEUX

475 Gratieux fils, 1907

LE PARISIEN

476 A. Lafosse, 1892

LE PETIT CHERUBIN

477 Rémignard, 1888

LE PETIT FRANÇAIS

478 F. E. Marseille, 1888

LE PETIT PARISIEN
BÉBÉ

479 J. N. Steiner, 1889

Le P'stt intrigant.

480 C. Rossignol, 1890

LE RÊVE DE BÉBÉ

481 Migault, 1899

LE SÉDUISANT

482 S.F.B.J., 1903

Les Nouveaux Jeux
DU
XXeme Siecle

483 Rambour, 1899

L'HEUREUX

484 L'Heureux, 1905

L'Idéal

485 Fouillot, 1906

L'IDÉAL

486 Abrahams, 1909

Liliput

487 E. U. Steiner, USA 1894

Lilliput

488 Pabst, 1899

LILLIPUT

489 Thurnauer, 1899

Liliput
REGISTERED GERMANY

490 Geyer, 1902

LINON

491 Landshut, 1895

"L'INTRÉPIDE BÉBÉ„

492 Roullet et Decamps, 1893

Lithoid

493 Nockler & Tittel, 1901

LITTLE PET

494 Eisenmann, 1908

Little Snookums
The Newlywed's Baby

495 Schelhorn, 1910

Little Sweetheart.

496 M. Illfelder, 1902

LITTLE SWEETHEART"

497 B. Illfelder, 1905

„Little Tich"

498 Zimmer, 1908

499 E. U. Steiner, 1894

500 Kämmer & Reinhardt, 1902

501 Hamburger, 1901

Mausi

502 Carl, 1908

„Mein Goldherz"

503 B. Schmidt, 1904

Mein Liebling

504 Kämmer & Reinhardt, 1902

MENAGE PARISIEN

505 Monteux, 1891

Merry Widow

506 M. Illfelder, 1909

MICHU

507 Fleischmann & Bloedel, 1909

508 Bushow & Beck, 1900

MINERVA

509 Vischer, 1894

510 Bushow & Beck, 1905

MIRCO

511 Midland Rubber Co., 1903

MOKO

512 Kohnstam, 1900

MY DARLING

513 Kämmer & Reinhardt, 1904

My·Playmate

514 Borgfeldt, 1903

Noris

515 Debes, 1905

OHO

516 Lehmann, 1909

OLD ENGLAND

517 J. Reid, 1887

OLD GLORY

518 U. Wislizenus, 1902

OLD GLORY

519 Hamburger, 1900

ONDINE

520 E. Martin, 1878

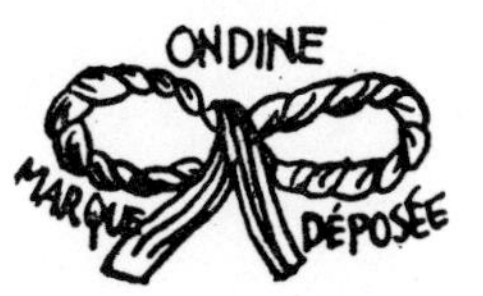

521 Bertran, 1878

522 Kennard, 1892

PALADIN BABY"

523 Hartmann, 1904

PALAIS ROYAL

524 Lisner, 1890

525 McKensie & McBurney, 1876

PARIS
BÉBÉ

526 Danel, 1889

PERSÉPHONE

527 Lindauer, 1910

528 Samstag, 1908

'PETIT-BÉBÉ'

529 Leconte, 1888

PETIT PIANISTE
AUTOMATIQUE

530 Bousquet, 1901

PLAYTIME

531 Rouech-Bowden, 1907

Polait

532 Polock, 1902

POUPÉE FRANÇAISE

533 Toulouse, 1894

POUPÉE MERVEILLEUSE

534 Mettais, 1900

POUPÉE NANA

535 Gregori-Olivier, 1879

Poupée Parisiana

536 Comptoir Général, 1905

537 Gosse, 1908

POUPÉE SANVER'S

538 Vercasson, 1903

POUPÉE-SATIN

539 Marignac, 1894

Poupon Parisiana

540 Comptoir Général, 1905

Princess

541 Borgfeldt, 1897

542 Strawbridge & Clothier, 1906

„PROWODNIK"

543 Russian French etc., 1910

QUEEN

544 A. Wislizenus, 1910

Queen Louise

545 L. Wolf, 1910

Rex

546 R. Schilling, 1901

Rosebud

547 M. Illfelder, 1903

ROYAL

548 Strobel & Wilkin, 1902

Salta

549 Wasmuth, 1900

SANTA

550 Hamburger, 1900

Santa

551 Hamburger, 1901

552 Klen & Hahn, 1910

„Spielwarenhaus Puppenkönig"

553 Birnich, 1907

Splendide Bébé

554 Cosman Frères, 1893

Struwelpeter

555 Anhalt, 1905

Sunny Jim

556 Kohnstam, 1904

'TALLY-HO'

557 Dare, 1878

TAUSENDSCHÖNCHEN

558 F. Schmidt, 1910

The Flirt

559 Kämmer & Reinhardt, 1908

560 Strawbridge & Clothier, 1906

561 Heaton, 1910

THE WISP

562 Upton, 1908

TINY TOTS

563 Roberts, 1908

Tootsie

564 Borgfeldt, 1906

TOYS

565 A. Bergmann, 1872

Tuff-A-Nuff

566 Schuldt, 1910

TWINWIN

567 Mountain, 1907

Uwanta

568 Borgfeldt, Berlin, 1899

UWANTA

569 Borgfeldt, New York, 1899

VELVOKIN

570 Chatanooga, 1910

VIOLA

571 Hamburger, 1903

VOX POPULI

572 Phillips, 1909

WALKURE

573 Klen & Hahn, 1902

WALLYPUG

574 Chapman, 1906

WEKO

575 Weiss, 1909

WOOLLYBAMBOLLY

576 British Ever Ready, 1910

"Y-Do-I."

577 Ackermann, 1905

YUM-YUMS.

578 Geen, 1903

579 C. Bergmann, 1910

580 1895

581 1902

582 1898, 3 Labels by Heinrich Handwerck

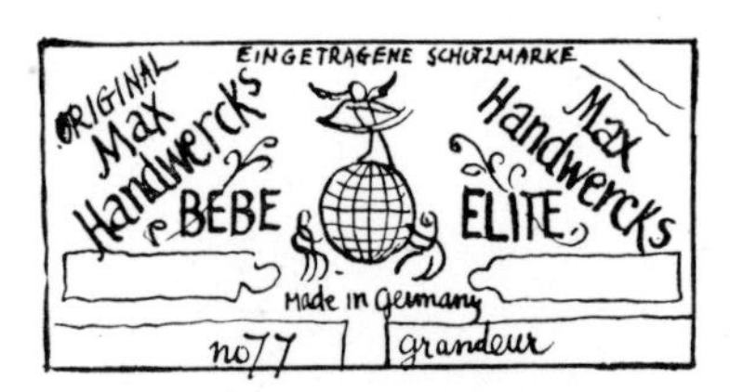

583 Max Handwerck, 1901

584 Kaulitz, 1909

585 Schnitz, 1893

586 Jumeau, 1896

STEINERS

MAJESTIC

DOLL

587 E. U. Steiner, 1902

UNION DES FABRICANTS

de Jouets, Articles de Paris et Objets Artistiques

MUSÉE COMMERCIAL

588 Antonin Debrieu, 1893

UNION FRANÇAISE

DES

Fabricants de Jouets et d'Articles de Paris

589 Guillet, 1894

BOX LABELS WITH MAKERS' NAMES

590 Landsberger, 1908

591 U. Wislizenus, 1910

592 Eugène Gibon, 1895

593 Rivaillon, 1900

594 Gerbaulet, 1910

595 Gans & Seyfarth, 1910

596 1902

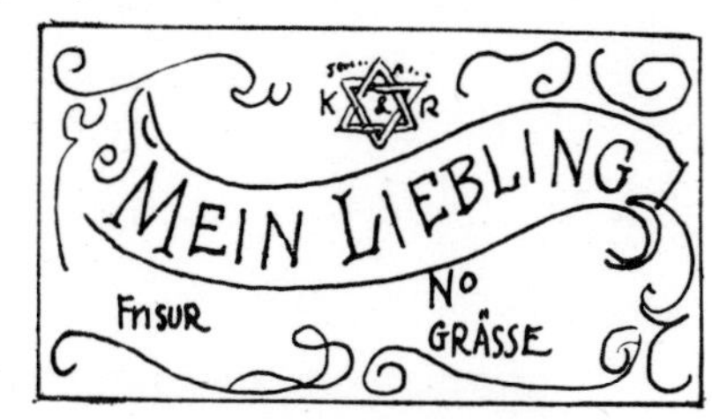

597 1902

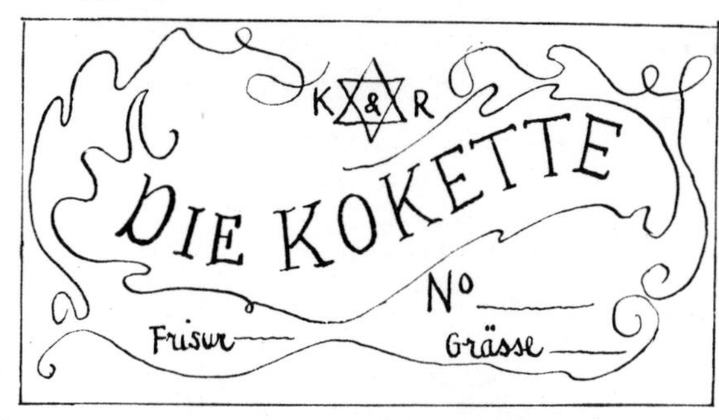

598 1907

599 1910, 4 Labels by Kämmer & Reinhardt

600 Sauleau & Rouaud, 1910

BOX LABELS WITH MAKERS' INITIALS

601 Rèmignard, 1888

602 F. E. Marseille, 1888

603 Pätzig, 1877

604 Zierow, 1910

601–4 LABELS WITH MAKERS' MONOGRAMS

605 Pelletier, 1892

606 F. Schilling, 1903

607 H. Steiner, 1902

605–7 DECORATIVE ONLY

608 Winkler, 1899

612 Geyer, 1900

609 Dressel, 1909

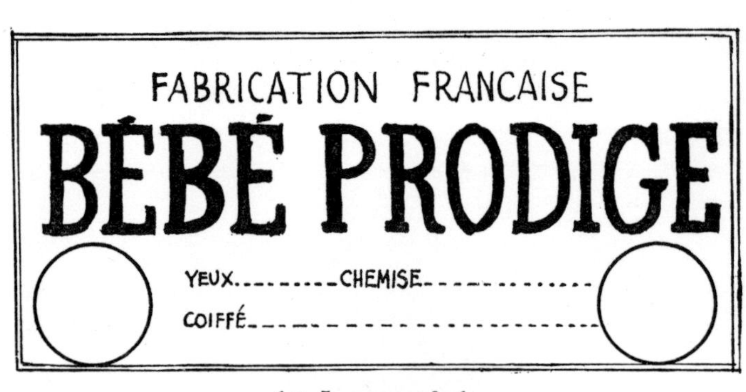

613 Jumeau, 1896

610 Handwerck, 1898

614 J. M. Guèpratte, 1891

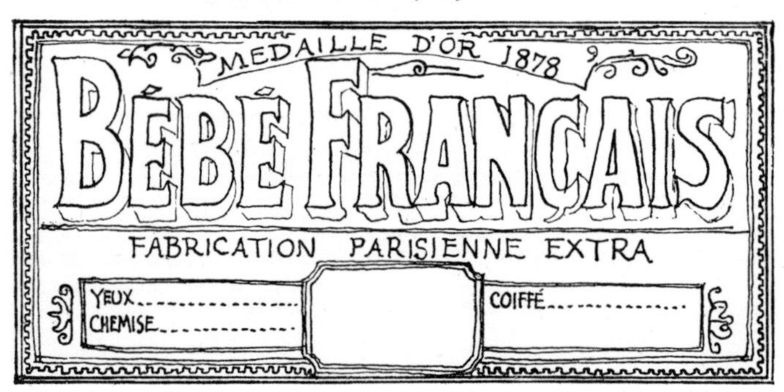

611 Jumeau, 1896

LABELS WITH DOLLS' TRADE NAMES

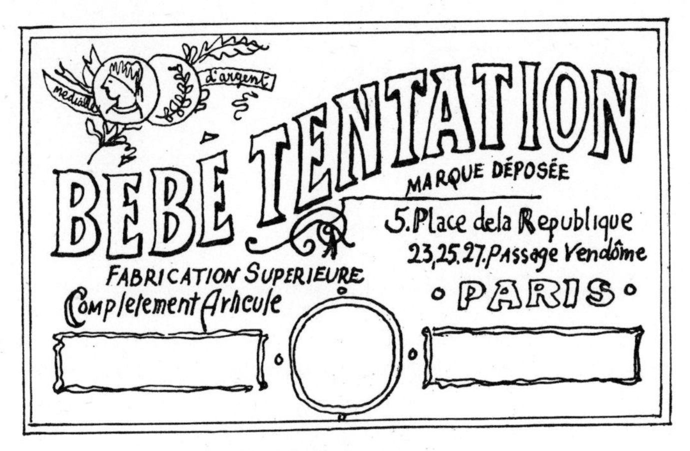

615 Thalheimer, 1900

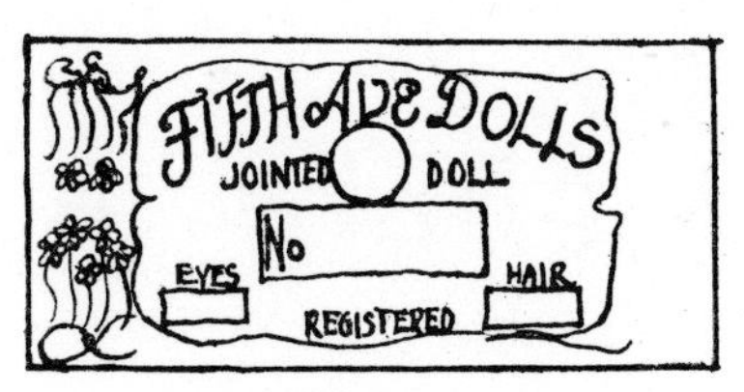

620 Dressel, 1903

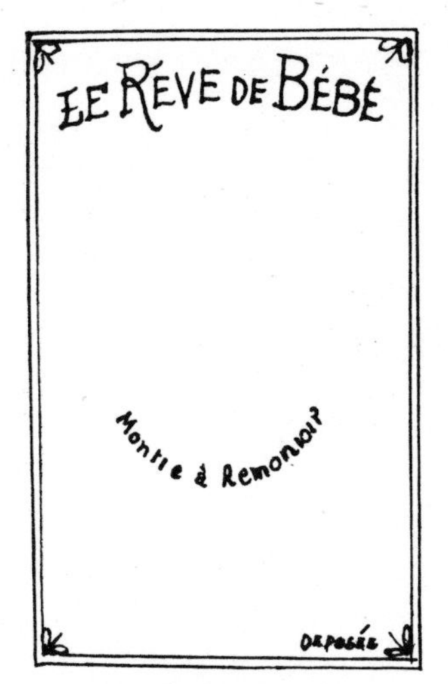

621 Mignault, 1899

616 Bach Bros., 1908

622 Landshut, 1895

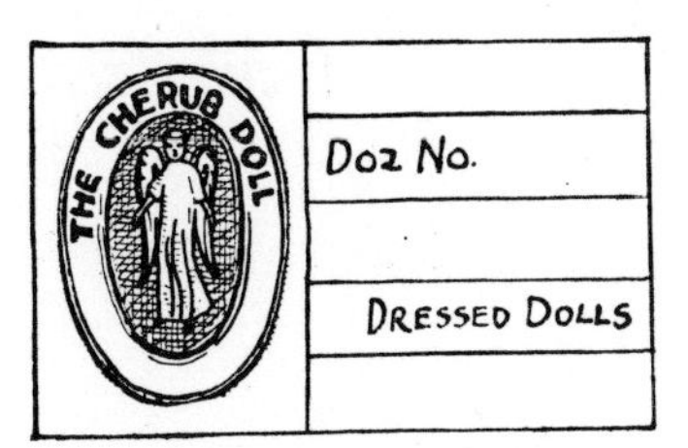

617 A. J. Isaacs, 1887

623 U. Wislizenus, 1902

618 C. Bergmann, 1897

PETER
PAN
PLAYTOYS

624 Max Fr. Schelhorn, 1907

619 Fleischmann & Bloedel, 1891

625 Borgfeldt, 1898

LABELS WITH DOLLS' TRADE NAMES

VARIATIONS OF MARKS

1894
AMODEP
Doll 15 in. long

48-94
AM 4 DEP

A.M.
1895

20
A.M. DEP.

600
A.M. DEP.

AM 1½ DEP
made in
Germany
Doll 15¾ in. long. c. 1895, closing eyes
Finland

1894
AM 1½ DEP
made in
Germany
Doll 15¾ in. long. Brown closing eyes
Finland

3200
AM5DEP
Doll 26 in. long. c. 1898

X made in Germany
3/0X
Doll 12 in. long. c. 1898
Photo no. 307 London Museum

370.
A.M.5/0XDEP
made in Germany
Doll 17 in. long. Photo no. 312
Mrs. Heather Fox

No. 3500
AM 1 DEP
Doll Mrs. Goodchild

370
AM 1 DEP
Doll 21 in. long

3200
AMODEP

Germany
Kiddiejoy
A O M
Doll Photo no. 308, 309, 310
Miss Christine Smith

DOLLS WITH KID BODIES

3200
AM 6 DEP
made in Germany
Doll 21½ in. long. c. 1895. Closing eyes, stuffed body
Finland

3200
AMO DEP
made in Germany
Doll 15¾ in. long. Closing eyes
Owner born in 1894 Finland

3200
AMODEP
made in Germany
Doll
Photo no. 318 Miss Moriarty

3700
A.M.3/0DEP
made in Germany
Miss Faith Eaton

370.
A.M.3.DEP.
made in Germany.
Doll 20 in. long. c. 1910. Stuffed cotton

370
AM 5/0 DEP
Armand Marseille
Doll 15 in. long. Body partly kid, partly cotton Mrs. Heather Fox

370.
A.M.4/0X.DEP.
made in Germany.
Doll 16½ in. long
Body of unglazed oilcloth
St. Albans Museum
Hair stuffed
Mark in blue on tummy

370
AM-0½ DEP.
Armand Marseille
Made in Germany
Doll 18 in. long. Stuffed body
Photo no. 313 Chester Museum

Made in Germany
Florodora
Doll A O M
Composition body. 1901.
Photo no. 314, 315 Miss Faith Eaton

A M
GERMANY
341/3

Doll Mrs. de Clifford

A M
Germany
5/6/3/2K

Doll 15 in. long. Photo no. 320
Bethnal Green Museum.

A.M.
Germany
351.5K

Doll Warwick Doll Museum

EARLY MARKS ON BABY DOLLS

Germany
971
A. 8. M.

Doll Miss Blair Hickman

Made in Germany
Armand Marseille
390
A 10/0M

Doll 8¼ in. long. Brown closing eyes
Owner born 1909 Finland

Armand Marseille
Germany
390
A.5M

Doll 22 in. long

A 11 M

Doll 27½ in. long. c. 1907
Saffron Walden Museum

Made in Germany
Armand Marseille
390
D.R.G.M. 346/1
A 4. M

Doll 20 in. long. c. 1905. Photo no. 317
Miss Alix Boyd.

Armand Marseille
Germany
390
A 0.M

Made in Germany
Armand Marseille.
390n.
D.R.G.M. 246/1.
A 1½ M

Doll 18 in. long. c. 1905. Photo no. 316
Chester Museum

Made in Germany
Armand Marseille
390n
DRGM 2',G/1
3 M

Doll Mrs. Goodchild

Made in Germany
Armand Marseille
390
A 8 M

Doll c. 1910 Mrs. Gordon Coles

MADE IN GERMANY
Armand Marseille
390n
A 9 M

Doll c. 1905 Mrs. Goodchild

Now that the Armand Marseille marks have been assembled, it can be seen that the early dolls with kid bodies were marked by the initials A M only. The size number usually appeared between the initials and the word D E P, with the exception of the baby dolls.

The full name Armand Marseille occurs about 1899 or 1900, the word D E P disappears, and gradually the cross-bar on the letter A is made in the form of a V.

About the time of the registration of the model FLORODORA in 1901, the initials A and M are separated by a number which refers to the size of the particular model. The kid bodies disappeared at the turn of the century and were then made partly of cotton. Some were of unglazed oilcloth, or of pink canvas with bisque forearms and stuffed legs. Later the limbs were of composition or of wood, and threaded.

The high numbers refer to the kind of model which is used for the head, but it is tempting to suppose that numbers like 1894 and 1895 refer to the time when the Marseille dolls were first produced, for none have been found previous to these years.

Doll 18 in. long. Mrs. Render

BRU-Jne

5

Doll 17 in. long. Photo no. 272, 273
Miss Betsy Dean.

Doll. Photo no. 108, 110
at Saffron Walden Museum

Doll 26 in. long. Photo no. 279, 280
London Museum

CUNO & OTTO DRESSEL.

Doll. Photo no. 282
Miss Faith Eaton

Doll. Photo no. 324
Saffron Walden Museum

MARKS OF CUNO AND OTTO DRESSEL, WITH MERCURY HELMET

Doll, kid body, cotton stuffed lower legs with black net stockings.
Mrs. Heather Fox

Black doll 15 in. long
Miss Blair Hickman

Doll $27\frac{1}{2}$ in. long. Brown closing eyes. Bought in Germany for a child born in 1891. Finland

Doll Miss Moriarty

Doll. Photo no. 297, 298
Mrs. Heather Fox

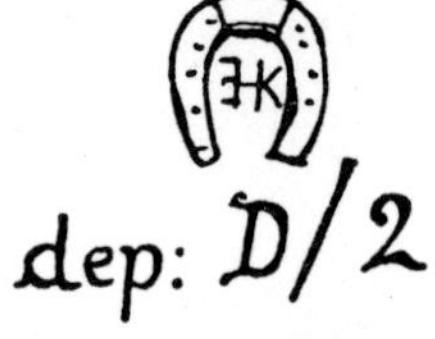

Doll. Photo no. 301, 302
Saffron Walden Museum

Heubach.
250-$6\frac{1}{2}$
Köppelsdorf.

Doll 24 in. long. Jointed body
Mrs. Heather Fox

11
Heubach
275 6/0

Doll 14 in. long. Photo no. 299
Bethnal Green Museum

Heubach-Koppelsdorf
300-3
Germany

Doll. Photo no. 304, 305
Miss Faith Eaton

MARKS OF ERNST HEUBACH

F. S & Co
1272/32 Z
Deponiert

Doll. Photo no. 277
Red House, Christchurch

FS & C
1253
39

Doll 15 in. long. c. 1910
Photo no. 278
London Museum

1295
FS & C
28

Doll
Miss Blair Hickman

MARKS OF FERDINAND SCHILLING

B 2 S

Doll bought in Paris in 1889
Haslemere Museum

DEPOSE
E J

Doll 14 in. long. Emile Jumeau
Photo no. 272 Bethnal Green Museum

Germany
HEINRICH HANDWERCK
SIMON & HALBIG

Doll Miss Jennie Polley

Germany
HEINRICH HANDWERCK
SIMON & HALBIG

Doll 26 in. long Mrs. Heather Fox

109 – 13
DEP

Mark on head

HANDWERCK
GERMANY

Doll Mrs. Goodchild

MAX
HANDWERCK
Germany
4

Handwerck

Mark on base of back
Doll Mrs. Goodchild

MARKS OF HEINRICH HANDWERCK

HURET

Mark of Mademoiselle Huret

Doll. Photo no. 327, 328 Miss Faith Eaton

K & R
53

Doll 20½ in. long. c. 1900
Photo no. 323
Pollocks Toy Museum

28
K & R
100

Doll 11 in. long
Bethnal Green Museum

K & R
114

Doll c. 1904
Mrs. Goodchild

K. made in
Germany 14
211
J.D.K.

Baby doll. J. D. Kestner
Mrs. Goodchild

MARKS OF KAMMER AND REINHARDT

Lilly
8/0
Made in Germany

Doll 16¼ in. long. Photo no. 306 Luton Museum

G K
34-26

Doll 14¾ in. long. Photo no. 248
Mrs. Graham Greene

Le Petit Parisien
BÉBÉ STEINER
MÈDAILLE d'OR
PARIS 1889

LE PARISIEN
Bte S.G.D.G
A 13

Doll 20 in. long. Photo no. 335
Miss Blair Hickman

L
17 72
Limbach
MADE IN GERMANY

Doll 24½ in. long.
Mrs. Goodchild

Doll 16 in. long. Photo no. 117
Mrs. Nina Davies

Doll. Photo no. 109, 111
Bethnal Green Museum

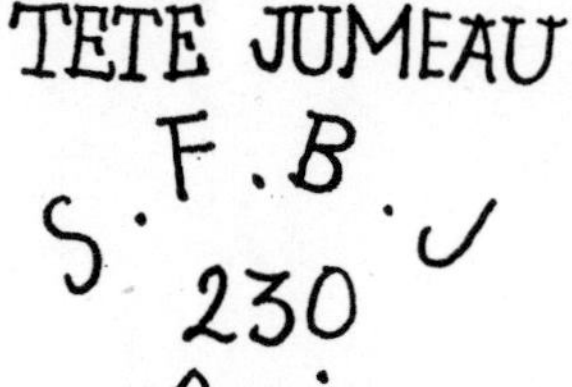

Doll Mrs. Goodchild

FRANCE
SFBJ
CO
PARIS
G

Doll Mrs. Goodchild

D
S.F.B.J
60
PARIS

Doll 20 in. long
Mrs. Heather Fox

42

S & H
K & R

Kammer & Reinhardt
Simon & Halbig

LORRAINE
No 0
AL & Co
LIMOGES

Doll, head $1\frac{3}{4}$ in. high
Late 19th century
Composition body
Bethnal Green Museum

Washable

Doll with turning head. Photo no. 180
Luton Museum

SH 1080 DEP. 7.

Doll $19\frac{3}{4}$ in. long. Closing eyes
Owner born 1894 Finland

SCH 769 DEP

Doll 13 in. long. Brown closing eyes
Bought in Munich in 1891 Finland

SH 4
905

Doll. Photo no. 285, 286
Miss Faith Eaton

S & H
10½

Doll $22\frac{1}{2}$ in. long. c. 1910. Photo no. 346
London Museum

S 12 H
939

Doll 22 in. long
Mrs. Wigmore

SH 1079-12
DEP

Doll. Photo no. 292
Miss Blair Hickman

Doll 18 in. long
Mrs. Goodchild

4000 4/0a
S. PB H

Doll $15\frac{1}{2}$ in. long
Photo no. 287
London Museum

S PB H
1906
14
Germany

Doll Mrs. Goodchild

S PB H
1909
3/0
Germany

Doll 15 in. long
Bethnal Green Museum

S PB H
1909
2/0
Germany

Doll
Mrs. Goodchild

MARKS OF SIMON AND HALBIG

31
3

Doll. Photo no. 99
Mrs. Hennessy

9
166

Doll
Miss Christine Smith

10B

Doll 10 in. long. Photo no. 91
London Museum

WD
3

Doll. Photo no. 275
Mrs. Heather Fox

4
151

Baby doll
Mrs. Graham Greene

3093

Doll $11\frac{3}{4}$ in. long. Fixed eyes. Owner born in 1880
Photo no. 250 Finland

OTHER MARKINGS

FABRICATION
FRANCAISE

AL e Cie
LIMOGES

Cherie 6

Doll 17 in. long
Mrs. Arthur Hunt

K & R
SIMON & HALBIG
117

Doll 26 in. long Mrs. Wigmore

SIMON & HALBIG
K & R
34

Doll Mrs. Arthur Hunt

MARKS FROM THE EDWARDIAN ERA

V Makers' Names

In the following list, a few abbreviations are used:

B. British
F. French.
G. German.
U.S.A. United States of America.
Pat. Patent Specifications.
Rep. Represented—used when a patent has been lodged in a foreign country by an agent.

The word '*bébé*' occurs throughout when it has been entered by the French maker, and means a child's doll or a baby doll. Although '*poupée*' is a doll, it is not necessarily a doll for a child.

Amongst the marks, the place names are spelt according to their respective registrations. Where the words '*Gebruder*' and '*frères*' appear, they are the German and French for Brothers, and are used in the same way as we have Hamley Brothers.

The dates given refer to the year in which the patent or the mark was lodged. Sometimes the patent will have been bought by a firm, and where a mark and a patent have been registered about the same time, they may refer to the same doll.

The descriptions of patents have been much abbreviated, but full specifications may be purchased from patent offices and will be in the language of the country in which they were lodged. The numbers of identical patents have been given so that readers can pursue them in the language in which they are most familiar.

The mark numbers refer to the illustrations which commence on page 95.

Abraham & Straus. Brooklyn, New York, U.S.A.
1906. Dolls. Mark no. 337

Abrahams, M. Paris, France
1909. Mark no. 486

Achenbach & Co. Hamburg, Germany
1891. Mark nos. 251–5

Ackermann, Cole. Co. Cleveland, Ohio, U.S.A.
1905. Mark no. 577

Adam, Carl. Konigsburg, Germany
1894. Mark no. 46

'Aeolus' Co. Strohhause, Hamburg, Germany
1910. Toys. Mark no. 1

Aetna Doll & Toy Co. U.S.A.
1910. Mark no. 403

Alderson, Mathew W. Braintree, U.S.A.
1890. G. pat. 56325, a doll's hand so that things may be picked up or released
F. pat. 208391, as above. Rep by Matray Frères, boul Henry IV, 31, Paris
USA pat. 440986, as above. Bozeman, Mont. Assignor to the American Doll Co. New York, N.Y.

Alexandre, Henry. Paris, France
1886. Toys. Mark no. 73

Anhalt, Wilhelm. Ostseebad, Kolberg, Germany
1905. Mark no. 555

Anquelle. France
1865. Doll

Arnaud. France
1852. F. pat. 13255, for jointed dolls
1864. F. pat. 61809, for movable arms and legs strung with elastic
(In 1908, a Celestin Arnaud lived in Marseille)
Arnold, Oscar M. Neustadt, Coburg, Germany
1904. B. pat. 11356, for a doll on wheels
F. pat. 343300, for a talking doll
1906. G. pat. 191962, for a speaking doll
USA pat. 820843, for a doll with a turning head
B. pat. 19614, for a phonograph doll, patented by E. C. R. Marks
1908. B. pat. 13824, for a phonograph doll
G. pat. 211232, as above
1909. G. pat. 231597, for a bathing doll
Arnold Print Works. North Adams, Massachusetts, U.S.A.
1876–1900. Rag dolls. Mark no. 3
Ascher, Adolf. Berlin, Germany
1892. G. pat. 66543, for a method of making mechanical dolls and hollow bodies in one piece, by pressing
F. pat. 220120, as above
1893. F. pat. 229703, for making parts of jointed dolls
Atwood, K. C. U.S.A.
1877. Pat. 186919, for a jointed doll of sheet metal
'Au Bébé Rosc'. Paris, France
1910. Designers of dolls. Mark no. 38, printed in violet
Aubert & Papin. Vésénet, Versailles, France
1907. Mechanical toys and others. Mark no. 156

Bach Bros. & Katzenstein. U.S.A.
1908. Rag dolls. Mark nos. 398, 616
Baculard. France
1860. F. pat. 43392, for rubber heads
Baer & Proeschild. Thuringia, Germany
1910. Material for dolls and for stands. Mark no. 395
Baker & Bennet Co. U.S.A.
1909. Mark no. 462
See also Hays
Baker, W. H. 98 Gosset Street, Bethnal Green Rd., London
1902. Toy manufacturers. Mark no. 153
Ballu, Ernest. Paris, France
1896. Merchant of Paris and designer of dolls. Mark no. 375
Barbe, Lechertier. France
1860. F. pat. 79722, for a paper doll

Barker, Florence Annie, Madame. Née Rees. Mirfield, Yorks., England
1906. B. pat. 7899, for a doll dressed to represent a flower, and filled with lavender, etc.
F. pat. 366560, as above
These dolls were composed of cloth, fabric or other flexible material, including face, etc., and were stuffed with pungent leaves and herbs. Mark no. 309
Bartenstein, Fritz. Hüttensteinach, Germany
1880. G. pat. 14429, for a doll with a turning head showing two expressions
1881. G. pat. 17327, for a method of making a doll-head lean backwards, the cord coming out at the side
G. pat. 14400, for dolls' heads of wax and composition
USA pat. 243752, for a doll with a double face
Barth. France
1856. F. pat. 34136, for moulded dolls
Barth & Wagner. Rodach, Coburg, Germany
1877. Toy manufacturers. Mark no. 45
Bastier, François Felix. Paris, France
1880. G. pat. 18595, for composition dolls
Batt, John & Co. London, England
1883. Mark no. 202
Bauersachs, Emil. Sonneberg, Germany
1895. Doll manufacturer. Mark no. 243
Bawo & Dotter. East Orange, N.J. and New York, U.S.A.
1910. Mark no. 332
Bazley, Frederick W. Highland Park, Mich., U.S.A.
1905. Dancing dolls. Mark no. 396, word used since 1904
Bazzoni, Antoni. Made wax dolls in England until 1868
Behu. France
1892. F. pat. 222152, for jointed dolls
Belton. Salle au Comte St. Paris, France
1844. Exhibited dolls at the Industries Fair, Paris
Benda, Anton. Coburg, Germany
1858. B. pat. 2283, for separate limbs of dolls joined by Indiarubber or elastic cords
Benda, G. Coburg, Germany
1872. USA pat. 129086, for a doll's head
Benoit fils et Romain. Paris, France
1885. Toys. Mark no. 43
Bensinger, Lenel & Co. Mannheim, Germany
1895. Washable celluloid dolls and toys. Mark no. 225
Berg. France
1898. Rep by Matray frères. F. pat. 273952, for a bubble-blowing doll

Bergmann, Althof. New York, U.S.A.
1872. Mark no. 565
1881. Mark, 'The horse enclosed in a circular border'
Bergmann, C. M. Waltershausen, Germany
1897. Mark no. 408
1910. Mark nos. 579, 618
Bergmann, Josef. Sonneberg, Germany
1888. G. pat. 46547, mechanism for dolls' eyes
1889. Rep by Casalonga, rue des Halles 15, Paris, France
F. pat. 202407, mechanism for moving dolls' heads in all directions
G. pat. 52573, for a method of moving a doll-head
Bergner, Carl. Sonneberg, Germany
1890. G. pat. 57035, for a doll to turn her head from side to side
1904. B. pat. 27919, for a doll's head made in two parts, so that several faces may be fixed to one body
1905. G. pat. 164535, for a doll's wig
Berlin, Joseph. Germany. Trading as Fleischmann & Bloedel, successors to J. Berlin, Nurnbergerstrasse, Furth, Bavaria.
1909. Mark no. 275. *See* Fleischmann & Bloedel
Bernard, Aristide. Saint Leger aux Bois, France
1894. Doll maker. Mark no. 281
Berner, Jacques. Paris, France
1888. Merchant. Mark no. 81, stamped on the boxes containing the dolls—the colour and size of the mark could vary. A '*Bébé Moujik*' is a little peasant. Mark no. 373
Bernheim et Kahn. Paris, France
1904. Mark no. 430
1905. F. pat. 351911, for a method of making dolls and bébés
1906. Mark no. 369
Bertal & Taffe. France
1861. Makers of historical dolls
Bertran, Charles. 4 rue des Archives, Paris, France
1878. Toys. Manufacturers of the swimming doll or '*Poupée Nageuse*', known as Ondine
1878. Mark no. 521. *See* Martin, E.
Bés. France
1868. F. pat. 83361, for a doll
Betzig, Edward Charles. 110 Fifth Avenue, New York, N.Y., U.S.A.
1894. Designer. B. pat. 25154, for a paper doll with detachable garments
Biddle, L. England
1897. B. pat. 24679, for a smoking doll
Bien. France. Rep by Armengaud, senior, rue St. Sebástien, 45, Paris
1889. F. pat. 200010, for jointed bébés
Bierer, F. L. England
1908. Rubber toys. Mark no. 278
Bing, Gebr. Nuremberg, Germany
1906. British mark no. 64
Birnich, Balthasar Paul. Cöln, Germany
1907. Toy maker. Mark no. 553
Bishoff, Josef. Nürnberg, Germany
1899. Tintoys. Mark no. 82
Bitner, H. U.S.A.
1906. Pat. 836296, for a hanging dolls' house
F. pat. 363018, for dolls' chairs
Blakeslee, C. F. New York, N.Y., U.S.A.
1865. Pat. 45691, for dolls' arms cut from leather
Blampoix. France
1855. Dolls with enamel eyes
Blank, Oscar. Hamburg, Germany
1891. Toy manufacturer. Mark no. 219
Blay. France
1888. F. pat. 188825, for a doll with movable head, arms and legs
Boisson Berrod, Jean Hermann. Dorton, France
1895. Mark no. 41
Boitel. France. Rep by Digeon, rue de Lancry, 56, Paris
1887. F. pat. 182616, for celluloid heads, arms and legs for dolls
Bonnal, Claude Valery. Vincennes, France
1904. Mark nos. 357, 359, 360, 362, 363
Bontempo, C. England
1898. B. pat. 14173, for Jack-in-the-box dolls
Borgfeldt, George B. & Co. Berlin, Germany
1897. Mark nos. 429, 541
1898. Doll manufacturer. Mark nos. 456, 615
1899. Berlin. Mark no. 568
1899. New York. Mark no. 569, registered in the U.S.A.
1901. Berlin. Mark no. 436
1901. Berlin. Retail sale of dolls. Mark no. 325
1903. Berlin. Mark nos. 437, 514
1906. Berlin. Joint stock Co. Mark no. 564
1907. U.S.A. Mark no. 400, used for ten years. Mark no. 461
1908. Mark no. 333
See also Steiner, Louis
Bortoli frères. Marseille, France
1895. Merchants and designers of dolls. Mark no. 453
Bouchet. Rue Cauchy, 24, Paris, France
1894. F. pat. 240889, for a new method for the heads and other parts of dolls

Boult & Gay, A. J. & William Alfred. England
1893. B. pat. 11063, for a doll with metal rods and a marble making musical sounds
F. pat. 230657, rep by Thirion, as above
G. pat. 73658, as above
A. J. Boult. *1893*. B. pat. 13084, for attaching hair to the heads of dolls. If the head of the doll to which the hair is to be applied is constructed of papier mâché, Indiarubber or hard rubber, the hairs are pricked in by needles and fixed with any suitable adhesive material. If the heads are of porcelain or other hard substance, recesses are formed which are filled with plastic material, the hairs being pricked in by means of needles

Bour. France
1892. F. pat. 218586, for perfecting dolls

Bourrillon. France
1876. Dolls

Bousquet. France
1901. F. pat. 317341, for a doll called '*Petit Pianiste Automatique*'. Mark no. 530

Boutard. France
1869. F. pat. 87264, for a flying doll

Bowden, Louise M. Newark, N.Y., U.S.A.
1893. Pat. 511111, for a piece of cloth with the outline parts of a doll

Boyer. Rue de Madrid, 25, Paris, France
1889. F. pat. 201648, for dolls with hollow rubber heads and various expressions

Breisson. France
1853. F. pat. 16220, for metal shoes for dolls
1859. F. pat. 39490, for a shooting device, whereby a flying doll is shot off into the air, making a sound as it takes off

Bremai. Rue St. Honoré, Paris, France
1803. Toyshop

Brentano, Arthur. Paris, France
1889. Marchant. Mark no. 40

Bretsch, Hugo. Berlin, Germany
1878. Toy manufacturer. Mark nos. 168, 169

Briens. France
1860. F. pat. 47573, for jointed dolls of various materials
1860. F. pat. 45269, for rubber doll-heads with enamel eyes and invisible joints
1862. F. pat. 252500, for a turning head with enamel eyes

Brierley, W. (J. Schön.) England
1886. B. pat. 10100, for dolls' heads made from stamped metal sheets

British Ever Ready Electrical Co. Theobalds Rd., London, W.C.
1910. Toys. Mark no. 576

Brock, William E. U.S.A.
1874. Pat. 149831, for hollow dolls' heads, the mould being lined with tinfoil or leather so that the glue-stiffened material does not adhere to the mould

Bromhead, S. S. *See* Treude & Metz

Brookes, A. G. England
1888. B. pat. 616, for a phonograph doll (W. W. Jacques)

Brooman, Richard A. England
1858. B. pat. 2639, for metal moulds for rubber dolls, made in two halves, a top half and a bottom half, the joins covered with a belt around the waist

Brouillet. France. A doll made of bread

Brouillet-Cacheleux. France
1856. Papier mâché dolls and composition consisting of cardboard paste mixed with resin and oils to make a plastic substance

Broullet. 116 St. Denis St. Paris, France
1844. Makes 'well-dressed dolls'

Brown Westhead, Marcus. England
1864. B. pat. 61, for a jointed doll walking down a plank

Browne, T. England
1899. B. pat. 345, for a fabric doll

Bru, Leon Casimer. France
1867. F. pat. 78844, for a turning head
1867. F. pat. 77084, for a crying doll with two expressions by turning the head
1869. F. pat. 84302, for the manufacture of dolls
1872. Madame Bru. F. pat. 95335, for a talking or singing doll, which could sing various airs, known as a 'Surprise Doll'
1878. F. pat. 126948, for a jointed rubber doll
1879. Casimer Bru, Junior. G. pat. 10536, for a feeding doll
F. pat. 129657, for leather dolls
F. pat. 132998, for feeding dolls, known as '*Bébés Teteurs*'
1891. Mark no. 342 registered by Paul Girard, trader at Paris
1891. Mark no. 343, as above, this mark put on the dolls and also on the boxes containing them
1891. Mark no. 381
1894. Mark no. 341

Bruchet. France
1852. F. pat. 13000, for a jointed bébé

Bryan, F. Bartholomew Close, London, E.C.
1877. Mark no. 215
Bub, Karl. Nürnberg, Germany
1899. Mark nos. 101, 102
Budwig, D. U.S.A.
1905. Pat. 788350, for an ornamental figure of a doll
Bull, Thomas Henry. Newington Causeway, Surrey, England
1888. Pewter Toys. Mark no. 320
Burnell & Hockley. England
1906. J. Hockley, B. pat. 13745, for patterns for rag dolls
Bushow & Beck. Nossen, Saxony, Germany
1900. Dressed and undressed dolls. Mark no. 508
1905. Mark no. 510
Butler Doll Stand Co. Chicago, Ill., U.S.A.
1904. Six doll stands resting on bases. Mark used since January 1895

Cacheleux. France. Dolls
Caillard, Varenne. France
1890. F. pat. 208172, for dolls' heads and other parts covered with plastic paste
Carette, Georges, et cie. Nuremberg, Germany
1909. Mark no. 65
Carl, Robert. Köppelsdorf, Germany
1908. Dolls and parts of dolls. Mark no. 502
Carpenter, W. B. U.S.A.
1880. Pat. 235933 and 237599, for celluloid dolls with real hair
Catterfelder-Puppenfabrik. Catterfeld, Thuringia, Germany
1910. Mark no. 160
Catusse, Clément. Paris, France
1893. Doll maker, dolls dressed and undressed, bébés, and sundry toys. Mark no. 349
Cavell. France
1869. F. pat. 79581, for a doll
Cayatte, E., Madame. Née Marie Mommessin. Paris, France
1909. Designer of dolls and bébés of all kinds. Mark nos. 233, 257, 376, 385
Chalory (Widow). France
1893. F. pat. 230739, for a doll known as the '*Bébé Leger sans rival*'. Mark no. 356
Chambon & Baye. Paris, France
1889. Doll makers. Mark no. 47, which may be incised or raised or done in colour
Chambre Syndicale des Fabricants de Jouets. France
1886. Mark no. 29
1897. Mark no. 30

Champson. France
1868. F. pat. 83211, for a paste for the manufacture of dolls
Chapman, Constance Mary. 'Rodean', Glossop Rd., Sanderstead, Surrey, England
1906. Artist. Mark no. 574
Charstone, W. J. England
1902. B. pat. 170, for a doll mounted on three wheels
Chase, Martha. U.S.A.
1890. Chase Stockinet Doll Co., Pawtucket, Rhode Island. Dolls. Mark no. 4
Chattanooga Medicine Co. Chattanooga, Tenn., U.S.A.
1910. Mark no. 570
Chauvière. France
1861. F. pat. 48415, for dolls of kid or other material jointed and stuffed
1870. F. pat. 88653, for a speaking doll
1870. F. pat. 48415, for a doll of kid or other material, stuffed and jointed. Rep by Bresson
Checalier & Venard. England
1850. B. pat. 9346, for a mechanical doll
Checkeni, Dominico. Marion, Conn., U.S.A.
1866. Pat. 52782, for a 'Fancy Doll' with a pivoted head, with four faces, so that either face may be brought to the front, a suitable wig covering the entire head, excepting for one face
Chevallier et Brasseur. France
1868. F. pat. 80827, for a doll made of artificial wood
Christie, Walter Edward. 41 Charterhouse Square, London, E.C.
1907. Merchant. Dolls. Mark no. 314
Clark, William. England
1861. B. pat. 1664, for a walking doll with step by step movement
1862. B. pat. 2672, for a doll
1865. B. pat. 1068, for a composition for making doll-heads with glue 4 lb., nutgall, etc. 3 oz., glycerine 8 oz., acid 1 lb.
Clarke, George Pemberton. New York, N.Y., U.S.A
1871. Pat. 118435
Clarke, Nicholls & Coombe. Hackney Wick, Middlesex, England
1870. Toys, games, figures and the like, also edible figures. Mark no. 319
Clarkson, T. C. England
1867. B. pat. 2630, for dolls made of West Indian corkwood, made by covering a mould with netted fabric, cementing on sheet cork with Indiarubber solution, and covering the whole with leather,

calico or felt, the surface of which may be painted or enamelled after the removal of the mould

Clausthal, William Rohde. Oberharz, Germany
1910. Mark no. 242

Clavell, J. S. England
1866. B. pat. 2897, for a dancing doll
1867. B. pat. 1334, for a doll

Clay, Robert J. New York, N.Y., U.S.A.
1871. Pat. 112550, for a creeping doll, having the arms and legs connected by a rod and propelled by wheels

Clement. France
1866. F. pat. 70283, for a doll of leather

Cohn, G. England
1899. B. pat. 4356, for dolls of sheet metal, etc., or of cardboard, in which the tongue comes out through a hole

Cohn, P. Breslau, Germany
1898. G. pat. 102151, for movable dolls and doll-heads

Colin. France
1890. F. pat. 205621, for unbreakable dolls and bébés made from artificial wood

Comptor General de la Bimbeloterie à Paris. France
1905. Mark nos. 380, 536, 540

Consterdine, H. England
1903. B. pat. 4586, for a jointed doll

Continental Caoutchouc & Gutta-percha Co. Hannover, Germany
1893. Mark no. 48

Cook, Henry & Solomon, John. Barbican Court, London
1902. Mark no. 438

Cordier. France
1889. Rep by La Société Marillier et Robelot, boul Bonne-Nouvelle, 42, Paris, France. F. pat. 198928, for jointed toys for children, dolls, bébés, and pantins

Cordonier. France
1880. F. pat. 134583, for a doll statue
F. pat. 135438, for stands for dolls

Cosman frères. France
1891. Designers of dolls and other toys. Mark nos. 348, 355
1893. Rep by Thirion. F. pat. 227174, for a doll to walk and turn the head, and talk by a simple compression on the shoulders
1893. F. pat. 227264, for a doll to walk and turn the head
1893. Doll makers of Paris, designers of bébés, jointed or otherwise, and also dolls, clowns, etc. Mark no. 554

Coube, Emma Butter. Myrtle House, Warwick Rd., Worthing, England
1909. Having no occupation. Toys. Mark no. 399

Couturier. France
1891. F. pat. 214501, for a toy called '*La Poupée Volante*'. Mark no. 473

Craemer & Heron. Sonneberg, Germany
1893. Dolls. U.S.A. mark no. 336

Crandall, J. S. Brooklyn, U.S.A.
1878. Mark using the words 'Child's Benefactor'. Mark no. 406

Cremer & Sons. London
1862. Exhibited dolls
1868. They were doll manufacturers at 210 Regent St., London
W. H. Cremer, Junior. *1867*. Exhibited in Paris
1873. Exhibited in Vienna
1874. Known as 'The Toyman of Regent Street'

Cruchet. France
1862. Doll

Dallimore, W. H. England
1893. B. pat. 21268, for a dancing doll made of cardboard and wire

Damas-Lajon. France
1868. F. pat. 85644, for a holder for a doll

Damerial, Jules and Charles. Paris, France
1910. Designers of dolls. Mark no. 458

Danel et cie. Montreuil-sous-Bois, France
1889. Doll makers. Mark no. 54
This sign was stamped on the boots and on the shoes, in the middle of the sole. Mark no. 526
1891. Mark no. 350

Dannhorn, Max. Nürnberg, Germany
1895. Mark no. 121

Dannin et Paulet. Paris, France
1908. Mark no. 56

Dare, Charles W. F. Brooklyn, U.S.A.
1878. The words 'Tally-Ho'. Mark no. 557

Darizard. France
1860. Doll's head

Darrow, F. E. Bristol, Conn., U.S.A.
1866. Pat. 54301, for dolls made from raw-hide, saturated with steam generated from a solution of caustic alkali, and then pressed into form between dies. Mark no. 5

Daspres. France
1902. Rep by Ch. Thirion & J. Bonnet
F. pat. 323175, for a walking and talking doll

D'Autremont. Paris, France
1858. F. pat. 37537, for Indiarubber dolls

Dawson, Peter. Glasgow, Scotland
1903. Mark no. 391
Deans Rag Book Co. 18 Paternoster Square, London, E.C. Publishers
1903. 'A Big Baby Doll', printed on a linen sheet with instructions in three languages
1908. H. S. Dean. B. pat. 25452, for dolls made from six pieces of printed fabric, 2 front, 2 back, and 2 soles for the feet
1909. Toys, namely Dolls, Toy animals, Birds and other Toy Figures. Mark no. 212
Debertrand, J. Paris, France
1905. Mark, a crowing cock with the initials J.D.
Debes, Carl & Sohn. Bavaria
1905. Dolls. Mark no. 515
Debrieu, Antonin. Paris, France
1893. Merchant, toys of all kinds. Mark no. 588
Décamps, Jean Maurice. Bordeaux, France
1908. Mark no. 6
Decker, Gussie D. Chicago, Ill., U.S.A.
1903. Pat. 724822, for a leather doll with stained features
Decoeur, A. England
1890. B. pat. 9515, for a talking doll with a rubber ball for a sounding bell, producing words such as 'Mama'
Degen, Elsa Beatrice. Finsbury Square, London
1908. Dealer in games. Mark no. 186
Dehler. France
1888. F. pat. 192456, for a doll to talk by telephone
Dehors. France
1866. F. pat. 70941, for doll with bust joints
Delcroix, Henri. Montreuil, France
1887. Doll manufacturer. Mark no. 193 engraved on the dolls' heads. Mark no. 194
Delhay frères. Paris, France
1896. Designer of toys. Mark no. 93
See also '*Les Jeux*, etc.', mark no. 16
Delphieu. France
1856. F. pat. 29606, for the use of pink textile instead of kid for dolls' bodies
Denancy, Paul. France
1891. Mark no. 128
Deropkine, La dame Alexandrine. France
1886. Mark no. 28, which was stamped on the dolls and also on their clothes
Deuerlein, Josef. Nürnberg, Germany
1908. Manufacturer of toys. Mark no. 449
Distler, Johann. Nürnberg, Germany
1910. Metal toys with the exception of dolls. Mark no. 83

Doebrich, George. Philadelphia, Pa., U.S.A.
1895. Pat. 551630, for dolls of composition
Dolffs & Helse. Braunschweig, Germany
1893. Toys and rubber works. Mark no. 52
Dorft, Fa. Julius. Sonneberg, Germany
1907. Dolls and animals. Mark nos. 175, 176
Dorn, A. & Crandall, C. M. U.S.A.
1881. Pat. 243873, for a doll house in box form
Dotter, Charles T. Brooklyn, Kings County, New York State, U.S.A.
1880. Pat. 235218, for a doll with a printed corset and with an imported head from Germany
Douglas, Anne Marie. Dalkeith House, Leamington, Warwicks., England
1894. B. pat. 19850, for a pivoted double reversible doll which could be weighted or held in the hand
Drechsel & Stroebel. Markleuthen, Bayern
1900. Porcelain factory. Mark no. 57
Dressel, Cüno and Otto. Sonneberg, Germany
1875. Dolls, Dolls' heads of wood, Glass, Porcelain, Raffia, Marbles, slates and slate pencils. Mark nos. 161, 162
1895. Dolls etc. Mark no. 316
1903. Mark nos. 435, 610
1907. Mark no. 460, for double-jointed dolls
1909. Mark no. 338. Sonneberg. Mark no. 609
Dressel Kister. Passau, Bavaria, Germany. Hard-paste porcelain
1840. Mark nos. 53, 178, 260, 308
Dumerey. England
1848. B. pat. 6829, for jointed feet for dolls
Dunn, Ralph. Barbican, London
1906. Toy game called 'Dolly's Post'
Dürfield, Victor. Osternhau, I.S. Germany
1877. Toy manufacturer. Mark no. 149
1888. Nachfolger, Friedeburg, Germany. Mark no. 261
Du Val, Alberic. Paris, France
1890. Mark no. 94

Eadie, Junior. France
1898. F. pat. 275915, for perfecting dolls
Eaton, F. E. England
1895. B. pat. 897, for making dolls' faces or heads of dental enamel and sheet Indiarubber, worked on a porcelain model while hot, and the surface coloured.
1901. B. pat. 7583
1904. B. pat. 24846, for a doll of papier mâché made to resemble china

Eck, Berthold. Unterneubrunn, Thuringia, Germany
1876. Dolls. Mark no. 289
1877. Dolls. Mark no. 290
Eckert, H. England
1901. B. pat. 23650, for a doll with ball-and-socket joints
F. pat. 316550, as above
1902. B. pat. 8798, for ball-and-socket joints
F. pat. 316550, rep by Thierry, for jointed dolls
1904. B. pat. 12803, for ball-and-socket joints
Edison, T. A. England
1878. B. pat. 1644, for a phonograph doll in which the lips of the mask move
Edwards, John. 43–45 Waterloo Rd., London, S. Model dolls of wax, rag, composition, dressed or undressed
Egrefeuill. France
1865. F. pat. 67276, for a doll in the form of a box
Eisenmann & Co. Fürth, Germany
1895. Dolls. Mark no. 277
1908. 46 Basinghall St., London, E.C. Toys and dolls not composed wholly or partly of metal. Mark no. 209
1908. Dolls and Fancy Goods Merchants. Mark no. 494
Eisenmann, J. England
1905. B. pat. 20301, for rag dolls with moulded cardboard faces, covered with gauze and with inset eyes
Eisenstadt, Isador. Waltershausen, Germany
1899. G. pat. 115408, for walking dolls
Eisenstaedt, Paul. Waltershausen, Germany
1901. G. pat. 127696, for a walking doll
Eldridge, Stuart. Yokahama, Japan
1883. USA pat. 278240, for a speaking doll. Assignor of one half to Ethel C. Hine and Richard W. Beyrich, Brooklyn, N.Y., U.S.A.
Ellis, Joel A. H. Springfield, Vt., U.S.A.
1873. Assignor to the Co-operative Manufacturing Co. Pat. 139130, for joints for wooden dolls, some having lead or pewter hands and feet
Engel, Adolph. Berlin, Germany
1879. G. pat. 7644, for a child's toy known as the 'Hampelmann'
Engel, Louis. Blumenau, Germany
1898. Mark no. 264
Engelfred, Arthur. Rue de Saint Quentin, Paris, France
1889. Mark no. 27. Rep by Fleischmann & Bloedel
Erdmann, Joseph. Paris, France
1891. Mark no. 86
Escher, E. Junior. Sonneberg, Germany
1880. G. pat. 12547 for a composition for dolls
1881. Dolls, etc. Mark no. 310
1896. Mark no. 311
Esparza. France
1888. Rep by Armengaud, Jeune. Boul de Strasbourg, 23, Paris, France
F. pat. 194738, for a method of painting dolls of pasteboard to imitate porcelain

Falck, Adolphe. Paris, France
1885. Mark no. 62 stamped on the dolls and also on the boxes containing them. Mark no. 374
Falck Roussel. France
1892. F. pat. 220366, for a method of putting together the joints of dolls
Farjasse. France
1890. F. pat. 207697, for rubber dolls
Faugier, Eugénie. (Mlle) Resident of Belgium
1909. F. pat. 405786, for a doll with two faces
Fausel, Charles. Chicago, Ill., U.S.A.
1896. Pat. 553643, for dolls with universal joints
Fayaud, A. England
1894. B. pat. 5937, for rubber dolls
Fehr, Hugo. Hamburg, Germany
1891. Mark no. 246
Fell. England
1894. B. pat. 25154, for detachable garments for dolls
Fiedeler, Hermann. Döhren, Hannover, Germany
1905. G. pat. 187473, for a forward and backward movement in dolls' bodies
G. pat. 178746, for a nodding movement
1907. USA pat. 863270, for an apparatus for turning and bowing the heads of dolls
Fischer Naumann & Co. Ismenau, Germany
1876. Papier-mâché figures and playthings. Mark no. 61
Fitch, D. A. England
1909. B. pat. 2369, for dolls' eyes
Flechter, Wolf. Covington, Ky., U.S.A.
1887. Pat. 371751, for a device for stuffing dolls
Fleischmann, Gebr. Nürnberg, Germany
1903. Manufacturer of swimming toys. Mark no. 66
Fleischmann & Bloedel
1889. Known as 'Toymen of Paris'
1890. Rep by Cahen, boul Saint Denis, 1, Paris, France
F. pat. 204739, for a method of putting elastic into jointed dolls
1890. Rep by Fayollet
F. pat. 205174, for a jointed doll, using wire and elastic. Also no. 210529

1890. Toymakers of Paris. Mark no. 424
1891. Fürth, Germany. Doll manufacturers. Mark nos. 427, 619
1892. G. pat. 68282, for a doll with forward movement, and turning of head simultaneously
See also Thompson, W. P.
1892. Rep by Engelfred, rue de Saint Quentin, Paris
F. pat. 221685, for an unbreakable composition for dolls
1894. Fürth 1, Bayern, Germany
G. pat. 83684, for a talking doll
F. pat. 236162, for a sleeping doll
F. pat. 236639, for a walking doll
F. pat. 239230, for mechanical dolls
F. pat. 239738, for a walking doll
F. pat. 241365, for mechanical dolls
F. pat. 243005, for a walking doll
1895. G. pat. 88335, for automatic dolls
1895. Manufactures at Paris. Mark no. 258
1896. F. pat. 241365, for kissing and talking dolls
Fürth. Mark no. 425, registered in Paris
1897. F. pat. 263708, for dolls which talk, walk and move their lips
1897. Mark no. 324
1898. Mark no. 388, Paris
1903. Mark no. 259
1909. Mark no. 507
1909. Mark no. 275, registered under J. Berlin, Nürnberger Strasse, Fürth, Bavaria. Address for U.K.: c/o Marks & Clerk, Lincoln's Inn Fields, London

Fleischmann, A. & Craemer. Sonneberg, Germany
1881. Toy manufacturer and dolls, etc. Mark no. 241

Fleischmann, Julius and Paul. U.S.A.
1892. Pat. 477892, for moulded portions of dolls, connected by wire staples

Flint, W. G. San Jose, California, U.S.A.
1902. Pat. 712786, for a tumbler doll with an ovoid base

Flynn, Olice A. Tacoma, Wash., U.S.A.
1910. Pat. 958387, for a clown doll

Foote, M. C. W. Plainfield, N.J., U.S.A.
1909. Dolls both dressed and undressed. Mark no. 434

Forster, Thomas. England
1844. B. pat. 10092, for rubber dolls with the heads and other parts made in moulds, using Indiarubber, shellac, gum opal, asphaltum, arsenate of potash

Fouillot, Blanche. Mlle. Paris, France
1906. Designer of dolls. Mark no. 485

Fouquet et Dorville. France
1891. F. pat. 212114, for eyes which can move at will, and in any direction
1893. F. pat. 227796, by Fouquet, for eyes worked by weights for dolls and bébés

Fourot, Paul Toussaint. Paris, France
1909. Mark nos. 129, 182

Franken, P. 35 rue de Nazareth, N.D., Paris, France
1893. Mark no. 183
See also Schmitz

Fuchs, Paul. Berlin, Germany
1904. USA pat. 754861, for dolls on rolls, a mechanism for walking. Assignor to the firm of Treude & Metz

Furch, J. England
1898. B. pat. 11167, for a doll printed on cardboard

Galibert. France
1860 and *1861*, for moving dolls

Gamage, A. W. Holborn, London
1910. Mark no. 402

Gans & Seyfarth. Waltershausen, Germany
1910. Dolls and doll parts. Mark nos. 72, 595

Gauthier. France
1872. Doll-head

Gay, William Alfred. Corry, Erie, Pennsylvania, U.S.A.
1893. G. pat. 73658, for a musical doll
1903. Terryville, Conn.
USA pat. 721948, for a doll with an extending body, permanently filled with air
See also Boult, A. J.

Gebaulet frères. Paris, France
1910. Designer of dolls. Mark nos. 67, 409, 594

Gedney, M. T. England
1897. B. pat. 30600, for a doll which runs and falls down

Geen, Evison, Stutchbury & Co. 6 Bevis Marks, London
1903. Japanese importers and manufacturers. Mark no. 578

Gems, J. F. & Nicks, W. F. England
1908. B. pat. 14081, for doll bodies formed with solid discs and covered with material

Geradin. France
1874. A rubber doll with moving eyes

Gerabon. France
1874. A grimacing doll

Germain. France
1899. F. pat. 291017, for a telephoning doll

Gesland. France
1898. Rep by Chaussevent, boul Magenta, 11, Paris
F. pat. 282752, for unbreakable dolls
Geyer, Carl & Co. Sonneberg, Germany
1885. Mark no. 269, for jointed dolls
1900. Mark no. 274, for dressed dolls
1900. Mark no. 353, for dressed dolls. Mark no. 612
1902. Mark no. 490, Dolls
Gibbons, Charles Kendrick. Surbiton, Surrey, England
1907. Engineer. Mark no. 329
Gibon, Eugène. Marseille, France
1895. Mark nos. 58, 592
Gibson, Edward Tinkham. 629 South 8th Street, Minneapolis, Hennepin, Minnesota, U.S.A. Physician *1895.* B. pat. 14496, for a paper doll with a change of clothes
F. pat. 249291, as above
1897. USA pat. 585092, for a paper doll, known as a 'Roundabout Doll'
1910. USA pat. 952731, for a doll of cloth, cut out and stuffed to the body, with the skirt to hang loosely
Gifford, Squire D. Terre Alta, W. Va., U.S.A.
1906. Pat. 817055, for an eye mechanism for dolls. Assignor of one half to Jacob P. Shafer
B. pat. 9900, for dolls' eyes and eyelids by means of weights
Gilbert. France
1885. Rep by Thirion, boul. Beaumarchais, 95, Paris
F. pat. 170370, for perfecting dolls and pantins
Gilbert, W. V. England
1905. B. pat. 19728, for cardboard cut-outs of dolls
Gill'o, Pierre Bois. Lyon, France
1898. Artist and designer of automatic figures. Mark no. 472
Girard, Paul. France. Rep by Blétry, senior
1891. F. pat. 214359, for a method of combining the eyes and the eyelids in the heads of dolls and bébés
1891. F. pat. 216294, for a doll which can walk and talk, known as '*Bébé Marcher*' and '*Bébé Petit-pas*'
1891. For marks. *See* Bru
1892. F. pat. 220001, for a talking and sleeping doll
1895. F. pat. 247060, for a kissing doll
1897. F. pat. 264955, for a doll with many movements, walks, talks, moves lips, and turns head
See also Soc. Inter., etc.

Giroux, Auguste. Paris, France
1888. Mark no. 32
Globe Supply Co. Islington, London
1902. Mark no. 148
Gobillot et Samson. Paris, France
1891. Their mark is of a figure rather like Mr. Punch, carrying toys. Mark no. 282
Goblet, A. Monroux, France
1891. Mark no. 31
Godfrey, Emily Dorcas. Also Sarah & Catherine Maria Godfrey. 30 George St., Croydon, Surrey
1880. Doll manufacturers. Mark no. 141
Goldsmith, Philip. Covrington, Kenton, Kentucky, U.S.A.
1885. Pat. 332248, for a doll body with corsets, the doll being of kid or cloth, with an imported china head from Germany
Goodyear, Charles. Woburn, Mass., U.S.A.
1839. Pat. 1851, for dolls made of rubber. Assignee of Nathaniel Haywood
Gorguet. France
1875. A toy parasol for dolls
Gosse, Marie-Félicienne. Clefs, France
1908. Designer of dolls. Mark no. 537
Goye, J. S. U.S.A.
1879. Pat. 220606, for a doll on wheels
Graeser, Heinrich. Germany
1890. G. pat. 54262, for a doll's head with a moving bottom lip
F. pat. 209238, for doll's head with pivoted eyeballs and pivoted lip-carrying block
USA pat. 440706, as above
Gratieux fils, Fernand. Paris, France
1907. Designer of toys, etc. Mark no. 475
Gray, W. England
1896. B. pat. 27072, for a doll dancing on a platform
1898. B. pat. 23304, for a dancing toy
Greffier, François. France
1855. Baby dolls, known as 'Japonese type'
Gregori-Olivier. France
1879. F. pat. 133538, for a toy called 'Poupée Nana'. Mark no. 535
Greiner, Ludwig. Philadelphia, Pa., U.S.A.
1858. Pat. 19770, for strengthening the seams and protecting the exposed parts of dolls' heads, by cementing or pasting on those parts muslin, linen, silk or other equivalent material, so that the heads are more or less unbreakable
Grieszmeyer, George. Nürnberg, Germany
1902. Dolls. Mark no. 68

Grimm, E. A. & Co. Hamburg, Germany
1889. Mark no. 307
1891. Toy factory. Mark no. 279

Grin. Place du Commerce, 17, Paris, France
1889. Leather merchant
F. pat. 200506, for a doll to turn round with a cord through the body

Grosbrütenbach. Thüringia, Germany. Porcelain factory
1770. Mark nos. 235, 236, 237
1855. Mark no. 234

Grumeau. France
1886. Rep by Armengaud jeune, boul de Strasbourg, 23, Paris
F. pat. 175687, for dolls and bébés

Gruss, R. & Brückner, A. Jersey city, N.J., U.S.A.
1901. Pat. 678244, for a layer of paper and a layer of textile fabric moulded

Guépratte, Jean Marie. Paris, France
1891. Doll maker. Mark no. 386. Mark no. 614 stamped on the dolls and on their boxes

Guhrauer, Ludwig. Hamburg, Germany
1893. Mark no. 113

Guichard, Edward. England
1854. B. pat. 1455, for applying flock by means of gums to the surface of the dolls, in order to imitate skin

Guillet, Louis. France
1894. Trustee of Paris, manufacturer of toys for the garden, etc. Mark no. 589
1896. Designer of dolls. Mark no. 328

Guilliard. France
1853. F. pat. 17054, for a talking doll, made of wood

Gutmann & Schiffnie. Nuremberg, Germany
1907. Designer of dolls and bébés. Mark no. 354

Gutsell, Ida. Ithaca, N.Y., U.S.A.
1893. Pat. 503316, for a doll-producing blank, consisting of a sheet showing a cut-out doll of cloth

Haag, Gebrüder. Sonneberg, Germany
1886. Dolls in imitation biscuit and all kinds of dolls. Mark no. 270
The words '*Marque de Fabrique*' appear along the base of the mark

Haas, Albert F. England
1860. B. pat. 1866, for stuffed dolls with porcelain heads, for the company of Fischer Naumann, Saxe Weimer, Germany. The doll's legs bend and hang from the knee when sitting in the position of a living person

Hachmeister, Hermann. Sonneberg, Germany
1908. Mark no. 268

Hacker, Christian. Nürnberg, Germany
1875. Wooden playthings. Mark no. 159

Haddon, Herbert & Co. Bedford St., London
1906. Agent in the U.K. for Kämmer & Reinhardt

Haffner's J. Nachf. Nürnberg, Germany
1899. Tin figures. Mark no. 90
(Nachf. is an abbreviation for successor)

Hager, J. Nürnberg, Germany
1875. Playthings. Mark nos. 171, 172

Halbig, Carl. Germany. Sole proprietor of the house of Simon & Halbig
1903. Rep by Thirion & Bonnet, 95 boul. Beaumarchais, Paris, France
F. pat. 335403, for a doll's head with moving eyes
1905. Graefenhain, Germany
USA pat. 796419, for a doll's head with eyeballs loosely mounted therein, and controlled by weights

Hamburger & Co. New York, U.S.A.
1895. Dolls. Mark no. 55
1898. Dolls. Mark no. 454
1900. Dolls. Mark no. 550
1901. Dolls. Mark no. 551
1901. New York, and two places in Berlin, manufacturers of dolls. Mark no. 455
1902. U.S.A. Mark no. 519, used since 1900
1902. U.S.A. Mark no. 501, word used since 1901
1903. Mark no. 571, and also for the two places in Berlin
1907. Nürnberg. Mark no. 419

Hamburger, A. & Coston, H. London
1908. B. pat. 22925, for dolls made from distorted photographs

Hamley Bros. 512 Oxford St., London
1904. Mark no. 397
1908. 86 High Holborn, W.C. Register their name as Toy Merchants

Hammond. France
1858. F. pat. 37616, for mechanical flesh-coloured rubber dolls with invisible joints

Handwerke, Heinrich. Waltershausen, Germany
1891. Mark nos. 75, 76
1895. Doll factory. Mark no. 344, entered in 1891
1895. Mark no. 77. On the boxes containing the 'Bébé Cosmopolite' are directions thus—Eyes are tied through the mouth, cut the string on the corner of the mouth, and they will open and close. Mark includes the word '*Supérieure*'. Mark no. 580
1897. G. pat. 100279, for a doll with ball joints and elastic

1898. Mark nos. 7, 345, 582, 610
Doll factory, and dolls with ball-bearings
1900. G. pat. 116025, for parts of dolls
G. pat. 123848, addition to '*Bébé Cosmopolite*'
1902. Mark no. 581
Handwerke, Max. Waltershausen, Germany
1901. Doll maker. Mark nos. 346, 583
Hannebelle, Auguste. Paris, France
1909. Mark no. 33
Hannoversche Caoutchouc. Linden, Germany
1893. Rubber goods of all kinds. Mark no. 207
Hannoversche Gummi-Kamm-Compagien (Acting company). Hannover, Germany
1899. Mark no. 394
1904. British mark no. 8
Harmus, Carl, Junior. Sonneberg, Germany
1909. Mark no. 203
Harratsz, B. Böhsen, Thüringia, Germany
1890. Mark nos. 158, 292
1894. Mark nos. 167, 293
Harrison. England
1903. B. pat. 19348, for a paper doll
Hart, William J., Junior. Philadelphia, Pa., U.S.A.
1874. Pat. 157394, for a paper doll, the body in several parts constructed to assume the appearance of walking. It may be fitted to various dresses
Hartmann, Carl. Neustadt, Coburg, Germany
1899. Dolls and jointed dolls. Mark no. 443
1904. Mark no. 523
Harwood, William A. Brooklyn, N.Y., U.S.A.
1877. Pat. 189935, for a talking and crying doll with a reed mouthpiece
Häuser, Carl. Leipzig, Germany
1887. Mark no. 283
Hausmeister, Paul & Co. Göppingen, Germany
1909. Dolls' heads. Mark no. 222
Hawkins, G. H. New York, N.Y., U.S.A.
1868. F. pat. 83285, for a moulded doll
USA pat. 81999, for a doll of textile fabric, stiffened with glue, and pressed between heated dies
1869. USA pat. 85589, for the manufacture of dolls' heads
Hays, Frank A. Overbrook and Philadelphia, Pa., U.S.A.
1909, for the Baker & Bennet Co. New York, N.Y., U.S.A. Mark nos. 392, 420
Heaton, Mary. Arosfa, Trefuant, R.S.O. Vale of Clwyd, North Wales
1910. (Of no occupation). Toys Mark no. 561
Hecht. France
1885. Rep by Chaussevent, boul. Magenta, 11, Paris
F. pat. 167650, for a method of putting whistles into rubber dolls
Heinrich, Johann Georg. Fürth, Germany
1896. Mark no. 89
Heinrichmaier & Wünsch. Rothenburg, Germany
1892. Mobile dolls. Mark no. 79
Heller, Alfred. Meiningen, Germany
1903. Dolls' heads, manufacturer and distributor of metal doll-heads. Mark no. 415
U.S.A. mark no. 414. The word used since 1902
Hende, Hermann. Dresden, Germany
1910. Dolls, dolls' wardrobes, and dolls' stands. Mark no. 170
Hendricks & Schrum. England
1904. B. pat. 1298, for dolls from woven mesh wire
Herbillon. France
1858. F. pat. 35090, for dolls improved by the use of cork
Herland. France
1861. F. pat. 68122, for musical and jumping dolls
Hermann, Carl Albert Georg. Allemagne, France
1906. F. pat. 369146, for unbreakable heads of plastic, covered with leather
Herrick, Lizzie. Iowa, U.S.A.
1880. Pat. 232403, for a doll support
Heubach, Ernst, or Heuback. Köppelsdorf, Thüringia, Germany
1887. Hard paste porcelain. Mark no. 59
Heubach, Gebruder. Lichte, Coburg, Germany
1880. G. pat. 11153, for a porcelain figure with moving parts
Heublein, Bernard. Malmarz, Sonneberg, Germany
1901. G. pat. 123847, for sleeping dolls
Hickisson, J. England
1873. B. pat. 2463, for dolls' heads of rubber, to assist in the teething of infants
Hillman, Friedrich. Sebnitz, I.S., Germany
1909. G. pat. 218858, for a padded doll
Hinckley, Henrietta R. Waterbury, Conn., U.S.A.
1896. Pat. 569333, for a stand for a doll
Hincks, E. T., U.S.A.
1907. Pat. 853639, for a doll
Hinde, John Lord. 1 City Rd., Finsbury, London
1888. Doll maker and Brush manufacturer
B. pat. 9080, for dolls made of pressed pulp in two halves and then joined, the dolls wear canvas-lined paper clothes. Mark no. 417, for Hinde Bros.

Hinrichs & Co. New York, N.Y., U.S.A.
1894. Dolls Mark no. 74, used since 1890
Hinrichs & Bemis, Edward Augustus & Frederick Pomeroy. Davenport, Scott, Iowa, U.S.A.
1896. Crockery dealer and Insurance agent
USA pat. 564563, for pivoted eyeballs
G. pat. 91888, as above
F. pat. 257993, as above
B. pat. 15166, as above
Hockley, J. Burnell & Hockley. England
1906. B. pat. 13745, for patterns for rag dolls
Hodgson, Ellen. Sheraton, Fortrose, Inverness, North Britain
1896. Wife of Major General Hodgson, Bengal Army, retired
B. pat. 20116, for a clockwork swimming doll, or it could be wound with a length of elastic string. The doll to be of Indiarubber, tin or other metal
Hoffmann, Solomon D. Moscow, Russia
1892. USA pat. 480094, for dolls of composition
Hölbe, Richard Hugo. Oberlind, Sonneberg, Germany
1880. G. pat. 16502, for a stand for a doll
1883. G. pat. 26082, for a musical doll
1890. G. pat. 62868, for a talking doll which says Papa-Mama, or Mama-Papa
Holland, Annie J. U.S.A.
1893. Pat. 503967, for a doll in which the eyelids move over the eyes
F. pat. 232496, for perfecting eyes
Horne, Elizabeth. Female toymaking depôt, 9 Greencroft Gardens, South Hampstead, Middlesex
1890. A maker of toys, but not dolls' houses. Mark no. 317
Horne, J. W. U.S.A.
1906. Pat. 834981, for a doll's head
Horsman, E. I. Co. Broadway, New York, N.Y., U.S.A.
1910. Games of all kinds. Address in U.K.: c/o William E. Peck & Co., 31 Bartholomew Close, London, E.C. Mark no. 334
Horstmeyer, Madame. Née Hedwig Burkhardt. France
1899. Rep by Borame et Julien
F. pat. 290492, for dolls
Hotchkiss, Arthur E. Cheshire, County of New Haven, State Connecticut, U.S.A.
1875. Pat. 167899, for a clockwork walking figure
Hover, Andrew C. Paterson, N.J., U.S.A.
1908. Pat. 903573, for a mechanism for dolls' eyes
Howard, George H. U.S.A.
1882. Pat. 268020, for an extensible doll with tubes and pins which could be driven by clockwork
Hughes, Herbert Edward. 9 Long Lane, London
1902. Toy dealer. Mark no. 432
1905. Mark no. 464. Words mean 'Bead in Ear'
1910. Goswell Rd., London. Toy dealer. Mark no. 466
Hulot, Lucien. 1 rue de la Lune, Paris, France
1904. F. pat. 347487, for a doll toy
Huneaus, P. Linden, Hannover, Germany
1900. G. pat. 123967, for moving eyes for dolls
1901. G. pat. 126409, for celluloid dolls. Mark no. 184
Hunter, Rudolph Melville. Philadelphia, U.S.A.
1899. Pat. 634143, for pivoted eyes
B. pat. 19447, for eyes that turn laterally with or without the means of shutting the eyelids
F. pat. 292914, as above
G. pat. 110812, as above
Huret, Mlle. France
1850. F. pat. 10936, for a jointed doll with a moulded body. Dolls are marked HURET or MAISON HURET
Hyatt, John Wesley. Newark, N.J., U.S.A.
1862. The Celluloid Manufacturing Company

Illfelder, B. & Co. New York, N.Y., U.S.A.
1905. Mark no. 497
Illfelder, Max. Fürth, Bayern
1902. Dolls. Mark no. 496
1903. Mark no. 547
1909. Bavaria. Dolls. Mark no. 506
Imhof, Ferdinand. Berlin, Germany
1898. G. pat. 113509, for a walking doll
1899. G. pat. 109368, for a method for a self-moving doll
B. pat. 19002, for a walking doll, and pat. 18408
F. pat. 293185, as above
1900. B. pat. 18408, for a walking doll
G. pat. 119857, as above
Indiarubber Co. U.S.A.
1851. Use Goodyear's patent for dolls
Indiarubber, Gutta-percha and Telegraph Works Co. Ltd. Cannon St., London
1908. Manufacturers of Indiarubber and gutta-percha, Mark no. 247
Internationale. *See* Soc. Int., etc.
Isaacs, A. J. 33 Houndsditch, London
1887. Wholesale doll importers and dressers. Dolls both dressed and undressed. Mark nos. 405, 617
Ismenau, or Ilmenau. Thüringia Porcelain Factory
1786. Mark nos. 80, 238

Ivimey, Annie Alice. Manor Rd., East Molesey, Surrey
1906. Dolls. Mark no. 418
Izon, Thomas. Birmingham, England
1906. Toy manufacturers. Mark no. 428

Jaboulay. France
1892. F. pat. 226431, for a dancing doll
Jacob, Leopold Emil. London Wall, London
1893. Importer of toys. Mark no. 227
Jacques, William W. Newton, Middlesex, Mass., U.S.A.
1888. Pat. 383299, for a combined doll and phonograph
1889. Rep by Brandon, rue Lafitte, 1, Paris
F. pat. 197149, for talking dolls
B. pat. 5573, for a phonograph doll
See also Brookes, A. G.
James, Arthur William. 29 Gloucester Terrace, Hyde Park, London
1907. Physician. Mark no. 322
Jeanson, Jules-Joseph. Paris, France
1891. Mark no. 91
Jefferson, William T. New York, N.Y., U.S.A.
1895. Pat. 535621, for a paper doll
Jeidel, Julius. France
1908. Rep by Assi, 41 rue des Martyrs, Paris
F. pat. 388564, for a doll
1908. Frankfort, Germany. Dolls. Mark no. 389
Jenkins, Raymond. Brooklyn, U.S.A.
1875. Dolls. Mark no. 459
Jeux et Jouets Française. Paris, France
1904. Mark no. 177
See also Les Jeux et Jouets Français
Jewitt, Henry. 141 Leighton Rd., Kentish Town, Middlesex, England
1870. Mark no. 78, Dolls and toys
1874. B. pat. 1866, for a wooden doll
He made many wooden toys with carved figures. One of his patents was a communication from abroad of William W. Rose, of New York, U.S.A., and possibly the letter R in his sign stands for Rose
Joanny, Joseph. France
1889. Rep by Albert Cahen
F. pat. 198668, for a doll with two faces, talking and crying, the dolls being hollow or solid
1907. 202 rue de Rivoli, Paris, France. Mark no. 92
Johnson, C. C. U.S.A.
1882. Pat. 267212, for a doll's head of wood covered with a plastic substance
Johnson, Rebecca. Brooklyn, N.Y., U.S.A.
1887. Pat. 366730, for rag dolls, made of waxed cloth and strengthened
Joliet. France
1867. F. pat. 76520, for a jointed doll
Jouet de Paris. *See* 'Le Jouet de Paris'
Jourlait. France
1892. F. pat. 220752, for a method of making celluloid heads for dolls without soldering
Judge, E. S. U.S.A.
1875. Pat. 166111, for dolls' heads made from sheets or layers of paper, treated with paste and moulded
Jumeau. France
1844. Exhibits dolls at the Industries Fair, Paris
1851. Wins medals for dolls' dresses
Jumeau, Emile. France
1878. An unbreakable doll body of papier mâché, jointed
1878. Awarded gold medal. Mark no. 9, sometimes stamped on the backs of the dolls near the waist
1885. Awarded Diploma of Honour, Antwerp. Mark no. 10. This mark is stamped on the dolls' bodies in dark blue, on a cream background
1886. Emile Jumeau, manufacturer of Paris. Mark no. 11
1887. Nr. 8 rue Pastourelle, Paris
G. pat. 41373, for hemispherical shaped eyes, with movable eyelashes for a sleeping doll. Rep by Delage, rue Saint Sebastien, 46, Paris
F. pat. 182307, for dolls' eyes
1888. The words 'BEBE JUMEAU' were registered, but they had been used since 1840, this date being given at time of registration. U.S.A. Mark no. 11
1888. Mark no. 296, stamped on the dyed skins of the dolls, and registered by Emile Jumeau, Tenturier de Paris. This mark is 0.065 high, and 0.065 broad, the original being in black
1891. Mark no. 204, stamped on the shoes of the 'Bébé Jumeau', by Emile Jumeau, maker of dolls and bébés, Paris. This mark is made on the soles with a punch
1896. E. Jumeau et cit. Rep by Armengaud
F. pat. 260167, for movable eyes for dolls and bébés
1896. Mark no. 613, printed in black on a white background, on the boxes, cases and packets containing dolls or bébés
1896. Mark no. 586, printed on a gold background, with the surround white with a black border, the cartouche being partly in gold, with the large letters in white and black

1896. Mark no. 611, printed in gold and black on a reddish background
1896. Mark no. 12, printed on the boxes. Background of gold, a blue, white and red band, with the letters in gold and black
1896. Mark nos. 351, 352, 384

Kämmer & Reinhardt. Waltershausen, Germany
1896. Dolls and doll parts, and papier mâché animals. Mark no. 107
1902. Doll manufacturers. Mark nos. 500, 596, 504, 597
1903. Mark nos. 108, 109
1903. Mechanical dolls
1904. Mark nos. 110, 513
1905. Mark no. 504
1906. Schlanmgasse, 107, Waltershausen. Doll and doll parts. Mark no. 111
1907. Mark nos. 416, 598
1908. Mark no. 559
1910. Mark nos. 404, 599

Kaulitz, Marion. München, Germany
1909. Dolls, dolls' heads and dolls' clothes. Mark no. 584

Kelson, George Mortimer. Westminster, England
1904. Mark no. 13

Kennard Novelty Co. Baltimore, U.S.A.
1892. Playthings. Mark no. 522

Kestner, A. Germany
1892. B. pat. 13985, for dolls' limbs attached by hooks
B. pat. 9562, for making dolls so that new limbs can be substituted for broken ones

Kestner, J. D., Junior. Waltershausen, Gotha, Germany
1889. Jointed dolls. Mark no. 272
1892. Firm of J. D. Kestner
G. pat. 70685, for fastening and strengthening the heads of jointed dolls
G. pat. 69020, as above
1896. J. D. Kestner, junior. Mark no. 84 for dolls, leather dolls, jointed dolls, and nankeen dolls, i.e. made of cotton. Mark no. 85
1896. U.S.A. mark no. 228

King, Jean Paul. Philadelphia, Pennsylvania, U.S.A.
1893. Pat. 486014, for a crying doll
G. pat. 73316, as above
G. pat. 70417, as above
F. pat. 226882, as above, rep by Armengaud, Poissonnière, 21, Paris

Kintzback, Martin. Philadelphia, U.S.A.
1869. Pat. 95489, for a method of fastening a leather arm to a doll with a porcelain head

Kirn, Hugo & Co. Nürnberg, Germany
1888. Mark no. 206

Kister. *See* Dressel

Kleinig & Blasberg. Leipzig, Germany
1899. Mark no. 103

Klen & Hahn. Ohrdruf, Thüringia, Germany
1902. Doll manufacturers. Mark nos. 104, 573
1909. Mark no. 100
1910. Mark no. 552, for jointed dolls, character dolls and leather dolls

Knight, Arthur Bertram. 63 St. Charles Square, Notting Hill, London
1893. B. pat. 19692, for a celluloid doll made in two halves, which when thrown to the ground, opens to show a doll's face

Kochendörfer, F. Sonneberg, Germany
1891. G. pat. 61965, for a method of substituting parts of dolls

Kohnstam, Moses. London, England
1900. Mark no. 512
1904. Bavaria. Mark no. 556
1909. 55 & 56 Nürnberger Strasse, Fuerth, Bavaria. Mark no. 411, and 24 Milton St., London, E.C. Dolls and toy manufacturers
1910. German mark no. 313. British mark no. 312, for dolls and toys at 21 Milton St., London

König, Fritz. Köhn, Germany
1884. G. pat. 28562, for puppet figures

Köring, Adolf. Allemagne, France
1907. F. pat. 378721, for doll clowns

Krampe, Otto. Schalksmühle, Germany
1902. Doll manufacturer. Mark no. 421, for sleeping dolls
USA pat. 720703, for an oscillating eye lever

Kratz-Boussac, Henri-Othon. Paris, France
1892. Designer of dolls
F. pat. 221627, for celluloid heads for dolls made in one piece
1906. Mark no. 469
1907. Mark no. 431
1910. Mark nos. 433, 471

Krausz Mohr & Co. *See* Mohr

Krausz, Samuel, or Krats. Rodach bei Coburg, Germany
1875. Papier mâché and wood, toy factory, dolls' heads, etc. Mark nos. 14, 291

Krenkel, Frederick Robert. Nürnberg, Germany
1875. Toy manufacturer. Mark no. 15

Kubelka, Josef. Wein, Germany
1884. G. pat. 31189, for a method of inserting hair into the heads of wax dolls
1889. Vienna, Europe
USA pat. 397463, for heads and busts of dolls made of hard material wherein are formed recesses of plastic, so that hairs may be inserted therein

Lacman, Jacob. Philadelphia, U.S.A.
1871. Pat. 113532, for a doll's hand. Elastic flexible cores in combination with the fingers and thumb
1874. USA pat. 148835, for papier mâché hands and feet, covered with leather or other suitable material
Lacoruchy. France
1864. Doll
Lafosse, Amédée-Onésime. Paris, France
1892. Designer of dolls and bébés
F. pat. 221582, for talking dolls. Mark no. 476
1893. F. pat. 229995, for movable eyes for dolls and bébés
F. pat. 234713, for a walking and talking doll
1894. F. pat. 238710, for a walking doll
La Fosse, Madame Marie Lambert. Paris, France. Designer and maker of dolls
1895. Mark no. 382
1897. (Widow) F. pat. 264464, for a doll to talk, cry and move the lips
1898. F. pat. 276458, for a method of making dolls and parts of dolls and bébés
Lake, W. R. England
1868. B. pat. 2859, for dolls' heads of buckram, muslin or other textile stiffened with starch, size or other glues, and pressed between heated dies. The heads are formed in two halves which are placed together with the edges overlapping
1882. B. pat. 1635, for a musical doll, where the note is made by means of bellows
1886. B. pat. 11845, for an educational toy, known as the *Yankee Schoolmaster*
Lambert. France
1893. Rep by Louis Gudman et cie, boul. de Strasbourg, 6, Paris
F. pat. 238207, for a mechanical bébé doll
Lambert, T. B. England
1902. B. pat. 9906, for phonograph dolls
Lamour. France
1863. Automatic doll
Lanagnère, Théophile. Paris, France
1887. Mark no. 146
Landsberger, Fa. Adolf. Magdeburg, Germany
1908. Dolls. Mark nos. 34, 590

Landshut, Hermann. & Co. Waltershausen, Germany
1895. Dolls and parts of dolls. Mark nos. 491, 622
Lazarus & Rosenfeld. 4 Houndsditch, London
1867. Register an 'ornamental doll's hat' in the Earthenware class
Lechertier Barbe. France
1860. F. pat. 79722, for a paper doll
Lecomte-Alliot. France
1886. Doll
Leconte. Rue Charlot, 35, Paris, France
1888. F. pat. 190960, for a new toy to be called '*Petit-Bébé*'. Mark no. 529
Lee, David Thorpe. England
1866. B. pat. 1579, for joints for dolls on the ball-and-socket principle. Move in any direction and stay by action of the springs
Lefferts & Carpenter. Marshall C. & W. B. New York, U.S.A.
1881. Pat. 237559, for celluloid dolls moulded in separate sections
Legrand. France
1891. Rep by Marin
F. pat. 203156, for a method of fixing movable eyes of enamel in dolls and bébés
Legros, Marie Dégene Tais. Saint-Maur-les-Fossés, France
1890. Mark nos. 117, 468
Lehmann, Ernst Paul. Plauerstrasse, Brandenburg, Havel, Germany
1892. B. pat. 2827, for a top in the form of a dancing doll
1901. B. pat. 11604, for a doll on wheels
1902. Mark no. 185
1904. B. pat. 17439, for a walking doll
1909. Sheet metal toys, manufacturer of toys and metal ware. British mark no. 516
'Le Jouet de Paris'. Paris
1902. Mark no. 98
Lemon & Page, D. M. and E. V. England
1910. F. pat. 417335, for perfecting toys and dolls
B. pat. 14922, for a doll with tears falling from the eyes and with various eye and mouth expressions
L'Epine. France
1890. F. pat. 208322, for perfecting the heads and parts of dolls
Leredde. (Widow.) Née Leonie-Alphonsine, and Charles Eugène Sonnet, i.e. Leredde et Sonnet, France
1888. Mark no. 126 which can be incised or raised
Les Jeux et Jouets Français. France

1909. Mark no. 16. Formed by the Société Levy, Perret, Simonin-Cuny, Alphonse and Alexandre Delhaye, Paris
See also Jeux et Jouets Française
Letort. England
1849. B. pat. 8759, for dolls' heads and feet which are detachable. Used by linen drapers and milliners
Léve, Prosper. Paris, France
1909. Mark nos. 143, 144
Leverd et cie. France
1869. F. pat. 85557, for a jointed doll
Levy. *See* Les Jeux et Jouets Française
L'Heureux, Louis. Paris, France
1905. Designer of dolls. Mark no. 484
L'Hotte. France
1874. F. pat. for an automatic doll
Liebermann, G. N. & Liebermann, L.
1903. F. pat. 331629, for a doll's head
Liedel, Theodor. Sonneberg, Germany
1894. G. pat. 82712, for a feeding doll
Limbach, Thüringia, Germany. Porcelain factory
1855. Mark no. 115. Combined with the Porcelain factory at Grosbrutenbach in 1772. Mark no. 114
Lindauer, Jules. Paris, France
1910. Toys of all kinds. Mark no. 527
Lines, G. & L. Ltd. 457 Caledonian Rd., London, N.
1910. Toys made of wood, toy manufacturers. Mark no. 69
Lipatoff, Jacques. Paris, France
1908. Designer of toys. Mark no. 321
Lisner, Rose. New York, U.S.A.
1890. Dressed dolls. Mark no. 524
Lloyd, F. G. England
1894. B. pat. 24378, for a walking doll which moves when pulled along on a string
Longbottom, John. England
1865. B. pat. 1775, for dolls made from a composition called Kampakaon
Lonquet, Anne Huet, & Eléonore Strady. Paris, France
1908. Mark no. 239
Luis, J. England
1858. B. pat. 2683, for wires in the drawers of dolls thus dispensing with the use of crinolines. The wires were threaded through tucks
L'Union des Fabricants de Jouets. France
1884. Mark no. 87, which can be either in relief or in colour
Lutticke, G. F. England
1876. B. pat. 3888, for juggling toys

Lynd, William J. California, U.S.A.
1886. Pat. 351785, for a doll connected by a speaking tube to the operator

McAdam, Constance Clyde. New Kent Rd., London
1909. Authoress. Toys and Noah's Arks. Mark no. no. 323
McCalmot, R. England
1895. B. pat. 22211, for paper dolls with gummed paper loops
McElroy, Daniel S. New York, N.Y., U.S.A.
1894. Pat. 525716, for a doll with movable arms and legs
McKenzie & McBurney. Dundee, Scotland
1876. Toys. Mark no. 525
Maelzel, Jean. Paris, France
1824. Mechanic. Patent for the first speaking doll
Maillard, Demoiselle. France
1883. F. pat. 155805, for a doll's sleeve
Maillard, Victor. Paris, France
1897. Mark no. 151
Malepart. France
1891. F. pat. 214985, for a walking doll
Mally, Joseph Robert. Bridgewater Square, London
1896. B. pat. 8937, for movable eyes in wax faces
B. pat. 15678, for clothing for dolls and dolls' heads of celluloid
Mandel & Sichert. France
1893. F. pat. 234019, for dolls and dolls' heads of celluloid
Marignac. Rue Oudinot, 6, Paris France
1894. F. pat. 235438, for an unbreakable doll called the '*Poupée Satin*'. Mark no. 539
Marks, E. C. R. *See* Arnold, O.
Marseille, Armand. Germany. Dolls of kid and bisque. Mark nos. 2, 35
Marseille, Armand. Kopplesdorf, Germany. Pottery founded in 1865. Mark no. 36
Marseille, François Emile. Maker at Maisons-Alfort, France
1888. Mark no. 119. Mark no. 602, is stamped on the boxes containing jointed dolls, and can be of various dimensions and colours. The words '*Bébé incassable articule*' along the base of the mark signify unbreakable jointed dolls. Mark no. 478
Marsh, Charles. 114 Fulham Rd., London
1879. Mark no. 17. This is stamped in pale blue and varies somewhat, often having the words 'Corinthian Bazaar', Argyll St., London, W. added
Martin, Auguste. Moncel sur Seille, France
1896. Toy manufacturer. Mark no. 37
1900. Paris, France. Mark no. 470

Martin, E. Paris, France
1863. F. pat. 57795, for a sitting doll with swivel joints
1876. F. pat. 115897, for a swimming doll
1878. In Paris, J. Brandt & G. W. v Nawrocki, in Berlin, for the swimming doll known as 'Undine', a 'Schwimmpuppe'
1878. F. pat. 159427, for a mechanical doll known as 'Ondine', and distributed by Charles Bertran
1878. Mark no. 520
Martin, Frank D. Springfield, Windsor, Vermont, U.S.A.
1879. Pat. 214830, for wooden dolls with ball and socket joints, and with elastic or spiral springs
Martin, S. F. England
1900. B. pat. 5978, for a walking figure
Mason, C. G., Forster, F. A., Elms, J. C. and Sprague, S. England
1894. B. pat. 20611, for wearing apparel for dolls, printed on fabric ready for cutting out
Mason, Henry H. & Taylor, Luke W. Springfield, Windsor, Vermont, U.S.A.
1881. Pat. 242210, for a method of a turning head of wood or of composition
May Bros. Paris, France
1890. Manufacturers and designers of jointed dolls. Rep by Cahen. F. pat. 207291, for a method of joining the metal parts of jointed dolls, bébés and pantins
1890. Mark no. 365
Mead, Madge Lansing. Philadelphia, Pennsylvania, U.S.A.
1900. Pat. 661185, for a rag doll with gussets
Mechtold, George & Chillingworth, Thomas. Oberlind, Sonneberg, Germany
1894. G. pat. 84059, for a doll with an inset wardrobe
Meech, H. J. 70 Willmington Rd., London, S.E.
1870. Doll maker to the Royal Family
Meier, A. & Co. Yokohama, China
1892. Dolls and playthings. Mark no. 208
Meier, H. W. U.S.A.
1906. Pat. 818842, for jointed dolls
Meisel, Aloys. U.S.A.
1878. Mark no. 6088 registered as a Coat of Arms, but with no illustration recorded in Britain
Meissen. Germany. The name given to the wares from the Königliche Porzellanmanufaktur zu Meissen. The initials K P M stand for this, and the initials A R used between 1709 and 1726 are for Augustus Rex. Complete marks are given here though few are for dolls

Mark no. 221	used 1712–19
Mark no. 106	used 1720–30
Mark no. 297	used 1720–30
Mark no. 298	used 1720–30
Mark no. 299	used 1730–3
Mark no. 300	used 1733–63
Mark no. 301	used 1763–74
Mark no. 302	used 1744–1814
Mark no. 303	used 1814–75

Mark no. 304 is that of the factory at Tournay, 1750–1800, and is shown because it might be confused with that of Meissen
Melchers & Co. Shanghai, China
1888. Mark no. 120
Merlin, Alphonse. Paris, France
1887. Toymaker. Mark no. 49
Mermod frères. Ste. Croix, Schweiz, Germany
1887. Clocks and playthings. Mark no. 123
Mettais, Jules. Paris, France. Maker and designer of dolls and bébés
1900. Mark no. 534
1901. Mark no. 368
Mewburn, J. C. England
1871. B. pat. 3494, for a doll's head
Mewman, A. M. England
1906. B. pat. 6220, for a phonograph doll
Meyer, Louis. Komotau & Karl Ring, Deutsch-Kralup, Böhmen, Germany
1892. G. pat. 71240, for a doll's head with moving eyelids
Meyerstein, William. 6 Love Lane, Aldermanbury, London
1876. Toys. Mark no. 214
Midland Rubber Co. Birmingham, England
1903. Mark no. 511
Migault, Albert. Paris, France
1899. Mark nos. 481, 611
Migault et Papin. France
1908. Mark no. 124
Miller, Wesley. New York, N.Y. U.S.A.
1875. Pat. 164582, for a hollow, flexible rubber doll with wire inside
Mohr, Krausz. & Co. Nürnberg, Germany
1900. Mark no. 105
Mohrhardt, Thomas Christo. Nürnberg, Germany
1897. Mark no. 245
Monteux, Gaston. Paris, France
1891. Mark no. 505
Montgomery-Moore. England
1889. Rep by Sautler & Mestral, rue Ballif, 11, Paris. F. pat. 200554, for a dolls' house

Monroe, Ansil W. Rahway, N.J., U.S.A.
1874. Pat. 159437, for a rubber doll with a ball-shaped head, resting in a socket and secured by a rubber band. The doll has a wig of the pelt of an Angora goat, which is tacked directly to the hard rubber

Montanari, Augusta. 29 Upper Charlotte St., Fitzroy Square, London
1849. Maker of wax dolls
1851. Medals for wax dolls, dressed
1852. She registers a drawing in the Earthenware Class of the Design Registry. This was 'an Ornamental Design for a Doll'
Mark no. 18 was found on the front of a doll's body in faded brown ink

Montanari, Napoleon. Charles St., Soho Square, London
1859. B. pat. 2358, for a child's walking aid. He also made children's toys and wax figures

Montanari, Richard Napoleon. Son of the above
1855. Makes wax dolls covered with fine muslin

Moody, E. Soho Bazaar, London
1870. Sells dolls

Mora, Antonio Luigi. London, England
1887. G. pat. 42282, for a jumping doll

Moret, Jules. Lyon, France
1908. Designer of toys. Mark no. 95

Morgenroth, Otto. Sonneberg, Germany
1905. Dolls. Mark no. 327

Morillot, Pierre. Paris, France
1889. Agent. Mark no. 217

Moteurs, Gnome. Paris, France
1910. Mark no. 444

Mothereau. France
1880. An unbreakable jointed bébé

Motschmann & Hufner. France
1886. Rep by Blétry frères boul. de Strasbourg, 2, Paris
F. pat. 179449, for perfecting dolls

Mougin, Jean. Barcelonnettes and cradles for dolls and children

Mountain, Henry. Liverpool, England
1907. Mark no. 567, for inflatable toys

Muller, Andr. Sonneberg, Germany
1896. Mark no. 229

Muller, E. & A. Schwarza-Saalbahn, Thüringia, Germany. Hard paste porcelain
1890. Mark nos. 192, 410, 180
1904. Mark no. 125. Schönwald, Bavaria

Muller & Co. Volkstedt, Germany
1870. Hard paste porcelain
1907. Mark nos. 112, 122, 181

Müller & Froebel. Sonneberg, Germany. Playthings
1884. Mark no. 284

Müller, O. Madame. Née H. Buttner. England
1905. B. pat. 21418, for eyelashes of 'hairs' attached to elastic material, or of the clipped edges of feathers

Munn & Cobb. England
1863. Joseph Munn
B. pat. 40, for an automatic walking doll

Musée Commercial. *See* Debrieu, Antonin

Naneau, Hippolyte. Paris, France
1905. Mark no. 440

Naumann. *See* Fischer Naumann

Neubart, Heinrich. Charlottenburg, Germany
1893. G. pat. 72737, for a stuffed rag doll

Neumann, Louis. Germany
1887. Mark no. 179

New Eccles Rubber Works. Monton Rd., Eccles, England
1905. Dolls, etc. Mark no. 127

Newell, E. G. U.S.A.
1900. Pat. 643385, for a rag doll

Newton, Alfred Vincent. England
1862. B. pat. 3408, for a mechanical walking doll
1871. B. pat. 2942, for a crawling doll

Newton, H. E. England
1876. B. pat. 2465, for clothes to conceal the joints on dolls

New York Hamburger Gummi Waaren Co. Hamburg, Germany
1899. Mark no. 422

Nicholas, Maurice. Paris, France
1907. Mark no. 474

Nicholson, Andrew N. Brooklyn, N.Y., U.S.A.
1869. Pat. 88197, for a walking doll

Nockler & Tittel. Schneeberg, Germany
1901. Manufacturers of dressed and undressed dolls. Mark nos. 448, 493

Nörregaard, A. Hamburg, Germany
1885. Playthings. Mark no. 265

Nube. France
1895. Rep by Jaffeux, boul. Saint Denis, 15, Paris
F. pat. 249167, for movable shoulders for dolls' heads

Nuttall & Maden. England
1894. B. pat. 21052, for celluloid dolls prepared in sheets, and moulded while hot
J. H. Maden, B. pat. 20186, for dolls' dresses on which are printed pictures

Offene Handels Gesellschaft Morisz Puppe. Leignitz, Germany
1908. Mark no. 256
Ohlenschläger, K. England
1897. F. pat. 264361, for a jointed doll. Rep by Blétry
B. pat. 5320, for a jointed doll like an acrobat
Ott, Gebhard. Steinbühl, Germany
1883. Mark no. 70. An interesting entry because of the Toymaker of Nürnberg, called Ott in 1413 A.D.
Otte, Janns & Co. Hamburg, Germany
1891. Mark no. 216

Pabst, G. J. Nürnberg, Germany
1899. Mark no. 488
1900. Mark no. 165
See also Thurnauer
Pannier. France
1872. A parasol with metal frame and joints
Parent. France
1871. Doll
Parquet. France
1888. Rep by Albert Cahen, boul. St. Denis, 1, Paris
F. pat. 189791, for dolls' heads of blown glass and decorated
Pätzig, R. & Co. Niederneuschönberg, Germany
1877. Maker of wooden playthings. Mark nos. 190, 603
Payne, John Edward. England
1849. B. pat. 12643, for dolls of moulded India-rubber, and certain gums, the dolls being hollow and then joined
Péan frères. France
1887. Metal toys. Article Français. Mark no. 130, which can be in relief or in colour
Pecclet. France
1887. Rep by Blétry frères
F. pat. 181922, for imitation hair wigs for dolls
1890. F. pat. 204241, for a wig machine for dolls and bébés
Peck, David. 9 Pembroke Rd., Norwood, Surrey, England
1902. Toy maker. Mark no. 305
Peck, Lucy. 131 Regent St., London
1902. Wax dolls with inset hair
Peck, William E. & Co. Bradford Rd., London
1906. Toys & American merchants. Mark no. 451
Pelletier, E. Marseille, France
1887. Rep by the Société Assi et Génès, boul. Voltaire, 36, Paris
F. pat. 184148, for movable dolls from the waist
1892. Mark no. 605, stamped on the boxes containing the dolls
Peloubet, Francis W. Newark, N.J., U.S.A.
1886. Pat. 335302, for a walking doll
Pencke & Rascher. Hamburg, Germany
1892. Mark no. 224
Pepper, John. England
1866. Gymnastic figures
Perret, Paul. Paris, France
1892. Mark no. 280
See also 1909, Les Jeux et Jouets Français. Mark no. 16
Petit, Jacob. Belleville, France
1790. Mark no. 96
1843. Fontainebleau. Hard paste factory. Mark no. 97, in blue
He made biscuit figures, and patented improvements in porcelain
F. pat. 15159
Pfeifer, Emil. Wein, Germany
1904. Doll manufacturer. Mark no. 285
1907. Mark no. 19
Pflaumer, J. F. & Co. Weitzenberg, Germany
1890. Mark no. 88
Philippart, Gustave. France
1907. Mark nos. 331, 339
Phillips, J. A. & Co. Birmingham, England
1909. Mark no. 572
Pierotti, H. England
1854. Wax doll maker
1861. Inventor of the 'Royal Model Dolls'
1862. Wins Bronze medal at the International Exhibition
1880. 'Crystal Palace Gallery', Oxford St., London, maker of wax dolls
Many of their dolls were sold by Hamleys as French dolls, made by an Italian
Pinnock, Young F. Hymer, Kans., U.S.A.
1904. Pat. 758469, for a doll dancing on a box
Pintel. France
1890. F. pat. 203385, for jointed dolls of composition
Pollak, H. England
1884. G. pat. 31189, for a method of inserting hairs into the heads of dolls; the heads could be of India-rubber, vulcanite, porcelain, papier mâché or of composition
Polock, Max. Waltershausen, Germany
1902. Dolls and parts of dolls. Mark no. 532
Poncet. La dame, Paris, France
1860. F. pat. 47867, for paper dolls and dolls of bread

Poulin. France
1861. F. pat. 50679, for dolls with metal heads and enamel eyes
Preston, A. M. England
1910. B. pat. 11434, for a dancing doll with a box for support
USA pat. 954341, as above
Pulvermacher, Albert. Sonneberg, Germany
1890. G. pat. 55484, for a method of jointing dolls
F. pat. 208291, Rep by Danzer, rue de Florence, 9, Paris, as above
1891. USA pat. 447034, for a doll with pins and spiral springs in detachable, hollow, jointed parts
Purvis, R. C. U.S.A.
1901. Pat. 681974, for a doll with a wire interior

Quinquandon, Jean Baptiste André. England
1854. B. pat. 2517, for a machine for making cork powder with which to stuff dolls

Rabery. France
1893. F. pat. 229555, for a talking and walking doll
Radde, Carl Heinrich Otto. Hamburg, Germany
1876. Toys. Mark nos. 187, 188
Rambour, Charles. Paris, France
1899. Mark no. 483
Rauly, Jean. France
1891. Mark no. 287
Ravenstein, Thüringia, Germany. Sometimes spelt Rouenstein
1760. Porcelain factory. Mark no. 132
1855. Mark nos. 133, 134
Rayer. France
1890. Rep by Thirion, boul. Beaumarchais, 95, Paris
F. pat. 205174, for a musical bébé doll
Reichmann, L. U.S.A.
1877 Pat. 187173, for dolls' heads of composition with an outer layer of beeswax, paraffin and turpentine, and an inner layer of sawdust, glue and paste
Reid, James. Paris, France
1887. Toys. Mark no. 517
Reid, J. A. England
1900. B. pat. 6176, for weighted dolls such as John Bull tumblers
Reidemester. Paris, France
1860. F. pat. 47756, for dolls with metal joints, the head and lower arms could be of porcelain
Reinhardt, Ernst. Sonneberg, Germany
1904. B. pat. 18089, for closing eyes made of pressed celluloid
F. pat. 345746, as above
G. pat. 171907, for sleeping eyes for dolls
Reinhardt, F. Waltershausen, Germany
1903. USA pat. 738628, for a mechanical doll with narrow strips secured to the legs
Reithoffer, J. N. Germany
1897. Mark no. 150, the initials stand for Vereingte-Gummiwaaren-Fabriken-Harburg-Wein, formerly Menier-Harburg
Rémignard, Frédéric. Paris, France
1888. Merchant. Mark nos. 477, 163. Mark no. 601 stamped on the boxes containing the dolls
Rémond. France
1883. F. pat. 158038, for a dancing doll
Restignat. Madame. France
1869. F. pat. 84707, for a jointed doll made of cork
Rheinische-Gummi-und-Celluloid-Fabrik. Neckarau-Mannheim, Germany
1899. G. pat. 120557, for celluloid dolls with hair
1899. Mark no. 226
1905. G. pat. 170308, for inserting glass eyes in dolls' heads of celluloid
Richard. France
1853. F. pat. 15918, for doll busts of cirico-plastic paste
Richter, Bernard. Cöln, Germany
1902. Mark no. 276
Richter, Frederick Adolphus & cie. Nürnberg, Germany
1879. Mark nos. 131, 199
1886. Nürnberg. Mark no. 223
1902. Rudolfstadt, Germany. Mark nos. 249, 330
1907. Dolls. Mark no. 244
Richter Tschuschner. *See* Tschuschner
Ring, H. & Co. Brieg 1. Schl. Germany
1889. G. pat. 49697, for a method of fixing eyes in dolls' heads
1897. F. pat. 267526, for a mechanism for closing dolls' eyes
Ring, Karl
1892. *See* Meyer, Louis
Ritter, Julius. Halle A.S. Germany
1895. G. pat. 85411, for a stand for a doll
Rivaillon, Caroline. Madame. Argenteuil, France
1900. Designer of bébés. Mark nos. 60, 367, 593
Robb, W. R. England
1899. B. pat. 25341, for cardboard dolls with magnifying lenses behind the eyes, on which are advertisements

Robert. France
1858. F. pat. 39282, for a crying doll in swaddling clothes, known as a '*Poupée-maillot*'
Roberts Bros. Glevdin Works, Gloucester, England
1908. Manufacturers of games. Mark no. 563
Robinson, Sarah C. Chicago, Cork, Illinois, U.S.A.
1883. Pat. 283513, for a stuffed doll of cloth or leather, made in sections, and stuffed with bran, sawdust or hair. The dolls' heads could be of bisque or composition
Rogier, Edouard. Roubaix, France
1908. Mark no. 189
Rohmer, Marie Antoinette Leontine. France
1857. F. pat. 31242, for joints for kid dolls
F. pat. 34123, for rubber arms for stuffed dolls, jointed or unjointed
F. pat. 17769, for jointed leather arms
1858. F. pat. 36531, for dolls of kid, linen, or rubber with a cord from the head, running down through the body
F. pat. 20616, for dolls' heads
Rosa, S. D. U.S.A.
1901. Pat. 688008, for a dolls' house
Rösing Bros. & Co. London, England
1891. Mark no. 240
Rossignol, Charles. Paris, France
1890. Toymaker. Mark nos. 51, 480
Rossignol (Veuve.) Widow of C. H. Rossignol, Paris
1905. Registers the same mark as that of her husband, i.e. Mark no. 51
Rostaing, Charles Sylvester. England
1859. B. pat. 2962, for dolls' heads of rubber, so hard that it replaces wood
Roullet & Decamps, E. France
1892. F. pat. 222661, for a walking doll by means of weights
1893. F. pat. 227522, for walking dolls and bébés
1893. Designers of dolls and bébés. Mark no. 492
Rousseaux, Germain. France
1891. Mark no. 147
Roussel. *See* Falck Roussel
Rousselot, Jean. England
1845. B. pat. 228, for a baby doll of kid, with wire inside so that it could lift and lower the arms when wound up. The doll had a German head, yoke, enamel eyes and teeth
Rouech, E. E. U.S.A.
1908. Pat. 875954, for a doll
Rouech-Bowden Co. Detroit, Mich., U.S.A.
1907. Mark no. 531
Roy. France
1857. F. pat. 30913 and 17624, for jointed dolls of '*pâté plastique*'
Rudd & Co. Ludgate Square, London
1905. Mark no. 306
Rügemer, Hans. Würzburg, Germany
1905. G. pat. 176717, for jointed dolls
Russian French India-rubber, Gutta-percha & Telegraph Works. Riga, Russia
1910. Mark no. 543

Sackman, L. A. U.S.A.
1908. Pat. 882422, for a doll
Sala, A. Berlin, Germany
1888.
Sallee, Lucretia E. Decatur, Macon, Ill., U.S.A.
1865. Pat. 46270, for a mode of constructing dolls' heads, the outer surface being made of leather, or tough material backed up by cement
Salt, Ellen. Hammersmith, London
1906. Toy dealer. Mark no. 20
Samhammer, Philip. 2 Butler St., Milton St., London
1888. Doll manufacturer
B. pat. 17702, for improvements in rag dolls
Samstag & Hilder Bros. New York, U.S.A.
1908. Mark no. 528
Sanders, G. W. U.S.A.
1880. Pat. 235300, for tenon and mortise joints for dolls
Sanford, T. W. U.S.A.
1910. Pat. 954544, for a nautical doll
Santy. 340 Long Room, Soho Bazaar, London
1850–60. Made wax dolls with real hair curls, and stuffed bodies
Sauer, Gebr. Nürnberg, Germany
1908. Metal toy factory. Mark no. 166
Sauerteig & Lutz. Johann & Lorenz Heinrich Friedrich. Sonneberg, Germany
1888. Toy manufacturers
G. pat. 15169, for a singing doll, where a musical box is played by the jointed arm of the doll
Sauleau et Rouaud. Paris, France
1910. Mark nos. 145, 600
Saunier et Caux. Paris, France
1889. Mark no. 136
Schab, S. M. England
1893. B. pat. 17143, for dolls made from two pieces of fabric
Schachne, Albert. Nürnberg, Germany
1909. G. pat. 223397, for a doll with tears formed by pressing a rubber ball concealed in the body
Schelhorn, Max Frederick. Sonneberg, Germany
1907. Dolls, etc. Mark no. 614

1908. Dolls and their parts. Mark no. 439
1909. Dolls' rooms. Mark no. 191
1910. Mark no. 495
Scheller & Co. Bohrmühle, Schmalkalden, Germany
1877. Toy manufacturer. Mark no. 266
1888. Gebrüder Scheller. Mark no. 267
Scherf, George. Allemagne, France
1908. USA pat. 906566, for a doll knee joint, for leather and rag dolls with the knee-pan made of wood, held together by rubber cords
F. pat. 391740, as above
B. pat. 13104, as above
1910. USA pat. 979573, as above
Schiller, Dosogne et cie. France
1887. Mark is a 'gladiator'
Schilling, Ferdinand Max. Sonneberg, Germany
1893. Mark no. 262. Dolls and dolls' heads of papier mâché, paper, wood, rubber and composition
1895. Mark no. 263
1903. Mark no. 606
Schilling, Stephan Max Ferdinand. Sonneberg, Germany
1884. USA pat. 295435, for a doll with a fixed transverse tube at the shoulder portion, with jointed arms, and elastic cords connecting to the said tube
1889. G. pat. 52783, for a talking doll
Schilling, Rudolf. Hamburg, Germany
1901. Mark no. 546
Schimansky, H. 10 Brücken Strasse, Berlin, S.O. Prussia, German Empire
1888. B. pat. 5530, for dolls made of cast metal, molten tin or zinc, and wearing pasted wigs
Schlopsnies, Albert. München, Germany
1909. G. pat. 228275, for jointed dolls and marionettes
Schmetzer, Louis. et cie. France
1875. A dancing doll
1876. Rothenberg, Germany. Playthings. Mark no. 116
1895. F. pat. for a doll
Schmidt. France
1887. Rep by Chassevent, boul. Magenta, 11, Paris
F. pat. 185062, for making dolls
Schmidt, Bruno. Waltershausen, Germany
1904. Dolls. Mark nos. 44, 503
1908. Mark no. 248
1910. Mark no. 401
Schmidt, Franz. Georgenthal, Saxe-Coburg-Gotha, German Empire
1891. B. pat. 1218, for sleeping dolls which close their eyes when laid in a recumbent position. A swinging lead weight and wire framework enable the doll to close the upper lid faster than the lower lid
F. pat. 210940, for a new method for dolls' heads
1899. Franz Schmidt & Co.
G. pat. 108361, for jointed dolls
1910. Doll manufacturer. Mark nos. 450, 558
Schmit, Franz. & Co. Georgenthal, Thüringen, Germany
1902. Dolls, etc. Mark no. 63
Schmitt Père et fils. France
1879 F. pat. 130416, for porcelain bébés
1886. Rep by Blétry frères, boul. de Strasbourg, 2, Paris, for dolls with moving eyes
Schmitz, P. H. Paris, France
1893. Mark no. 183, put on the dolls and also on their boxes and packages
Schneider fils (Benoist). Paris, France
1888. Merchant. Mark no. 138, stamped on both leather dolls and on the bébés
Schnepff, Albert. Coburg, Germany
1904. G. pat. 170775, for a movable dolls' head
1906. G. pat. 186250, as above
Schnitz, P. H. Paris, France
1893. Mark nos. 370, 585
Schoenhut, A.
1903. B. pat. 24185, for a jointed doll
Schön, Joseph, or Schoen. Reichenbach, Schlesien, Germany
1886. G. pat. 38714, for dolls' heads stamped from metal sheets
1887. USA pat. 361453, for dolls of sheet metal made in halves, riveted or soldered together, and coated with enamel
Schönhut, W. Fr. Hernrannstadt, Siebenbürgen, Germany
1890. G. pat. 55305, articulations for dolls' heads, etc.
Schramm. Mille, France
1895. Rep by Neuhardt, boul. Magenta, 30, Paris, for a doll's room
Schuldt, Ad. Ernst. Hamburg, Germany
1910. Mark no. 566
Schultz, Adolphe L. G. Paris, France
1893. USA pat. 500682, for an apparatus for moulding the heads of dolls in a single piece from a tube of celluloid or other material
Schultz, Frederick B. New York, N.Y., U.S.A.
1893. Pat. 504627, for dolls jointed by means of springs and swivels
1894. Pat. 526667, for a doll with tubular jointed parts

Schultze, Gebruder. Hamburg, Germany
1886. Mark no. 318
Schwickart, H. U.S.A.
1908. Pat. 896048, for a doll's head
Scott & Seymour, F. M. & A. F. U.S.A.
1893. Pat. 508770, for making dolls
Seligmann, A. Berlin, Germany
1892. Playthings. 'Berliner Patent-Spielwaaren-Fabrik'. Mark no. 42
Sevette, Paul. Paris, France
1884. Maker of toys. Mark no. 50
S.F.B.J. *See* Soc. Française, etc.
S.G.D.G. '*Sans Guarantie Du Gouvernement*'
Sharples, A. England
1894. B. pat. 11144, for sweetmeat, hollow moulded dolls of sugar and chocolate
Sheperd, George Henry. Brighton, England
1909. Mark no. 423
Sherwood, Katherine Mary. 8 Seaside Rd., Eastbourne, Sussex, England
1910. Of no occupation. Three mechanical dolls. Mark nos. 445, 447, 452
Siemroth, A. Böhsen, Germany
1888. Mark nos. 157, 294
S.I.I.M. *See* Soc. Internationale, etc.
S.I.J.I.M. *See* Léve, Prosper
Simonne. Passage Delorme, rue de Rivoli, 188, Paris, France
1863. Maker of dolls and dressed bébés. Mark no. 21
Simms, Henry. Hamburg, Germany
1887. Mark no. 230
Simon & Halbig. Gräfenhain, Herzogth, Gotha, Germany
1890. G. pat. 56562, for a doll with moving eyelids
1890. Grafenhain, bei Ohrdruf
G. pat. 62880, for dolls' heads, with eyes which move from left to right
1890. G. pat. 75652, as above
1905. Manufacturer of dolls' heads. Mark no. 142
See also Halbig, Carl
Simon, Wilhelm. Hildburghausen, Germany
1875. Porcelain and Toy factory. Mark no. 220
Simonot. France
1892. F. pat. 223223, for a mechanism for jointed dolls
Simpson, W. S.
1887. B. pat. 14754, for dolls on a wheeled toy
S.J.J.F. *See* Soc. des Jeux, etc.
Slade, Charlotte L. U.S.A.
1874. Pat. 156382, for a doll's trousseau, consisting of a packet of miniature patterns for wearing apparel
1877. USA pat. 193674, for a doll's hat, trimmed with relief pictures of flowers
Slevogt & Co. Shanghai, China
1889. Mark no. 137
Smith, C. England
1893. B. pat. 20870, for rag dolls in two pieces, and stuffed with cotton
Smith, E. U.S.A.
1905. Pat. 800333, for a doll
Snequireff, Leon. Paris, France
1906. Mark no. 465
Société des Jeux et Jouets Française. Paris, France
1904. Mark no. 177
Société Française de Fabrication de Bébés et Jouets. Paris, Seine, France
1901. F. pat. 309788, for talking dolls
1902. Mark no. 379
1903. Mark nos. 371, 482
1904. F. pat. 341108, for moving eyes
1904. Mark no. 378
1905. F. pat. 351423, for a mechanical doll
1905. F. pat. 353622, for a talking doll
1905. F. pat. 354337, for a jointed doll
1905. F. pat. 360100, for a doll's head with moving eyes, worked by weights
1905. Mark no. 139
1905. Mark no. 426. Renouvellement de dépôt
1906. Mark no. 205, as above
1909. F. pat. 399883, for a talking doll
1910. S.F.B.J. Société Anonyme, 8 rue Pastourelle, Paris, Toy manufacturers. Address in U.K.: c/o G. F. Redfern & Co. 15 South Street, Finsbury, London. Mark no. 140
Société Industrielle de Celluloid. 326 rue Saint Martin, Paris, France
1909. F. pat. 405227, for a celluloid swimming doll, called the '*Poupée Nageuse*'.
G. pat. 227544, as above
1910. B. pat. 16732, for an improved floating doll
Société Internationale des Inventions Modernes. France
1891. A doll known as '*Bébé-Petit-Pas*'. Mark no. 381
Soehlin et Bailliart. Paris, France
1902. Designers of toys. Mark no. 315
Sommer, Jacques-Adolphe. Paris, France
1886. Manufacturer. Mark no. 271. The mark is stamped on the dolls in colour, and is 0.016 in diameter
Sommereisen. France
1898. Rep by Caron
F. pat. 273785, for aluminium heads for dolls

Soret, Jean. France
1847. B. pat. 5198, for bébés' heads of papier mâché, and for milliners' models

Soulard. (Widow.) France
F. pat. 255918, for a doll known as 'La Charlotte'. Rep by Good, rue de Rivoli, 70, Paris. Mark no. 467

Souty. France
1862. F. pat. 56106, for dolls with heads and arms of porcelain, bisque or pipe clay, and otherwise of pumice stone coated with glue, painted, and then washable

Stallarde & Co. 37 Commercial Rd., London, E.
1905. Manufacturers of toy dolls. Mark no. 463

Standfusz, Karl. Deuben, Dresden, Germany
1909. G. pat. 226324, for a bathing doll

Staples, A. U.S.A.
1886. Pat. 352161, for a doll supporter

Statham, S. E. England
1893. B. pat. 23342, for dolls of seamless rubber

Steiff, Margarete. Giengen, Brenz, Würtemberg, Germany
1907. Felt goods. British mark no. 23, German mark no. 22
1907. Mark no. 210. Firme Margarete Steiff, Würtemberg Dolls and stuffed toy figures
1908. Mark nos. 24, 25, 211
1909. Mark no. 390

Stein et cie. Paris, France. Merchants
1888. Mark no. 295, registered by E. Stein. The background is white or any other tint, the coat of arms is blue, white and red, the lion and the inscription on the original drawings are black. Mark no. 446

Steiner, Edmund Ulrich. Citizen of the U.S.A., Brooklyn, New York, Kings. N.Y., U.S.A.
1902. Pat. 695121, for a walking doll, the child takes it by the hands and draws it gently forwards, and the doll moves alternate legs
1902. Sonneberg, Germany. Manufacturer of dolls. Mark no. 587
1902. U.S.A. Mark no. 499. The word used since 1894
1902. U.S.A. Mark no. 487. The words used since 1894
(A scroll with an eagle perched thereon)
1903. Mark no. 412

Steiner, Heinrich. Schalkau, Germany
1902. Dolls. Mark no. 607

Steiner, Jules Nicholas. France
1862. Rep by Ricordeau, Paris
1862. F. pat. 57863, for a mechanical doll
F. pat. 52929, for a speaking doll, known as '*Bébé Parlant Automatique*'. Mark no. 377
1869. 25 rue de Saintonge, Paris, Toy manufacturer, velocipedes and automatic toys
1880. 60 rue Davron, Paris
F. pat. 137333, for movable eyes for bébés and poupées
G. pat. 14292, as above
1881. F. pat. 140916, for artificial eyes
1884. Rep by Blétry frères, boul de Strasbourg 2, Paris. For a method of moulding by compressed air, dolls and bébés of pasteboard or other material
1889. Rep by Blétry frères
F. pat. 199084, for unbreakable heads of porcelain or biscuit, for dolls and bébés
1889. Doll maker, Paris. Mark no. 26, stamped on the boxes containing the dolls, in various colours and sizes
1889. Mark no. 479
1890. Rep by Blétry frères
F. pat. 206131, for a walking doll known as '*Bébé Premier Pas*'. Mark no. 383
1890. Mark no. 358

Steiner, Louis. Sonneberg, Germany
1910. Assignor to G. Borgfeldt & Co. New York, N.Y.
USA pat. 952716, for a doll's head with inset eyebrows of hair on a strip

Steiner, Rudolf. Sonneberg, Thüringia, Germany
1889. G. pat. 14534, for a feeding doll, which sits on a chair and feeds by means of a syphon
1890. USA pat. 427927, as above

Steuber, M. A. U.S.A.
1878. Pat. 205314, for a doll's leg, complete with a stocking

Stevens, G. England
1861. B. pat. 1146, for rubber dolls coated with glue and then with natural skin, thus avoiding the use of paint. These rubber dolls were sometimes covered with silk

Stiefel, William. Berlin, Germany
1901. G. pat. 132849, for dolls of composition, doll parts, walking dolls, hollow bodies, etc.

Stöter, Otto. Cöln, Germany
1906. G. pat. 178012, for fixing the eyes in dolls' heads by means of an axle

Strady. *See* Lonquet

Stranders, Walter & Perry, Joseph. Holborn Viaduct, London

1889. Designers and steel pen manufacturers
B. pat. 14356, for a mechanical doll which could crawl, row or swim
About this time, J. C. Morrell of Oxford St., London, sold crawling dolls
Strawbridge & Clothier. Philadelphia, U.S.A.
1906. Dolls. Mark no. 335. The words 'Princess Royal', printed on a streamer. Mark nos. 542, 560
Strobel & Wilkin Co. New York, N.Y., U.S.A.
1902. Dolls. Mark no. 326, the word used since 1895
1903. Mark no. 548, the word used since 1902
Süszenguth, Gebruder. Neustadt, Coburg, Germany
1900. Dolls of all kinds. Mark no. 413
1904. Mark no. 71, the name '*Puppe der Zukunft*' meaning Doll of the Future
Süszenguth, S. England
1898. B. pat. 18871, for a strengthened paper doll
Süszkind, Jos. Hamburg, Germany
1905. Dolls and dolls' theatres. Mark no. 393

Taumeyer & Co. Shanghai, China
1890. Mark no. 250
Thalheimer, Sylvian M. et cie. 5 Place de la République, 23, 25, 27 passage Vendôme, Paris, France
1900. Designer of bébés, dolls, etc. Mark nos. 387, 615
Awarded a silver medal for their dolls
Théroude. France
1852. F. pat. 13748, for mechanical dolls with voice and movement
1854. F. pat. 18834, for a doll to raise the arms, open and shut eyes, and to say 'cou-cou'
1890. Théroude, Père. Rep by Thirion
F. pat. 208609, for a jointed doll
Thompson, R. A. & Freeman, W. S. England
1898. B. pat. 25883, for mechanical dolls
Thompson, W. P. England
1887. B. pat. 9941, for dolls prepared from leather board, cut and shaped in moulds, in two parts and joined by glue
1892. B. pat. 23958, for dolls to imitate walking, and to turn their heads from side to side at the same time
(This doll was for Fleischmann & Bloedel)
Thowless, Arthur J. Newark, N.J., U.S.A.
1904. Pat. 752607, for a doll with a hollow body
Thurnauer, Emil. Albrecht Durer Strasse, Nürnberg, Germany
1899. Wood and papier mâché toys. Mark no. 489, registered in Britain
Thurnauer, Emil. & Neumark, Max. Trading as G. I. Pabst. Solgerstrasse, 16, Nürnberg, Bavaria
1906. British mark no. 442
Timm & Schrumf. Hamburg, Germany
1890. Mark is a 'Dragon on a black ground'
Toulouse. Rue Saint Merri, 24, Paris, France
1894. F. pat. 241865, for a jointed doll, called the '*Poupée Français*'. Mark no. 533
Trautmann, F. O. England
1909. B. pat. 5624, for a skipping doll
Tredoulat. France
1858. Dolls' heads of strong rubber
Treude & Metz. Laasphe, Westphalia, Germany
1902. B. pat. 16700, for a walking doll. (Entered by S. S. Bromhead)
F. pat. 322998, for a mechanical doll
Trufant, Bertha A. England
1895. B. pat. 2002, for paper dolls
USA pat. 537791, as above
Tschuschner, Richter & Co. 2 Falcon Square, London
1902. Toys. Mark no. 135
Tuchmann, Victor & Co. Invicta Works, London
1891. Toys and dolls. Mark no. 273
Tuck, A. England
1893. B. pat. 11367, for a baby doll of paper
B. pat. 23003, for a paper doll with changeable dresses

Uhrig, R. England
1903. B. pat. 3071, for a jumping doll
Upton, Florence Kate. 76 Fellows Rd., Hampstead, London
1908. Artist and author. Mark no. 562
Union des Fabricants de Jouets. *See* Debrieu
Union Française. *See* Guillet

Vallée & Schultz. Louis V. & Adolphe L. G. Paris, France
1893. USA pat. 500682, for an apparatus for moulding the heads of dolls in a single piece, from a tube of celluloid or other material
Véraine, Renée de. Mille
1907. F. pat. 383919, for a doll with a double face
Vercasson, P. et Cie. Paris, France
1903. Mark no. 538
Verdier & Gutmacher. Rudolf, Verdier, 10 rue d'Angoulême, Paris, France, was a hat manufacturer. Sylvain G. Gutmacher, 7 rue des Petites Ecuries, Paris, was a fancy goods importer
1897. G. pat. 100771, for unbreakable dolls made from glued layers of felted material, etc.
B. pat. 22691, as above
F. pat. 269564, as above
1900. USA pat. 652497, as above

Verdier, R. et Cie. Paris, France. Doll makers and designers of dolls and bébés
1899. Mark nos. 347, 361, 366, 372
F. pat. 291188, for mechanical dolls
Vangel, A. L. Wein, Germany
1879. G. pat. 7162, for dolls and doll parts made of composition
Verpillier & Graves. Emil and Charles Watson. Newark, Essex, N.J., U.S.A.
1892. G. pat. 69976, for dolls with ball-and-socket joints
1892. E. Verpillier
USA pat. 487861, for jointed dolls
F. pat. 224809, for spherical joints for dolls
1894. Addition to the above
1895. USA pat. 546791, for jointed dolls
G. pat. 83728, as above
1898. Verpillier & Graves & O. Zeh
USA pat. 604243, for a doll with tubular portions and ball joints
USA pat. 603216, for a process of colouring dolls' heads, in order to produce a dull effect
Vervelle. France
1876. Metal doll
1879. F. pat. 115279, for metal heads for dolls
Vichy. France
1862. Automatic doll
Vincent Fils et Neveu. Paris, France
1888. Mark no. 200, done in various colours and sizes
Vines, José. Roda, Paris, France
1909. Mark no. 99
Vischer, A. & Co. New York, U.S.A.
1901. Metal doll-heads. Mark no. 509, used since 1894
Vogel, Fritz. Sonneberg, Germany
1879. G. pat. 12676, for a new method of constructing dolls' heads and limbs covered with stretched leather
1879. G. pat. 7446, for dolls and parts of dolls covered with leather
1882. G. pat. 19495, for dolls' heads made from layers of various compositions
Voigt, Bruno. Olbernhau, I.S. Germany
1891. G. pat. 63491, for a doll of paper to tell fortunes
Voirin. France
F. pat. 151201, for dolls' heads made of '*Cuir moulé*', i.e. a kind of moulded leather
Voit. Hilburghausen
1855. Dolls' heads of cardboard with 'hair dressed with taste'

Waite, Frederick Adolphus. Bridge St., Manchester, England. Toys. Mark no. 441, used for 20 years before 1876, i.e. 1856
Walker, Izannah F. U.S.A.
1873. Pat. 144373, for a stuffed rag doll, consisting of layers of stuffing with an external webbing
Wannez et Rayer. Paris, France
1891. Mark no. 364
Warmuth, Heinrich William. Dresden, Germany
1893. Mark no. 152. Rubber factory
Warncke, A. Hamburg, Germany
1887. Mark no. 286
Wasmuth, Auguste-Louis-Martin-Albert. Hamburg, Germany
1900. Merchant and designer of toys. Mark no. 549
Wattilliaux, Charles-Auguste. Paris, France
1891. Toymaker of Paris. Mark no. 457
1896. Merchant of Paris. Mark no. 155
Wear, I. O. U.S.A.
1909. Pat. 912637, for a sleeping doll
Webber, Rand & Given. William Augustus Webber of Medford, Edward Lyman Rand of Boston, John Leslie Given in Cambridge, Mass., U.S.A.
1884. G. pat. 20938, for a singing doll. This doll sang patriotic songs, such as 'The Old Grey Goose is Dead'
Webber & Webber. Willy and Hans. 21 Schwedter Strasse, Berlin, Germany. Sculptor and mechanician respectively
1894. B. pat. 9811, for a doll with a turning head and eyes to move in a natural manner
Wedeses Co. Hamburg, Germany
1892. Dolls. Mark nos. 213, 232
Weidmann, Carl. Leipzig, Germany
1901. G. pat. 130942, for dolls' bodies with metal parts
Weigel, A. England
1899. B. pat. 24044, for hopping dolls
Weiss, Auguste. Paris, France
1909. Mark no. 575
Weisz, Heinrich. Sonneberg, Germany
1895. Jointed dolls. Mark no. 218
Wellington, M. L. Brooklyn, Mass., U.S.A.
1883. Pat. 285448, for a doll made from a wire frame, covered with stockinette, stuffed, painted and sewed
Wessel, Ludwig. Popplesdorf, Bonn, Germany
1755. Mark nos. 118, 201
West, Sylvester A. Rock Port, Mo., U.S.A.
1907. Pat. 849588, for a doll with movable arms
Wheeler, John. 15 New Gate St., London
1879. Toys, dolls and dolls' dresses. Mark no. 231

Whyte, Robert. Trading as Whyte & Risdale, 73 & 74 Houndsditch, London
1876. Toys and fancy goods. Mark no. 154. The motto is '*Ingenio et Labore*'
Wicks, W. England
1852. Maker of composition dolls
Wiegand, Carl. U.S.A.
1876. Pat. 177777, for dolls' heads made from layers of textile with an intermediate layer of paper
Wilcox, A. B. U.S.A.
1892. USA Pat. 478481, for a doll support
Wilmer, Margaret E. Brooklyn, N.Y., U.S.A.
1897. Pat. 575749, for a doll made from a sheet of paper
Wilson, G. L. England
1894. B. pat. 14984, for a hot-water bottle in the shape of a doll
Winkler, Friedr. Edmund. Sonneberg, Germany
1899. Manufacturer of dolls and jointed dolls. Mark nos. 340, 608
Winterbauer, Martin. Nürnberg, Germany
1910. Mark nos. 195, 196, 197
Wishard, Lucinda B. J. Indianapolis, U.S.A.
1883. Pat. 280986, for a doll with a flexible body, stiffened with wires
Wislizenus, A. Waltershausen, Germany
1901. G. pat. 127697, for jointed dolls
G. pat. 126901, for dolls with hollow bodies
1910. Mark no. 544
Wislizenus, U. Waltershausen, Germany
1902. Jointed dolls. Mark nos. 518, 623
1910. Mark nos. 39, 591
Wolcot & Rider. H. G. and J. P. England
1895. B. pat. 24169, for hollow rubber dolls
Wolf & Co. Louis W. U.S.A.
1897. Dolls and dolls' costumes
1897. Mark no. 407, used since 1892
1910. Mark no. 545
Wolff. France
1890. F. pat. 206345, for a doll saying 'Papa-Maman'
Wollheim. England
1899. B. pat. 12246, for dolls' heads of bossed cardboard
Work, Henry C. Brooklyn, N.Y., U.S.A.
1873. Pat. 140605, for a walking doll, which raises her dress enough at the side to show but one pair of feet at once. A multipedal wheel is pivoted at the knee and is moved by friction
Worsnop, Arthur. 25 Union St., Halifax, England
1907.
Wynne, William R. London, England
1895. G. pat. 86808, for a feeding doll
1897. B. pat. 24679, for a doll 'bubble-blower'

Young, I. U.S.A.
1905. Pat. 79043, for a detachable doll's head

Zehnpfenning, A. England
1904. B. pat. 26858, for a weighted doll
Zeuch & Lausmann. Sonneberg, Germany
1896. Mark no. 288
Ziegler, W. München, Germany
1879. G. pat. 9800. His toys were known as '*Mechanischer Reiter*', i.e. mechanical riders or horsemen
Zierow, P. R. Germany
1910. Doll manufacturer. Mark nos. 198, 604
Zimmer, Fa. S. D. Fürth, Bavaria
1908. Mark no. 498

Glossary

F: French, G: German

Appliqué en creux (F). Sunk or intaglio. Applies to the marks on bisque dolls.
Appliqué en relief (F). Raised.
Apposée sur des poupées (F). Stamped on the dolls, and applies to marks and labels.
Articulate. The manner in which the bodies are joined to the limbs, etc.

Baby doll. In England means a doll dressed as a baby.
Badepuppe (G). Bathing doll.
Bamboo. Used for the hands on some 'Queen Anne' dolls.
Bébé (F). Doll, a child's doll or a baby doll.
Bébé-baiser (F). Kissing doll, where the doll touches the lips and throws a kiss.
Bébé de chant (F). Singing doll.
Bébé nus (F). Naked dolls, i.e. undressed.
Bébés porte-bonheur (F). Name given to those dolls which are hung in motor cars for luck.
Bébés Teteurs (F). Feeding dolls.
Beweglicher Unterlippe (G). A moving bottom lip.
Biedermeyer or *Biedermeier* (G). A homely or Early Victorian type, 1820–48, often used to describe a doll with a bald pate.
Bimbeloterie (F). The toy trade—*bimbelot* is a plaything, a *bimbelotier* is a toyman.
Biscuit. Unglazed china usually referred to as bisque.
Bisque. The name given to all china dolls with a matt surface.
Bonnet dolls. Dolls complete with moulded bonnets or hats.
Breveté (F). Patented. *Breveté* is a male patentee, *Brevetée*, a female.
Buckram. A stiff coarse linen cloth often used for heads of rag dolls, and for doll masks which are sold separately (F=*Bougran*).

Calico. A fine cotton cloth used for the bodies of wax and porcelain dolls (F=*Calicot*).
Carton-pâte (F). Pasteboard.
Celluloid. Made by treating cellulose with a solvent such as camphor, and is highly inflammable.
Ceramic. The general word given to any fired clay object.
Cheveux (F). A head of hair, as opposed to a wig.
China. I.e. glazed china or porcelain, all unglazed china dolls being classed as bisque.
Cirico-plastic. A composition imitating china.
Composition. The name given to various substances including papier mâché. Sometimes known as 'compo' (F=*Composition*, G=*Stoffgernische*).
Cork. Used for filling the hollow of a porcelain or bisque head, for lightness owing to custom duty, for affixing the hair wig and also for the bodies of some swimming dolls.
Crawling dolls. Those which crawl along the ground by means of a string or by clockwork.

Crying dolls. With faces screwed up as if crying or weeping, others made to produce actual tears. *Pleurer* (F) for crying. *Schreipuppen* (G) for a crying doll, or one which cries out.
Cuir (F). Leather, *cuir moulé* being moulded or printed leather.

Dancing Jacks. Flat dolls of cardboard with separate limbs joined to the bodies by strings (F=*Pantins*, G=*Hampelmann*, U.S.A.=*Proteans*).
D.E.P. *déposé* (F), *deponier* (G).
Detachable limbs. Those which are joined to the body by wires or strings, and can usually be replaced if broken.
Docke (fifteenth-century G). Doll.
Doll. *Bébé, poupée* (F), *Puppe* (G).
Doll's head. *Puppenköpfe* (G).
Dolls in general. *Puppen im allegemeinen* (G).
Doppelgelenk (G). Double-jointed.
Doublefaced. When the head of a doll has a face at the back as well as at the front, usually one crying, one smiling, but can be one awake and one asleep.
D.R.G.M. (G). Made in Germany, i.e. a German registered design, the letters standing for *Deutsches-Reichsgebrauchsmuster*.
Dutch dolls. The name comes from the German word *Deutsch*. The word was formerly used for the German people quite as much as those of Holland, and now is used for any of those little jointed dolls made in the regions of the Black Forest, and even in North Italy. They may still be purchased in England, notably at Stratford-on-Avon, and Pollocks Toy Museum, London.

Edible dolls. Those made of bread, chocolate or sugared almonds, which are made in the form of dolls and are handed round at Christening ceremonies.
Elastic. Used for joining limbs to bodies.
Email (F). Enamel, used for eyes and for teeth.
Emballages (F). Packages or boxes in which the dolls were packed, each doll often having its own specially printed box.

Fabricant (F). Manufacturer.
Fester Masse (G). All other substances.
Flanders Baby. A name given to the 'Dutch' dolls from Europe.
Flirting eyes. U.S.A. name for those eyes which move from side to side.
Flock. A method of using minute fragments of wool to adhere to a surface in order to make it matt and velvety like peach skin (F=*Velouté*).
Flussigkeit (G). Fluid.
Four faces. Dolls which have heads made up of four faces, one showing, the others usually covered with a close fitting bonnet with a frill; the four faces may be smiling, laughing, crying, sleeping, or cross.
Frozen Charlotte. U.S.A. name for little dolls made without joints.

Gelenkpuppen (G). Jointed dolls.
Georgian dolls. Those dolls following on from the Queen Anne type, often with protruding round glass eyes, usually blue.

Gutta-percha. Elastic substance obtained from the gutta-percha tree in Malaya.

Hohlkörpern (G). Hollow body, used when referring to the inside works.
Holz (G). Wood.

Imperméable à l'eau (F). Used to describe those dolls which are watertight, including swimming dolls.
Incassable (F). Unbreakable.

Jeux (F). Games.
Jouet (F). Toy or plaything.
Junior. *Jeune* (F), also *Jne.*

Kugelgelenk (G). Ball-and-socket joint.

Lederpuppen (G). Leather dolls.
Léger (F). Light, nimble, active.
Lustre or luster. High glaze.

Maches. U.S.A. for papier mâché dolls.
Marques de Fabrique (F). Trademark.
Metallpuppenköpfen (G). Metal doll-heads.
Migault (F). Dream of a baby.
Milliner's models. Parisian fashion dolls which may be dated by their coiffure.

Nageuse (F). Swimming.
Négociant (F). Trader.

Pandora. A large fashion doll in full costume, a smaller one often in négligé.
Pantins (F). Dancing Jacks, very popular in France, 1746.
Paper dolls. Flats dolls of paper or cardboard cut-outs on which dresses may be put.
Papiermasse (G). Papier mâché.
Papierstoff (G). Pulp, made from paper.
Parian. Dolls with heads made of fine white china-clay. Fair 'hair' is usually in one with the head. A kind of fine white porcelain named after the island of Paros, famous for its white marble.
Poupard. A doll which can be twirled around on a stick, usually without legs.
Poupée (F). Doll, often a lady-doll, but also a doll for a child.
Poupée-maillot (F). A doll in swaddling clothes.
Poupée-parlant (F). A talking doll.
Poupon (F). Chubby-cheeked baby.
Pouty. Dolls with drooping mouths.
Puppe der Zunkunft (G). Doll of the future.
Puppenteile (G). Parts of dolls.

Rawhide. Used by Darrow in his patent for doll-heads.

Saugpuppe (G). Feeding doll.
Schlafpuppen (G). Sleeping dolls.
Schneewittchen (G). Snow-white.
Schutz (G). Trademark.
S.G.D.G. (F). Without government guarantee, i.e. *Sans Guarantie Du Gouvernement.*
Silesia. Fine linen or cotton fabric originally manufactured in Silesia, a province in the east of Germany, 1727. It is a thin twilled cotton and was used for linings as well as for the soft bodies of dolls.
Sleeping doll (F=*poupée-dormant*, G= *Schlafpuppen*). Applies to dolls which can close their eyes.
Slit-head. Dolls in which hairs have been inserted in a centre parting groove.
Sprechmaschine (G). Speaking apparatus.
Spielen (G). Toys.
Ste. (F). Abbreviation for *société*, meaning a company or firm.
Swivel-neck. Dolls with turning heads.

Threaded. Dolls with limbs joined by cords or elastic.
Three faces. Usually crying, sleeping or awake.
Tocka (Old High German). Doll. *Tocke* is a small block of wood.
Tournure (F). Bustle.
Trademark. F= *Marque de fabrique*, G= *Waarenzeichenblatt, Schütz-marke.*
Turning head. F= *à tete tournaille.*

Upside-down-doll. An apparently normal doll wearing a long skirt, but when turned upside down, instead of legs a different head is revealed. The coloured lining of the skirt will show as the skirt itself, the result appearing to be an entirely different doll.

Veuve (F). Widow.

Waschbar (G). Washable.
Wassendichten (G). Watertight.
Wimpern (G). Eyelashes.

Yoke. The head and shoulder-piece

Zappelmann (G). Dancing Jack.
Zinnfiguren (G). Metal figures.

Bibliography

Allemagne, H.R.d' *Histoire des Jouets*, Paris, 1903
Boehn, Max von. *Dolls and Puppets*, London, 1932
Canning-Wright, H. W. *Peeps at the World's Dolls*, London, 1923
Claretie, Leo. *Les Jouets*, Paris, 1894
Coleman, E. *The Age of Dolls*, 1965
Daiken, Leslie. *Children's Toys Throughout the Ages*, London, 1963
Early, Alice K. *English Dolls, Effigies and Puppets*, London, 1955
Fawcett, Clare Hallard. *Dolls, A Guide for Collectors*, New York, 1947
Freeman, Ruth. *American Dolls*, New York, 1953
Gerken, Jo Elizabeth. *Wonderful Dolls of Wax*, U.S.A., 1964
Gordon, Leslie. *Peepshow into Paradise*, London, 1953
Grôber, Karl. *Kinderspielzeug aus alter Zeit*, Berlin, 1928
Children's Toys (English Edition), London, 1929
Helsingfors. *Dockor och Tennsoldater*, 1961
Holme, Geoffrey. *Children's Toys of Yesterday*, London, 1932
Jackson, F. N. *Toys of Other Days*, London, 1908
Johl, Janet. *The Fascinating Story of Dolls*, New York, 1941
More about Dolls, New York, 1946
Still More about Dolls, New York, 1951
Lehmann, Emmy. *Die Puppe in Wandel der Zeiten*, Sonneberg Spielzeugsmuseum, 1957
Low, Frances H. *Queen Victoria's Dolls*, London, 1894
McClintock, Marshall and Inez. *Toys in America*, Washington, D.C., 1961
Rijksmuseum Booklet, Amsterdam, 1955
Victoria and Albert Museum Booklets:
A Picture Book of Dolls and Dolls Houses, London, 1926
Dolls and Dolls Houses, 1950
Dolls, 1960
White, Gwen. *Ancient and Modern Dolls*, 1928
A Book of Dolls, 1956
Dolls of the World, 1962
Young, Helen W. *Toys and Games*, A London Museum Booklet, 1959

Index

The figures in bold type refer to the plate numbers

Index

Index

Index

DISCARDED